D1295866

THE
Courage
OF
Judgment

.

OTHER BOOKS

BY GEORGE A. PANICHAS

Adventure in Consciousness:
The Meaning of D.H. Lawrence's Religious Quest

•

Epicurus

•

The Reverent Discipline:
Essays in Literary Criticism and Culture

•

The Burden of Vision:
Dostoevsky's Spiritual Art

•

Mansions of the Spirit:
Essays in Literature and Religion (editor)

•

Promise of Greatness:
The War of 1914–1918 (editor)

•

The Politics of Twentieth-Century Novelists (editor)

•

The Simone Weil Reader (editor)

•

THE
Courage
OF
Judgment

ESSAYS IN CRITICISM,

CULTURE,

AND SOCIETY

•

George A. ⌊Panichas⌋

with a Foreword by Austin Warren

THE UNIVERSITY
OF TENNESSEE PRESS
KNOXVILLE

•

Library of Congress Cataloging in
Publication Data
Panichas, George Andrew.
  The courage of judgment.
  Includes index.
  1. Literature—History and
criticism—Addresses, essays, lectures.
I. Title.
PN511.P158   809   81–4050
ISBN 0-87049–325–6   AACR2

TO

David S. Collier

IN RECOGNITION—IN APPRECIATION—IN FRIENDSHIP

Contents

Foreword by Austin Warren .... *ix*
Introduction............................... *3*

Part I. Definers and Defenders

1. The Challenge of Simone Weil............. *19*
2. The Critical Mission of Irving Babbitt *54*
3. T.S. Eliot and the Critique of Liberalism....*85*

Part II. The Religious Idea

4. A Note on Religion and Literature *111*
5. Without One False Note................. *115*
6. Voyage of Oblivion..................... *125*
7. The New Logos........................ *148*

Part III. Metaphysics of Politics

8. Politics and Literature.................. *159*
9. Dostoevsky's Political Apocalypse........ *177*
10. The Modernist Impasse................. *189*
11. Presenting Mr. Marx *193*
12. Conservative Expositors *203*

Part IV. Modes of Sensibility

13. The Jamesian Mirror *211*
14. D.H. Lawrence's War Letters............. *220*
15. In Retreat *232*
16. Testaments of Devotion *238*
17. A Family Matter...................... *245*

Part V. Teachers and Critics

18. Creative Questioner.................... *253*
19. Voice in the Wilderness *268*
20. A Constant Dimension................. *273*

Acknowledgments *279*

Index *281*

Foreword

BY AUSTIN WARREN

PROFESSOR GEORGE PANICHAS has wished me to introduce his latest book; and this I do in deference to his modesty, meanwhile reflecting that, at this midpoint in his dedicated literary career, he and his work need no sponsorship.

Panichas and I have been friends for upwards of ten years, our relation beginning when, after reading his essay on the Cambridge Platonist, Henry More, and the Greek spirit, I wrote him an appreciative letter. Our friendship, growing ever warmer, has progressed through occasional meetings and occasional telephone conversations, but most frequently, and to our mutual edification, through the exchange of letters. What I like to call, in echo of my early studies in neoclassicism, the "epistolary art," is dear to us both; and letters we both write with the same assiduous care as our essays tended for publication. I know my friend best, I think, from his meditations, couched in epistolary form.

Friendship is cardinal for us both, ranking next to adherence to principles. Loyalty to persons and loyalty to principles—sometimes these two high loyalties painfully conflict, as our letters testify; and occasionally we have differed over matters of what my old master, Irving Babbitt, might have called "mediation," over matters of practical policy, or what medieval thinkers would have called "prudence." But then we have each practiced patience with the misjudgment of the other.

In his new book Panichas demonstrates his loyalty to earlier admirations: he adds heroes without subtracting or substituting others, transcending by including; F.R. Leavis, D.H. Lawrence, and Dostoevsky stay in, while first Simone Weil and then Irving Babbitt is added, included. It is difficult to see how all these admirations, all these loyalties, can be reconciled; but it is an engaging task for the friendly critic, and critical friend, to work out the unnamed, uncommon denominator.

Panichas thinks of himself as a conservative, but if "conservative" can cover both Lawrence and Babbitt, or even Simone Weil and T.S.

Eliot (who wrote a sympathetic preface to Weil's *The Need for Roots*), what can the term mean? That we may say, with Panichas in his introduction to the *Courage of Judgment*, is just the function of the critical spirit to explore. The very word "conservative" proves as slippery, when examined, as other terms in constant use. Perhaps one thinks of it first as a political term; but, if one is a generalist, only at first thought, for subsequent thoughts show it to be of universal application,—notably, however, to religion and education, to the *paideia* and culture which shape us all. A conservative, in Panichas's sense, is not a reactionary, an unmitigated finance-capitalist, else he could not approve of the Christian Socialist, Simone Weil. The conservative is not necessarily a Christian, for Lawrence, the vitalist, was no more of a Christian than Nietzsche, and Babbitt was a New Humanist and, unofficially, a crypto-Buddhist; but, in the deepest sense, he must be devout.

Whatever else it is, Panichas's conservatism is neither doctrinaire nor programmatic. Deeply concerned, as his anthologies and the essays in his book both show, with politics and religion, and their relation to literature, he does not proselytize for any specific ecclesiasticisms, though presumably his taste is for the more traditional and orthodox varieties; and politically he is neither a monarchist, nor, necessarily, a Republican. He stands for man's recognition of his dual citizenship in church and state, society visible and invisible, for man's recognition that all we are we owe; that we do not, and cannot, begin *ab ovo* and *de novo* but are heirs to a great inheritance of tradition and wisdom, represented in the West by our joint indebtedness to the Greek philosophers, the Hebrew prophets, and the Christian saints.

Panichas admires monolithic men who attack and expose the sins and follies, the errors and heresies, of the modern age; yet, for the most part, he does not himself appear in that role of enemy, but rather as guide and as the sympathetic expositor of the great exponents of positions he admires,—preeminently Leavis, the moralist; Babbitt, the humanist; and Weil, the prophetic and spiritual seeker. In his humility he calls our attention to his own masters. Though his discipleship is selective,—that is to say, discriminating and critical,—he dwells not on any restrictions he may put upon his approval but upon those aspects of his heroes to which he can give reverence.

Panichas's *The Reverent Discipline* is subtitled "Essays in Literary Criticism and Culture." "Literary" criticism is "reverent" because it is ancillary to imaginative literature (i.e., poetry, the novel, and drama), and because its prime object is the appreciative illumination of writers and works selected by the taste of the critic. *The Courage of*

Judgment represents, for Panichas, a shift of emphasis: here, the essays are in "criticism—and culture and society." In both titles, "culture" stands halfway between Arnold's use of the term, which we might now gloss or paraphrase as "high culture," and "culture" in the quasi-sociological sense the term bears in our time: the common matrix of habits and attitudes shared by a society, the matrix out of which more specialized and professional emphases develop.

Courage of Judgment is a title complementary to *Reverent Discipline*, for the critic—whether a literary critic or a critic in the readily intelligible larger sense which covers men like José Ortega y Gasset, Lewis Mumford, and Babbitt—needs both reverence and courage of judgment: reverence in the presence of persons and principles he deems higher than himself and in the presence of masterpieces of art and thought, and courage of judgment to make his own assessment of what are those higher values. Panichas praises Sir Harold Acton, an aesthete, for his "reverence for beauty"; and, since we may assume that our critic's supreme values are the so-called Platonic trinity of the Good, the True, and the Beautiful, reverence for beauty, though beauty be the least of these values, is itself a virtue.

Henry James speaks, in a phrase of which both Panichas and I are fond, of "the ceaseless wear and tear of discrimination" required by the act of judgment. It indeed takes courage to face, in one's own silent thought, in one's speech, in one's letters and in one's published writings, this ceaseless and fatiguing discrimination,—never to allow oneself to slip into easy compliance with the currently accepted compromised standards of one's neighborhood, one's university (academics are not noted for their courage), one's inherited nation, one's church or religion. There can be no relaxation of the critical spirit, no unbending of the bow; and no sphere is exempt from its operation—if the critical spirit be justly joined to the spirit of reverence. It is a "vulgar error" to suppose that conservatives need accept whatever is; and Panichas's conservatism, like Babbitt's (though it often judges differently), is highly critical. Any position can be taken hastily, on grounds of temperament or tradition; but it can also be taken reflectively, after experience, observation, meditation, and judgment, as Panichas does.

Earlier I have said "All we are we owe"; but I should have added, "all save our present act of judgment and commitment." In ecclesiastical terms, we are baptized into the faith of our parents but "confirmation" awaits some degree of maturity, some time at which we are capable of ratifying the decision provisionally made for us.

It is the supreme merit of *The Courage of Judgment* that it covers almost the whole of man's basic categories,—political theory, religion, literature, and education,—that its "criticism" is so unspecialized, so general and generalist. Its prime virtue will not be grasped if one reads only the essays on the subjects of one's own professional and temperamental competence. I can myself testify how such a total reading has forced me, in my old age, to reexamine, rethink, rejudge, reflect upon the range and repertory of my own intellectual positions. Panichas's book might thus be called what Coleridge called one of his, *Aids to Reflection*.

On the first page of his penultimate *Democracy and Leadership*, Irving Babbitt wrote: "When studied with any degree of thoroughness, the economic problem will be found to run into the political problem, the political problem in turn into the philosophical problem, and the philosophical problem itself to be almost indissolubly bound up at last with the religious problem"; let us add, somewhere along the line, the problem of education, to which Babbitt devoted his keenly sound first book, *Literature and the American College*. The critic, as distinct from the purely literary critic, is deeply aware of this interpenetration of values—as was Matthew Arnold, in his *Essays in Criticism* as well as in his books on culture, society, and religion, as was T.S. Eliot, in all his later books. Such is the ancestry, in the English line, to which Panichas belongs.

Like all thoughtful men, Panichas esteems knowledge as a good, but fears its substitution for wisdom (*sapientia*): indeed wisdom, and its Latinized adjective, *sapiential*, appear often in his book. Knowledge and specialized expertise are not enough without wisdom and what is inseparable from it, character, responsibility, integrity. These qualities, of which the world stands in such dire need to-day, cannot be acquired just by taking college courses, or just by reading whatever comes to hand: reading as such may be an opiate, a more refined version of watching whatever emerges on the TV screen. For the development of character, the "elective system" of Harvard's President Eliot will not suffice. It is not true that any subject, any course, is as valuable as any other. There must be a rigorous selection of what is truly basic, balanced, central—one is even tempted to say: of traditional value.

We live, fifty years after Babbitt, in a time when his predictions have come true. The modern world goes on its deterministic way. Novelty, whatever its kind, is prized over continuity (a central conservative word); bigger is equated with better (though surely, "small can be beautiful"); change of whatever kind is identified with progress, or improvement, though it is often just the reverse.

The courage of judgment is the prime virtue of the critic, his *unum necessarium*. To criticize is to take a stand,—it is not necessarily to damn or to deride, as popular usage would have it; much of the best criticism is considered and selective celebration. If detachment is requisite, so is empathy,—each in its place. Experience and a certain degree of learning are the prerequisites to detachment; just as an unabashed openness to new experiences and further learning are to enlightened empathy. All this suggests the necessity for balance; but balance (which so easily may seem calculation and compromise) is not to be sought for as such.

The critic must work out his decisions with fear and trembling, for he must be a responsible guide, if not an actual leader, in a world which, most of all in America, but increasingly in the whole Western world, becomes quantitative. In an age given over to all manner of polls, so that one can discover the "trend" and, lest one prove eccentric, follow it, the critic must judge for himself, and then be possessed of the final courage to utter his judgment.

A.W.

THE
Courage
OF
Judgment

·

*We fight for lost causes because we know
that our defeat and dismay may be the
preface to our successors' victory, though that
victory itself will be temporary; we fight
rather to keep something alive than in the
expectation that anything
will triumph.*

—T.S. ELIOT

Introduction

THE ESSAYS IN THIS BOOK can, for purely catalogical purposes, be called essays in criticism, culture, and society. Or, for purposes of purely descriptive summary, they can be put under the rubric of literary and social criticism. Or, too, for the purpose of adverting to the particular critical system and methodology being employed, they can be viewed as selected instances of the teacher and critic conversing on subjects he seeks both to teach and to criticize. One's critical thought, however, cannot be easily classified if it is sufficiently critical. Indeed, the central concern of this book is ignited by the need to challenge and to resist precisely those habits of mind that lead to the ascendancy of quantifying criteria at all levels of life and letters. What unifies the critical theory and practice of these essays is, in fact, a deep and constant concern with this double need in all its urgency. On occasion this sense of urgency is echoed in the militant tone of the essays. But militant is a word that presumes a far greater adjectival force within the contexts and directions of these essays in their totality. Courage and judgment, the two emphases covered by the title of the book, indicate not only the book's aims and ideas but also the internalities of its preoccupation with what is considered of urgent importance in the modern world. Those conditions of criticism, and of culture and society, that are viewed as urgent are those that require a persistent examining response. Such a response, if it is to convey any evidence of truth, must revolve around the necessities of courage and judgment that must be met as necessities.

Throughout, the courage of judgment will be seen working on two, interconnected dimensions: that which includes great teachers, critics, and creative writers, who serve as protagonists of the critical function; and that which depicts the major critical problems confronting civilization, as well as the humanistic values that have come under threat and attack. The literary and the sociohistorical situations delineated here are subjected to critical verdicts and, more specifically, verdicts as to significance. Criticism is an adjudicative process, and the critic, in his struggle for verbal consciousness, must speak to others. When that struggle occurs in a period of crisis and unbelief, he strives to understand what is happening. Essentially, then, his critical responses are reports about the struggle that rages in the world—and in himself. Such reports catch something of the danger and the friction found in that struggle. They also catch something of the critic's search for the idea of value. Standards of criticism and the responsibilities of the critic, in their reciprocal relations, must designate the first acceptance of the office and province of criticism. If in the dialectic terms of his experience of literature the critic must meet the necessity of analysis and judgment, he must also meet the necessity of courage. For one who is responsive to these necessities, the criticism of literature inevitably entails the criticism of culture and society, in which literary ideas have their counterpoise in moral or social or religious ideas. Critical discourse emerges from and makes essential a triadic experience of life, literature, and thought. The critical function embraces human and spiritual values and mobilizes sensibility and moral perceptions. It is a consummate process, all the more positive and critical in its recognition of the wider contexts that go beyond the immediate text; of the permanent things that transcend the impermanent things; of the enduring wisdom, the right use of reason, and the habit of order that proceed from a qualitative and selective fusion of literature as a reverent discipline and of criticism as the courage of judgment.

Identifying the critical function, as both necessity and centrality, as a force for life, calls attention to a related need: that of defining and defending the critic's main responsibility. The mission of the critic is compromised as a result of either a misconception or a displacement of its integral values. In particular, this failing is to be seen in the attempt, which in time changes into bad critical habits and practices, to absolve the critical function of any ethical or moral dimension. Such an abdication results in an erosion of the critic's responsibility. Authentic fulfillment of critical responsibility demands a rigorous commitment to principles of order, to the making of hard choices and categorical decisions, to the selection and the espousal not merely of aesthetic, literary, or linguistic values but of ethical and moral derivatives—and imperatives. There exists, then, what can be called not so much the business but rather the character of criticism, not only as it arises from and discloses criteria and discriminations but also as it opposes the lures of critical *divertissements* and avocations. Insofar as we refuse to recognize this character of criticism as sapient, we must continue to fail to locate, in life as in literature, a center of values. Such a failure harbors the seeds of nemesis. The consequences, for civilization, are disastrous; and the major, and ultimate, questions with which literature and thought are concerned are ignored, or scorned, or dismissed in favor of peripheral and, indeed, extraneous questions that too often occupy students and even scholars. One's choice of a critical pathway reveals the character of the criticism and of the critic. It tells us much about how one views his world and himself; how one bears the burden of one's critical responsibility; in short, how one wrestles with literary values as these inevitably relate to cultural values. The character of criticism must emerge from a serious, deliberate attempt, finally, to answer at least two paramount questions: What does the critic care about, if he cares about anything at all? And does he show that what he cares about is something that matters?

Implicit in assessing an answer to these questions is the position one ultimately takes concerning the critical pursuit in its humanistic dimension. The critic stamps the character of his criticism in the framework of his perception of humanistic values. One of the crises in the twentieth century, and it is surely a crisis that we are now experiencing in its final and most fateful phase, is the decline or even the disappearance of the humanistic tradition. The ethos of this tradition is centrally and singularly ethical and moral, stressing as it does the sanctity of human worth. In effect the humanistic ethos validates, qualitatively, man's destiny and resists the relentless attempts to technicalize, to objectify, and to dehumanize man's significance and, indeed, his essentially spiritual being. Critical concerns, as humanistic concerns, are precisely those that resist what one might call the statistical-sociological preoccupations that have increasingly moved to the center of intellectual life not merely as a replacement of the humanist ethos but as the creed of a new reality. The alteration of the idea of value in modern times is best described not by the critic as humanist, but by the critic as ideologue, as one who has renounced the old principles of wisdom, synonymous with the abiding One, so to speak, in favor of experiment and change, in their relativistic values. Inevitably this alteration reduces ethical and moral humanism to ineffectuality and makes it dispensable and thus inoperative. Thingness, in its various departmentalizing critical guises and smatterings, with each new vogue invariably blown out of all proportion, has become the critic's dogma. Outer values replace, with an appropriating arrogance, the inner values with which the humanistic ethos is associated. Measurement and not valuation now characterizes the critical act. As critical humanism has been usurped, a quantum criticism, as it might be called, has surged forward. Such a criticism can be no less pluralistic and technical than modern culture itself, with which it enjoys a mechanistic alliance of means and ends.

The critical function should not belong to an exclusive category of thought or to an exclusive class of persons. Nor should it be viewed as an activity of the mind that is self-regulating and self-sufficient, some autonomous concern to be pursued for its own particular sake or even for its own idiosyncratic excellence. To believe that the critical function should, for instance, be reserved by and for the academic mind is to perpetuate the mythical aura that has often come to surround it and that has, in fact, further removed it from its rightful and necessary place in life. The values of critical thought are in themselves life-values; they contain a connective absoluteness and viability that endow them with a universality that defies formalistic boundaries separating life from literature and literature from life. Such boundaries are synthetic and dangerous. In the end, they inhibit thought as a primary substantive element, without which any consideration of life and literature remains meaningless. To be sure, there is always a need to apprehend and define the critical function in terms of standards. The critical function requires a discriminatory process in and by which standards are formulated, affirmed, and applied. But standards of thought should in no way mislead one to accept the formation of boundaries—the boundaries that become barriers—between the realm of life and the realm of literature. Life, literature, and thought are inclusive and cohering entities, simultaneously revolving around standards and transcending boundaries. That is to say, the critical function is not to be seen as an isolate act circumscribed by its own special province, by its own special practitioners, by its own special set of standards, by its own special audience, or by its own special time and place. Such an insistence on these individuating prerogatives of the critical function as a specialist function diminishes radically, perhaps fatally, its potentiality as a positive value relevant to the meaning of literature and of life in their totality of human experience.

Critical chimeras and sophistries in their present proliferation, often solipsistic and sometimes even pathological, point to the consistently aggressive attack on the idea and the value of *humanitas.* In this respect, they are centrifugal symptoms and portents of an age increasingly dissociating itself from the intellectual and spiritual excellences that the humanistic temper, as essentially a vision of order, contains. The call to greatness one associates with the voice of humanism is heard of less and less. The identification of the soul of man with the soul of culture is repudiated, as pervasive cynicism, narcissistic conundrums, and vagaries (often in the form of a pitiable *angst*) are given unending importance at all cultural levels, a disproportion violating even the most modest standards of discrimination, let alone of civilization. The permanent things, as transcendent and metaphysical constituents of humanism, are renounced to the point of extinction. The eternal questions are reduced to the level of commercialism—or to a maddening self-pity and self-deception. Critical pedagogy, or *paideia*, in the best humanistic sense of comprehensiveness, gives way to surrogate specialisms of the most parochial forms, particularly to a contemporary critical rhetoric that rarely manages to escape the violence of its aberrations and fragmentation.

These are certainly not, for the critic, happy conditions to view, let alone report. To be silent (or defensive) about them is for some no doubt the preferable and less consequential choice. In either case the conditions of disarray are allowed to multiply, to the detriment not only of the dignity of literature but also of civilization, of life itself. Thought, intelligent critical thought, suffers in the process, and this is a concomitant that, for anyone at all concerned with the survival of *homo humanus*, poses the most disturbing problem. Survival may seem to some a needlessly alarming word to use, and it may signal to others yet another occasion for ugly rebuttal and the sanctimonious display of irreverence, a double negation that so much of contemporary academic and journalistic criticism dictates. Such reactions, in their abundance, in their display of power, and in their command of strategic power centers, register not merely a reigning orthodoxy of enlightenment. They are reactions that underline dramatically the diminution of the pertinence of a critical humanism as an ethical and moral reference to human life and education.

A critical humanism without a metaphysical basis—or reality without a consciousness of beginnings and endings and of first and last principles—remains incomplete, ineffectual. It fails, in short, as a totality of spiritual value. Any absence of spiritual value, as a reverence for fundamental experience and moral distinctions, must inevitably result in the search for synthetic social values. The endless, captive attention that many artists and critics, in alliance, now give to the things of the world—to the trivial, the skeptical, the irreverent, the demeaning, the obscene, the blasphemous, the nihilistic—is symptomatic of a regnant positivistic temper (as opposed, for instance, to a classical temper). Moral neutrality too often permeates an approach to the problems of criticism, as well as to problems of culture. As critical reductionism gains in importance and influence, critical humanism wanes. In the process we notice the blanket dismissal of ethical and moral values as unverifiable, as empirically meaningless. Academic criticism, by endorsing the vulgar commercial criticism of the literary marketplace, corroborates and abets the empirical. It, too, indiscriminatingly synthesizes with the prevailing climate of opinion. And it, too, views itself as a science or a sociology of criticism, not as a humanistic discipline of intelligence and a training of sensibility. The critic's educating function, under the circumstances, falls into eclipse, a tendency that cannot be other than disastrous to man's possibilities. Diagnostic and judgmental truths are discredited; the quantifiable and the measurable become the informing principles of intellectual arrogance. Conditions of criticism, no less than those of civilization, are relegated to technical dictates and computerized efficiency. The morally (and metaphysically) neutral or relativistic thrives as the standards and traditions of critical humanism are abolished. It is hardly necessary to observe that, for such a transposition (of the idea of value, of orientation) to occur, the religious concept of life is one of the first theoretical foundations to be allowed to deteriorate, or, as has often happened since 1917, to be grossly radicalized. As such, the crisis of criticism is related to the continuing crisis of faith, which in turn leads to the crisis of humanistic civilization.

Today there is an insistent concern with means and ends that overshadows what should be a concern with causes and effects. This concern with means and ends, inescapably functional and technical, cannot be recognized as a legitimate critical concern insofar as it severs ties to the humanistic critique of existence. It is impelled and shaped by elements foreign to human destiny in its moral perspective. Criticism that removes itself from moral transcendences, in terms of choices, discriminations, and tacit cause-and-effect estimations, must simultaneously lose the moral impulse that originates with belief in standards and values. Under the circumstances, the derivative categories of moral distinctions and hierarchies are robbed of their diagnostic and judgmental capacities. That which is integratively absolute in humanistic, and qualitative, value slides into quantitative technique: into a quantum criticism that assists the equations of physics; that is stereoscopic, computative, and molecular in conception and application; that draws its atomic modes and bases of observation and conclusion from empirical science. The organic properties of criticism belong less and less to a critical humanism and more and more to a quantum mechanics, to quantum mechanical analyses. Criticism finds itself increasingly, perhaps even terminally, in a crisis situation as humanistic judgments of value become mere appropriations of basic physical laws and mathematical relationships.

Subsumed in this process of a unified hierarchy of science are not only other branches of science (physics, chemistry, biology, and medicine) but also other human fields in addition to criticism: psychology, anthropology, sociology, and politics. What is so frightening about this subsumption is the twin tyranny of the secular and the material, measuring the meaning of existence and the act of judgment by exclusionary units, or quanta. The humane element in criticism, with its overarching verities, thus becomes still another victim of a continuing fragmentation. Identifying character as a centripetal element of the critical function becomes an utter impossibility.

A commitment to the critical process is an exercise in responsibility that predicates belief, thought, and judgment. Insofar as the critical process is evaded or allowed to deteriorate, the pursuit of truth is considerably weakened. The structure of commitment and the act of judgment impel and complement each other. An act of commitment and an articulated judgment conjoin to signify a daring at once intellectual and spiritual. Such a nexus constitutes a profession of faith. But in an age of equivalence the critical process loses these qualitative distinctions, as the critical element and the democratic sentiment are progressively confused in terms of both the specifics and the primacy of the value that each conveys. It is not unpatriotic, surely, to assert that the critical spirit as a conceptual framework is ultimately judgmental and not democratic. At every literary and cultural level the critical process, if it is to be authentic and to mean anything, must maintain a transcendent position and exert a transcendent value. As such it cannot be a mere acceptance of democratic idols or a mere acquiescence to shifting popular enthusiasms. Where such surrender is made and implemented, especially in the name of pluralism, the results are manifestly alarming—and damaging to critical intelligence and to humane civilization. In the most reductive, because subservient, ways, we choose to equalize critical judgment with the climate of opinion. That element of character that validates and orients the critical act, such as courage of judgment, is, under the circumstances, subordinated, materialized in the most disintegrating ways. Critical disorientation portends cultural disorientation. Where the critical function, critical thought, is devalued, where standards of discrimination, both intellectual and moral, are spurned, cultural life must inevitably deteriorate. An age of anxiety too easily becomes an age of doubt. This doubt now approaches monolithic proportions and becomes a universal nightmare of doubt as fundamental beliefs are everywhere questioned and assaulted.

The humanistic studies, including the critical discipline, are the most vulnerable victims of this assault. In terms of consequences and results (for it is no longer just a matter of recognizing symptoms and portents), modern man's situation becomes one of extremes. Beliefs, convictions, and judgments, when ravaged by doubts—particularly doubts as to their verification and essential validity—lead to unceasing innovation, change, experiment, aggregation; on the other hand, nihilistic self-doubt inevitably leads to a moral vacuum. Judgment, above all, becomes a prey of the collectivist view, of pragmatic tests, of empirical procedures. Judgmental concerns are forcibly transformed into what are called job-related situations. The capable communicator (or, worse, coordinator) is the man of today. Literature, as a reverent discipline, and criticism, as the courage of judgment, are reduced to marketable communications skills. As mere gradients, thought, language, and creativity are tailored to the crass extremisms of the new reality, in which doubt turns into denial. At no point, then, is there greater displacement of humanistic value than at the point of denial, since it produces not so much a disequilibrium as a complete loss of value or possibility of transcendence. The total human situation testifies to the grim repercussions in terms not only of diminished mind but also of crippled soul. First principles, as such, are rejected. Ideas of discipline and of hierarchic values, as sources of civilizing power and truth and as concordances of judgment, are ignored. Spiritual interests and needs become irrelevant. Insofar, then, as these needs in both realms are needs of integration, their diminution must ultimately weaken the act, let alone the courage, of judgment. The results of such a decrease—desacralization, demoralization, disorientation—affect the entire culture and force it more and more into fragmented states of extremism. In time, disequilibrium becomes full-scale retreat. Denial of judgment manifests precisely those uncentered extremisms that proliferate in every sector of life.

The act of judgment is, to reiterate, an act of courage. It is a decision to speak responsibly, spiritually, to the matter of value; to the necessity for forming, expressing, transmitting, and continuing a definable position; to the affirmation of transcending direction and principle; to the willingness to respond to a test of conscience and thought; to a perception of origins and goals, beginnings and endings. The courage of judgment is an irreducible event, a turning point. Where it is absent or lost, where it is surrendered to the power of the world, corrosion and negation become the most evident debilitations of life and thought. There is no end to the consequences of the neglect or the absence of judgment. Yet, as an old Hasidic saying reminds us, if man does not judge himself, all things will judge him, and all these things will also become the messengers of God. In this respect, the pursuit of judgment is a tacit affirmation of belief. It affirms a belief in value greater than in its immediate self or circumstances; thus it makes judgment an intrinsic dimension of a higher framework. It is not excessive to claim that the critical mission, no less than the imagination, is at its maximum a religious process, whatever resistance or scorn this claim may arouse in the apologists for a secular dynamism. It is all too evident that with the eclipse of belief in the idea of value there is also a lessening concern with judgment. Certitudes are much less in demand in a period that delights in irreverence and desanctification. The crisis of criticism, no less than the crisis of the imagination, mirrors this breakdown. The critic, no less than the imaginative artist, possesses neither centrality nor authority. If we are to see, as we must, the critical function in intimate connection with the educational task, perhaps the most alarming symptom of the deterioration of the office of the critic is the concomitant deterioration of the mission of the educator. Damage to one does damage to the other. Inevitably the cultural drifts and shifts that are in such widespread evidence are direct embodiments of this dual deterioration. Fragmentation, insofar as it erodes the reciprocal, unifying function of critic and of teacher, can hardly conduce humanistic and spiritual renewal on either a personal or a social level.

The consequences are inescapable as the critical and cultural situation hardens into a stasis. Intellectual and moral greatness are absent, but academic (and political) ideologists and their power enclaves, self-regulating and self-serving, thrive. Inevitably the entire cultural situation reflects the apodictic extremisms emerging from localizing concepts of human experience. Secular and specifically political and liberal experience, as opposed to noetic experience, is everywhere ascendant. The critic as publicist and not the critic as teacher creates and dictates policy; definers and defenders of critical and cultural discriminations (and integrations) are in retreat as sundry idolatries, particularly that of a modern gnosticism in education, are constituted—and reconstituted. Criticism, which should provide informing standards and bearings, falls into the same solipsism that grips so much of the contemporary literary imagination. The belief, for example, that the study of literature embodies a reverent discipline, ethically and morally, as well as critically and culturally, is increasingly difficult to communicate and even at times to express. But it is not only the critical function that flounders, and along with it the allied but necessarily diluted task of education. The concept of the religious significance of man is another major casualty of disorientation. Demystification, which is a singular form of specious grace and worth, abrogates universals and solidifies the process of secularization. What can be called critical fictions, in the form of quantitative demonstrations, dislodge those transcendent values that one identifies with some organic spiritual truth, or some principle of unity, or some perception of fair judgment, or some intrinsic discipline of idea. The dislodgements emerge gradually (too gradually, it seems) as new dogmas, which are, in reality, the mechanisms that prevail against any judgment of values. These circumstances are not so much brutally paradoxical in substance as they are destructive in direction. It is precisely this individuating destructiveness that transforms a metaphysics of values into a chaos of values that goes beyond nihilism. In such a process critical thought is a principal victim. When the process becomes a situation, then the conditions of both a critical and a cultural disorientation assume an irreversible, circumscribing primacy.

These dangerous and adverse conditions are clearly in need of being recognized for what they are; however circumscribing in their strengths, they should not deter a dissenting scrutiny. In the recognition of these conditions is to be found the possibility that goes with opportunity: the opportunity for noticing the dangers and adversaries that should not go unchallenged. The expression of reservations and complaints, or the call for moral imperatives, undoubtedly will be resented. The critical function, insofar as it posits particular standards and asserts the autonomy of particular qualities of life and thought, represents a form of austerity that is obviously incompatible with an age fundamentally opposed to registering any conditions of restraint. Adjustment to the democratizing norms of relativity, sentimentalism, expansionism, uniformism, and egalitarianism is demanded. These norms, in fact, are the defining and quantifying criteria that shape pedagogy and intellectual and sociopolitical life as a whole. The concept of restraint is, for the majoritarian ethos, both an implicit and an intended attack on the security of an open society. Resistance to anything that questions the meaning and degree of regulative norms, that requires us to be transparent to ourselves and to our institutions, becomes intense and categorical. Even some commentators who would in principle support the courage of judgment as discrimination, proscription (if necessary), correction, and redirection exhibit a tendency to hesitate when it is time to give a final accounting that is not commensurate with the way things are. This is especially true for those who would isolate the office of criticism, citing the sacred priority of the delicacy of judgment. This argument, if altogether sincere, can be self-delusive and compromising. It exemplifies the desire not only to avoid naming names, imputing motives, or saying what is in one's mind, but also to avoid confronting basic issues that relate to the very survival of intelligent thought and civilization. Criticism is by its very nature confrontation—confrontation that ultimately rests on the courage of judgment. In such a framework one can neither deny nor abjure an element of violence, if by violence one means repudiating the canons of a collective, imperialistic mediocrity.

That for some persons a critical approach, especially one developed in the contexts of a censorial inspection, is too negative goes without saying. But no excuse is needed for holding to any approach that concerns itself with ultimate questions and with a sensibility of principle; with, above all, the need to generate qualitative, fundamental considerations, decisions, and judgments that enlarge and sharpen an awareness of life and that accentuate values, humanistic and spiritual, superior to those of the marketplace. These integrant values contain moral essences, transcending mere conditions of locality or pragmatic demand; and they belong to the large, or comprehensive, view of culture and society, transcending the flux and the temporal. In fact, such a critical approach, far from being negative and destructive, seeks to conserve precisely those values of character in life, in literature, and in thought that modern empirical radicalisms seek to twist and destroy. It is time for such a criticism to assert its central tasks—circumspection, meditation, correction, and conservation; to assert, in effect, the presiding constituents of the process of judgment—necessities rather than expediencies, instruction rather than power, restraint rather than expansiveness, reverence rather than mockery, order rather than chaos.

The need to foment and instill critical leadership is a moral need. It is, decline and debasement being what they are in modern civilization, a desperate and final need. Theories of criticism, no less than applied theories of literature (as the latter abound in and incite so much of the literary imagination, at times to the point of perverse esotericisms and sensations), revolve around peculiarly academic specialisms and psychologies increasingly detached from the deeper meaning of life as judgment, as conduct, as character. A random glance at the conditions both of modern pedagogy and of the sociopolitical situation is enough to indicate the failure of mind and of nerve to an extraordinary degree. The vices of criticism and the frenzy of imaginative literature have, as the twentieth century wanes, left us burdened with a legacy of distempers. It is time for the critic who believes that he has a real, moral function to assume the corrective work he has to do on the basis of principles and not theories, with the courage of judgment that combats noncritical enthusiasm for innovation.

A combative dissenting criticism is especially needed in a time when critical standards and cultural values are under heavy attack, when change and innovation are upon us everywhere. If a critic can do nothing but warn of lost bearings and wrong directions, while at the same time instancing the moral infirmities of any human situation in which rights replace obligations, he is fulfilling his function. Our obsession with rights, with the freedom that becomes license, has become as pervasive as it is fanatical. The democratizing yearning, expansive in root and reach, to oppose whatever restrictive view may be proffered ultimately leads to the abdication of any abiding principle or any rule. In this respect, it needs reiterating that the expansionist view is not the genuinely far view. Yet what prevails with such stubborn and arrogant consistency, what so often creates policy and legislates taste and thought, is precisely this expansiveness that promises freedom, at no matter what cost.

It is profoundly disquieting to note the dominance and the arbitrariness of the lords of the new disorder. Undoubtedly, the expression of critical dissent is condemned in many quarters not only as negative but also as pessimistic. Forever riding on the wave of the future, liberal optimists will cite, for example, the sales and the consumption of items of high culture as proof of progress, or of joy, or of vitality. Even by dividing criticism into pessimism and optimism, they abandon the judgmental process by reducing it to statistical tests. This argument is self-congratulatory. It is a pragmatic approach of free acceptance, not a critical approach of conviction. To invoke its merits as creative self-criticism is merely to repeat a euphemism, as well as an ideal thesis, that breaks upon individual and collective romanticisms. It is, in a word, criticism as self-indulgence. Secular in its concern and direction, it relegates fundamental things to secondary or tertiary importance. Questions of value and the judgment of values, found inoperable on a positivistic or a mathematical basis, are dismissed by relativists who now go under the name of revisionists. For the latter, it seems, incorrigible optimism heralds glad tidings even in the midst of the breakdown of moral and sociopolitical standards. At its worst this is a form of indiscriminating intellectual hedonism; at its best it is a muddle; either way it is a clear and present danger to the function of criticism.

It may very well seem to some that to hold to a critical position, which, in short, means both identifying and combating the debasing conditions found in a place and at a time that scorn discrimination, definition, significance, and value as principles of order, has no relevant worth—no "viability," as the word is now so often used. Lacking the courage of judgment, they have forcibly reconciled themselves to these new conditions, even as they express serious reservations concerning the changes that are swiftly, furiously occurring. Others have enthusiastically enlisted in the ranks of those who herald the new Logos, insofar as they refuse to accept (even to under-stand) the role of moral imperatives in imagination, in criticism, in thought, and in culture and society as a whole. For them there is only the one certainty of the ebb and flow of all things; moral constants are unverifiable abstractions that belong to an ungraspable and unde-monstrable order. For still others, there is the thrill of inaugurating change, of endlessly experimenting for the sake of experimentation. They recognize no limits and, therefore, no idea of value. For them, the critical function does not exist in a substantive or a fundamental form. It is neither seen nor respected as a discipline of thought, as a process of discrimination, as the embodiment of enduring principles and standards; it is shorn of any moral meaning in the contexts of self-criticism and self-restraint. The consequences of this nihilism are inescapable, for the weakening and defacement of the critical function go far beyond the immediate problems of criticism, which must inevitably relate to economic, social, political, philosophical, and, above all, religious problems in all their complexity.

Failures of criticism reflect failures in these other key areas of life and thought. What should be a continuous interplay between the critical function and the other realms of life dissolves in the absence of basic humanistic standards. When the critical function lacks def-inition and has little authority, when it is made subordinate to the idols of the marketplace, to the vaunting spirit of equivalence, to the demands of shifting doctrines and drifting states of mind, dispersion-ary tendencies arise to presage collapse and to create a void. These tendencies are the enemy of humane civilization. If they continue to be allowed to multiply and to advance indiscriminatingly, the break-down will be complete and invincible. To challenge and to resist the collectivist enemy are commands that the humanistic critic must accept, no matter how great the perils or the costs. In waging his fight and in fulfilling his mission, he has need of no greater courage than the courage of judgment.

Part 1

DEFINERS AND DEFENDERS

•

It is out of reverence for the moral ideal that we must fight against its greatest enemies, which are perverse moralities.

—JOSÉ ORTEGA Y GASSET

1

The Challenge of Simone Weil

I

No one who reads about the life of Simone Weil (1909–1943) can escape the consequences of the process of reflection, a process that, in her own words, "presupposes a transformation in the orientation of the soul."[1] Insofar as it can be said that reflection is an initiation into wisdom, then Simone Weil's value is extraordinary. We live neither in an age nor in a society conducive to reflection. Our modernism has so pitilessly conditioned us against this process that it is hard to turn away from our new little habitats and new little hopes. We remain prisoners within the very walls that we have built in and around a century that we so confidently cite as being progressive. This confidence is undeserved and unjustified, for the instances, as well as the possibilities, of escape from our modern fate—one of spiritual littleness or blankness—become rarer. We have perhaps reached the point where we can no longer perceive the truth about the desperate nature of our captivity and emptiness. No helpers are on the scene to lead us out of the wasteland. No prophetic voice can be heard reminding us of our true spiritual destiny. The voices that we do hear are, on the contrary, ugly and scornful. It is the Voice of the World that rages. And that Voice is damned, something that we refuse to admit. Diabolism, which Simone Weil defined as "the empire of might," dictates the conditions of our imprisonment. To battle or protest against this diabolism involves risks of increasing magnitude. Few dare to take these risks. Since we have no Simone Weil in our midst today, we must try to recall her authentic witness, even if it means only glimpsing her shadow at the edge of eternity. We need to reflect on her witness, for we need her help.

To reflect on Simone Weil is to see that she achieved in life what others merely imagine (or, as the case may more often be, fear to imagine). What her life reveals is great spiritual courage and tough-

---

1. All quotations from Simone Weil's writings come from the volume I edited under the title *The Simone Weil Reader* (New York, 1977).

ness: the refusal to surrender to or compromise with those modern forms of imperfection that go under the name of mediocrity. In Simone Weil, the spirit of Hellenism and the prophetic faith attained a Christian synthesis, no easy attainment, and one that requires moral strength of will and definiteness of purpose and character. That she had so much courage "in sight of chaos" tends to intimidate those who, even as they may respect her, view her personal and spiritual example as "unrealistic" and "inhuman." The fact is that we are accustomed to so much spiritual cowardice and ambivalence that when a real religious visionary does appear we become resentful. The discomfiting problem that Simone Weil presents to her critics is that in her own life and beliefs she never deviated from the standards, from the perfectionism, that she defined as being necessary to spiritual faith. Hers was an indefatigable journey in search of the pure absolute. Her scruples and scrupulousness, as her life and work amply demonstrate, were maintained no matter what the cost. If this maintenance gave moral and spiritual centrality to her life, to those coming into contact with it it discloses a standard that must be strained for if it is to be reached. What makes Simone Weil so difficult to understand, let alone to accept, is her requirement that, in one's spiritual journey, one must continuously strain for spiritual progress and purification. "There is a distinction," she avers, "between those who remain inside the cave shutting their eyes and imagining the journey, and those who really take it." These brave words epitomize the challenge of Simone Weil, as they perhaps epitomize the reasons modern man is not yet ready to receive her witness.

Her life must be viewed as a supremely consummate spiritual effort. Though it is quite true that, until the early 1930s, she was frenziedly involved in radical political activity of a decidedly Marxian cast, she was not so much a political ideologue as a sensitive sympathizer with everyone and everything in life that suffered oppression in any form. "I envied her for having a heart that could beat right across the world," wrote Simone de Beauvoir in *Memoirs of a Dutiful Daughter* (1959). Simone Weil was both a friend of man and a "friend of God," and no doctrine could ever come before this reciprocal allegiance. If there is any centralizing dogma, any rooted principle of unity, that encompasses Simone Weil's life and thought, it is her sensitivity to affliction: "Human existence is so fragile a thing and exposed to such dangers that I cannot love without trembling." Throughout her life, in whatever capacity, whether as teacher, political dissident, factory and farm worker, or religious visionary and philosopher, all roles she combined with a profound devotion and a tenacious purity of purpose, she never forgot the fallen and broken men and women whom she called her brothers and sisters and with whom she sought to share what she termed "the religion of slaves." If her own life was bereft of physical love, if passion was something that she could never experience, could never share with another person, she strove to translate this lacking physical love into a greater fellowship of spiritual love. Her deep admiration of Antigone is pertinent here. Not unlike the ancient Greek heroine she chose to love on a transcendent plane.

Contact with Simone Weil's life is contact with spiritual heroism. This is no ordinary human life, but rather, in T.S. Eliot's words, "a woman of genius, of a kind of genius akin to that of a saint." For a woman who was so often sickly it is remarkable that her life contained so many and such intense actions, commitments, conflicts, and involvements, of which her brief participation in the Spanish Civil War is a notable example. (It is not surprising that she was nicknamed the "Terror.") More than anything else she wanted to identify, and thus to penetrate and understand, the human condition: its travail, its burdens, its suffering—its ultimate spiritual meaning. This yearning led her into the depths. No abyss could restrain her courage or overtax her perseverance; her experience of the abyss was her experience of passion. Driven as she was by this passion, she was also devoured by it. Such an experience was not only prophetic but also Christlike. "It is very difficult to judge from above," she said, "and it is very difficult to act from below. That, I believe, is in general one of the essential causes of human misery. And that is why I myself wanted to go right to the bottom and will perhaps return there." Others, we know, have touched bottom, but too often their aims revolve around acts of self-justification that transpose into adventures in consciousness. But for Simone Weil the view of the bottom contained divine glimpses, hints, shocks, connections, in which gravity and grace became a purifying experience of God.

"She had the poverty of those who are searching." This is how Sister Colombe described Simone Weil in a letter recalling their meeting.[2] Almost from the beginning of her life, self-sacrifice and self-denial were her most constant companions. She reminds us that there can be no mysticism without asceticism. Since, as she believed, our age is one of real and not simply metaphysical affliction, she chose to bear this affliction in whatever way she could. Especially during the early years of World War II did her yearning to share human suffering heighten. She sought furiously to avoid any kind of

---

2. See Simone Pétrement, *Simone Weil: A Life,* trans. Raymond Rosenthal (New York, 1976).

comfort that removed her from peril and hunger. She sought to experience "a different kind of tension." To Maurice Schumann, a former classmate who was serving with the Free French government in London, she wrote: "The suffering all over the world obsesses me and overwhelms me to the point of annihilating my faculties, and the only way I can revive them and release myself from the obsession is by getting for myself a large share of danger and hardship." Even during a brief stay in New York City, in 1942, she found the distance from the arena of combat unbearable: "I can't go on living like this. If this must go on, I'll go to work in the south with the blacks, and there I am sure I will die because I can't stand this life." Nothing, she believed, should impede the purifying process of dispossession, of disincarnation, or "decreation," as she phrased it. If her personal habits were those of a religious solitary—eating little, dressing cheaply and inelegantly, sleeping on floors, giving away most of her material and financial possessions—her deepest spiritual needs dictated, and depended upon, a consuming participation in man's visible warfare. Her search for God became emblazed in the shadow of the Cross.

She saw her own destiny as being inseparable from human destiny. Her life testifies, in the paths that it took, to the anguish and suffering of dark times. Toward the end of her life she was to declare: "All human beings who love real peace are strangers now in a strange world and must find consolation from each other." But no matter how much she felt for even the smallest suffering in life, she never surrendered to romanticizing or sentimentalizing the human condition or to underestimating the power of evil. Her contacts with, and penetration into, the depths of "real life" enabled her to see things that others see only through the eyes of poets and novelists. "Above all," she wrote to one of her former students, "I feel I have escaped from a world of abstractions to find myself among real men—some good and some bad, but with real goodness and badness." Her distrust of the life of abstractions was closely tied to her distrust of the life of sensation: "For the reality of life is not sensation but activity—I mean activity both in thought and in action. People who live by sensations are parasites, both materially and morally, in relation to those who work and create." With the necessity of religious belief Simone Weil increasingly identified the necessity for responsible work, a theme and conviction that became prominent in her life and writings: "I regard physical work as a purification—but a purification in the order of suffering and humiliation. One can also find in it, in its very depths, instants of profound, nourishing joy that cannot be equaled elsewhere." Matter and spirit, no less than gravity and grace, are interdependent and interactive. In affirming this great eternal truth she refused to succumb to the all-pervading poison of material progress.

Her intense concern with a social transformation advantageous to the less fortunate must in no way be seen as an endorsement of secularization. Indeed, one discovers in her life a deepening spiritual recognition that was gradually attained only through liberation from the sin of self-will and self-worship. How does one ascend from the human to the superhuman level? This, for Simone Weil, constituted a fateful existential religious question. Her own life-experience is an answer to it. Against the scientific-empirical ethos of modern civilization, which she saw as being untrue to the nature of man, she dramatized the meaning of the life of the spirit. And she proclaimed precisely this higher meaning in its deepest spiritual dimensions, confessing her responsibility in ways that were relentless, irrevocable, and irreversible. The driving power of her witness was nothing less than staggering in both its rigor and vigor. We have a sense of a woman carving her vision of the Stations of the Cross, and doing so with impersonal grandeur, finality, nobility, and always with great purity and precision. Throughout, a wonderful hardness of purpose and execution sustained this transcending vision. Where does one find the strength to overcome the paradoxes, the compromises, the ambivalence, the illusions that forever remain the quicksand of human effort? For Simone Weil such a question was somehow irrelevant. Even her own appearance underscored the special sanctity of her hardness. Gustave Thibon said of his first meeting with her in 1941, "I don't want to talk about her physical appearance—she was not ugly, as has been said, but prematurely bent and old looking due to asceticism and illness, and her magnificent eyes alone triumphed in this shipwreck of beauty."

Inevitably it is an impelling religious sensibility that both illuminates and encompasses Simone Weil's life. Perhaps the most disciplining and pervasive characteristic of this sensibility is her capacity for contemplation—contemplation won through experience. Her view of history, as well as her vision of man's fate, was to be colored more and more by her contemplations, often thorny and always uncompromising in their formulation and expression. For Simone Weil contemplation was no soft or sloppy action. It dictated undiminishing and ascending attention, a complete giving and opening of one's self to those supernatural powers that she associated with attention and patience. Her preoccupation with the contemplative-sacramental essences of religion, above all with Christianity ("above all" because she also gave much of her attention to other religious philosophies, eastern as well as western), deepened as her disenchantment with political revolutionism increased in the late 1930s. (Conor Cruise O'Brien rightly calls attention to "the anti-politics of Simone Weil.") Her condemnation of the Roman Empire—"I believe the Roman conquests, with their atrocious material or spiritual annihilation of entire peoples, to have been history's great disaster"—catches the tone of her developing political attitude as a whole, and as it informs her sociopolitical writings in *Oppression and Liberty* and in her only full-length book, *The Need for Roots.* Even in the years of her greatest political militancy and involvement in the syndicalist movement (trade unionism without bureaucracy being her highest ideal) she insisted, as Simone Pétrement observes, "that the Church and its ceremony did the soul good by wisely predisposing and preparing the body." In any case Simone Weil had a haunting fear of the "Great Beast," whether as a political or as a religious collectivism. ("Is There a Marxist Doctrine?," one of her last pieces of writing, sums up the prophetic political relevance of her fear.) The more she came to contemplate the social idolatry that the "Great Beast" symbolized, the more she became aware that modern man, if he is to survive, and survive in her defining structural contexts of rights and obligations, needs something more than bread alone. She allied this need with the needs of the soul: "The people have as much need of poetry as of bread. . . . They have a need that the daily substance of their lives might itself be poetry. . . . And this poetry can only be religion."

The canonicity of Simone Weil's Christianity will remain perplexing and controversial. She herself, as the following representative excerpt confirms, repeatedly stressed that she was Catholic in the etymological sense:

> I adhere totally to the mysteries of the Christian faith, with the only kind of adherence that seems to me appropriate for mysteries. This adherence is love, not affirmation. Certainly I belong to Christ—or so I hope and believe. But I am kept outside the Church by philosophical difficulties that I fear are irreducible. They do not concern the mysteries themselves but the accretions of definitions with which the Church has seen fit to clothe them in the course of centuries and above all use in this connection of the words *"anathema sit."*

Her refusal of baptism was no doubt to stress the theological position that she enunciated in the words above. (She detailed the whole matter in her *Letter to a Priest.*) She chose, in short, to see herself as "the bell which tolls to bring others to church." Throughout, the intellectual formulation of her Christianity never wavered. "I do not recognize any right on the part of the Church to limit the workings of the intellect or the illuminations achieved by love in the domain of thought," she insisted. For some, such a position must smack of arrogance. Yet her heterodoxy was prompted by her suspicion of any influence or orientation that she considered dangerous to gaining a pure and perfect religious faith. Her fear of an exclusive Christianity sanctifying a Romanism that leads to the abuse of power and of a Judaism that leads to sectarianism or fanaticism never abated. Indeed, it contributed first, always, and finally to a standard of spiritual perfection that forced her to halt at "the intersection of Christianity and everything that is not Christianity."

To view Simone Weil during the final year of her life is to view a modern saint, seeking alone, until the hour of her death, to bear the grief of the world. Her death in England on August 24, 1943, brought on by pulmonary tuberculosis and also by starvation, for she refused to eat because her compatriots in German-occupied France were dying of hunger, tells us something about the conditions of our times. There is also something apocalyptic about her last days, as those who visited her in the hospital later testified. In appearance, she had become, despite the ravages of illness, very beautiful, ethereal, transparent, and purified of all materiality. She was, according to Maurice Schumann, "a spirit almost completely released from the flesh, a spirit who was the Word." In ways that bring to mind Pascal, she seemed, even though she admitted that she was "finished, broken, beyond all possibility of mending," to be affirming joy, certainty, and peace. To one of her visitors, probably at the sanatorium in Ashford, Kent, where she spent her last days, she cried: "You are like me, a badly cut-off piece of God. But soon I will no longer be cut off; I will be united and reattached." In a letter, written a few weeks before her death, she expressed doubts that she could hand on the pure gold deposited in her soul. But she was to add: "This does not distress me at all. The mine of gold is inexhaustible." The ending of one journey now marked the beginning of another, fulfilling what she called "the supreme act of total obedience." For her funeral in Ashford's New Cemetery, in the section reserved for Catholics, a priest had been invited. He never arrived. Schumann, who had a missal, knelt and read the prayers, while another friend made the response. Newspapers in the area reported Simone Weil's death, with one account carrying the headline, "Death from Starvation: French Professor's Curious Sacrifice."

II

Simone Weil's life was all too short. But in its achievement and meaning it was a life of consummate spiritual intensity, revealing the need for the "new saintliness" required by modern times. What impresses one most in studying the various fragments of her autobiography is her prophetic awareness of the human condition in the twentieth century. Her reactions, her judgments, are at once spiritual and moral, fearless and devastating. In a sense she saw too much, as an early essay, "Sketch of Contemporary Life," shows, evoking as it does, though it does much more than just this, the destructive and self-destructive energy loosed in a world in which "everything is disequilibrium." Containing her "inventory of modern civilization," this essay also contains her vision of evil. "Our present situation more or less resembles that of a party of absolutely ignorant travellers who find themselves in a motor-car launched at full speed and driverless across broken country." There could be a no more apt image of man's fate in collective, technological, industrial society, of man subordinated to and oppressed by new and vast mechanisms. "Machines do not run in order to enable men to live, but we resign ourselves to feeding men in order that they may serve the machines." Nothing could be more prophetic of the legioned diabolisms of the modern age than this stark and frightening declaration: "The powerful means are oppressive, the non-powerful means remain inoperative."

Her prophecies were more than divinations. They were also derived from her personal destiny: from her own fervent involvement in the cruel historical process. However short her life, Simone Weil filled it with purposive spiritual action, which in turn nourished and intensified her social, intellectual, and religious sensibility. In quest of the absolute she experienced the inescapability of the world. "This world into which we are cast *does* exist," she wrote; "we are truly flesh and blood; we have been thrown out of eternity; and we are indeed obliged to journey painfully through time, minute in, minute out." From the age of five, when she refused to eat sugar because the French soldiers fighting the Germans on the Western Front had none, until her death in 1943, she chose "to journey painfully through time." "Contact with affliction" is invariably at the heart of Simone Weil's experience of the world. It is also a primary condition of her conception of "a new saintliness," even as it permeates her view of the ultimate worth of a "Christianity [that] should contain all vocations without exception since it is Catholic." The truly redemptive function she found in "knowing the world's affliction and contemplating its reality."

In her life and work, and in her search for the principle of spiritual unity, Simone Weil sought to conjoin knowledge and contemplation.

26

For her the life of action was a prelude to the life of prayer. She was as much an "activist" as she was a mystic. During the 1930s she was a revolutionary idealist who championed the working class and the oppressed. Picketing, refusing to eat more than people on relief, distributing most of her earnings to the poor, writing for radical journals: such actions made her suspect in the eyes of the authorities and led to her being characterized as "a mixture of anarchist and nun." A remarkable, if enigmatic, teacher, she served in various French lycées; philosophy and classical philology were her academic specialties. One need only read her "Reflections on the Right Use of School Studies with a View to the Love of God" to grasp the uniqueness of her pedagogical concepts, particularly the special values that she placed on, and demanded of, the educative process as a preparation for a spiritual life. "Although people seem to be unaware of it today, the development of the faculty of attention forms the real object and almost the sole interest of studies." "Never in any case whatever is a genuine effort of the attention wasted. It always has its effect on the spiritual plane and in consequence on the lower one of the intelligence, for all spiritual light lightens the mind." A kind of *supra*pragmatism also informs her view of the tasks of learning: One should have as one's purpose not only "increasing the power of attention with a view to prayer," but also acquiring the virtue of humility, "a far more precious treasure than all academic progress." "When we force ourselves to fix the gaze, not only of our eyes but of our souls, upon school exercises in which we have failed through sheer stupidity, a sense of our mediocrity is borne in upon us with irresistible evidence. No knowledge is more to be desired." Her educational views can best be summed up as those of a spiritual progressivist.

The factory was yet another of Simone Weil's classrooms, as the essay "Factory Work" makes clear. This essay augments and, more particularly, objectifies "Sketch of Contemporary Life." It underlines another personal "contact with affliction," which is at the same time free of spiritual pride and of presumption, as she herself conveys in a confessional letter to Joë Bousquet, a disabled veteran of the Great War: "I worked for nearly a year [1934–35] in engineering factories in the Paris region. The combination of personal experience and sympathy for the wretched mass of people around me, in which I formed, even in my own eyes, an undistinguishable item, implanted so deep in my heart the affliction of social degradation that I have felt a slave ever since, in the Roman sense of the word." "Factory Work" marks an important and meaningful station in Simone Weil's spiritual pilgrimage. No mere sociological report, it is a spiritual offshoot of everything that she connotes with the words "concentrated attention." It is also an excellent example of a sustained attempt at spiritual analysis, a difficult task that Simone Weil saw as condemning oneself to moral loneliness, to lack of understanding, and to the hostility of both the enemies and the servants of an existing order. If her critique of factory work has finally a meditative impact, it also has implicit common sense. Who, today, can find fault with her condemnation of a "productive process" in which "things play the role of men, men the role of things. There lies the root of the evil"? And who can deny the insightfulness of this observation on human misery that brings to mind Dostoevsky: "Humiliation always has for its effect the creation of forbidden zones where thought may not venture and which are shrouded by silence or illusion." Or this insight that can be placed with the finest diagnostic insights of "brave men" like William Blake and D.H. Lawrence: "It is high time that specialists, engineers, and others concerned, should be exercised not only to make objects, but also not to destroy men." In "Factory Work" one hears the most intimate, anguished voice of a saint "proper to the present moment."

Though Simone Weil was a pacifist—"I do not love war; but what has always seemed to me most horrible in war is the position of those in the rear"—she could not prevent herself from participating morally in a great human struggle. ("The effect of a moral symbol," she wrote to Maurice Schumann toward the end of her life, "is independent of statistics.") In the summer of 1936 she joined an anarchist unit fighting in the Spanish Civil War. She spent about two months (her stay was brought to an end by an accident) in the remote Aragonese countryside on the banks of the Ebro, about ten miles from Saragossa. Useless bloodshed, atrocities, and the smell of blood and terror convinced her of the dehumanizing effects of applied and calculated might. "One sets out as a volunteer," she recalled in her letter to Georges Bernanos, "with the idea of sacrifice, and finds oneself in a war which resembles a war of mercenaries, only with much more cruelty and with less human respect for the enemy." This, she realized, was no moral, no authentic and pure struggle, a war of exploited peasants against landed proprietors and their clerical allies, but rather a political war between Russia on the one side and Germany and Italy on the other. Here, in this fleeting "contact with affliction," Simone Weil deepened her moral vision and enlarged her spiritual destiny. Above all, she witnessed man's "animal nature": "this mechanical necessity [which] holds all men in its grip at every moment." Her experience in Spain was even more important as a self-recognition that was simultaneously self-cleansing: "I was ten years old at the time of Versailles, and up to then I had been patriotically thrilled as children are in war-time. But the will to humiliate the defeated enemy which revealed itself so loathsomely everywhere at that time (and in the following years) was enough to cure me once for all of that naïve sort of patriotism. I suffer more from the humiliations inflicted by my country than from those inflicted on her."

Even as Simone Weil could not escape the awesomeness of the affliction of the world, she could not escape the central spiritual fact, "Faith is the indispensable condition." Hers was a life of consecration, as her "Spiritual Autobiography" with its integrity, simplicity, humility makes clear. What we have in this long letter to the Reverend Father J.-M. Perrin, her Dominican friend and adviser, is the testimony of a mystic and saint completing her pilgrimage. Through it the reader can make connection with this pure soul, finding ample proof for Simone Weil's informing declaration that, "as to the spiritual direction of my soul, I think that God himself has taken it in hand from the start and still looks after it." Surely a Divine Presence radiates as the epiphanies of Simone Weil's mystical ascent crystallize here. One of these relates her experience during a visit to Assisi in 1937: "There, alone in the little twelfth-century Romanesque chapel of Santa Maria degli Angeli, an incomparable marvel of purity where Saint Francis often used to pray, something stronger than I compelled me for the first time in my life to go down on my knees." Another relates her experience at Solesmes, where she followed all the liturgical services in 1938, from Palm Sunday to Easter Tuesday: "I was suffering from splitting headaches; each sound hurt me like a blow; by an extreme effort of concentration I was able to rise above this wretched flesh, to leave it to suffer by itself, heaped up in a corner, and to find a pure and perfect joy in the unimaginable beauty of the chanting and the words." Still another relates her experience in the course of reading George Herbert's poem "Love": "I learned it by heart. Often, at the culminating point of a violent headache, I make myself say it over, concentrating all my attention upon it and clinging with all my soul to the tenderness it enshrines. I used to think I was merely reciting it as a beautiful poem, but without knowing it the recitation had the virtue of a prayer. It was during one of these recitations that . . . Christ himself came down and took possession of me."

These religious experiences were epiphanic and not conversionary. They stamped and reinforced what was for Simone Weil an "implicit faith" in a Christianity that had chosen, even "captured," her. The daughter of freethinking Jewish parents, she was brought up "in complete agnosticism." "I have never been in a synagogue, and have never witnessed a Jewish ceremony," she notes in her interesting letter "What Is a Jew?" From the very beginning hers was the Christian, French, and Greek tradition. With special reference to her cultural roots, she recalls: "Since I practically learned to read from Racine, Pascal, and other French writers of the 17th century, since my spirit was thus impregnated at an age when I had not even heard talk of 'Jews,' I would say that if there is a religious tradition which I regard as my patrimony, it is the Catholic tradition." In her "Spiritual Autobiography" she further refers to her instinctive choice of a Christian outlook. "I always adopted the Christian attitude as the only possible one. I might say that I was born, I grew up, and I always remained within the Christian inspiration." Her Christian attitude was not only implicit but also strict and pure, and helps to explain her admiration of twelfth-century Catharism, which she opposed to the influence of the Old Testament and of the Roman Empire—a tradition she saw as being continued by the Papacy—and in which she pinpointed the two essential sources of the corruption of Christianity. Since, as she defined it, Christianity is Catholic by right but not in fact, she considered it legitimate on her part to be a member of the Church by right but not in fact. "So many things are outside it, so many things that I love and do not want to give up, so many things that God loves, otherwise they would not be in existence." Until Christianity became Catholic in the sense that she defined it, she chose to remain "on the threshold of the Church." An explanation of her refusal to be baptized is found in her reiteration that "the love of those things that are outside Christianity keeps me outside the Church." A truly Incarnational Christianity must be inclusive, impartial, universal, and thus genuinely catholic. One reads in her "Last Thoughts" (comprising another letter to Father Perrin that complements and refines her "Spiritual Autobiography"), "The children of God should not have any other country here below but the universe itself, with the totality of all the reasoning creatures it ever has contained, contains, or ever will contain. That is the native city to which we owe our love."

Only when Christianity is at last free of social trappings and temptations can it arrive at its most authentic and destined point of witness. ("I do not believe that I am outside the Church," she wrote toward the end of her life, "as far as it is the source of sacramental life; only insofar as it is a social body.") Only when a Christian actualizes what the value of his spiritual destiny prescribes can he be a Christian by right and in fact. The true measure of our Christianity must finally and fully comprise the capacity, "in contact with the affliction of other people," to extend ourselves in an act of disincarnation that forces us to come out of ourselves. This act requires the greatest religious courage and signifies the power of miracle that Simone Weil envisioned when she wrote: "Those who are unhappy have no need for anything in this world but people capable of giving them their attention. The capacity to give one's attention is a very rare and difficult thing; it is almost a miracle; it *is* a miracle." No statement brings into sharper focus the life-impelling obligation that Simone Weil embraced and that has earned her the right to be called "the saint of the churchless," "the Outsider as saint, in an age of aliena-tion."

III

Simone Weil believed that "the social order, though necessary, is essentially evil, whatever it may be." Yet, however bleak her conclu-sions regarding social organization, she devoted deep thought to its manifestations. No less than her spiritual meditations, her sociopolit-ical reflections are fraught with prophetic meaning and are the result of a rigorous critical process in which vision and wisdom prevail. Her political awareness is exceptional for its sensitive and comprehen-sive response to the mechanisms of social power. Her insights are relevant and incontrovertible when one studies in particular her two main contributions to political theory and thought, *Oppression and Liberty* and *The Need for Roots.* (This latter work, undertaken in exile at the invitation of the Free French authorities in London, is the only full-scale book that she wrote, the remainder being compila-tions of essays, letters, notes, *pensées.*) It should be noted that her sociopolitical reflections are not limited to these two works; that they occupy her most diligent attention. Richly blending high intelli-gence and spiritual strength, she explores the depths of modern sociopolitical systems, problems, issues, and ideologies. The condi-tions of contemporary culture and politics distressed her, but she insisted on confronting them directly and honestly, fully and re-sponsibly. Her critique of these conditions, though harsh, inevitably discloses intrinsic compassion and sympathy. "If, as is only too possible," she asserts, "we are to perish, let us see to it that we do not perish without having existed." Her vision of hell is never without her vision of heaven. More than anything else it is the oppression and debasement of the human spirit that arouse her greatest protest, as well as her Christlike anguish for "the lame, the halt, the blind." Certainly there is much truth, and much to recommend, in the description of Simone Weil as "a prophet of grace."

Her critique of the sociopolitical structure of contemporary society, and of modern theories of evolutionism, progressivism, and secular humanism, is at once antiempirical and antimaterialistic. It is informed and impelled by faith in spiritual creativity. In this respect her indictments both of capitalism and of Marxism are equally damning, insofar as she sees in both political systems the deification of social matter, or as she wrote in one of her most piercing observations: "And the materialist is a man. That is why he cannot prevent himself from ultimately regarding matter as a machine for manufacturing the good." Faith in matter, especially as it has been embraced and espoused by modern-day liberals, preceded the brutal uniformity and the standardization that left little room for thought and thus in the end for either justice or prudence, which she saw as required conditions of the spiritual life. "We are only geometricians in regard to matter," she wrote; "the Greeks were first of all geometricians in the apprenticeship of virtue." In the materialistic view of life she saw the fundamental causes of the kind of uprootedness that appears in an age and in a society in which money and the state replace all other bonds of attachment and in which morals cease to play any part: "Workers need poetry more than bread. They need that their life should be a poem. They need some light from eternity. Religion alone can be the source of such poetry. It is not religion but revolution which is the opium of the people."

Oppression, Simone Weil concluded, is the reigning monarch of all social organization. Hence the true emperor is the empire: the modern centralized state as the final, the absolute and despotic authority and as the real object of worship. "Human history is simply the history of the servitude which makes men—oppressors and oppressed alike—the plaything of the instruments of domination they themselves have manufactured, and thus reduces living humanity to being the chattel of inanimate chattels." In ancient times Rome personified the imperialistic spirit. Spiritual life in Rome was hardly more than an expression of the will to power, she maintained. Even the Christian sect emerged as the struggle of the Greek spirit against the Rome of "an unlimited and shameless brutality," of "the shrewd employment of cruelty." In modern times Hitlerism became Rome's royal successor. "Everything that disgusts and also everything that shocks us in his [Hitler's] methods is what he has in common with Rome," she observed. Her analysis of oppression was tough and relentless. She confronted facts and delineated sociopolitical conditions with an uncompromising argumentative ferocity, that same ferocity, in fact, that even some of her friends detected (and feared) in discussions with her. Her sociopolitical writings reveal Simone Weil as a critic of considerable power, vigorously and rigorously applying and demanding high standards of discrimination and arriving at judgments of a stern moral character. She was as tough, it could be said, as a modern saint should be. The power of Satan lies at the heart of all forms of human oppression, she maintained. Against the prince of this world one has to fight with all of one's might.

The religion of power, Simone Weil insisted, is inseparable from the conditions of servitude, of oppression. It is something that is inevitable and common with all totalitarianism—with Romanism, Marxism, Hitlerism; with the "collective values" promulgated and enforced by all principalities of oppression from ancient through modern times. Oppression is the substance of power; power is the form of oppression. But it is also its fatality, "the most fatal of all vicious circles," insofar as power always cuts both ways: against the one who commands as much as against the one who obeys. It is an ongoing process that enslaves everybody, strong and weak alike. Yet no oppressive social system ever escapes or defeats the internal contradiction, "like the seed of death," contained within itself: "It is made up of the opposition between the necessarily unlimited character of the material bases of power and the necessarily unlimited character of the race for power considered as relationship between men." Simone Weil, it should be noted, respected Marx's deep concern for human misery and his concomitant belief that weakness also can be a social mechanism for "producing paradise." Yet she saw the absurdity of his position, as she was to emphasize in perhaps the last words she ever wrote, in the spring of 1943: "Marx accepted this contradiction of strength in weakness, without accepting the supernatural which alone renders the contradiction valid." In the religion of power she saw the willful, unceasing destruction of the true elements of spirituality; the violation of all reverence for the integrity of mind and for man created in the image of God. In her delineation and condemnation of the uses of power Simone Weil spoke on the basis of spiritual, and Christian, standards. Failure to satisfy such standards, whether on the Left or the Right, aroused her unrelenting anger. To the politicians (who, as Shakespeare has said, would circumvent God Himself), indeed to all political theorists and thinkers who bow down to the dictates of a so-called realpolitik, Simone Weil is something of an enfant terrible. That soldier-politician extraordinaire, Charles de Gaulle, even pronounced her crazy!

Perhaps at no other point in her sociopolitical commentaries does

Simone Weil better reveal the greatest triumph of Spirit than in her classic essay "The *Iliad*, Poem of Might," which, in 1941, was the first of her writings to reach the English-speaking world. In its truths and humanity it catches the horror of war not only in its immediate historical situation but also in its universal contexts. Containing her apex-thought, it is an essay that repays frequentation, such is its truth and relevance. Bringing together ancient and modern experience, it probes the lessons of history in the clear light of the wisdom of the ages. The battle being fought on the plains of Troy is no local war but a universal, a total war that has no end in human consequences—and costs. War is diabolism that oppresses victor and vanquished. War becomes the objective correlative of the "empire of might," as she terms it: "Such is the empire of might; it extends as far as the empire of nature." Its cruel, rending effects are not to be counted only in terms of human casualties. In war, as in the heart of man, God and Satan are locked in combat. The spiritual dimension of such ultimate struggle is as immeasurable and portentous as the physical dimension is measurable and concrete. The opening sentences of her essay bring most to mind the poetic power and insights of Leo Tolstoy: "The true hero, the real subject, the core of the *Iliad*, is might. That might which is wielded by men rules over them, and before it man's flesh cringes. The human soul never ceases to be modified by its encounter with might, swept on, blinded by that which it believes itself able to handle, bowed beneath the power of that which it suffers."

Simone Weil shows the nature of might to be such that it transforms man into a thing and violates, differently but equally, the souls both of the victim and of the victimizer, "brothers in the same misfortune." "Might suffered at the hands of another is as much a tyranny over the soul as extreme hunger at the moment when food means life or death." It first denies and then kills life, for, "when exercised to the full, it makes a thing of man in the most literal sense, for it makes him a corpse. There where someone stood a moment ago, stands no one. This is the spectacle which the *Iliad* never tires of presenting." If might crushes the soul of the weak, it also does irreparable damage to the strong: "And so pitilessly as might crushes, so pitilessly it maddens whoever possesses, or believes he possesses it." "The strong man is never absolutely strong, nor the weak man absolutely weak, but each one is ignorant of this." More prodigious than the power to kill outright is the power of might to reify life. This is always a greater condemnation since it is the greatest humiliation of the life of the soul. In war the human soul is subordinated to might, that is to say, to matter. There can be no human heroes; might is the only hero. Yet there always exists the possibility for another hero, that spiritual hero whom Simone Weil must surely have had in mind when she wrote: "Only he who knows the empire of might and knows how not to respect it is capable of love and justice."

The necessity that belongs to war is both onerous and terrifying. No one can escape for long the fact of defeat or of death. "The day comes when fear, defeat or the death of beloved companions crushes the warrior's soul beneath the necessity of war. Then war ceases to be a play or a dream; the warrior understands at last that it really exists. This is a hard reality, infinitely too hard to be borne, for it comprises death." What Simone Weil goes on to say about the ever-present specter of death in, and the insensibility induced by, the experience of war discloses the same high degree of lucidity, of purity, and of simplicity that she worshiped in Hellenism. "The thought of death cannot," she says, "be sustained, or only in flashes from the moment when one understands death as a possible eventuality." What survivor of a great war dares to deny the truth of a statement like this: "That men should have death for their future is a denial of nature. As soon as the practice of war has revealed the fact that each moment holds the possibility of death, the mind becomes incapable of moving from one day to the next without passing through the spectre of death"? In these circumstances, the tragedy of soul ensues, which for Simone Weil is the greatest of all tragedies: "That soul daily suffers violence which every morning must mutilate its aspirations because the mind cannot move about in a time without passing through death." A sense of doom for the soul that is dominated by death prevails with a double intensity: "The despair which thrusts toward death is the same one that impels toward killing." Hector's plea to Achilles for deliverance—"I am at thy knees, Achilles; have pity, have regard for me; / Here as a suppliant, O Son of Zeus, I am worthy of respect"—holds a truth that rings far beyond the Scaean gates: "And how should he who has destroyed in himself the very thought that there may be joy in the light, how should he respect such humble and vain pleadings from the vanquished?"

T.S. Eliot placed Simone Weil's sociopolitical writings "in that category of prolegomena to politics which politicians seldom read, and which most of them would be unlikely to understand or to know how to apply."[3] Never much of an optimist, he was nonetheless quite right in his conclusion. Politicians are forever thinking or scheming for technic victory, in war or in peace. Not unpredictably they forget

3. From his preface to Simone Weil's *The Need for Roots: Prelude to a Declaration of Duties Toward Mankind,* trans. Arthur Wills (New York, 1953 [1949]).

that, as Simone Weil expresses it, "The winning of battles is not determined between men who plan and deliberate, who make a resolution and carry it out, but between men drained of these faculties, transformed, fallen to the level either of inert matter, which is all passivity, or to the level of blind forces, which are all momentum." Intent on sociopolitical transformations at any price, they forget the state of man's soul and man's relation to spiritual principle. These politicians, "geometricians in regard to matter," are blind to that indefinable existence that is our soul and our God. In this respect, whether or not they know or admit it, most people are politicians. They continue to erect the "wall of partition" between life and soul, endlessly, but needlessly, constructing barriers and bolting doors. But in the end they forget a central spiritual fact, containing the greatest revelation and the infinite possibility that are at the heart of these words of Simone Weil, words that modern man should ponder even unto his peril: "The world is the closed door. It is a barrier. And at the same time it is the way through."

IV

Critical, no less than religious, standards of discrimination inform the demands Simone Weil makes of her own as of all human thought. Her critical thought shows astonishing consistency in fusing reverence and discipline, in creating a reverent discipline. In her writings, through a common allegiance to standards, the critic and the mystic religious philosopher come together. Unfailingly, her criticism is founded on a vision of order and never stops seeking clarity of expression and balance of thought. The critical function is a close ally of spiritual life. A failure in either dimension is detrimental to the other, causing a breakdown in the total process of making responsible judgments. Intelligent thought requires a constant discipline if it is to avoid the pitfalls of sloppiness, sentimentality, and disorder. When the critical process retreats before such adversaries, the total effect on intelligence, and consequently on civilization, is lamentable, for, as Simone Weil wrote, "when the intelligence is ill-at-ease the whole soul is sick." In her writings the critical process emerges from, and is simultaneously molded and refined by, the application of a firm and constant pressure on the need to mediate and to conjoin intellect and soul. Her essays, at once critical and religious, illustrate the goals of the evaluative process of critical thought that becomes transcendent and impersonal in that ultimate sense that Simone Weil was aware of

36

when she wrote, "The human being can only escape from the collective by raising himself above the personal and entering into the impersonal." Yet there is a tendency to ignore or to dismiss Simone Weil's view of the critical function, or to subordinate it to the mystical dimension of her life and thought. This leads to misreading and misunderstanding the critical powers of analysis that she brings to bear on all her writings.

A modern saint, she was also a modern critic when one considers the questions, doubts, concerns, and issues that preoccupied her; the religious and cultural criteria she formulated; and the relevance and truth of her diagnosis of (and prescriptions for) "man in the modern world." In her critical thought she insisted on both communication and transcendence. She also steadfastly insisted that critical concepts that refused to acknowledge the interdependence of the physical and the spiritual nature of man were categorically incomplete. The failure to acknowledge this interdependence is tantamount to the failure to recognize, and hence to discriminate between, good and evil. "In all crucial problems of human existence the only choice is between supernatural good on the one hand and evil on the other." Her thought never lost sight of this criterion, which became for her a pivotal moral and critical centrality in the light of which all human problems, accomplishments, and aspirations are to be viewed and judged. Critical judgment is for her spiritual judgment. Any separation of the two must result in a fictionalization of the direst consequences. In her religious, sociological, and literary reflections she never failed to address the intellect in order to reach the soul. Her criticism both expresses and advances a spiritual principle of unity. To some readers and commentators, no doubt, such criticism may sound conservative, even reactionary. To Simone Weil it was criticism with deep roots in Hellenism—in the Greek view of life that she especially admired and that she saw as being increasingly absent in the modern world: "Real genius is nothing else but the supernatural virtue of humility in the domain of thought."

Her concern with and her own careful use of language are always apparent. "Where there is a grave error of vocabulary it is almost certainly the sign of a grave error of thought," she emphasized. In the debasement of language she detected one of the serious causes of modern breakdown. Indiscipline, formlessness, nihilism, and blasphemy she associated with the careless use of language. The adverse effects of this carelessness on human thought, as she clearly indicated in her exquisite essay "The Power of Words," are immense: "To clarify thought, to discredit the intrinsically meaningless words, and to define the use of others by precise analysis—to do this, strange though it may appear, might be a way of saving human lives." She was not hopeful of improvement or reform insofar as "our age seems almost entirely unfitted for such a task. The glossy surface of our civilization hides a real intellectual decadence." Problems of language cannot be separated from political problems, as she brings out in a sentence that rings with recurring truth in the sociopolitical arena: "On inspection, almost all the words and phrases of our political vocabulary turn out to be hollow." Her perception of the corruption of language was intrinsically a moral (and a religious) one: The more blatant and callous the secular state became, the more decayed language itself became. And the more language became separated from its intrinsic connection of responsibility to human worth. Hence, as Simone Weil lamented, "language is no longer equipped for legitimately praising a man's character." Moral loss—moral immobilization—is the consequential, far-reaching loss of this destructive process, as she asserted: "In every sphere, we seem to have lost the elements of intelligence: the ideas of limit, measure, proportion, relation, comparison, contingency, interdependence, interrelation of means and ends."

Other writers, critics, philosophers, and "new theologians" have also perceived the deteriorating life of language in society and culture. (The remarkable diagnoses and continuing warnings of George Steiner come especially to mind.) But their concerns are, for the most part, humanistic, positivistic, rationalistic, existential, or academic, confined to and, in the end, circumscribed by a labyrinthine secularity that makes the modernist impasse all the more evident. Their solutions are not much better. In contrast, in her examination of the problems of language and thought, Simone Weil concentrates judgmentally on the accelerating loss of the spiritual idea of value in the twentieth century. Her concern revolves around the total effect of spiritual bankruptcy and of the profanation of "the good" in the religious sense that she identifies with such bankruptcy when she asserts: "The good is the only source of the sacred. There is nothing sacred except the good and what pertains to it." The enfeeblement and disappearance of the criterion of value, she stresses in her essay "The Responsibility of Writers," is pervasive in all aspects of society and culture. "Such words as spontaneity, sincerity, gratuitousness, richness, enrichment—words which imply an almost total indifference to contrasts of value—have come more often from their pens than words which contain a reference to good and evil," she says of modern writers. Words particularly related to the sacramental concept of good—virtue, nobility, honor, honesty, generosity—have been so twisted and debased that they have become almost impossible to use. The degradation of language is concomitant with and reflective of the despiritualization of man, especially as it is rendered in literature: "The fate of words is a touchstone of the progressive weakening of the idea of value, and although the fate of words does not depend upon writers one cannot help attributing a special responsibility to them, since words are their business."

Literary creativity, she insisted, cannot be absolved from moral and spiritual responsibility. Because the connection between literature and morality is equally endemic and binding, she believed it impossible to exempt literature from those categories of good and evil to which all human actions are referable. Modern creative writers, even if they bear a burden of vision, must also bear a burden of responsibility to the moral values of which they have been immemorially the guardians and which they have lost in various degrees of seriousness. Singling out the surrealists, she underlines their "non-oriented thought" and their dangerous and portentous choice of "the total absence of value as their supreme value." There has not always been a literary sacking of towns, she says, but "surrealism is such an equivalent." Many modern writers, she goes on to claim, have in one way or another surrendered the value of the spiritual principle of unity. They have converted twentieth-century literature into what is essentially psychological, "and psychology consists in describing states of the soul by displaying them all on the same plane without any discrimination of value." Her main, most vigorous complaint, and one that lacks neither legitimacy nor examples, she expressed in words that can hardly be dismissed except by those who, negating the idea of value, preach "the absolute absence of the absolute" (as Samuel Beckett expresses the moderns' spiritual malaise): "Writers do not have to be professors of morals, but they do have to express the human condition. And nothing concerns human life so essentially, for every man at every moment, as good and evil. When literature becomes deliberately indifferent to the opposition of good and evil, it betrays its function and forfeits all claim to excellence."

In her critical and aesthetic views, Simone Weil was morally severe. Unhesitantly she could state: "I believe in the responsibility of the writers of recent years for the disaster of our time." We have in this statement an illustration of the kind of sternness that one commentator equates with her total outlook, "half icy intellectual, half mystic." Yet, it is always the primary need to recognize the difference between good and evil which she demands that we confront, whatever the consequences. In much of modern literature, she observes, values are reversed. Evil becomes attractive; good tedious. She distinguishes between literary genius oriented toward the good—

Homer, Aeschylus, Sophocles, Racine, Villon—and the "demoniacal geniuses" of whom Rimbaud is an example and symbol. A writer who shirks his moral responsibility, who in effect refuses to give meaning to human action, refuses to recognize the difference between good and evil. This refusal constitutes a fundamental failure of responsibility. And insofar as he has occasion to influence human behavior, she claims, "it ought to be recognized that the moment a writer fills a role among the influences directing public opinion, he cannot claim to exercise unlimited freedom." She especially laments the loss of spiritual direction since the time of the Enlightenment, with the usurpation of spiritual and moral authority by men of letters who introduced "into literature a Messianic afflatus wholly detrimental to its artistic purity." With the waning of sharply defined moral standards, discriminating judgments and critical intelligence have been incalculably blunted. Writers must satisfy the standards of moral vision. When they do, then "their contemplation is the ever-flowing source of an inspiration which may legitimately guide us. For this inspiration, if we know how to receive it, tends—as Plato said— to make us grow wings to overcome gravity."

The value of a work of art must be judged according to the way it discloses the moral real and relates to the human soul. In what can well be called her metaphysics of art Simone Weil returns to this aesthetic principle: "Art is an attempt to transport into a limited quantity of matter, modeled by man, an image of the infinite beauty of the entire universe." An artist who continuously attempts to make connection with the depths of mystery discovers that grace and nature are inseparable and indivisible. It is the Catholic sacramental view of life that she no doubt has in mind when she says: "Every true artist has had real, direct, and immediate contact with the beauty of the world, contact that is of the nature of a sacrament." (A modern Catholic novelist, Flannery O'Connor, was saying something analogous to this when she wrote: "The artist penetrates the concrete world in order to find at its depths the image of its source, the image of ultimate reality.") For Simone Weil, the artist who distances himself from the ultimate divine source dissociates himself from the permanent things and falls into sin. Such artists become, in T.S. Eliot's phrase, "promoters of personality," seekers "after strange gods." These artists Simone Weil finds unworthy, for they defile the sacred consciousness and banish man's religious need. (Her admiration of *The Brothers Karamazov* is closely tied to Dostoevsky's perception of man's inexhaustible and indispensable religious needs.) The artist as *homo viator* must travel the road to transcendence. His achievement must be an achievement in transcendence, beyond himself and beyond personality. "Perfection is impersonal," she stresses in one of her most astute essays, "Human Personality." "Our personality is the part of us which belongs to error and sin." Truth and beauty thus reside in the impersonal and anonymous, "in the realm of the sacred." An artist of the very highest genius is a spiritual artist. But, she exclaims, "there are not very many of them."

An artist, and anyone whose function it is to advise the public on what to praise or to admire, should strive to plant in man "the invisible seed of pure good." Artists who believe that their work is a manifestation of personality are "the most in bondage of public taste" and hence captives of collectivity. Artists who respect and affirm the clear and present existence of standards higher than their personal selves and talents recognize limits that are finally resolved in absolutes: "Justice, truth, and beauty are the image in our world of this impersonal and divine order of the universe. Nothing inferior to them is worthy to be the inspiration of men who accept the fact of death." Simone Weil was clear in her mind and firm in her conviction that art must make visible the search for the absolute, the courage of belief, the operation of grace, the vindication of the holy, the salvation of the soul. Not unlike all the needs of life, art must have a constant reference to the theological truths, as well as to the eternal standard that "in all crucial problems of human existence the only choice is between supernatural good on the one hand and evil on the other."

V

How does one pass from critical intelligence into the beginning of wisdom? This is a question that Simone Weil never stops asking. Nor does she hesitate to provide hints and suggestions challenging both believer and unbeliever. Hers is not the mere voice of a religious apologist. What distinguishes her writings and thought is an interiorizing spiritual strength, which is equally distinguished by manifest qualities of certainty and of judgment. In some ways she is a tantalizing propagandist who, using all her powers of strategy, of tact and tactic, knows that she must engage anyone willing to listen to her. She can be likened to a religious artist who strives to trap and bribe one's attention. ("All art is propaganda," claims that charismatic English sculptor, engraver, and essayist Eric Gill, "for it is in fact impossible to do anything, to make anything, which is not expressive of 'value.' ") Simone Weil knows that she is playing for the highest of stakes, the fate of the soul. One finds in the tone of her appeal the inevitable traits (and habits) of a dedicated didactician. Man's total predicament requires a total concentration on her part. If on occasion she seems unreasonable in her demands and relentless in her judgments, for she is always driving toward a perfect Christianity, she at the same time conveys complete sincerity. This sincerity has the final virtue of redemption. Simone Weil, speaking of and to herself, speaks of and to others. Her writings are dialogues with her soul and with the souls of others. Her inner life contains the outer world. A mystic without a church, she knows that there are countless others who share her affliction. She also knows that affliction is, by its very nature, inarticulate. "Thought revolts from contemplating affliction, to the same degree that living flesh recoils from death." To this affliction she seeks to lend a contemplative voice, a voice that must be convincing if it is to be believed. And belief must have substance since it must seek to satisfy a test, a principle, a rule, a canon, or a standard by which value is valued. One's spiritual life, in both its limitation and its possibility, must be continuously judged; and the spiritual life continuously posits criteria. In her writings Simone Weil provides criteria for contemplation.

Criteria of themelves are never adequate. They need refining, assimilating, so as to take on that added dimension which mere intellectual fact and fate preclude. A positive understanding of criteria must lead to an internal transformation of life and faith. Wisdom is the revealed spiritual zenith of this transformation. It is part of, a reflex of, the divine and, as such, is always alive. Wisdom is not only the world-thought, it is God. It is God and Man, for it is Christ, as one theologian predicates. For Simone Weil, this signifies divine wisdom. The faculty of judging attains its spiritualization in wisdom. Wisdom transforms criteria by turning them from a finite toward an infinite direction. It has precisely those powers of transcendence that, in Simone Weil's spiritual vocabulary, distinguish gravity from grace. Gravity is the evil that drags down and cloys the human soul; it can be both an oppressive and a repressive force. Grace is the opposing force of good that makes possible the release and ascent of the soul. When criteria lose sight of wisdom it is the pull of gravity that predominates. Human experience is in a state of crisis as these two forces remain in a state of perpetual contention. The human condition is ever in the throes of descent and yet at the edge of ascent. When grapsed in their full meaning and fatefulness, spiritual criteria enable one to measure one's perilous situation, specifically what existentialists speak of as the limit-situation. Wisdom is cognition, profound insight into the meaning and tasks of life. It is the revelation of and the emanation from God, a radiation of his eternal light, a half-celestial, half-terrestrial being, a mediatrix between God and man, to use an apocryphal image. Acquiring wisdom is no easy job for the catechumen. Criteria, Simone Weil believes, stipulate the recognition of value precedent to the realization of God. "Earthly things are the criterion of spiritual things. This is what we generally don't want to recognize, because we are frightened of a criterion."

Connect: this is Simone Weil's unceasing admonition. Separations can become links. Breaks can be healed. Barriers can be surmounted. Distances can be overcome. Streams can be crossed. "The essence of created things is to be intermediaries. They are intermediaries leading from one to the other, and there is no end to this. They are intermediaries leading to God. We have to experience them as such." The connection—the intermediary—that she sees existing between criteria and wisdom is one that defies division and produces spiritual unity. Once man accepts the meaning of this connection he is able to see what hitherto he has not seen; he is capable of understanding the true relationship of things. The criteria of wisdom can serve as doorways to the eternal, but only at that point where interconnection is made. "To re-establish order is to undo the creature in us." "We have to be nothing in order to be in our right place in the whole." "Belief in the existence of other human beings as such is *love*." Knowledge such as this is the revelation of wisdom. In learning something about ourselves, she is saying, we begin to approach the divine. In wisdom, then, beginning and ending harmonize. "It is a fault to wish to be understood before we have made ourselves clear to ourselves." Christian Hellenism informs in the most decisive ways Simone Weil's ideas of making connection between the secular and the sacred. Her otherworldliness is rarely without a sense of that same refining proportion that she appeals to when she says: "Proportion can be defined as the combination of equality with inequality, and everywhere throughout the universe it is the sole factor making for balance." The criteria of wisdom that recur in her "thorny creed," as it has been described, serve as qualitative guidelines to matters of life and faith. The goal is self-understanding, crystallizing into self-purgation. Simone Weil carefully, strictly, plots her criteria in the light of wisdom. Wisdom is the final criterion, its consummation.

Her criteria of wisdom point the way toward spiritual development. They have a substantively active goal: life's acquisition of virtues, which become links to God Himself. Friendship, of which she writes in the best tradition of Hellenism, is for her one of the greatest paradigms of virtue. Her essay of the same title is an illustration of the way in which she amalgamates Hellenism, Platonism, and Christianity. It is also an illustration of the criterional method of her thought as it blends with those forms of knowledge leading to wisdom. It is a perfect illustration of her Christian Hellenism. Here the strictness, the purity, of her contextual thought—the trenchancy and rigor of the criterion that she is arguing—is made clear in her definition: "Friendship is a supernatural harmony, a union of opposites." Her stress on clarity and precision of language and critical thought informs her criteria of friendship: "There is no friendship where there is inequality." "Friendship has something universal about it. It consists of loving a human being as we should like to be able to love each soul in particular of all those who go to make up the human race." Her intellectual grasp and delineation of criteria make her intuitive insights into the realities of interpersonal relations sharp and unsentimental: "When the necessity which brings people together has nothing to do with the emotions, when it is simply due to circumstances, hostility often makes its appearance from the start." She therefore constantly warns against the necessity that is the principle of impurity. Criteria identify moral and spiritual guides that must translate into an ethos of life and faith. The full meaning of what Simone Weil is pronouncing, and of the wisdom she is communicating in her view of friendship as a sacrament, is contained in these faithful, prevenient words: "Pure friendship is an image of the original and perfect friendship that belongs to the Trinity and is the very essence of God. It is impossible for two human beings to be one while scrupulously respecting the distance that separates them, unless God is present in each of them. The point at which parallels meet is infinity."

Simone Weil helps us not only to approach wisdom but also to contemplate it. In contemplation, pervaded by the attitude of looking and waiting, the real presence of God is felt. It is a form of contact with the beautiful, a sacramental experience by which one passes from the flesh to the soul. "The beautiful is the experimental proof that the incarnation is possible," she says. The beautiful and the good irradiate the realm of wisdom. As such, wisdom touches infinity. When the act of judgment coheres with the grace of wisdom a spiritual entity is born. It is at this juncture that one is made more aware of the vices that are subject to gravity. When such an awareness is attained, spiritualized so to speak, it is possible for one to fathom the crisis of meaning encountered in Simone Weil's distinction between evil and good: "Evil is multifarious and fragmentary, good is one; evil is apparent, good is mysterious; evil consists in action, good in non-action, in activity which does not act." The recognition of the power of evil, as a necessity and a duty, is tantamount to the transcendence of a criterion of wisdom. It is a point of arrival at which one can say that one must live for one's soul. Now, Simone Weil says, the attendant experience of suffering can be apprehended in its true, or pure, significance: "The false God changes suffering into violence. The true God changes violence into suffering. Expiatory suffering is the shock in return for the evil we have done. Redemptive suffering is the shadow of the pure good we desire." Now, too, we are ready to see that good is good and sin is sin. This knowledge "leads to a knowledge of the distance between good and evil and the commencement of a painful effort of assimilation." Divine wisdom proclaims this ineradicable and universal criterion: "Evil has to be purified—or life is not possible. God alone can do that." The fearsomeness of evil can never be underestimated: "We cannot contemplate without terror the extent of the evil which man can do and endure."

Insofar as the devil governs the social order, says Simone Weil, all that man can do is limit the evil of it. Man wants the absolute good; but "that which is within our reach is the good which is correlated to evil." Only in the idea of relationship can one break out of the social: "To relate belongs to the solitary spirit. No crowd can conceive relationship." Man must have the courage to test, to judge, and to meditate on the social order so as to detach himself from it. "To contemplate the social is as good a way of detachment as to retire from the world," she writes. "That is why I have not been wrong to rub shoulders with politics for so long." The social element is one in which the pull of gravity is supreme. She identifies Rome, a society "absolutely without mysticism," with this gravity, as she also does the Hebrews, since "Their God was heavy." The distinction between "social morality" and "supernatural morality" is equivalent to that between gravity and grace, between knowledge and wisdom. Rootedness must be centered in something other than the social. "A nation as such cannot be the object of supernatural love. It has no soul. It is a Great Beast." For Simone Weil the Great Beast, "the only *ersatz* of God," is the devil disguised. Submission to the former is submission to the latter. The consequences of the social are forbidding. Conscience is deceived. Judgment falters. Meditation, as a phase of purification, ceases. Wisdom vanishes. And the soul is deprived of life and death. The power of Satan is unassailable in the abyss of gravity. "It is only by entering the transcendental, the supernatural, the authentically spiritual order that man rises above the social. Until then, whatever he may do, the social is transcendent in relation to him."

Simone Weil's contemplations consist of spiritual directions, spiritual counsels, and spiritual exercises. But they also transmute into spiritual life. A glimpse of beauty, a purity of soul, a realization of wisdom, a sense of the holy: these are the encountered constituents of this experience. Her thoughts are never without a higher purpose. In their formulation they necessarily impose a discipline of attention, of a devotional rather than an essentially ascetical character. Not the laceration of the self but the "decreation" of the self is the goal. "May that which is low in us go downward so that which is high can go upward. For we are wrong side upward. We are born thus. To re-establish order is to undo the creature in us." Human misery is at the core of human experience. "The curtain is human misery: there was a curtain even for Christ." The anguish of Job and the symbol of the cross are constants of her religious vision. So that the love of God may penetrate the depths of what she calls "vegetative energy," nature must undergo the ultimate violence. The acceptance of this spiritual fact is the recognition of "this world, the realm of necessity, [which] offers us absolutely nothing except means." No violence, she believed, can make purity less pure, though it can inflict suffering on it. Hence, the consequences of suffering can be dangerous, leading to imbalance, distortion, degradation. The virtue of patience, the innermost essence of wisdom, is indispensable to spiritual warfare, visible or invisible: "Patience consists in not transforming suffering into crime. That in itself is enough to transform crime into suffering." "Waiting patiently in expectation is the foundation of the spiritual life." The need for patience, like the need for roots, is a divine need. To ignore or to reject this need is to glorify a broken world. "We are like barrels with no bottom to them so long as we have not understood that we rest on a foundation."

VI

Simone Weil chose to remain "a stranger and an exile" at the threshold of the Church, yet she did pass through the sacred doors of infinity. Ultimately, miraculously, her life and thought instance a spiritual victory that is perhaps unparalleled in the twentieth century. The paths of her unceasing meditations led her out of herself to God. Destiny made it impossible for her not to bear "the mark of the experience of God." To judge by the allegory of her life, written a few months before her death, her encounter with the divine seems foreordained: "He entered my room and said: 'Poor creature, you who understood nothing, who know nothing. Come with me and I will teach you things which you do not suspect.' I followed him." In its unalterable direction and in its shaping form her lifework is itself a divine meditation. It is her passageway to God. "God is attention without distraction," she wrote. Action and contemplation seek for and find a point of perfect harmony and unity in God. "The silent presence of the supernatural here below is that point of leverage. That is why, in the early centuries of Christianity, the Cross was compared to a balance." Any true relationship between means and ends must exist in God. This relationship must be one of reciprocal forgiveness: "If we forgive God for his crime against us, which is to have made us finite creatures, He will forgive our crime against him, which is that we are finite creatures." One's spiritual transformation depends on the attainment of this reciprocity. The value of one's conception of life is then completely altered, illuminated, for the soul has "passed through the fire of the love of God": "When a man's way of behaving towards things and men, or simply his way of regarding them, reveals supernatural virtues, one knows that his soul is no longer virgin, it has slept with God; perhaps even without knowing it, like a girl violated in her sleep."

Since God is not in time, Simone Weil specifies, man is abandoned in time. Creation itself is an abdication; God must wait patiently for man to love him. God is the good, and "the good which is nothing but good can only stand waiting." Whatever speaks to man of time conveys God's supplication to man. "God waits like a beggar who stands motionless and silent before someone who will perhaps give him a piece of bread. Time is that waiting." The very nature of creation hinders the drawing closer together of God and man. "Time, which is our one misery, is the very touch of his hand. It is the abdication by which he lets us exist." In the grip of this paradox, in which exists the possibility of divine mystery, one can make contact that helps to place oneself in what Simone Weil calls "the third dimension": "Contact with human creatures is given to us through the sense of presence. Contact with God is given to us through the sense of absence. Compared with this absence, presence becomes more absent than absence." Indeed, one should not dare to speak about God, or to pronounce the word, "except when one is not able to do otherwise." But precisely at that point at which "one is not able to do otherwise," when infinite possibility becomes divine certainty and one has truly imitated the patience and humility of God, one's experience of God transcends both affirmation and denial. "We can only know one thing about God: that he is what we are not. Our misery alone is the image of this. The more we contemplate it, the more we contemplate Him."

Simone Weil's meditations on the Cross belong to the highest expression of her mystic genius and of her "supernatural knowledge." In the Passion of Christ she saw a correlation with, and

expression of, suffering humanity. Christ is proof that human affliction is irreducible, "that it is as great in the absolutely sinless man as
in the sinner." He also epitomizes abandonment. Man, in his misery,
shares in the distance placed between the Son and his Father. This is
also his participation in the Cross of Christ, which should become
the very substance of life. As she wrote in one of her most astonishing, if not her greatest, meditations, "The Love of God and Affliction": "The Trinity and the Cross are the two poles of Christianity,
the two essential truths: the first perfect joy; the second perfect
affliction. It is necessary to know both the one and the other and their
mysterious unity, but the human condition in this world places us
infinitely far from the Trinity, at the very foot of the Cross." The
contemplation of Christ's Cross alone enables man to accept and
endure affliction. This contemplation should also teach man not to
feel compassion for himself or even others, but rather to extend
compassion to slaughtered innocence, to the Christ "across the centuries." Only Christ is capable of compassion. And only by looking
upon the symbol of the Cross can man love God. "The Cross of Christ
is the only source of light that is bright enough to illumine affliction.
Whenever there is affliction, in any age or any country, the Cross of
Christ is the truth of it." Repeatedly Simone Weil identifies the Cross
and necessity. Human destiny and the Passion of Christ are one.
"There is not, there cannot be, any human activity in whatever
sphere, of which Christ's Cross is not the supreme and secret truth."
"If you have to choose between Christ and truth choose truth, and
you will immediately find yourself in His arms."

If the knowledge of affliction is, as Simone Weil contends, the key
to Christianity, it is also the key to her religious meditations. In his
acceptance of affliction man consents to God's grace and accepts the
decreative process of "expiation," "to want not to be any longer" and
to know that "we are totally mistaken" in the presumption, the
arrogance, "that the world is created and controlled by ourselves."
Decreation, a purgative inner state of soul, indicates progress in
man's self-knowledge of his nothingness. Affliction and decreation,
in terms of acceptance, the acceptance of humility really, are interdependent spiritual states. In the act of accepting suffering, man
accepts the gift of grace and begins to climb the ladder of transcendence, or as Simone Weil writes: "Affliction, when it is consented to
and accepted and loved, is truly a baptism." As such, it is an uproot-
ing of life, "a more or less attenuated equivalent of death" that takes
possession of the soul. In the course of this possession God is absent.
This absence accentuates death, darkness, horror, lovelessness,
accursedness, inertia. Men who are struck down by affliction, she

goes on to stress, are at the foot of the Cross, the point of greatest possible distance from God. "One can only accept the existence of affliction by considering it as a distance," she reflects. But, for those who love, this distance is only separation; and separation, though painful, is a good because it is love. "This universe where we are living," she continues, "and of which we form a minute particle, is the distance put by the divine Love between God and God." Man can never escape obedience to God. He must learn to feel in all things the obedience of the universe to God: "As soon as we feel this obedience with our whole being, we see God." Simone Weil equates this process with an apprenticeship, involving not only time and effort but also, inevitably and indispensably, joy and suffering.

Perhaps more than any of her great meditations, her meditation on God, whatever its theological sources, or validity, or orthodoxy, breathes a coalescent inspiration and profundity. It is as if a divine passion possesses and overwhelms her every word and thought as she fervently probes the divine questions: "How can we seek for him? How can we go towards him?" The very essence, the justification of her fate is caught in those two obsessive questions. The paths of her meditation, of her mystic quest, lead her to and merge with them. Her answers to them are an intermediary between divine passion and divine revelation: "We are incapable of progressing vertically," she confesses. "We cannot take one step towards the heavens. God crosses the universe and comes to us. Over the infinity of space and time the infinitely more infinite love of God comes to possess us." To those who refuse, God returns again and again, like a beggar, until "one day he stops coming." "If we consent, God places a little seed in us and he goes away again. From that moment God has no more to do; neither have we, except to wait." She does not hesitate, nevertheless, to stress that "the growth of seed within us is painful." There are always weeds to pull up and grass to cut: "This gardening amounts to a violent operation." But when the seed does grow of itself there comes a time when the soul belongs to God. It is now the soul's turn to cross the universe to go to God. Now, too, the love within the soul is divine and uncreated; "it is the love of God for God which is passing through it. God alone is capable of loving God." A tremendous transformation is effected in us, for the soul comes into the actual presence of God. "It is at the point of intersection between creation and Creator. This point is the point of intersection of the two branches of the Cross."

Always it is the right orientation of the soul toward God that counts for Simone Weil. This orientation contains the divine possibility of transfiguration. It also clarifies and, in the end, deifies affliction, or "the possibility of affliction," which she considers "a marvel of divine technique." She likens extreme affliction, consisting of physical pain, spiritual distress, and social degradation, to a nail being struck by a hammer. The shock, which is ultimately religious, spiritual, and infinite, travels from the nail's head to the point. "The point of the nail is applied to the very centre of the soul, and its head is the whole of necessity throughout all space and time." This nail pierces through creation, through the veil, or screen, separating the soul from God. And the soul enters a different, totally other dimension. "The man whose soul remains oriented towards God while a nail is driven through it finds himself nailed to the very centre of the universe; the true centre, which is not in the middle, which is not in space and time, which is God." Affliction serves both as spiritual revelation and as opportunity. We pass through the divine fire, and we have things disclosed to us that hitherto have been divine secrets. A divine synthesis in purgation transpires; our spiritual blindness is lifted; the laws of gravitation are put aside by divine grace. Affliction is a supernatural process. To pass through the experience of affliction is "to know it in the depths of one's being." It is to know, that is, the death of the soul, as well as the acceptance of that death, by finally placing one's treasure and heart not merely "outside one's person but outside all one's thoughts and feelings and outside everything knowable, in the hands of our Father who is in secret."

Simone Weil's theological-metaphysical meditations never fail to attain a point of balance. In its totality her thought is identified, and identifiable, by its intrinsic sense of harmony. In this she is a true Christian Hellenist. If she emphasizes "the love of God and affliction," she equally emphasizes the "love of the order of the world" (the title of another of her great meditative essays). Her sensuous vision of living life, of "the country of here below," "the city of the world," is not as denuded, or as harsh, or as one-dimensionally dialectical as some of her commentators like to think. Affliction is not her last or only word, or, if it is, it is mediated by her supreme appreciation of beauty, in which she sees a redemptive capacity for incarnation. Beauty is another indicator of the divine, or as she notes: "Beauty is eternity here below." It assists us in finding answers to the divine questions and makes us more perceptive of time, values, and being. Beauty can conduce spiritual transformation in the sacred forms that Simone Weil underscores when she writes: "By loving our neighbour we imitate the divine love which created us all and all our fellows. By loving the order of the world we imitate the divine love which created this universe of which we are a part." She especially singles out for praise the beauty of the world as it is expressed by

Greek Stoicism, by parts of the Old Testament (the Psalms, the Book of Job, Isaiah, and the Book of Wisdom), by Saint John of the Cross, and by Saint Francis, who "stripped himself naked in order to have immediate contact with the beauty of the world." But for the most part, she complains, the beauty of the world, as a central inspiration, is absent from the Christian tradition. Her criticism is not, in our present impoverished circumstances, without either its sociological or its ecological validity or relevance; she observes, in that prophetic vein that recalls D.H. Lawrence: "Today one might think that the white races had almost lost all feeling for the beauty of the world, and that they had taken upon them the task of making it disappear from all the continents where they have penetrated with their armies, their trade and their religion."

Her sense of beauty can hardly be overestimated. It underlines her most explicit feelings about, her "filial piety" toward, the tangible world—feelings that are characteristically selfless. Any estimation of her thought has to take these feelings, in all their sensuous reverence, into full account since they comprise an essential dimension of her thought. What she has to say about beauty comes not so much from some rapturous, ecstatic inner source of vibration, but from a deep and sensitive passion for creation. Ultimately she writes of the beauty of the world from a religious imagination. It can be said that in her appreciation and evocation of the beautiful she writes as a great artist who sees beauty as the most natural approach to God. Though the modern secular world has debased beauty, she affirms its wondrous sacramental potentiality. "If it were made true and pure, it would sweep all secular life in a body to the feet of God; it would make the total incarnation of the faith possible." Beauty, a mysterious emanation of the divine, is also a "divine enticement," a "trap," and a "labyrinth": "The soul's natural inclination to love beauty is the trap God most frequently uses in order to win it and open it to the breath from on high." An attribute of matter, beauty is to human sensibility a supernal essence of the world: "The beauty of the world is the co-operation of divine wisdom in creation." At the same time, beauty can be painfully tantalizing, drawing us toward it without our knowing what to ask of it. Even when we possess it, we still desire something more of it, even to feed on it. But looking and eating are two different operations, except "in the country inhabited by God," where they are one and the same. "It may be," she thinks, "that vice, depravity, and crime are nearly always, or even perhaps always, in their essence, attempts to eat beauty, to eat what we should only look at." Our love of beauty, if it is to transcend the slavery of matter, must finally intersect with our pursuit of wisdom, at last breaking through the curtain that separates us from the ultimate real. It is this truth that we must contemplate: "We cannot contemplate without a certain love. The contemplation of this image of the order of the world constitutes a certain contact with the beauty of the world. The beauty of the world is the order of the world that is loved."

Simone Weil's concept of carnal love having the beauty of the world as its object shows a profound sympathy of compassion. She can, in her judgments, be hard; but she is never heartless. How can we diminish and transcend our coarseness, our vulgarity, and our cruelty? She helps us to confront this question, to come to grips with it—and with ourselves. She arouses in us the redemptive process in all its possibilities. Her special relevance to the modern human predicament is inestimable when one reflects on statements such as these: "The longing to love the beauty of the world in a human being is essentially the longing for the Incarnation." "The different kinds of vice, the use of drugs, in the literal or metaphorical sense of the word, all such things constitute the search for the state where the beauty of the world will be tangible. The mistake lies precisely in the search for a special state." "The only true beauty, the only beauty that is the real presence of God, is the beauty of the universe. Nothing less than the universe is beautiful." "To destroy cities, either materially or morally, or to exclude human beings from a city, thrusting them down to the state of social outcasts, this is to sever every bond of poetry and love between human beings and the universe. It is to plunge them forcibly into the horror of ugliness. There can scarcely be a greater crime." Her understanding of the human condition is always one of control and order; sentimentalism in no way subverts her view of the created universe in which, "under a thousand different forms, grace and mortal sin are everywhere." A purity of thought, conveyed with absolute sincerity and sympathy, informs and shapes her judgments, her deeper vision, of the supernatural presence in all life.

"Concerning the Our Father" marks the culmination of Simone Weil's meditations. It is her spiritual epitome, the final resolution and the final consecration of her life's thought. All approaches to Simone Weil must end here in her approach to God. Passage from time into eternity and release from the prison of self are gained in this meditation. Consent to grace becomes eternal in the supreme supplication, "Our Father." One arrives at the highest spiritual moment when he asks for "supernatural bread." Divine possibility is realized. "The prayer began with the word 'Father,'" Simone Weil points out in a paradigmatic passage of great beauty, "it ends with the word 'evil.' We must go from confidence to fear. Confidence alone can give us strength enough not to fall as a result of fear. After having contemplated the name, the kingdom, and the will of God, after having received the supernatural bread and having been purified from evil, the soul is ready for the true humility which crowns all virtues." Her meditation on the most sacred of prayers, the source of all prayers according to Saint Augustine, is the sacred point at which all her paths of meditation converge. It is the point from which a modern saint gives her final testimony, her witness. Her concluding sentences summarize the worth of her meditation, in its depth and warmth, even as they can confirm for us why, in the history of spirituality, it is comparable to some of the greatest works on the "Our Father," including that of Origen in the third century or of Saint Teresa in the sixteenth century: "The Our Father contains all possible petitions; we cannot conceive of any prayer not already contained in it. It is to prayer what Christ is to humanity. It is impossible to say it once through, giving the fullest possible attention to each word, without a change, infinitesimal perhaps but real, taking place in the soul."

Simone Weil's life was a gesture of spiritual destiny. Her devotion was unhesitant. Her faith was unshakable. "My heart, I hope, is transferred forever into the Holy Eucharist," she wrote a year before she died. In her meditations we are in the presence of a modern saint, a mystic and religious philosopher, who seeks for and attains unity across the gulf of "infinite separation." In the end we must stand before this spiritual attainment deeply humbled. Our experience of her vision, a vision that is surely one of the great miracles of the twentieth century, becomes a lesson in humility that allows us to enter the "warm silence," the "true silence," when, as she believed, God's love can speak and be heard.

2

The Critical Mission of Irving Babbitt

"FIGHTING A WHOLE GENERATION is not exactly a happy task," wrote Irving Babbitt (1865–1933), recognizing the painful costs of his mission as a teacher and critic. These are brave words not often heard in the academy, where judgments that are at once critical and moral are neither fashionable nor expedient. If uttered, they are frequently received with haughty skepticism. The critic who makes moral judgments meets with a resistance that, in amoral or immoral critical contexts, turns into acceptance or even acclamation. But if Babbitt had been seeking academic standing, he would never have written as he did. Fortunately he had more important matters to attend to than worrying about executing a calm and prosperous passage in the academic world. Neither compromise nor timidity was a quality that Babbitt ever adopted. He had hard and threatening, as well as prophetic, truths to deliver to a world that, for him, extended far beyond that of "the hustling scholar" and his "productive scholarship." Babbitt chose to be, within the educational community, something of an outsider. In time he also came to be treated as an outlaw by those academics who watch over their special provinces. The values implicit in Babbitt's teachings and writings were increasingly incompatible with those of his contemporaries. He equated their values with "the democratic absurdity" and other forms of a failure of authority—and of nerve.

Babbitt was a brave man whose example must remind us that nothing else is worth having. Perhaps one of the most extraordinary characteristics of his thought is that he was a man without doubts. Some teachers confess, reproachfully, to themselves, or perhaps to their students or to their colleagues, doubts concerning their work, or the worth of their work, or the influence of their work. Some critics, and even some great authors, come to see their writings as just so many words to be forgotten or to be preserved only for the specialists or, as Babbitt called them, "the throng of scholiasts and commentators whom Voltaire saw pressing about the outer gates of the Temple of Taste." Such confessions may come out of humility, or exhaustion, or disappointment, or uncertainty. But whatever their source, they stem from self-doubt. Feelings of meaninglessness often prelude gestures of renunciation—both for the teacher who would be a savior and for the writer who would be an evangel. For Babbitt such confessions would have constituted routes of escape and self-indulgent solace unworthy of and unwelcome to one who steadfastly taught the Socratic, the humanistic, doctrine—"the discipline of a central standard"—and who affirmed Goethe's admonition that "anything that emancipates the spirit without a corresponding growth in self-mastery, is pernicious." It could be said that Babbitt never lost his vision of the One, in the absence of which there is inevitably, as he declared, "a disquieting vagueness and lack of grip in dealing with particulars."

A man of firm confidence, he never lost his own "grip in dealing with particulars." While so many teachers, critics, and thinkers were busily questioning, even destroying, the traditional values, and at the same time creating new abstractions or avoiding valuations, Babbitt admonished that it was urgent to create "That aristocracy of character and intelligence that is needed in a community like ours to take the place of an aristocracy of birth." The act of valuation, as a courage of judgment, was for him not only a serious but also a moral matter that qualitatively affected not only the individual but also the whole of society, of civilization. In place of a policy of expansionism, he counseled one of retrenchment, hardly a popular program to recommend to a nation boastful of its optimism. He realized fully the difficulty of advocating the aristocratic principle at a time when "all the ideas which I know to be most vital for man have more and more declined." Nor did his stress on the disciplinary and selective "truths of the inner life" find favor in a secular age glorifying the gospel of progress and bigness and promising to open "the gates of Eden," as daring a promise as any that, Babbitt would go on to say, pushes pluralism to excess and assaults the supreme law of life—the law of measure. Babbitt chose to fulfill the function of the critic, which Matthew Arnold had formulated: ". . . whoever sets himself to see things as they are will find himself one of a very small circle; but it is only by this small circle resolutely doing its own work that adequate ideas will ever get current at all." That he would not substitute miscellaneous sympathies for firm principles of judgment; or cower before the imperial power of what he labeled "a cheap contemporaneousness"; or view the human problem as merely a socioeconomic one—these were brave refusals that distinguished Babbitt from his contemporaries.

The thrust of his judgments, enhanced by his penchant for polemics and repartee, alienated many of his contemporaries and continues to alienate those who now sneer at him for his "one-sided erudition of doctrinaire propaganda." The animus against him, always lingering (and even at times unscrupulous), and in itself a symptomatic phenomenon, springs to attack at the mere mention of his name. Daring to speak favorably of him, especially among teachers and scholars, has a curious way of eliciting, in print or viva voce, a double damnation: both of the embattled defendant and of his wary defender. Babbitt's ideas touch sensitive nerve centers. His whole critical approach, etched as it is by strenuous self-assurance, has about it a kind of direct and unguarded fearsomeness, pushing aside cozy collegial loyalties engendered by the "associational process," as Henry James once described it. Babbitt's final goal, he wrote, was "to define types and tendencies, and not to satirize or even label individuals." What he wanted to show was "not that our contemporary scholars are lacking in humanistic traits, but that the scholars in whom these traits predominate are few. . . ." Babbitt had a way of expressing things, of hitting the mark, with a sparseness, a cutting simplicity, an honest severity, and a robust, even racy, authoritativeness. The aphoristic quality of his writing has, unfortunately, been largely ignored. His writing was cast very much in the mold of a New England mind preaching the New England virtues of conviction, self-control, and good character. A sturdy, if inelegant, sermonic note pervades Babbitt's writing, reinforced at every step by his desire to persuade men's intellects and to awaken their hearts. His "sermon" possesses the plain style of the Puritans.

Babbitt's greatest achievement, Walter Jackson Bate has stated, was "to recall an entire academic and critical generation to consider primary questions."[1] Since 1952, when this statement was made with rare and grateful fairness, much has occurred in American intellectual and cultural life to substantiate Babbitt's persistent warning that modern man is "treading very near the edge of sudden disaster." Insofar as we are still witnessing both its concomitants and its consequences, we find it difficult to estimate the ramifications of this disaster. Our difficulty is exacerbated by the fact that, for many, the disaster has never happened; possibly it only has happened for the priests and the prophets and the moralists for whom disaster is necessarily an occupational hazard. The yearning to await the promise of a "new deal" or to relay the "good news" is, for some, an unsacrificeable illusion. Yet Babbitt saw the contemplative life and

1. *Criticism: The Major Texts*, ed. Walter Jackson Bate (New York, 1952), 547.

the permanent things deteriorate into what he termed "a delicious epicureanism," as the need for "a juster judgment and richer selection" became a victim of "the furious and feverish pursuit of mechanical efficiency." Essentially a "destructive critic," he opposed the cock-a-hoop tendencies of modern man and called them errors. This was hardly a popular role. It never is for the critic who attempts to act as the conscience of the race. To academics Babbitt became an embarrassment, for he charged them with betraying their moral function. To critics he was an oddity, for he demanded criticism with a centrality and a direction. To the intelligentsia at large he was essentially a persona non grata, for he demanded a discipline that they could not meet.

No reader of Babbitt can come away without having gained an awareness of the qualities that shaped his mind and character. A sense of contact with a major force, a major critic, is inescapable. Even when one resists or disagrees with his ideas, one cannot dispense with them without assessing them. Babbitt has a power of forcing reaction, of requiring some kind of analytical exertion. It is not merely that he forces one to deal with overwhelming issues, but that his criticism becomes a source of reflection, as well as, in the end, a path of meditation. Babbitt's criticism is concerned with something more than the so-called business of criticism, since for him the critical pursuit transposes into the pursuit of criteria of wisdom. To read Babbitt and to discover the value of his critical mission is to be reminded of ultimate human questions—and answers. He is a severe critic whose driving force of thought and whose moral purposes are never confused about their target, possessing as they do a defiant confidence and a cosmopolitan rightness, as intimidating as they are earnest. Babbitt invariably addresses himself to the catechumen. He neither makes empty promises nor incites tempting illusions. In an age when creator and critic have been subjected both to an overriding skepticism and to a general softness of standards, Babbitt taught a doctrine of human centrality, of sentience and responsibility. What some take to be the singlemindedness, or even the narrowness, of his critical views is in reality a persevering toughness.

Babbitt was a great man in the Emersonian sense that "great men exist that there may be greater men." He was to attain and to personify the kind of disciplined transcendence that enabled him to inhabit a higher sphere of thought, a sphere to which, to quote Emerson again, "other men rise with labor and difficulty." In Babbitt one finds no tormenting paradoxes, complexities, anomalies, conundrums, or enigmas; he admits to no baffling deflections in his critical ideas.

Indeed, he reveals in many and astonishing ways a mastery—a command—of analytical thought that underscores attained resolutions. Order and control, two of his principles, impel and inform his ideas. Constancy and consistency register the moral rhythm of his thought. The life and health of the mind remain his absorbing purpose. He does not explore new pathways. He is no critical adventurer. Adventure in itself he finds suspect: a Dionysian quest that too easily becomes uncertainty and dissolution. His work is not addressed to those who want a journey of discovery. One of his goals is to discourage man from distorting himself in the pursuit of the unknown—for Babbitt the epitome of fantasms, lost bearings, and "great confusion." He affirms man's need to husband his resources, to plot his way, to affirm character rather than temperament, adhering to both restraint and constraint. Babbitt's emphasis on limits is never without a recognition of the need for humility. It is the austere voice of the schoolmaster that speaks in Babbitt—a New England schoolmaster of a nation during extreme times.

Particularly within the progressivist ethos, that which inspires the modern gospel of humanitarianism dependent on technology and pluralism on the one hand and allied to compassion and social hope on the other finds staunch opposition in Babbitt. The continuing refusal to recognize Babbitt's significance stems in large part from a commonly held view of him as a hard, elitist-oriented "antimajoritarian." Insofar as from the turn of the century he condemned the growing obsession with socioeconomic capabilities and arrangements, he chose to reject a way of life that, especially in more recent history, is increasingly controlled—programmed, in today's parlance—by precisely the social scientists whom Babbitt early recognized as sabotaging the values of humanistic culture. In countering this movement Babbitt was challenging powerful forces ("the wave of the future"). Against them he posited what he believed to be saving principles of order, insisting that unless a sound and qualitative dialectic is able to come to the rescue, all the terms expressive of the higher values of human nature are in danger. As a teacher and critic, then, he chose to devote himself to the greater moral issues rather than to the sophomoric intellectual discourses that other academics are usually content with pursuing. It would be fair to say that Babbitt was to be another (and by no means the last) victim of the by now all too familiar alliance between academics in the liberal arts, who distrust a moral critic's diagnostic insistences, and social scientists, who detest his cultural convictions and his stress on the need for standards.

To include Babbitt's writings, so long neglected, among the major texts of American criticism, and to place Babbitt, so long relegated to an orphan status, among the major critics—among, that is, the "keen-sighted few" (to use his own term)—form a dual necessity that has been ignored. The failure to recognize Babbitt's critical contribution instances a shameful episode in the history of American intellectual life. At a time when lesser critics amass reputations and influences in excess of their achievement or their intelligibility, it is imperative to salute Babbitt's contribution and to demand that it be given its due. Babbitt died nearly fifty years ago, but his critical thought is very much for our time. Yet it is not easy to rescue him from the fate assigned to him by no less than Edmund Wilson, who stated, in a letter to Burton Rascoe of April 8, 1930, "that Humanism is now a flattened corpse over which the whole army of American intelligence has passed, and that it might as well be left for dead."[2] The prejudices and fallacies inherent in Wilson's denigration are repeated just as fiercely by today's hardened literary politicians of revolution, who oppose what they see as the Arnoldian "administration" of literature and who yearn desperately for the final and irrevocable "demystifica-tion of authority." Against this prevailing climate of a new absolut-ism, the task of winning recognition for Babbitt's critical relevance is formidable.

But such a task is essential. Babbitt's steadfastness, in the face of an orthodoxy of messianic pragmatism, should serve as an example to those who would dare to believe that the teacher's and the critic's main goal is the achievement of a wisdom that points to positive insight, to self-mastery rather than to solipsistic self-assertion and self-liberation. For Babbitt, what is important about one, and what identifies one in the contexts of a controlling purpose and value, is whether one's point-of-view is Socratic or sophistic. It was this that impelled, stamped, and interrelated Babbitt's standards of judgment in his outlook and overview, in his valuation of the life of literature, and in his perception of ideas and the world. Babbitt harbored no delusion about the possibility of training the ideal critic in the mod-ern world or of attaining standards of order that resist what he termed "the disillusion of decadence." He saw his mission as one defining and conveying corrective judicial measures. To this end he worked in the hope that "some progress might at least be made towards temper-ing with judgment the all-pervading impressionism of contemporary literature and life." What most characterizes Babbitt as a teacher and critic is that he spoke out. In an age that has seen the abridgement of

2. *Letters on Literature and Politics, 1912–1972,* ed. Elena Wilson (New York, 1977), 195.

the heroic spirit, Babbitt's willingness to face hard problems and to make discriminations provides a much needed lesson in critical conviction and courage.

II

An unceasing vigilance characterized Irving Babbitt's mission as a teacher and critic. Whatever he observed or looked at in the human world—particularly in literature, politics, education, philosophy, and religion—he saw with a rigorous and vigorous exactness, at once perusing, inspecting, and appraising an issue in a constant critical process. In both his outlook and his overview he was painstakingly discriminating. He was not afraid to define and to pronounce his value judgments on matters that he believed profoundly affected the human fate. The need to look not only at things but also beyond them constituted for Babbitt an urgent critical responsibility. Enthusiasms and impressions of the hour, or of the season, or of the age, he dismissed as the consequences of "free temperamental overflow." At the vortex of this overflow, impelling and molding it, and as the cause of what might be termed the crisis of modern civilization, he placed Jean-Jacques Rousseau. Babbitt characterized Rousseau's achievement, in its continuing influence on modern life, as immense and far-reaching. In Rousseau's contention that "man is naturally good and it is by our institutions alone that men become wicked," Babbitt pinpointed what he believed to be the "new dualism," replacing the "older dualism" and thus transferring the struggle between good and evil from the heart of man to society. In this transference Babbitt saw a portentous and epochal yielding to the sociological view of life. It was to signify a consequential shifting of standards and traditions favoring the humanitarian over the humanistic and the immediate over the transcendent. It marked the ascendancy, if not the triumph, of the vital impulse (*élan vital*). And for Babbitt it was to mark the elimination of the principle of control (*frein vital*), without which spiritual anarchy prevails.

Throughout his life Babbitt devoted all his energy to stressing the need for recovering spiritual discipline. He stressed that, to attain this ultimately unifying discipline, the development of a humanistic attitude was necessary. He associated this attitude with the will to refrain, which he opposed, strenuously, to "dogmatic naturalism" and, less strenuously, to "dogmatic supernaturalism." In relying on social dualism, the naturalist, he believed, was evasive and superficial in his treatment of evil; the supernaturalist, on the other hand, ultimately sought total renunciation, containing an ascetical quality that Babbitt found excessively mystical and even morbid, as well as remote from "the actual data of experience." "The right use of grace and similar doctrines," he says, "is to make us humble and not to make us morbid or discouraged." Babbitt's ideological perspective should be approached in the special light of his embracement of these words from *The Dhammapada*, Buddha's Sermon on the Mount: "Work out your own salvation with diligence." The humanistic virtues that he proffered had as their chief aim "not the renunciation of the expansive desires but the subduing of them to the law of measure." In short, Babbitt sought to teach a humanism that he considered to be both positive and critical. Failure to recover the true dualism or its equivalent, "a reaffirmation of the truths of the inner life in some form—traditional or critical, religious or humanistic," he asserted, would have tragic consequences for civilization. In dealing with the problems of the intellect and the will, he counted as crucial the need for the definition and application of standards. The neglect and discrediting of "the analytical intellect" were disturbing developments that Babbitt located within the modern movement from Rousseau to Henri-Louis Bergson. (He was severely critical of Bergson, in whom he saw a representative of the modern thinker, "a new Protagoras," who rejoiced in novelty for its own sake, wanted nothing better than "to whirl forever on the wheel of change," and constructed a metaphysics of "intoxication with the future.")

Tied to and symptomatic of the discrediting of the analytical intellect, Babbitt further believed, was an irresponsible use of general terms. Two such terms, to which he returned repeatedly, were "classicism" and "romanticism." Babbitt's entire thought revolved around not only the use but also the informing ethos of these words, insofar as each makes concrete a "life-attitude," or an idea of value. Without an understanding of these two key words there can be no understanding of Babbitt's teaching and criticism. He believed that one's own definition and applied understanding of these words epitomize one's perception and concept of life. The nature of one's understanding, in fact, helps to identify the measure of one's own quest for meaning and value. To Babbitt the capacity to identify the discrete qualities that characterize classicism and romanticism denoted a qualitative, critical act of responsible self-recognition, if not of self-perpetuation, and beyond that, an awareness of the very quality of civilization itself. That is to say, what one says about, the response he makes to, the weight and significance that he attaches to these words, the defining essences, requirements, possibilities, and functions that he locates in each, help to determine the difference between discrimination and indiscrimination, between triumph and failure, order and chaos, civilization and barbarism. The need to distinguish between classicism and romanticism constituted, for Babbitt, a judgmental process that centers, and insists, on fundamentals: on fundamentals that must posit critical standards and discipline in an age that has witnessed the weakening of traditional beliefs. In emphasizing the need for clear-cut definitions, for precise critical analysis and "hard consecutive thinking," Babbitt hoped to bring attention to the allied need for affirming an enduring scale of values, in the permanent framework of which the job of definition and analysis must be done. "Unless a sound dialectic comes to the rescue," he warned, "all the terms expressive of the higher values of human nature are in danger of being discredited."

Romanticism the term—no less than its great evangelist, Rousseau—finds in Babbitt a formidable antagonist. Neither the definition nor the comprehension of this word can be complete without some reference to Babbitt's thoughts on the subject. His consideration of romanticism, whether as an idea or as an intellectual movement, is incessant and categorical. Babbitt was never one for shirking the burden, or the courage, of his judgment. ("All children, nearly all women and the vast majority of men always have been, are and probably always will be romantic," he wrote in words that capture that polemical and uncompromising tone, as well as that tough honesty, that permeates Babbitt's critical opinions.) In romanticism and in the romantic, Babbitt found something that is wonderful rather than probable; something that "violates the normal sequence of cause and effect in favor of adventure." In particular he detected the romantic attitude in writing, and in what he called "imaginative unrestraint," that he found synonymous with the thrilling, the marvelous, the melodramatic, and with that which leads to imagination superseding judgment and reason, in short, to "the despotism of mood." "Romantic impressionism" is another term that Babbitt often used to pinpoint what he believed to be excesses of the imagination. "Writing that is romantic," he asserted, "writing in which the imagination is not disciplined to a true centre is best enjoyed while we are young. The person who is as much taken by Shelley at forty as he was at twenty has, one may surmise, failed to grow up." We hear in these words the voice, disciplined and disciplining, of the didactician; the fact remains that Babbitt never separated his vocation as a teacher from his mission as a critic. Closely scrutinizing the consequences of the romantic attitude, in literature as in society, he was unrelenting in his view of it as lacking sufficient qualitative discrimination and as erring inevitably on the side of emotion, and worse, of anarchy: "The romanticist . . . revels in the mere picturesqueness of the facts or else takes refuge in the past from the present, uses it . . . to create for himself an alibi. But the past should be regarded primarily neither as a laboratory for research nor as a bower of dreams, but as a school of experience."

Babbitt was fully aware that classicism can degenerate into the pseudoclassicism of the eighteenth century (when form, for instance, became formalism) and, in turn, into an artistic Pharisaism: "the romantic view . . . is too much the neo-classical view turned upside down," he asserted. The classicism he championed had to be a classicism of standards, in essence not local or national or relative, but universal and human. Such a classicism affirms "a general nature, a core of normal experience" and possesses an abiding element, an intrinsic, unifying principle, in the midst of the flux of circumstance. Its sources and its paradigms are in Hellenism, where, in theory and in practice, it attained its apogee. It is best revealed in and exemplified by Aristotle. Aristotle and classicism contain Babbitt's answer to Rousseau and romanticism. The Hellenic, the classical, spirit underlines the doctrine of measure, a law to which all of man's religious, ethical, and aesthetic values must finally be referred. Classicism supplies models for imitation. Ignoring or rejecting them leads to "the progressive decline of standards." For Babbitt, then, the classical spirit emphasized the recognition of limit, whereas the romantic spirit was a yearning for the infinite. The decline of the classical spirit in the modern world, as he was to show, was not restricted merely to the decline of the moral imagination. Inevitably it instanced a much wider and more serious decline that spilled over into ethical action, into the sociopolitical realm. The end that Babbitt sought, despite the severely magisterial tone of his pronouncements (if not his fiats), was one of reconciliation appropriate to the modern age: reconciliation of the creative enthusiasm of romanticism with the disciplined strength of classicism—that achieved great middle ground where "man may combine an exquisite measure with a perfect spontaneity, that he may be at once thoroughly disciplined and thoroughly inspired."

The critic's battle against romanticism can no more cease than can the priest's battle against sin. In waging this war against inveterate and unforgiving enemies, who from the beginning attacked his work as an example of "the neo-pseudo-bluestocking variety"—"the more earnest the moralist, the more justly suspect the historian," Arthur O. Lovejoy, philosopher and critical realist, said derisively of Babbitt's interpretations—he persisted in his contention that moral contexts and moral effects are inseparable. In this respect he insisted on the operative value, the "imitation," of a standard—a standard of discrimination as well as a standard of conduct: What one says about literature and how one judges its significance and value should also tell us much about what one thinks of life. It is this moral correlation between literature and life that Babbitt posited and that challenged and unsettled those who refused to see the correlation or, if they did see it, chose to see it as a curious form of "the smuggest puritanism." In his outlook, as in his overview, Babbitt was immovably ethical. "When first principles are involved," he said, "the law of measure is no longer applicable. One should not be moderate in dealing with error." His criteria were not metaphysical dreams. In his introduction to *Rousseau and Romanticism (1919)*, considered by some critics his chef d'oeuvre, he wrote: "But, though strictly considered, life is but a web of illusion and a dream within a dream, it is a dream that needs to be managed with the utmost discretion, if it is not to turn into a nightmare. In other words, however much life may mock the metaphysician, the problem of conduct remains." Analytical reason, which Babbitt viewed as belonging centrally to the humanistic level of experience (as opposed to the materialistic and the religious levels), when appealed to, distinguishes between "the law for thing" and "the law for man." In his writings, therefore, Babbitt sought "to trace main currents as a part of my search for a set of principles to oppose to naturalism." "A student of main tendencies," he planted himself, sturdily, on the humanistic plane, seeking, at the same time, "a truly ecumenical wisdom" and being, at all times, a good humanist and ethical positivist, "moderate and sensible and decent." "It is much easier for a man," he reflected, "to deceive himself and others regarding his supernatural lights than it is regarding the degree to which he is moderate and sensible and decent."

Babbitt believed that the modern mind tends to reject everything that has the appearance of being nonessential. His first published essay, "The Rational Study of the Classics," appearing in the March 1897 issue of *The Atlantic Monthly*, decried some of the trends he detected in higher education, especially the movement away from the classics in particular and away from the Hellenic spirit in general, and the emphasis on specialization. The latter, he claimed, was a crude American imitation of the German scientific spirit. And for the rest of his life he kept on hammering at the trends that lead to a loss of intellectual symmetry and a sense of proportion. "Men have recently shown their fitness for teaching the humanities by writing theses on the ancient horse-bridle and the Roman doorknob," he scornfully and prophetically declared. Focusing on the study of philology, which he saw as diminishing the critical role of the study of classical literature, he warned of the damaging effects of "an epidemic of pedantry": "In the classics more than in other subjects, the fact should never be forgotten that the aim proposed is the assimilation, and not the accumulation, of knowledge." Echoing Emerson, Babbitt maintained that the goal of the true scholar, and of the whole educational task, is to combine analysis and synthesis. If the European man, he noted, is sometimes excessively tied to the past, the American is unduly absorbed in the present. Addressing himself to the progressivist and pragmatist, Babbitt sought to show that "movement is not necessarily progress, and that the advance in civilization cannot be measured by the increase in the number of eighteen-story buildings." He believed that the study of classical literature (in its historical and comparative contexts) should alert us to causes leading to the greatness or the decline of an ancient society. In the end it should help us to grasp the essences of a moral discipline, those ordering and civilizing virtues of restraint and proportion without which one's mind and character cannot be effectively formed.

"The Rational Study of the Classics" was later to be included as a chapter in Babbitt's first book, *Literature and the American College: Essays in Defense of the Humanities* (1908). Charles Eliot Norton, American scholar and man of letters, praised this book in these words: "It is a great misfortune for us nationally that the tradition of culture is so weak and so limited. In this respect the advantage of England is great. But I hail such a book as Mr. Babbitt's as an indication of a possible turn in the tide. . . ." For some readers, especially humanist educators, this book has always been Babbitt's most tempered, his "best and most finished piece of writing," according to Paul Elmer More. That it should inspire admiration is not difficult to understand. Containing the seeds of Babbitt's whole critical thought, it argues in favor of literary, as opposed to scientific and utilitarian, studies. But literary study, Babbitt also stipulated, must be conducted selectively and discriminatingly—always one of his central tenets; ultimately, too, it must have a formulating reference to absolute standards of literary values. His ideal of the educated man, of the *honnête homme*, was humanistic: a man morally responsible and intellectually responsive; exclusive and select in his sympathy and tastes; keenly aware of a scale of values. Education, Babbitt declared, must revolve around an integrating principle of concentration and selection, as well as of assimilation and reflection, if it is not to capitulate to the evils of specialism or to the centrifugal tendencies in human nature. Education and *humanitas* were, for Babbitt, consubstantial. The college and the university should offer not "training for power and service," but training for wisdom and character.

It was as a diagnostician of cultural decay that Babbitt fulfilled his roles as teacher and critic. Diagnosis, however, was not his sole or even his last word. His was, as his angry antagonists realized, a combative humanism, even as his books have been described as "so many combats all full of honorable contention." Though essentially he aimed his attention at the American scene, he was not a provincial critic in the least, but a generalist whose achievement takes on universal qualities of wisdom, as well as of vision—vision of order. He formed his diagnoses and waged his battles on the basis of his reading of and reflection on ancient, medieval, and modern literatures. A favorite phrase of his (from Matthew Arnold), "the imperious, lonely thinking power," best expresses the depth and intensity of Babbitt's examinations of the human situation. That his "system" is stringent, that he perhaps lacked appreciation of the gentler virtues, that love was not a word he used fondly or delicately are aspects of his thought that cannot be ignored. He made no pretense of denying either the stringency or the toughness of his position. "I should define myself as a realist according to the human law," he averred. His final stress was on the discipline of the mind and of the will, "the type of will that can alone raise one above the naturalistic level." He was not an idealist in the Wilsonian sense or even in the Platonic sense, as he freely admitted; he never failed to point out how "we are altruistic in our feelings about ourselves and imperialistic in our practice." To get rid of the selective and aristocratic principle, as the equalitarian democrat wanted, he warned, would create the cult of commonness. One must distinguish, Babbitt insisted, between the *hombre medio* and the *honnête homme*—between the man who makes for a chaos of values and the man who seeks a discipline of standards.

III

Literature and life, Babbitt insisted, are indivisible: literary studies need to be justified on cultural and disciplinary grounds. The study of literature must, in effect, become a discipline of ideas: a discipline that must distinguish between significant and insignificant literature, between literature that has an ethical or moral center and literature that is subservient to the flux of relativism. Babbitt saw literary studies as an integral part of the larger educational process, specifically of the "old education" aiming for a humanistic training for wisdom and not for a humanitarian training for service and power. In this respect his critical aims can best be termed sapiential rather than sociological. He sought quality and standards and not quantity and ideals: "True democracy consists not in lowering the standard but in giving everybody, so far as possible, a chance of measuring up to the standard." Insofar as he regarded the modern age as revolutionary and expansionist, with the traditional supports disappearing in society, he believed that the qualitative and selective idea in cultural life must be sustained. In the study of literature, as in the whole of education, he saw a common problem that relates to the even greater crisis of modern civilization. "What seems to me to be driving our whole civilization toward the abyss at present is a one-sided conception of liberty, a conception that is purely centrifugal, that would get rid of all outer control and then evade or deny openly the need of achieving inner control." Without a sufficiently stringent discipline of ideas, Babbitt believed, the temper of the sham "liberals" would triumph, spurning the past and barely tolerating the present—"the true home of their spirit is that vast, windy abode, the future." The main task of education, and of the teacher of literature, as he envisioned it, was that of defining general terms; the ideas for which the terms stand should be studied positively, critically, and concretely, especially as reflected in major literary currents and works.

For Babbitt the critic's central task, no less than the teacher's, was one of selection and judgment, and only secondarily one of comprehension and sympathy. That the final test of art is not its originality but its truth to the universal constituted for Babbitt a transcendent standard of criticism. Particularly in nineteenth-century art and literature did he detect eccentric and centrifugal, even pathological, tendencies. He felt that these tendencies, continuing into the twentieth century, signaled a rejection of those representative qualities of vision (and of permanence) that he found in ancient Greece: "The original man for the Greek was one who could create in the very act of imitating the past. Greek literature at its best is to a remarkable degree a creative imitation of Homer." Above all he thought that original genius must not allow the synthesizing process of humility and decorum to be outstripped by temperamental excesses of self-expression and restless self-concern. Babbitt thought it important that a work be assessed not in terms of the fulfillment of a particular aesthetic aim but in terms of whether its aim is intrinsically valuable in relation to achievement and intelligibility. The main business of the critic must be one of rating "creation with reference to some standard set above his own temperament and that of the creator." Original genius must rise to ethical standards and be disciplined to reality: "Once eliminate the high impersonal standard, the ethical norm that sets bounds to the eagerness of the creator to express himself, and the eagerness of the creator to thrill to this expression, and it is hard to see what measure of a man's merit is left save his intoxication with himself; and this measure would scarcely seem to be trustworthy."

The role of the "ethical imagination," insofar as it possesses a literary conscience, or high seriousness in the Aristotelian sense, was for Babbitt a defense against the lures of "decadent aestheticism." Relentless in his censure of "romantic eleutheromaniacs," "the corrupters of the conscience in general," he held that "we must begin by creating standards." A reverence for boundaries and limits was, for Babbitt, essential; he endorsed fully Goethe's words that in limitations one first shows himself the master. But in much of modern art and literature, he argued, expression triumphs over form, a process that he associated with the Rousseauistic view of art. Such a view he saw as leading to a breakdown of standards: "There is no place in the process for the sharply drawn line of demarcation, for the firm and fast distinction. Definite standards are swallowed up in a universal relativity." The creator's need to mediate between "the outward push of expression" and "the circumscribing law" remained for Babbitt (and for "those who have thought correctly about art") a crucial one, particularly if beauty is to be acquired that is pertinent to man. The need for mediation, in its achievement and in its truth, underlined Babbitt's view of extremes that are barbarous. Form and symmetry, then, he cited as properties essential to beauty. The epithet "beautiful," he emphasized, must not be applied indiscriminatingly. A skyscraper, he noted, is hardly beautiful: "Now sky-scrapers may be picturesque, or vital, or what you will, though they are usually not much more than a mixture of megalomania and commercialism."

If Babbitt was concerned with first principles, he was also concerned with final directions. That is, he was fearful of the dehumanization of life and literature in the absence of absolute principles. In Oscar Wilde and Paul Verlaine, for example, he saw the Rousseauistic side of romanticism: "The latest romanticists have discredited themselves, which is not perhaps a serious matter; but they have also thrown a certain discredit on art and literature, and this is far more serious." For Babbitt there was no special mystery or paradox regarding the genres and the boundaries of art: ". . . a clear-cut type of person, a person who does not live in either an emotional or intellectual muddle, will normally prefer a clear-cut type of art or literature."

And always, too, it was to the ancient Greeks, to the *exemplaria graeca*, that Babbitt referred for our emulation: to their redeeming way of mediating between the One and the Many; to their intrinsic forms of "vital unity, vital measure, vital purpose"; to their high standards of art, which at its best is a triumph of restraint. The law of measure, as taught by Aristotle, should be, first and always, the impelling principle of life and literature. In life it helps us to distinguish the incongruity between appearance and reality; in literature it acts as a defense against the excesses of the romantic imagination, and particularly of the romantic religion of love: "There is in fact no object in the romantic universe—only subject. This subjective love amounts in practice to a use of the imagination to enhance emotional intoxication, or if one prefers, to the pursuit of illusion for its own sake." All this leads, Babbitt felt, to the confusion of ethical values, found, for example, in William Hazlitt, who "converts criticism itself into an art of impassioned recollection," with "its cult of Arcadian illusion and the wistful backward glance to the vanished paradise of childhood and youth when illusion was most spontaneous."

In the literature of the modern world, as in life, Babbitt perceived the consequences of a human situation when "things are in the saddle and ride mankind." For the individual and for society the consequences epitomize anarchy. The critic, and especially the moral critic, Babbitt believed, is in a position to resist and to diminish tendencies and habits of mind. Precise analysis, clear definitions of general terms, firm application of fixed principles and standards, keen awareness of the value of traditional beliefs: these are some of the qualities that a critic must bring to bear in pursuit of his task. Matthew Arnold exemplified for Babbitt precisely the pursuit of the critical function that he himself sought to fulfill in America: "Arnold always assumes a core of normal experience, a permanent self in man, and rates a writer according to the degree of his insight into this something that abides through all the flux of circumstance, or, as he himself would say, according to the depth and soundness of this writer's criticism of life." (At the same time Babbitt did not fail, as his most famous student, T.S. Eliot, did not fail, to point to Arnold's inability to rise far enough above the naturalistic level in his dealings with religion.) Arnold had worked out a positive and critical humanism, pertinent, Babbitt averred, to the modern concepts of democracy. Thus he saw in Arnold a critic who was ahead not only of his own time but also of ours: "Not to get beyond the idea of material organization as a remedy for moral anarchy is still to linger in the zones of illusion peculiar to the nineteenth century." Arnold's belief in a high quality of leadership, in terms of secured (and secure) standards and discipline, through the interaction of education and government, is also the belief that Babbitt argues for in his *Democracy and Leadership*. The real enemy of democracy is anarchy, and the corrective of anarchy is not a material and naturalistic efficiency but a humanistic or religious discipline. To have such a discipline, Babbitt noted, there must be standards, but in order to attain standards there must be critics who are concerned with defining and applying them. To be sure, he confessed, "We have no end of clever people, but clever people without standards."

Babbitt considered Arnold's essay on Joseph Joubert "one of the best critical essays ever written in English." Babbitt was sparing in outbursts of admiration; he was not, as has been observed, "an easy prey to imaginative enchantment of any kind." His standards were usually so strict that he excluded more than he included when passing judgment and assigning value. With Arnold, he recognized in Joubert a great critic, at once simple, brave, studious, and severe; one who, as Arnold wrote in the very last sentence of his essay, "nourished on some secret tradition, or illumined, perhaps, by a divine inspiration, kept aloof from the reigning superstitions, never bowed to the gods of Canaan." Joubert, Babbitt said, possessed a true spirituality, "far removed from a man like Coleridge who retired from his actual obligations into a cloud of opium and German metaphysics." Babbitt's estimation of Joubert appears in *Masters of Modern French Criticism* (1912), which, as Babbitt described it in his preface, is a criticism of critics. The sieving discussion of Joubert (and of other leading French critics of the nineteenth century, e.g., Chateaubriand, Sainte-Beuve, Taine, Brunetière) shows Babbitt at his best as a literary critic. His qualities of mind and of critical discrimination, of style, methodology, and scholarship, are immediately evident and provide an index to the integrity of his achievement, as well as a rebuttal of repeated charges by his detractors that he was an unsound critical thinker and a petulant writer. ("Professor Babbitt frowns a good deal and thrusts viciously," claimed one commentator.) His combination of courage of judgment and pithiness of statement radiates throughout this essay (and throughout the book itself). He never indulges in the kind of uncritical praise that, in Babbitt's own words, becomes "too full of admiration for unregulated sympathy": "Joubert tends to see only the benefits of order just as Emerson tends to see only the benefits of emancipation. In the name of what he conceives to be order, he would be too ready to deliver society over to the Jesuits and fix it in a sort of hieratic immobility." Perhaps no two consecutive sentences could better illustrate Babbitt's mastery of words or his powers of condensation and concentration. What Joubert wrote of himself can also be applied to Babbitt: "If there is a man tormented by the accursed ambition to put a whole book in a page, a whole page in a phrase, and that phrase in a word, it is I."

If Joubert leaned too much on the side of reaction in his politics and religion, he nevertheless preserved, as Babbitt emphasized, remarkable poise and balance in his literary opinions: "He did not, like so many moderns, go mad over the powers of suggestiveness." Joubert exemplified the merits that Babbitt required of a judging mind and that raise the art of criticism above impressionism and relativity. He knew how to combine sympathy with selection; how to temper expansion by concentration—"Joubert has not a trace of our modern megalomania." Babbitt called him "the critics' critic much as Spenser has been called the poets' poet" and recognized his remarkable literary perceptiveness: "Like Emerson he possessed the gift of vision, 'the eye of the spirit, the instinct of penetration, prompt discernment; in fine, natural sagacity in discovering all that is spiritual.' " Babbitt valued in Joubert the critic as sage, who joins to his sense of unity a fine perception of the local and impermanent. His overall quality as a critic is revealed by the fact that he had standards but held them fluidly. He was willing to concede much to the element of relativity without seeing literature merely as an expression of society or as the reflection of mobile conditions. Joubert perceived an "enduring something in man and aimed at it"; he focused on abiding relations. ("*Il y a quelque chose d'immuable dans l'homme!*") In short, Joubert exemplified both humanistic criticism and the dignity of criticism. In his appraisal of Joubert, Babbitt offered a "collective criticism," not only a theory of criticism but also a theory of conduct, a theory of education, and a philosophy.

In art as in criticism, Babbitt contended, one must always be on guard against the impressionism that culminates in "the fatality and finality of temperament." The impressionist cancels the principle of judgment; he slides into a quagmire of illusion and relativity. To counter the existing conditions that conduce such a vulgarization of sensibility, Babbitt appealed on an international scale to "the judgment of the keen-sighted few": "What we are seeking is a critic who rests his discipline and selection upon the past without being a mere traditionalist; whose holding of tradition involves a constant process of hard and clear thinking, a constant adjustment, in other words, of the experience of the past to the changing needs of the present." He pointed to Emerson as a model of this critical spirit, as one who can help us delineate critical standards, despite the fact that Emerson also contains a baffling blend of Rousseauism ("in denying intrinsic evil in human nature") and of insight. ("The oversoul that Emerson perceives in his best moments is the true oversoul and not the undersoul that the Rousseauist sets up as a substitute.") The "humanistic Goethe," the Goethe who renounced Rousseauistic reverie and turned from dreaming to doing, is still another model of one who can initiate us into the critical habit. In Goethe, Babbitt saw a modern who taught man the need to live and to think on the human path, one who attained and personified that existential wisdom for which Babbitt himself always sought: "No inconsiderable part of wisdom consists in just this: not to allow the mind to dwell on questions that are unprofitable in themselves or else entirely beyond its grasp." The problem of finding discipline and standards comprised for Babbitt the modern predicament, analogous, if one is to conceive fully of its ramifying difficulties and results, to the problem that faced Socrates and the ancient Sophists: how to "recover that firm foundation for human life which a misuse of the intellectual spirit was rendering impossible."

Clearly Babbitt must be viewed as a generalist critic comparable with Carlyle, Arnold, and Emerson—inferior to them, as it is sometimes claimed, in literary quality, but superior in intellectual depth. "He is a defender of tradition, an historian of ideas and tendencies, a moralist, a popularizer of general ideas: anything and everything, in fact, except a critic or a student of criticism." So wrote a distinguished American literary critic, J.E. Spingarn, in 1913, his words epitomizing the charge so often leveled at Babbitt: that he had no aesthetic theory and failed to answer the central questions: What is art? What is literature? What is criticism? Spingarn, who undoubtedly spoke for many others, objected not to Babbitt's cultural value, which he found considerable, but to his aesthetic theory, which he claimed "is vitiated by moralistic and intellectualistic errors." Above all, Spingarn continued, Babbitt shows his "confusion of ethical bias with aesthetic thought": "He does not care what art or criticism is, but he does care that young men and women should have discipline, training, tradition, ideals." Babbitt does not see, according to Spingarn, that "disciplined art and undisciplined art are both art; or perhaps we should say that disciplined minds as well as undisciplined ones may express themselves in art." In short, what Spingarn and other opponents of Babbitt's method emphasized is that Babbitt's literary approach, in appealing to formulas, can be rejected at the same time that his ethical outlook can be praised. Babbitt was dismissed as doctrinaire, or pseudoclassic, as insensitive to the literary experience. Later another critic, perpetuating Spingarn's objections, was to write of Babbitt: ". . . his literary criticism was inquisitorial, shrill—*criticism manquée*—because he sacrificed aesthetic to ethical vision." Even admirers of Babbitt's critical ethos, of literary criticism that sees the continuation of literary questions into general questions, voiced the fear that a critical practitioner, by placing moral edification above appreciation of genius, might lose his detachment and become too much a servant of his mind.

"Experience . . . has other uses," Babbitt maintained, "than to supply furnishings for the tower of ivory; it should control the judgment and guide the will; it is in short the necessary basis of conduct." That he equated the sense of beauty with the moral sense; that his literary standards were ethical absolutes, involving a violation of immediacy; that he "fatally" separated two orders of intuitions, the sensuous or aesthetic from the spiritual or intellectual; that he placed inordinate stress on control of the artistic imagination; that he expounded his views with "a feverish quickstep that arises from almost an excess of earnestness":—these are summary charges continually brought against Babbitt. To some extent these charges are valid, but they are valid only if one decides to separate Babbitt as literary critic from Babbitt as social critic, a separation that he himself never condoned. The fact remains that he viewed, and appraised, literary situations as cultural situations. In the process he damned much, whether in art or in criticism, in the name of standards, a fact that must be taken into account in weighing the charges against him. "There are critics who have founded," he wrote, "a considerable reputation on the relationship that exists between their own mediocrity and the mediocrity of their readers." In his view of the critical function there was obviously no room for endearing diplomacy and niceties. The critical act of judgment—and a judgment is personal or it is nothing—requires a mental toughness that is both a rejection of "unprofitable subtleties," to use Bacon's term, and a refusal of elegance: "The significant struggle is between the sound and the unsound individualist." For the modern critic, Babbitt contended, the main problem was how to "escape from the quicksands of relativity to some firm ground of judgment." He had little tolerance for dilettantes and *jouisseurs littéraires,* leading one critic to observe, ". . . Babbitt never takes a holiday. There is 'work' to be done, ethical work, seven days a week."

IV

Irving Babbitt was a man of ideas, which he held to resolutely once he had evaluated and assimilated and then converted them into principles. His younger Harvard colleague and critic, Theodore Spencer (1902–1949), always remembered Babbitt as a brave illustration of one who knew how to use ideas as principles. "His opinion was a foundation—it was as solid as a piece of granite," Spencer observed. Even in his writing the tenacity of Babbitt's ideas and opinions was one of his most identifiable, even overriding, traits. "He wrote always not for display but for conviction," Paul Elmer More has remarked. But whatever the tenacity of his ideas, Babbitt never failed to discover hidden relationships between historical or literary ideas. He looked on the exchange of ideas as essential, though at the same time he insisted on value. "There can be no assigning of values except in terms of ends," he said, "and no discovery of universal ultimate values except in terms of universal ultimate ends." Consistently he was to echo Matthew Arnold's rejection of the "over-preponderance of single elements": a rejection, that is, of the claims of a Romantic monism. Babbitt insisted on the discipline of ideas and not on the adventure in ideas, or indeed, on the "adventure of ideas," to borrow Alfred North Whitehead's phrase. He never stopped trying to relate what he believed to be positive and critical to the modern world. What he saw all around him, and attacked, was a rampant, an "imperialistic" (to use his own word), secularism: a world, he believed, in which the central maxim of the humanists, ancient and modern, "Nothing too much," was in eclipse. "In the ancients we should look for beauties because we frequently miss these," he said. "In contemporaries we should see faults, for they are part of the very air we breathe, the *Zeitgeist,* and we are in danger of not noticing them." His teachings and writings, then, were both corrective and catechetical. How can modern man convert the idea of value into the life of value? For Babbitt, this was a paramount question that tended to be sidetracked, ignored, scorned.

To preserve the integrity of the inner life, Babbitt claimed, it is necessary to set up a world of entities, essences, or "ideas" above the flux. The idea of self-reliance is, in this regard, all-important, requiring the possession of sound standards and the freedom to act on them. To secure standards one needs intellect, that power in man that analyzes, discriminates, and traces causes and effects. To act on them one needs will. Spiritual strenuousness was one of Babbitt's principles of life, and it was his final answer to the utilitarian-sentimental confusion of values and also his equivalent of passion. ("Love is the fulfilment of the law and not, as the sentimentalist would have us believe, a substitute for it.") One's moral conscience, Babbitt maintained, can never be replaced by social conscience. The distinction between one's moral and social, or material, progress can hardly be overemphasized. Its presence leads to making sharp exclusions and discriminations, to principles and practices and examples that positively activate civilized life and thought and that instance and confirm what Babbitt termed the "higher will": "To give the first place to the higher will is only another way of declaring that life is an act of faith." Civilization, which depends on the forms of inner action, "is something that must be deliberately willed; it is not something that gushes up spontaneously from the depths of the unconscious." It is true, confessed Babbitt, that modern civilization has witnessed considerable material progress. But this form of progress does not necessarily promote moral progress; it even works against it, impoverishing the truths of the inner life in their traditional forms. As a result the idea of liberty has become confused, "to be conceived expansively, not as a process of concentration, as a submission to or adjustment to a higher will." The consequence of this confusion is, for Babbitt, catastrophic for the modern world inasmuch as there is a failure to attain adequate equivalents for the traditional controls. Standards of selection are surrendered in the name of "nature," even as the ethical will gives way to a "diffuse, unselective sympathy": "This tendency to put on sympathy a burden it cannot bear and at the same time to sacrifice a truly human hierarchy and scale of values to the principle of equality has been especially marked in the democratic movement, nowhere more so perhaps than in our American democracy."

Particularly in the American achievement of his, and our, time, Babbitt detected some alarming features. If in romanticism he saw the literary expression of naturalism, in democracy he saw its political expression, which is the subject of his *Democracy and Leadership* (1924), a book belonging to the fields of political and social science, in many ways containing a summary of Babbitt's thought and in some ways his most important contribution. Characterized by a perfect dialectic integrity, *Democracy and Leadership* is his most hard-hitting, perhaps even his most threatening, book, particularly in the chapter entitled "Democracy and Standards." It is the lack of standards, Babbitt claimed, that condemns the American experience to an expansive "frontier psychology." In no way did he shirk looking at issues foursquare; he certainly did not try to flatter his readers. It is to the mind, not to the heart, that he spoke; his polemical approach, inherently lucid and robust, never wavered, based as it was on first principles—on truths. Consider these statements: "When the element of conversion with reference to a standard is eliminated from life, what remains is the irresponsible quest of thrills." "The American reading his Sunday paper in a state of lazy collapse is perhaps the most perfect symbol of the triumph of quantity over quality that the world has yet seen. Whole forests are being ground into pulp daily to minister to our triviality." "One should, therefore, in the interests of democracy itself seek to substitute the doctrine of the right man for the doctrine of the rights of man." "People will not consent in the long run to look up to those who are not themselves looking up to something higher than their ordinary selves." Obviously, such statements were hardly designed to endear Babbitt to his critics. Reviewing *Democracy and Leadership* in *The New Republic*, a needling T.V. Smith (1890–1964), self-styled defender of "the liberal temper" and advocate of the principle of compromise as "the very moral genius of America," wrote: ". . . further notice of such a book in critical circles would need apology were it not so thoroughly representative of any number of wisdom books now issuing from the citadel that humanism has erected on the banks of our democratic stream as an asylum for retired aristocrats."

T.S. Eliot did not share T.V. Smith's view of Babbitt. "He saw connexions that no other mind would have perceived," Eliot wrote of his "old teacher and master." Certainly in his view of modern politics Babbitt never failed to see and make connections, to take, in a word, the long view. "When studied with any degree of thoroughness," he said, "the economic problem will be found to run into the political problem, the political problem in turn into the philosophical problem, and the philosophical problem itself to be almost indissolubly bound up at last with the religious problem." It is the business of the critic, Babbitt stated, to distinguish between things that are at the center different and to apply standards of judgment. He saw the "general will" and the "divine average" as false criteria. "The unit to which all things must finally be referred is not the State or humanity or any other abstraction, but the man of character. Compared with this ultimate reality, every other reality is only a shadow in the mist." The hope of civilization, he believed, resides in the saving remnant, which must be Socratic in its dialectic. In the end, he insisted, democracy will have to be judged by the quality of its leadership. What he especially saw as a crucial problem facing political democracy and leadership was that of placing rights before duties: "The proper remedy for an unsound individualism is a sound individualism, an individualism that starts, not from rights, but from duties." Government, he said, is power, and whether power is ethical or unethical depends finally on the quality of will disclosed by the leaders who administer the power. "The value of political thinking is therefore in direct ratio to its adequacy in dealing with the problem of power." In *Democracy and Leadership*, then, Babbitt was not afraid to identify fundamental problems that make for uncomfortable reading: "It is growing only too evident, however, that the drift towards license is being accelerated rather than arrested by the multiplication of laws." "What is disquieting about the time is not so much its open and avowed materialism as what it takes to be its spirituality." "The democratic contention that everybody should have a chance is excellent provided it means that everybody is to have a chance to measure up to high standards."

The problem of standards and leadership, as Babbitt was always careful to indicate, is not merely an American phenomenon; it must be placed against the larger background of "the slow yielding in the whole of the Occident of traditional standards, humanistic and religious, to naturalism." In many respects *Democracy and Leadership* returned to the basic issues in *Rousseau and Romanticism*. The configurative schema is an endemic feature of Babbitt's writings; he inevitably revealed the whole of his work in each of its parts. In his evaluation of Madame de Staël, he focused on her as a representative of an age expansive in taste and tendency and neglectful of discipline. Babbitt's view of her work is particularly revealing for its discussion of nationalism as a product of romanticism. In her concept of the relation of nationalities to one another he saw reproduced on a large scale the Rousseauistic conception of the proper relation of individuals: "The first law for nationalities as for individuals is not to imitate but to be themselves." Babbitt admitted that Madame de Staël appears as the ideal cosmopolitan who has done much to advance the comparative study of literature. Yet in her cosmopolitanism he found her most pervasive and dubious trait, her romantic enthusiasm, which led him to demur: "When individual or national differences are pushed beyond a certain point what comes into play is not sympathy but antipathy." "The modern cosmopolitan is to be blamed not for developing on a magnificent scale the virtues of expansion but for setting up these virtues as a substitute for the virtues of concentration." He agreed with Madame de Staël that it is excellent to be internationally comprehensive and sympathetic, but he also noted that, unless a new discipline intervenes to control the expansion, "cosmopolitanism may be only another name for moral disintegration." True cosmopolitanism, Babbitt declared, must be a mediation between extremes; must possess the centripetal force, "the allegiance to a common standard, that can alone prevail against the powers of individual and national self-assertion."

For Babbitt the passion for humanity that marked the dawn of the French Revolution was to culminate, nationally and internationally, in imperialism. The will to power was to prevail over the will to brotherhood. He believed that nothing was easier than to transfer the concept of free expansion from the temperament of the individual to the temperament of the nation. Humanitarian devices for lessening international friction Babbitt counted as useless, insofar as "men are not governed by cool reflection as to what pays, but by their passions and imagination." (He was fond of asserting, "the progress of modern culture is from humanity through nationality to bestiality.") The gap between human aspiration and human achievement remained for Babbitt a permanent aspect of the condition of life that utterly belies the belief of "enlightened" philosophers that the state of nature is Arcadia. As he wrote with special reference to the Great War of 1914–18, "An age that thought it was progressing towards Armageddon, suffered, one cannot help surmising, from some fundamental confusion in its notion of progress." He saw a certain likeness, in fact, between the Great War and the Peloponnesian War, "both wars of commercial and imperialistic expansion." In the Peloponnesian War the various Greek states exhausted each other to the advantage of Macedon. "In the same way," he goes on to observe— and his observation, it seems, has now transcended to prophecy— "the countries of Western Europe may exhaust one another to the ultimate advantage of a comparatively uncivilized Power—Russia." Babbitt never weakened in his belief that "the present imperialistic drift" could be checked by a recovery of the disciplinary virtues, the virtues of concentration, and the right use of the critical spirit—and "the inspired and imaginative good sense that one actually finds in the great poets and the sages." He did not fail to point out, too, that "the opposition between imagination and common-sense is one of the most vicious assumptions of the modern movement."

The national character of a people—the directions it takes, the habits of mind it discloses, the sensibility it asserts—fascinated Babbitt, alert as he was to ethical and moral dimensions. Particularly in the Spaniards did he discover the "intense play of light and shade," "the alternations of energy and inertia, . . . sudden vicissitudes of greatness and decay." He found lacking, or at least uncultivated, in Spain the intermediary elements of lucidity, good sense, and critical discrimination. The absence of a temperate imagination he found especially regrettable. His early essay on the Spanish character, published in 1898, is one of Babbitt's most sensitively and warmly written, the result of his own travels.[3] (Those who charge Babbitt with being too austere as a literary stylist would do well to study this

---

3. "Lights and Shades of Spanish Character," *Spanish Character and Other Essays,* ed. Frederick Manchester, Rachel Giese, William F. Giese (Boston and New York, 1940).

essay. The equivalent charge is also sometimes made against him personally. Wyndham Lewis, who met Babbitt at Harvard in the early 1930s, helped to correct such a charge when he wrote: "I found this highly controversial professor a very wise and gentle creature indeed: if all our kind were made at all upon his model, life would certainly be less eventful, but we should have little need for extraneous 'checks,' I think."] In this essay he combines, with exquisite balance, his ideological concern with his impressions of and insights into the Spaniard: ". . . he is overflowing with national pride without being patriotic. He still has in his blood something of the wild desert instinct of the Arab, and the love of personal independence of the Goth." He goes on to observe that Spain "does not share our exuberant optimism, and has misgivings about our idea of progress" and that "she is haunted at times by the Eastern sense of the unreality of life." Babbitt was disturbed, however, by Spain's choice of a guide for entering upon the path of modern progress. He believed it dangerous that, in the main, her ideas came, because of her geographical position, from France: "In that ideal cosmopolitanism of which Goethe dreamed, each country was to broaden itself by a wise assimilation of the excellencies of other nationalities. The actual cosmopolitanism which has arisen during the present century has perhaps resulted in an interchange of vices rather than of virtues." But what remains one of the most striking features of Babbitt's essay is its prophetic note, which no student of the Spanish Civil War (1936–39) and its aftermath can overlook: "Whatever comes to pass, we may be sure that Spain will not modify immediately the mental habits of centuries of spiritual and political absolutism. In attempting to escape from the past, she will no doubt shift from the fanatical belief in a religious creed to the fanatical belief in revolutionary formulae, and perhaps pass through all the other lamentable phases of Latin-country radicalism."

Between the humanist and the humanitarian, Babbitt emphasized, there is a clash of first principles. Between the humanist and the Christian, as well as the Buddhist, on the other hand, there always exists the possibility for cooperation. As the basis of such a cooperation he indicated their common agreement on man's continual need to exercise the power of vital control, with the failure to do so constituting a chief source of evil. Humanist mediation and religious meditation he viewed only as different stages in the same ascending "path," though he also stressed that each has its separate domain. Men, Babbitt observed, "tend to come together in proportion to their intuitions of the One. . . . We *ascend* to meet." Babbitt was the first to admit that humanism cannot replace religion, that, in fact, the latter can dispense with humanism rather than humanism with religion. But at the same time, he also noted that the man who seeks to live religiously in the secular world cannot do so without referring to humanistic wisdom and some new vision of the Absolute. "For my own part," he declared in a key passage, "I range myself unhesitatingly on the side of the supernaturalists. Though I see no evidence that humanism is ineffective apart from dogmatic and revealed religion, there is, as it seems to me, evidence that it gains immensely in effectiveness when it has a background of religious insight." Any attempt to fix a religious label on Babbitt is, nevertheless, bound to fail, or at least to fail to convey the full extent and the deepest facets of his humanistic faith. His concern was, first and last, with the expression of human reason and not with the revelation of the supernatural. His emphasis, insofar as it touches on the religious, is moral. The rational element, in the contexts of intellect and will, rather than the sacramental is for him of final significance. It should be remembered that Babbitt found objectionable what he called the "tremendous spiritual romanticism" of Saint Augustine and that he had a strong aversion to the concepts of the fall of man found in Pascal and in Jonathan Edwards, which he characterized as extreme "expressions of the theological terror."

It was in the religious thought of the Far East that Babbitt found an absence of that warfare between reason and faith that plagued Occidental culture: "Buddha and Confucius both managed to combine humility with self-reliance and a cultivation of the critical spirit." He applauded the two great religious teachers' affirmation of the truths of the inner life and of that permanent self that exercises control. Buddha, in particular, was free from those undesirable elements so often found in the Occident: intolerance, obscurantism, and casuistry. "The greatest of the Eastern analysts," he reminded Babbitt of Aristotle, "the master analyst of the West." (His thoughts on Buddha are found in one of his most remarkable essays, "Buddha and the Occident," written in 1927 but not published until 1936, when it was included in a volume with Babbitt's translation, from the Pāli, of *The Dhammapada*. His translation has been applauded as "an inspired re-creation, the result of a long love and deep conviction.") Only a Buddha, claimed Babbitt, can apprehend the whole, possessing as he does a "rounded vision." The Buddhistic act itself is a rigorous tracing of moral cause and effect, as well as a discriminating temper appearing in the use of general terms; "vision" is synchronous with the critical act of analysis. Babbitt admitted that Buddha's teaching is not easy for the Westerner to grasp: "Buddha is so disconcerting to us because doctrinally he recalls the most extreme of our Occidental philosophers of the flux, and at the same time, by the type of life at which he aims, reminds us rather of the Platonist and the Christian." He described Buddha as a critical and experimental supernaturalist, that is, one who starts from "the immediate data of consciousness" rather than from certain dogmatic and metaphysical affirmations about ultimate things. In consequence, Buddhism looks up to and deals with the Law, the law of control, the special law of human nature. Babbitt was careful to point out, too, that the Buddhist, like the Christian, is an uncompromising dualist for whom the problem of evil is immense and unending. As Buddha said: "This alone I have taught, sorrow and the release from sorrow." He taught, above all, the spiritual need to attain a wholeness that is related to holiness and is the result of a concentration of will, or as Babbitt observed: "He has succeeded in compressing the wisdom of the ages into a sentence: 'To refrain from all evil, to achieve the good, to purify one's own heart, this is the teaching of the Awakened.' The Buddhist commentary is interesting: When you repeat the words, they seem to mean nothing, but when you try to put them into practice, you find they mean everything."

The unity of life that Primitive Buddhism (Hīnayāna) sought for, according to Babbitt, is to be achieved by an exercise of will that checks the expansive desires and that substitutes the more permanent for the less permanent among these desires. In Buddha's assertion of this quality of will he saw the concentrated process of thought of a religious empiricist that belonged not to a philosophical system in the Occidental sense but to a "path." Only those questions of human existence that make for edification were allowed by Buddha. Man, he taught, must save himself: "Self is the lord of self. Who else can be lord?" Man, in effect, cannot rely upon divine grace, or upon rites and ceremonies, in short, upon the Church and Revelation. The Buddhist quest, Babbitt stressed, is not for mere cessation but for the eternal in the form of a present blessedness to be found within the human state, the "Nirvāna here and now," which is attained through the right use of meditation. Buddha stands for the idea of meditation as it is irrevocably and transcendently tied to the principle of control. The meditation of the Buddhist is also tied to the exercise of the transcendent will. In Buddhism Babbitt found not only "a great religious movement" but also one that "at its best confirms Christianity." In his interpretation of early Buddhism, Babbitt also sought to show a religious movement that was free from the romantic elements of strangeness and wonder ascribed to it by Friedrich Schlegel and from the pessimism that Schopenhauer found in it. Far from being either nihilistic or pessimistic, Babbitt maintained, Buddhism was emphatically a religious ideology of earnestness, seeking at all times to defeat the forces of evil within one's self; to quell the impulses of temperament (*pamāda*); and to induce the active exercise of control, the greatest of the virtues (*appamāda*). Buddha, as Babbitt pointed out with assent, summarized his doctrine in one word, "strenuousness," in which all salutary conditions have their root, or as Buddha himself said: "Strenuous among the slothful, awake among the sleepers, the wise man advances like a racer leaving behind the pack."

One must be careful, Babbitt steadfastly maintained, to distinguish religion from romanticism. In early Taoism (550–200 B.C.) he detected, and rejected, a pantheistic unity and a naturalistic and primitivistic tendency. Confucianism, he believed, contained a humanistic antidote to a romanticizing Taoism. It is not difficult to understand the reasons for Babbitt's preference. Confucian thought recognizes an eternal moral law (*tao*) that, if obeyed, lends dignity and value to human actions. It stresses that society does not exist as such but is only an extension of the individual, the result ultimately of the extension of personal virtues. It teaches the need of attaining a keen and discriminating intellect and an intellectual honesty without which there can be no moral development: "When you know a thing, say that you know it. When you do not know a thing, say that you don't know it. This is true knowledge" (*Analects*, II., 17). It insists that knowledge requires mental training and discipline; that natural desires and instincts need to be properly ordered and coordinated; that the law of inner control is the law of laws (*li*), leading to the perfected moral life (*ren*). Since he was not a sinologue, Babbitt had to rely on translations of Chinese religious writings, a fact that no doubt made him feel somewhat of a stranger in Confucianism. (He, of course, knew Pāli, which accounts for his more detailed emphasis on Buddhism.) But clearly Babbitt understood the transcending and timeless importance of Confucianism in its idea of humility, of "submission to the will of Heaven." In this important respect, Babbitt observed, Confucius recalls Christ: "Though his kingdom is very much of this world, he puts emphasis not merely on the law of measure, but also on the law of humility." No one, Babbitt wrote, insisted more than Confucius "on a right example and the imitation that it inspires as the necessary basis of a civilized society."

Babbitt's attempt to erect "a secular philosophy of life in our time," according to T.S. Eliot, was, no matter how admirable, symptomatic of an "individualistic misdirection of will" and "a philosophy without revelation." Eliot thus summarized a basic criticism prompted by the uneasy feeling that, from a Christian perspective, humanism is incomplete. Even Paul Elmer More, Babbitt's comrade-in-arms of long standing, as well as his closest friend, was to ask toward the end of his life: "The high value of being a man—is that *telos* attainable, is it even approachable, without religion?" "Will not the humanist, unless he adds to his creed the faith and hope of religion, find himself at the last, despite his protests, dragged back into the camp of the naturalist?"[4] Eliot and More were no doubt disquieted by Babbitt's ambivalent view of the supernatural as instanced by his disavowal of "dogmatic or revealed religion." The questions that More raised are not easy to answer, and when answers are suggested they often reflect not so much Babbitt's own position as that of the commentator. More himself, it should be pointed out, went on to trace the relations between Platonism and Christianity: in *Christ the Word* (1927) to defend Christian assumptions, and in *The Catholic Faith* (1931) to view Christianity as the complement and climax of the Greek tradition. (It should not go unnoted here that Babbitt saw as justified "the opinion of those who look upon Protestantism in all its forms as only an incident in the rise of nationalism.") Babbitt never ventured into the mystical realm, regardless of how much he esteemed orthodox Christianity, particularly the Catholic Church. More insisted that there should be no misunderstanding with respect to Babbitt's religious position: "The dogma of Grace, the notion of help and strength poured into the soul from a superhuman source, was in itself repugnant to him, and the Church as an institution he held personally in deep distaste, however he may have seemed to make an exception of the disciplinary authority of Romanism."

More's words, if too astringent, have the value of reminding us that Babbitt was not a religionist. Religious experience is not what his ideas communicate or conduce. The "self-regarding virtues," on the other hand—moderation, common sense, common decency—as mediatory forms of ethical and moral life occupy a consistently high and revered place in Babbitt's teachings. He saw that virtue is also a matter of one's personal attitude toward the world insofar as it contains the possibility of constraint, and in practice it makes for a harmony that leads to unity. In Aristotelian fashion he recognized the Law of the Mean as the secret of virtuous discipline. Virtue requires also a humanistic and critical view of life in the framework of the modern world and in the ideational contexts not of the West alone but also of the Far East, especially India and China. Babbitt believed that, with the decline of the age of theology, the age of sociology was in ascendancy; that, with the victories of both rationalistic and emotional ethics over the traditional dualism of the eigh-

---

4. "A Revival of Humanism," *The Bookman* (March 1930), 7, 9.

teenth century, modern man is in the last phase of a secular process. For Babbitt this process, in all of its ramifications and consequences, was the enemy. He identified this enemy in its Rousseauistic reinterpretation of virtue as an expansive rather than as a restrictive sentiment. The values of the inner life must inevitably retreat before the imperialistic drive of such an enemy. (He stressed again and again that what in the French Revolution had started out as a humanitarian crusade ended in Napoleon and imperialistic aggression.) "The results of the material success and spiritual failure of the modern movement are before us," Babbitt wrote. He maintained that the term "modern" should be reserved for the person who strives to be critical according to both the human and the natural law. In his own ideas and in his awareness of the world Babbitt was a thoroughgoing and complete modern who did not forsake the older view of unity in diversity. This virtue of spiritual percipience made him an American sage.

3

T.S. Eliot and the Critique of Liberalism

*"Are you aware that the more serious thinkers
among us are used . . . to regard the spirit of
Liberalism as the characteristic of the destined
Antichrist!"*
— JOHN HENRY NEWMAN

EXCEPT FOR FRAGMENTS, the critique of modern liberalism has not been written. It cannot be otherwise. Our experience of liberalism, whether at this point of cruel history it is that of a moribund liberalism or of a *meta*liberalism, remains dynamic. We can record the cumulative effects of the process, its inclusive progressions, but we can hardly determine its complete and final ending. We shall have to be content with the fragments that contain the substance of the critique of modern liberalism. Julien Benda, José Ortega y Gasset, and Nikolai Berdyaev on the Continent, T.E. Hulme and Christopher Dawson in England, Irving Babbitt and Paul Elmer More in the United States—it is to writers like these that we need to turn in order to compile such a critique. Unquestionably, the name of Thomas Stearns Eliot figures prominently in this hierarchic list, despite the fact that his social writings now seem to be read only by literary scholars. They are largely dismissed, except to be ridiculed or damned, by most critics and cultural historians. Yet Eliot's contribution to the critique of modern liberalism is considerable. That his contribution has been misunderstood and misrepresented as an example of "right-wing millennialism" reflects not upon the quality of Eliot's thought but rather upon twentieth-century intellectuals who, as Benda once pointed out, do not have enough moral stamina to carry the weight of their culture.

Modern man has still to acquire those high items of civilization that Eliot admired in Vergil's world, a "more civilized world of dignity, reason and order." Eliot was thoroughly aware of the dominance of those forces leading to the decline of Western culture. "The forces of deterioration are a large crawling mass," he said, "and the forces of development half a dozen men." From the beginning he knew on which side of the cultural argument he belonged. That is, he refused to accept indiscriminatingly the view that cultural change is the law of life—a view that liberal ideologues have stoutly defended. This view epitomized for Eliot precisely the heresy that leads to cultural breakdown. "The heretic," he insisted, "whether he call himself fascist, or communist, or democrat or rationalist always has low ideals and great expectations." Eliot chose to resist the liberal doctrine no less than the liberal trend that he saw ascendant in the world. He made his choice knowing its alienating consequences. "What Machiavelli did not see about human nature is the myth of human goodness which for liberal thought replaces the belief in Divine Grace," Eliot wrote in tough and unflinching terms that liberals have neither forgotten nor forgiven.

In essence, liberalism was for Eliot a temper and an attitude and a habit of mind culminating in a particular ethos of response to the human condition. He did not approach liberalism as a specifying ideology or dialectic in the way that, say, an aristocratic liberal like Bertrand Russell or a reform liberal like John Dewey did. Instead, he saw the crisis of liberalism largely from a religious and poetic perspective, not from a scientific and statistical one. His assessment of liberalism, though "disinterested" in delineating defined valuations—the disinterestedness of a "steady impersonal passionless observation of human nature"—was moral and not programmatic or administrative. Not the principles of liberalism so much as the pattern—the shaping forms, curves, and colors—that liberalism took in civilization were what concerned Eliot. In "The Literature of Politics" (1955) he said, "For the question of questions, which no political philosophy can escape, and by the right answer to which all political thinking must in the end be judged, is simply this: What is Man? what are his limitations? what is his misery and what his greatness? and what, finally, his destiny?"[1]

Eliot's response to liberalism must be seen not in the special and limiting framework of the unity or the continuity of his thought per se, with its development plotted, indexed, and aggregated, but in its totality, in what Eliot spoke of as "one's total harvest of thinking, feeling, living and observing human beings." What Eliot thought and said and wrote emerged from a profoundly reflective process: determining, contemplating, discerning, judging. In his critique of liberal-

1. Donald Gallup's *T.S. Eliot: A Bibliography* (New York, 1969) contains detailed bibliographical descriptions, including collations, of first English and American editions of books by or with contributions of T.S. Eliot, as well as the chronological order of his contributions to periodicals.

ism he employed no Alexandrian theological design. He did not set out to write a *contra Haereticōs*. As a poet-critic, not a man of action, Eliot in his cultural opinions was not concerned with the political attainment of influence or with the goal of effecting an immediate change in human affairs. When Eliot said that he belonged to "the *pre-political* area" rather than to the political, he particularized further "the stratum down to which any sound political thinking must push its roots, and from which it must derive its nourishment." Such an area encompasses ethics and, in the end, theology.

Eternal rather than pragmatic principles inform Eliot's assessment of liberalism. To say that Eliot's writings on liberalism bear the imprint of a religious philosophy is to say that in these he discloses an apocalyptic bent, for he sees that modern man lives in an apocalyptic time in which an internal judgment of history reveals itself. Within the strict, measured Bradleyan economy and scrupulosity of his pronouncements, there is an everpresent vatic energy that makes one aware of Eliot's judgmental view of man's destiny in the historical process. Against what he sees as liberalism's relativism he posits the absolute; against its meliorism he asserts the tragic element; against its naturalism he upholds the supernatural; against its secularism he places the Incarnation. For Eliot, then, liberalism is a creed equivalent to the collapse not only of "ancient edifices" but also of spiritual values and certitudes. Such a creed, with its methodological proclivity and its scientific image of man, leads to the kind of devaluation, or desacralization, that, according to Eliot, negates order and confounds moral law and spiritual authority. As such, liberalism "is a movement not so much defined by its end, as by its starting point; away from, rather than towards, something."

What some of Eliot's critics mistake for lifelessness and escapism (the "liberal conservative" Peter Viereck spoke of Eliot's advocacy of "an artificial clerical unity" as being a symptom of the Waste Land in "its self-hate") is actually a diagnostic exploration of the most serious problems confronting Western culture. It is the writer's task, Eliot declares in his essay "The Man of Letters and the Future of Europe," to speak out on issues affecting the fate of one's country, particularly its "cultural map," and "to take a longer view than either the politician or the local patriot." What "the man of letters" should guard against, according to Eliot, is what he associated with the technologico-Benthamite liberal view and what he saw crystallizing even more explosively at the end of World War II: ". . . the idea of peace is more likely to be associated with the idea of *efficiency*—that is, with whatever can be *planned*."

For Eliot the crisis of liberalism was tied inseparably to the greater crisis of culture. The methodology of liberalism had become the ontological substance, as discriminating standards of inclusion and exclusion were neglected or dissolved in the name of sociopolitical expediency. Nor did he fail to see that in its acceptance of instrumentalism the liberal mind in time surrendered to the technical spirit and ultimately, too, to the principle of an organized social order: "Not the least of the effects of industrialism is that we become mechanized in mind, and consequently attempt to provide solutions in terms of *engineering*, for problems which are essentially problems of *life*." Political and economic thinkers who embrace the idea of social engineering disregard cultural consequences; only "the man of letters is better qualified to foresee them, and to perceive their seriousness." The qualitative aspects of cultural life had to be upheld against a state of mind that measures all things by number and linear extension and that expects human and social perfection to emerge from the historical process. Eighteenth-century rationalism, nineteenth-century utilitarianism, and twentieth-century collectivism embodied for Eliot an evolving historic, secular process contributing to overcentralization and uprootedness, the two most rife conditions of this century's cultural malady. Eliot's rejection of liberalism as "the wave of the future" was total and incontrovertible.

From the standpoint of clarity and rhetorical economy, John Dewey's *Liberalism and Social Action* has classical standing for its espousal of liberalism in its history, its theory and doctrine, its problems and its promise. From the standpoint of connection with Eliot's indictment of liberalism, it also has the remarkable advantage of containing Dewey's Page-Barbour Foundation lectures, given at the University of Virginia and published in 1935. The publication of these lectures came a year after Eliot's own Page-Barbour lectures appeared under the title *After Strange Gods*, in which Eliot bluntly stated his position: "In a society like ours, worm-eaten with Liberalism, the only thing possible for a person with convictions is to state a point of view and leave it at that." No indication is found anywhere in *Liberalism and Social Action* that Dewey was attempting to answer any of Eliot's charges, though the first two sentences of Dewey's book must inevitably place Eliot in the hostile camp: "Liberalism has long been accustomed to onslaughts proceeding from those who oppose social change. It has long been treated as an enemy by those who wish to maintain the *status quo*." In any event these two books present the two sides of a great debate. There could have been no more appropriate or intellectually respectable spokesmen for their opposing judgments about values in Western civilization.

Now, nearly fifty years later, Dewey's arguments have a timely ring, nowhere better heard than in his declaration that "If radicalism be defined as perception of need for radical change, then today any liberalism which is not also radicalism is irrelevant and doomed." Much of the New Left ideology of the contemporary period is both a continuation and a variation of Dewey's theme, but it often lacks either his devotion to liberty or his courage of honesty. The difference between Dewey and his successors is the difference between true and false liberals, between, in Irving Babbitt's apt expression, a "spiritual athlete" and "cosmic loafers."

"Organized social planning," Dewey repeatedly emphasizes, "is now the sole method of social action by which liberalism can realize its professed aims." A gradual, nonviolent combination of "organized intelligence," "scientific method," and "technological application," we are told, will topple the old morality and bring about a social order that will free man from the coercion and oppression of a dead past and prepare him for a place in the "great society." Conquer material wants and deprivations, runs the all too familiar argument, and spiritual rehabilitation of man is inevitable. Dewey's portrayal of liberalism speaks volumes about the historical promise of a "new deal" to be reached in the twentieth century:

> Flux does not have to be created. But it does have to be directed. It has to be so controlled that it will move to some end in accordance with the principles of life, since life itself is development. Liberalism is committed to an end that is at once enduring and flexible: the liberation of individuals so that realization of their capacities may be the law of life. It is committed to the use of freed intelligence as the method of direct change. In any case, civilization is faced with the problem of uniting the changes that are going on into a coherent pattern of social organization. The liberal spirit is marked by its own picture of the pattern that is required: a social organization that will make possible effective liberty and opportunity for personal growth in mind and spirit in all individuals. Its present need is recognition that established material security is prerequisite of the ends which it cherished, so that, the basis of life being secure, individuals may actively share in the wealth of cultural resources that now exist and may contribute, each in his own way, to their further enrichment.

If these are the words of a philosopher of a continent, of the New World, and if, incidentally, they underline the perennial but parochial dream of an "American Eden" (for "We are," Dewey said, "a new body and a new spirit in the world"), they also have the implicit, the reminding and representative, power of summarizing so much that missionary technical liberalism, regardless of time and place, prescribes. It is this prescriptiveness of liberalism that Dewey, no less than such earlier political moderns as John Locke, Jean-Jacques Rousseau, or Jeremy Bentham, enshrined in his writings. Apostles of the liberal spirit all, they refused to be intimidated by the more strenuous concept of human limitation and fallibility. Dewey accepted what is modern in human civilization: the belief in change, in social organization, in the "law" of progress, in the planned human will. "The task is to go on," he proclaimed, "and not backward, until the method of intelligence and experimental control is the rule in social relations and social directions." Regardless of the insight and wisdom of its lessons, the historical past, Dewey maintained, was nothing compared with the new scientific method, which merely needed cooperative, experimental application. *"That history in being a process of change generates change not only in details but also in the method of directing social change"*: this was something that could not be overlooked, he insisted. Indeed, this was the revealed fact of the modern world, a fact for which he became one of the prophets of acceptance, leading him to posit a recurring question that in recent years was the subject of acerbic debate between F.R. Leavis and C.P. Snow: "And what is scientific technology save a large-scale demonstration of organized intelligence in action?"

Eliot's vision of the historical process was the vision of a *Weltdichter* unafraid to see the world as it exists both in and between illusion and disillusion. In this vision Eliot possessed the poetic insight that Dewey and his liberal precursors and successors have lacked and that makes the difference between the creative and the technical minds so startling. "But the essential advantage of a poet," we hear Eliot saying, "is not to have a beautiful world with which to deal; it is to be able to see beneath both beauty and ugliness; to see the boredom, and the horror and the glory." Combining what he called "a Catholic heritage, and a Puritanical temperament" and affirming the requirements of "prayer, observance, discipline, thought and action," Eliot may have given a picture of the death-motive in life, the loathing and horror of life. Yet, as Eliot stressed, "hatred of life is an important phase—even, if you like, a mystical experience—in life itself." His diagnostic truths resulted precisely from his possessing a *préoccupation morale*; his poetic vision of life could hardly sanction the blank kind of empiricism found in the legacy of Charles Sanders Peirce—that "truth is that concordance of an abstract statement with the ideal limit toward which endless investigation would tend to bring scientific belief."

Reverence for what Eliot called "permanent truths about man and God and life and death"—the permanent things that Bentham derided as "nonsense on stilts"—is at the center of *After Strange Gods.*

Seen together, Eliot's book and Dewey's *Liberalism and Social Action* present the quarrel between the pronouncement of tradition and the proclamation of revolt. *After Strange Gods* can be interpreted as a condemnation of the intellectual revolution that Dewey's thought crystallized. (In *After Strange Gods* Eliot points to China as "a country of tradition"—"until the missionaries initiated her into Western thought, and so blazed a path for John Dewey.") What Eliot condemns is the spirit of indulgence that pervades liberalism. The results of such a softness bring decay of cultural standards. Assuming "the role of moralist," Eliot stresses that what he has to say is not undertaken as "exercises in literary criticism." Rather, he is concerned with developing "certain ideas in illustration of which I have drawn upon the work of some of the few modern writers whose work I know." In delineating these ideas Eliot employs moral criteria, for he believes that "the struggle of our time [is] to concentrate, not to dissipate; to renew our association with traditional wisdom; to re-establish a vital connexion between the individual and the race; the struggle, in a word, against Liberalism."

After Strange Gods has been attacked as the most offensive of Eliot's socioreligious writings. Typically critics charge that the book is "full of inverted psychology and perverted sociology," a "defeatist" example of "neo-scholastic" reversion to "dogmatic theology" and "ecclesiastical orthodoxy." Eliot was aware of this reaction to his book, which, after two printings, he did not permit to be reissued. "I regarded the tone of much of its contents as much too violent and sweeping; some of my assertions I should qualify and some I should withdraw," he declared in 1960. Yet, although he may no longer have agreed with certain of his opinions in *After Strange Gods*, he did not repudiate their essence. In the development of a writer's thought later qualifications must not be equated with outright rejection of earlier views. In this connection, it is interesting to note that John Hayward edited, "with the author's approval," a selection of Eliot's critical writings under the title *Points of View*, published in 1941 by Eliot's own firm of Faber and Faber. "Designed as an introduction to the author's work in prose," the book contains representative passages, from a single paragraph to a complete essay, from Eliot's writings published between 1917 and 1939. Two passages from *After Strange Gods* are included: the first under the caption "'Romantic' and 'Classic,'" the second under the caption "Thomas Hardy."

With all its problematic history *After Strange Gods* remains a valuable clue to Eliot's critique of liberalism. His misgivings about the book, curiously blending humility and irony, resulted from literary considerations, not from basic theses. In applying "the standard of orthodoxy to contemporary literature," Eliot focused on some of the writings of Ezra Pound, William Butler Yeats, Thomas Hardy, and D.H. Lawrence. In these he detected "deviations from the inherited wisdom of the race," that is, a denial or neglect of "a living and central tradition"; an extreme individualism in views; an absence of moral principles stemming from growing disenchantment with the validity of religious tradition as maintained and refined by the supervision of orthodoxy. Poets and novelists have become "promoters of personality," who claim that for a man to achieve his "sincerity" he should " 'be himself.' " Such a view of personality was, for Eliot, an example of "heresy," which he coupled, as consequence and concomitant, with the glorification of personality: ". . . the *unregenerate* personality, partly self-deceived and partly irresponsible, and because of its freedom, terribly *limited* by prejudice and self-conceit, capable of much good or great mischief according to the natural goodness or impurity of man: and we are all, naturally, impure." What Eliot was attacking was the "organizing" ethos of liberalism, as proclaimed by Dewey, and its optimist ideal of personality, as defined by another liberal oracle, L.T. Hobhouse, who wrote in 1911: "Liberalism is the belief that society can safely be founded on this self-directing power of personality, that it is only on this formulation that a true community can be built. . . ."

Eliot never deviated from his condemnation of the liberal view of personality. Whatever regrets he later expressed came not from the substance of his traditionalist convictions but rather from the form in which he presented them. Thus Eliot acknowledged "errors of judgment" and "errors of tone: the occasional note of arrogance, of vehemence, of cocksureness or rudeness." No doubt Eliot remembered his infamous statement in *After Strange Gods* that "reasons of race and religion combine to make any large number of free-thinking Jews undesirable." Whatever the insinuations, usually from critics who fail to distinguish between dogma and prejudice, Eliot's anti-Judaism was not anti-Semitism. For a Christian to be racist and to hate Jews, he later said, is forbidden—"is a sin"; and no other modern poet has been more aware of sin. It is enough to assert in Eliot's defense that his was a kind of Christian anti-Judaism that is opposed not to the Old Testament but to Talmudic-rabbinic Judaism, which developed after the Jews' refusal to accept Christ.

Eliot no doubt also remembered the travesty of his attack on D.H. Lawrence in *After Strange Gods:* "The man's vision is spiritual, but spiritually sick. . . . I fear that Lawrence's work may appeal, not to those who are well and able to discriminate, but to the sick and debile and confused; and will appeal not to what remains of health in them, but to their sickness." Above all Eliot had toward the end of his life reappraised some of his hard-line Bloomsbury valuations of Lawrence. Lawrence and Eliot were, at least in their critical overview of the dialectic of liberalism, of the same party without, it seems, knowing it, though as Eliot did say, "it matters a good deal in what name we condemn it." Lawrence's critique of liberalism nevertheless has its echoes in Eliot: ". . . they want an outward system of nullity, which they call peace and goodwill, so that in their own souls they can be independent little gods, referred nowhere and to nothing, little mortal Absolutes, secure from question. That is at the back of all Liberalism, Fabianism and democracy. It stinks. It is the will of the louse."

"When morals cease to be a matter of tradition and orthodoxy— that is, of the habits of the community formulated, corrected, and elevated by the continuous thought and direction of the Church— and when each man is to elaborate his own, then *personality* becomes a thing of alarming importance": to this thesis Eliot was to return again and again. If his use of Lawrence was a tactical error in the struggle against liberalism, there were other writers who could better illustrate the pitfalls of liberalism. Could Eliot have had this in mind when he permitted the long paragraph on Thomas Hardy from *After Strange Gods* to reappear in *Points of View?* Hardy, he charges, is an example of a writer living "in an age of unsettled beliefs and enfeebled tradition" with no loyalty to any metaphysics or tradition; a writer extremely self-absorbed in his novels, in which most of his characters come alive only "in their emotional paroxysms": "This extreme emotionalism seems to me a symptom of decadence; it is a cardinal point of faith in a romantic age, to believe that there is something admirable in violent emotion for its own sake, whatever the emotion or whatever its object." Hardy exemplifies a form of what Eliot found to be the same indiscipline that his Harvard mentor Irving Babbitt and the other New Humanists equated with the absence of the "inner check upon the expansion of natural impulse." In circumscribing Hardy from this angle of criticism Eliot surely had in mind the limitations of the liberal doctrine; the ultimate as opposed to the scientific fact that, as Eliot wrote of Hardy's rendered *"personal view of life"* (which, he said, referring at the same time to liberalism, "is merely part of the whole movement of several centuries towards the aggrandisement and exploitation of personality"), "unless there is moral resistance and conflict there is no meaning."

That man should be free to regulate his own moral progress: such constituted the climate of relativism that was at the core of Eliot's critique of a flourishing liberalism. The liberal view that morals are a kind of humanistic science and that, in consequence, as the liberal ideologue would have it, "for the rational man, the world begins anew each moment," led to "a spirit of excessive tolerance" that, Eliot believed, "is to be depreciated." Whatever reservations Eliot was to have about the tone of *After Strange Gods* or about the harshness of its opinions as he came to see them, he was never to repudiate the social and religious perspectives he delineated in his "primer of modern heresy." His preoccupation with "orthodoxy of sensibility and with the sense of tradition" was to remain pivotal. Without this sense of tradition—"all those habitual actions, habits and customs, from the most significant religious rite to our conventional way of greeting a stranger, which represent the blood kinship of 'the same people living in the same place' "—instability and moral debilitation are inevitable. Eliot stamped his moral perspectives with "a definite and theological standpoint," that is, with a clear-cut and present Christian metaphysics, insofar as he said in his essay "Francis Herbert Bradley" (1927), "Morality and religion are not the same thing, but they cannot beyond a certain point be treated separately." Eliot's critique of liberalism could hardly be more explicit in all of its developing and informing referents in *After Strange Gods* than in these words: "If you do away with this [moral] struggle, and maintain that by tolerance, benevolence, inoffensiveness and a re-distribution or increase of purchasing power . . . the world will be as good as anyone could require, then you must expect human beings to become more and more vaporous."

In liberalism Eliot discerned another form of secularism, another of the seductive "philosophies without revelation," springing from "titanism, or the attempt to build a purely human world without reliance upon grace." Liberalism was to underline a contemporary example "of the permanent force of the world against which the spirit must always struggle," as Eliot expressed it in an acute but neglected essay that he contributed in 1937 to a symposium entitled *Revelation*, edited by John Baillie and Hugh Martin. As always in his probing of secular philosophies, he returned to the moral element, or, better, to the absence of "the possibility of that frightful discovery of morality." In facing the *données* of liberalism—for example, those of Bertrand Russell's "enervate gospel of happiness"—he unfailingly castigated the liberals' contention that only in the adventure of unrestrained experience will truth ever emerge. Such a conviction he associated with what he believed to be the elements of modernism, "newness and crudeness, impatience, inflexibility in one respect and fluidity in another, and irresponsibility and lack of wisdom." Ultimately he saw that the promise of liberalism was mechanistic, part of the great, secular experiment conspiring "to form a civilized but non-Christian mentality." In his major prose writings appearing after 1934, Eliot continued to answer the "liberal-minded," who, as he put it in his essay "Religion and Literature" (1935), "are convinced that if everybody says what he thinks, and does what he likes, things will somehow, by some automatic compensation and adjustment, come right in the end."

That this conviction is untenable is a subject of Eliot's *The Idea of a Christian Society* (1939). *After Strange Gods* offended readers because of its demarcation, from an overtly Christian position, of "the organisation of values, and a direction of religious thought which must proceed to a criticism of political and economic systems." The judgmental tone of this later book is no less severe than that of *After Strange Gods*. So relentless and uncompromising is it that the book infuriated liberal critics, especially, and predictably, one of Dewey's disciples, who denounced its tractarian stance as "a vulturous idea decked out in dove's words." But there could be no relenting tone, no easy choice of tactics or of tact. In *The Idea of a Christian Society*, consisting of lectures delivered at Corpus Christi College, Cambridge, in March 1939, Eliot said exactly what he thought about the nature, end, and function of social order at almost exactly the time when Winston Churchill was warning the House of Commons, "The danger is now very near . . . dark, bitter waters . . . are rising fast on every side." It was a time of history, even of judgment upon history, that, as Eliot said in his conclusion, provoked "a doubt of the validity of a civilisation," made already more anguishing for "many persons who, like myself, were deeply shaken by the events of September 1938, in a way from which one does not recover; persons to whom that month brought a profounder realisation of a general plight."[2] In an appended note dated September 6, 1939, Eliot wrote that the whole of *The Idea of a Christian Society* "was completed before it was known we should be at war." He emphasized, however, that since the possibility of war was always present in his mind, he wanted to make only two additional observations: "first, that the alignment of forces which has now revealed itself should bring more clearly to our consciousness the alternative of Christianity or pagan-

---

2. It was in the Bavarian city of Munich, in September 1938, that Adolf Hitler, Benito Mussolini of Italy, Edouard Daladier of France, and Neville Chamberlain of Great Britain held the meeting at which it was agreed that Germany would annex the Sudetenland from Czechoslovakia in return for "peace in our time." Munich has become a byword for a policy of appeasement.

ism; and, second, that we cannot afford to defer our constructive thinking to the conclusion of hostilities—a moment when . . . good counsel is liable to be obscured."

Here, too, Eliot continued his examination of the environment of modern society that, as he had written in *After Strange Gods*, was hostile to faith and produced few individuals "capable of being injured by blasphemy." A modern society without the "assurance of first principles" becomes either, like the United States, religiously "neutral" or, like Soviet Russia, "pagan." Eliot was unbending in his distrust of "secular reformers," whose reforms merely generalize man and impose a mechanistic psychology over moral philosophy. His quarrel with an emergent modernism therefore was a quarrel precisely with the liberal concept that morals evolve in direct relation to the concrete results of social action. This legislative view, as it might be called, signified for Eliot moral flabbiness. "But because Christian morals are based on fixed beliefs which cannot change," he wrote, "they also are essentially unchanging: while the beliefs and in consequence the morality of the secular world can change from individual to individual, or from generation to generation, or from nation to nation." The image of Eliot as an "anxious pilgrim" rather than an intrepid explorer is no doubt understandable in any appraisal of *The Idea of a Christian Society*. But for Eliot the impelling idea of human exploration always had its limits; indeed, the whole of Eliot's poetic and critical achievement, in principle and in intent, ultimately affirms sacral limits, that is, knowing when to stop in reverence before the "burning bush," or as Eliot phrased it: "For only in humility, charity and purity—and most of all perhaps humility—can we be prepared to receive the grace of God without which human operations are vain."

Eliot's remarks on liberalism in *The Idea of a Christian Society* were made in the course of his envisaging the end to which "the community of Christians" must be directed, "a society in which the natural end of man—virtue and well-being in community—is acknowledged for all, and the supernatural end—beatitude—for those who have eyes to see it." Indubitably the religious attitude that he affirmed was set against the secular attitude and, more specifically, against the liberalism that he saw permeating men's minds and affecting their attitudes toward life. His treatment here of liberalism is brief but devastating. There is no doubt that he had given long and careful thought to the subject, that he knew its magnitude, that he had to speak his mind on the subject clearly and categorically, for the record, for history. Eliot also knew full well the intricate power of the enemy and the evil of which it is capable: "It [liberalism] is a necessary negative element; when I have said the worst of it, that worst comes only to this, that a negative element made to serve the purpose of a positive is objectionable." The historical role of liberalism in the neutralization and paganization of modern society cannot go unchallenged or unpunished, Eliot seemed to be saying. Consequently, the section that he devoted to liberalism has such a concentrated power of thought, of controlled scorn, such care of expression and confidence of view, that it sounds like the bursting of a rocket in a war of faiths. No better example of Eliot's pronouncements against liberalism can be found than in this passage:

> By destroying traditional social habits of the people, by dissolving their natural collective consciousness into individual constituents, by licensing the opinions of the most foolish, by substituting instruction for education, by encouraging cleverness rather than wisdom, the upstart rather than the qualified, by fostering a notion of *getting on* to which the alternative is a hopeless apathy, Liberalism can prepare the way for that which is its own negation: the artificial, mechanised or brutalised which is a desperate remedy for its chaos.

At the same time, Eliot prophetically pointed out that liberal attitudes were disappearing, inasmuch as the sphere of private life which liberalism traditionally defends was steadily diminishing. For out of liberalism, he noted, come philosophies that deny it, as we move "from Liberalism to its apparent end of authoritarian democracy." Liberalism signified for Eliot the legacy of disorder, "and not the permanent value of the negative element," which he saw as essential to cultural growth and maturity, an integral aspect of what he later labeled "internal cultural bickering." Eliot disagreed with critical liberalism, as it might be termed, but for him this disagreement was a dimension vitally important to an emerging "definition of culture." He was too much the creative genius to discredit dialectical tension. Still, Eliot was to take a long view of things, to make his judgments and choices according to his concept of "last things," according to what he regarded as the needful return to an assurance of "first principles." Only these could overcome and transcend that "liberalised or negative condition of society [which] must either proceed into a gradual decline of which we can see no end, or . . . reform itself into a positive shape which is likely to be effectively secular." For Eliot there was a third possibility, "that of a positive Christian society." For him the dogma of "the primacy of the supernatural over the natural life" was irrevocable. Christian theology provided Eliot with the answers to why things are wrong in the world: "What is right enters the realm of the *expedient* and is contingent upon place and time, the degree of culture, the temperament of a people. But the

Church can say what is always and everywhere *wrong.*" He refused to accept what the secular mind speaks of as the urgent need for "greater plasticity and bolder exploration of human possibilities." Eliot sought permanent answers to ultimate questions.

Man's possibility for evil, as Eliot underlined in *The Idea of a Christian Society*, was unlimited; hence, the problem of man was the problem of motives and of law. Eliot could not accept the secularist's view that politics, being the art of the possible, especially when embodied in the highest forms of intellect and governance, was superior to the prior creation of a temper of mind in people equipping them to see and know "what is wrong—*morally* wrong—and why it is wrong." Eliot affirmed the teleological priority of Christian doctrine. Hence, the year 1939, which for W.H. Auden brought to an end "a low dishonest decade," for Eliot marked the epochal crisis of modernism in all of its ramifications. The war embodied for Eliot the most brutalizing consequences of the liberal spirit, in short, the modern offshoots of secularism either as the neutralization or as the paganization of civilization, or as both. In holding to such a view he resolutely opposed what John Dewey espoused as modern man's need "to translate the word 'natural' into 'moral.' " *The Idea of a Christian Society* was to contain Eliot's answer to the liberal concept of human nature; in it he included his world view. This view was hardly optimistic, but historical developments since 1939 (let alone since 1914, that penultimate year of crisis) validate what liberal critics denigrate as Eliot's "peculiar gloom." Dewey's belief that "the future of democracy is allied with the spread of the scientific attitude" cannot but be tinged today with a more deepening irony, as Eliot had foreseen.

Dewey's *Freedom and Culture* appeared in the same year as Eliot's *The Idea of a Christian Society*. The earlier debate now continued as the crisis of 1939 emerged. No other two books could more sharply focus on increasingly opposing viewpoints. The positions stated and defended, in terms of each writer's special sense of historical crisis, are irreconcilable. For Eliot the crisis of history and the problem of man conjoined in the need for "the perpetual message of the Church: to affirm, to teach and to apply, true theology." For Dewey the crisis instanced the basic failures of modern society to subscribe more fully and boldly to the "scientific attitude" and to the belief in the infinite adaptability of human nature. Neither man's corruptiveness nor man's avarice, which Eliot called "the dominant vice of our time," contained explanations for Dewey. It was not a matter of the tragic outlook but rather of man not plumbing his capacity or exploring his possibilities, to use the liberal's terminology. Employing the logic of argumentation that makes Eliot's critique of liberalism all the more understandable as its antithesis, Dewey surveyed the crisis of his time in terms of the surviving relics of coercion instead of cohesion. The threat to the cause of democratic freedom, Dewey observed, lay not in the existence of totalitarian states but in man's own attitudes and within man's own institutions: "A culture which permits science to destroy traditional values but which distrusts its power to create new ones is a culture which is destroying itself." Invoking the liberal's faith, Dewey was to stress in *Freedom and Culture* that no problem was too big nor crisis too overpowering if only man confronted it "with all the resources provided by collective intelligence operating in co-operative action."

Eliot's concept of the modern cultural situation is closely tied to his indictment of the liberal ethos, particularly its pragmatism, with its pluralistic, indeterministic, and melioristic habits of thought. Democratic liberalism presented Eliot with no theory or standards for the growth and survival of culture. "A democracy in which everybody had an equal opportunity in everything would be oppressive for the conscientious and licentious for the rest," he observes coldly in *Notes towards the Definition of Culture* (1948), his sequel to *The Idea of a Christian Society*. In this work he is still assaying, though on a broader level, the consequences of the liberal outlook. Here, too, his pronouncements remain consistently critical. Secularism is the enemy. "Culture . . . is of divine origin and must perish among people who lose belief in a supernatural world," he warns. Eliot marks his cultural views in irrevocably religious contexts insofar as, he claims, one cannot escape the religious point of view, "because in the end one either believes or disbelieves." For him culture is "the incarnation . . . of the religion of a people"; "what is part of our culture is also part of our *lived* religion"; "the formation of a religion is also the formation of a culture." The informing religious tone in *Notes towards the Definition of Culture* is one of reverence: the reverence that Richard M. Weaver epitomized in his *Visions of Order* (1964) when he wrote: "While culture is not a worship and should not be made a worship, it is a kind of orienting of the mind toward a mood, a reverence for the spirit on secular occasions."

Although Eliot retains an inherent concern with the process of de-Christianization, the chief concern of this book is with religious values in their cultural meaning. (There is some truth to Walter J. Ong's observation that "Eliot's writings are often concerned with 'religion' but seldom explicitly with Christ.") Eliot recognizes in *Notes towards the Definition of Culture* the expansion of the irreligious and antireligious tempers in the modern world. World War II, "a period of unparalleled destructiveness," must be seen as the background against which he defends his religious concept of culture. If this book discloses a certain and pronounced hesitancy, even an impreciseness of definition and of critical application, and if it lacks that force of assurance found in *The Idea of a Christian Society*, these weaknesses must be viewed against the backdrop of the war. The question that now plagued Eliot more than ever was: Had not the world since 1939 moved beyond chaos, into the zero zone in which spiritual devaluation and homelessness are absolute? If Eliot had had, through Prufrock and Sweeney, his vision of horror, he now understood it in its most radical implications. A tormented note of defensiveness was the communicated consequence of such an experience, and its scars were visible. Fear, too, was a feeling that Eliot revealed here, leading to almost agonized supplication:

> If Christianity goes, the whole of our culture goes. Then you must start painfully again, and you cannot put on a new culture ready made. You must wait for the grass to grow to feed the sheep to give the wool out of which your new coat will be made. You must pass through many centuries of barbarism. . . . But we can at least try to save something of those goods of which we are the common trustees: the legacy of Greece, Rome and Israel, and the legacy of Europe throughout the last 2,000 years. In a world which has seen such material devastation as ours, these spiritual possessions are also in imminent peril.

The problem of culture and religion, of "the whole way of life," had grown immensely difficult, as Eliot showed. The conflict between social tradition, as the maintenance and transmission of standards of culture, and the common standards enforced by the decrees of social planners and of politicians was moving toward a secular victory. In the aftermath, Eliot also saw the religious decline against which he was fighting. Again, the seductiveness of liberal theory was all too evident. Common standards result in "common faith," to use the title of John Dewey's credo published in 1934. According to Dewey, "A body of beliefs and practices that are apart from the common and natural relations of mankind must . . . weaken and sap the force of the possibilities inherent in such relations. Here lies one aspect of the emancipation of the religious from religion." The allurements of such a liberal dictum were (and are) no doubt mighty for the masses that naturally dislike "historic encumbrances" and succumb to the miracle of technics. Eliot's recognition of the cultural power of these "new methods of inquiry and reflection," as "the final arbiter of all questions of fact, existence, and intellectual assent," to use Dewey's own words, is inherent in *Notes towards the Definition of Culture*. The metaphysical essences of a transcendent "otherness" and otherworldliness, Eliot could hardly escape noticing, were jeopardized by a world in which a religious concept of culture would increasingly fall victim to the radical metaphysics of liberal doctrine, the metaphysical pluralism that one authority has described as follows: "There can be no ultimate system, for each new system must like all others be limited by its categories and hence must take its place in an infinite series."[3]

The purpose and function of education also figure prominently in Eliot's critique of liberalism. Liberalism, he stresses in his essay "Modern Education and the Classics" (1932), along with exciting a "superficial curiosity," has fallaciously tried to equalize subjects of study. Radicalism, the offspring of liberalism, has proceeded "to organize the 'vital issues,' and reject what is not vital." As a result, liberal concepts of education, as of politics, have led to the steady decline of standards. "In a negative liberal society," Eliot observes in *The Idea of a Christian Society*, "you have no agreement as to there being any body of knowledge which any educated person should have acquired at any particular stage: the idea of wisdom disappears, and you get sporadic and unrelated experimentation." The question of education is tied to the principles of order. To think of education in terms merely of adapting it to a changed and changing world is to ignore what must remain the inviolable "permanent principles of education." Education is not to be measured pragmatically or scientifically, "dominated by the idea of getting on" as "many ardent reforming spirits" believe. "A high average of general education is perhaps less necessary for a civil society than is a respect for learning," Eliot wrote in *Notes towards the Definition of Culture*. His view of the close relationship between education and culture is evident: If "culture can never be wholly conscious . . . it cannot be planned because it is also the unconscious background to our planning." Such a truth for Eliot more specifically accentuates "the delusion that the maladies of the modern world can be put right by a system of education." It underlines also the commensurate truth that in education, as in culture, "one thing to avoid is a universalised planning; one thing to ascertain is the limits of the plannable."

No less than other aspects of modern life, education, Eliot believed, was stamped by a secularist liberalism. In his essay in *Revelation* he wrote: "The whole tendency of education (in the widest sense—the influences playing on the common mind in the forms of 'enlightenment') has been for a very long time to form minds more and more

---

3. See Henry Alonzo Myers, *Systematic Pluralism: A Study in Metaphysics* (Ithaca, N.Y., 1961).

adapted to secularism. . . ." Such a liberalism can appeal only to the "experiential test," not to the permanencies of order, of unity, and of wisdom. "What happens in our thinking about education is, of course, only a special instance of what happens to human consciousness," Eliot told his audience in his lectures on "The Aims of Education" at the University of Chicago in November 1950. At the heart of his criticism here, as elsewhere, was Eliot's distrust of changes that have external, material ends. Educational reforms, as such, can neither "change the will of those who worship false gods" nor "sustain an entire society." Such reforms, as the products of liberal theory, remain unfinished, for their success is socially oriented and derivative, fostering surrogates that also create new perils: "The restoration of a kind of order in people's private lives . . . when it is made in the name of a social purpose only, furthers the reduction of men to machines, and is the opposite from the development of their humanity."

Eliot never wavered in his belief that liberalism contains the kind of secular faith that conceives of the evils of the world as external to man. He rejected the liberal view of the human condition. He refused to subscribe to the scientific concepts of the future of man, precisely that "new age" which John Dewey saw as inseparable from scientific knowledge as the paradigm of all reliable knowledge. Eliot readily admitted that his approach to education was "orthodox." It was, in other words, metaphysical and theological. "There are two and only two finally tenable hypotheses about life: the Catholic and the materialistic," he wrote in "Modern Education and the Classics." There were, then, limitations and retributions that no scientific liberalism could ever overcome. These limits were, whatever the temptations of liberal doctrine, implicit in the very fabric of life. No liberal educational theorist, he maintained, could afford to ignore the insoluble contradictions that Simone Weil, whom Eliot admired, saw "afflicting" the human condition. Eliot saw fit to quote from Simone Weil's *Gravity and Grace* in "The Aims of Education": "Our life is impossibility, absurdity. Everything that we will is contradicted by the conditions or by the consequences attached to it. That is because we are ourselves contradiction, being merely creatures. . . ." The key to much of Eliot's critique of liberalism is found in these words.

Eliot considered education a cultural rather than a social phenomenon. His concern was always with cultural health achieved through standards, a concern informed by this statement in *Notes towards the Definition of Culture*: "For it is an essential condition of the preservation of the quality of culture of the minority, that it should continue to be a minority culture." In holding such a view, and especially in the attendant indictment of modern collectivist social theory, of "mass-culture," Eliot continued his conflict with liberalism and specifically with the liberal educational views propounded by John Dewey, who once more helps provide a positive frame of reference through historical antithesis. "One needs the enemy," Eliot wrote in *Notes towards the Definition of Culture*. "So, within limits, the friction, not only between individuals but between groups, seems quite necessary for civilisation. The universality of irritation is the best assurance of peace." It is Dewey, of course, who in the twentieth century has presented the liberal philosophy of education at its best. But it was not just a philosophy of education but also a philosophy of ideals, the major ideal being Dewey's conception of education as an agency of social adjustment, one in which the individual's "privacy of reflective self-consciousness," as it has been put, is notoriously expendable. As a liberal ideologue of education, Dewey resisted any "externally imposed ends." All values, he argued in his influential *Democracy and Education* (1916), a work that Walter Lippmann hailed as expressing "the best hope of liberal men," come from experience and not from contemplation. All distinctions, moreover, are social. All matters of moral significance and discrimination are derived solely from the relations between man and man and not from what lies within man. To the question What is education?, Dewey therefore replied: "It is the reconstruction or reorganization of experience which adds to the meaning of experience, and which increases ability to direct the course of subsequent experience."

Such a reply obviously was a liberal fallacy that Eliot connected with the spread of the materialistic view and ends. The Deweyan view sought for "the wrong things." Inherent in his rejection of such a view was Eliot's belief that it was not only "wrong" but also abstract. He wrote in *Notes towards the Definition of Culture*: "Education in the modern sense implies a disintegrated society, in which it has come to be assumed that there must be one measure of education according to which everyone is educated simply more or less. Hence *Education* has become an abstraction." Eliot thought that a proper system of education should "unify the active and the contemplative, action and speculation, politics and the arts." For Dewey—for the liberal—this approach signified the kind of philosophical dualism that was unprogressive. Education, Dewey stipulated in "My Pedagogic Creed" (1897), which he was to refine and enlarge upon in his later educational works, "is a process of living and not a preparation for future living"; "is the fundamental method of social progress and reform"; is "the art of thus giving shape to human powers and adapting them to social service . . . the supreme art."

Such testaments incorporate the liberal creed. They also signalize the unfortunate fact that "we have always new problems, and the old ones in new forms," as Eliot observed in "The Aims of Education." He could hardly have been more right or the Deweyan liberals more wrong in their dismissal of Eliot's thinking on education (or, rather, his reflections—for he distrusted conclusions) as having only "an antiquarian interest." Eliot's picture of higher education in America in the early thirties, as he painted it in "Modern Education and the Classics," could not be more prophetic of the contemporary plight:

> And when you have sunk so much money in plant and equipment, when you have a very large (though not always well-paid) staff of men who are mostly married and have a few children, when you are turning out from your graduate schools more and more men who have been trained to become teachers in other universities, and who will probably want to marry and have children too; when your whole national system of higher education is designed for an age of expansion, for a country which is going indefinitely to increase its population, grow rich, and build more universities—then you will find it very difficult to retract.

Eliot was fully aware that there were forces in the late 1920s fighting the manifold consequences of the liberal doctrine of endless experiment and expansion. He particularly applauded the New Humanism of Irving Babbitt and his disciples for its diagnosis of the ills of the modern world, arising, at least in one major respect, from what Babbitt termed the liberal theory of "free temperamental expansion." Eliot shared with Babbitt a distrust of the liberal pragmatists and other philosophers. No less than the humanists was he critical of monistic postulates, and no less did he seek for what a humanist like Norman Foerster called the "principles of order and construction" to help contain "the tumult of the times disconsolate." But no less than they did Eliot insist on what Babbitt himself termed "a careful determination of boundaries." If, therefore, Eliot joined the humanists in opposing what the latter spoke of as the gospel of Occidental "naturism," he could not overlook their lack of a Christian standard or their voluntary alienation from a central spiritual tradition. For the humanists the struggle against liberalism had to rely on the staying power and persuasiveness of "ethical will." Humanism was essentially a nonreligious philosophy, though nobler in its aspirations as it stood against the materialism and the "naturism" of a profane age. This humanism, Foerster wrote in "Humanism and Religion" (in The Forum, September 1929), "attracts persons who are content to be human, but not worldlings." It provided, as both mediator and reconciler, an alternative to "the ideal of the religious man" by offering "the ideal of the civilized man." Its roots, Foerster stressed, were

Hellenic, pre-Christian: "... the choice of the humanist is that vision of a proportioned totality, that selective comprehensiveness, that just relation of the planes of life which was more nearly attained in the Greece of Pericles than any subsequent time or place."

Despite his support of humanism, Eliot found its forms, ancient and modern, inadequate, just another "attempt to devise a philosophy of life without a metaphysic." His essay "The Humanism of Irving Babbitt" (1927) centers on the "obscurities" of humanism, resulting from its primary failure to accept any dogma except that of human reason. The humanist, by suppressing the divine element as the revelation of the supernatural, was left with the ever-corruptible human element. Humanism was "sporadic" and "impure"—"merely the state of mind of a few persons in a few places at a few times"— rather than, in irreversible historical contexts, "continuous" and "constructive" like Christianity. To be sure, humanism was, Eliot confessed in "Second Thoughts about Humanism" (1928), "necessary for the criticism of social life and social theories, political life and political theories." But the battle against liberalism, against the chaos of the modern world, needed, Eliot believed, more than the positive and exclusive things that humanism offered: "breadth, tolerance, equilibrium and sanity." Here Eliot was as critical of Babbitt's humanism as he was of Matthew Arnold's philosophy of culture (he, in fact, believed Arnold to be a forerunner of humanism). In the positions of both men he condemned the great élan toward usurping the place of revealed religion. By no means did Eliot reject either the virtues or the values of humanism, but these, too, he was careful to define in the priority of their appropriateness: "Without humanism," he wrote in "Religion Without Humanism," an essay he contributed to Norman Foerster's *Humanism and America* (1930), "both religion and science tend to become other than themselves, and without religion and science—without emotional and intellectual discipline—humanism tends to shrink into an atrophied caricature of itself."

Only what Jacques Maritain called *"humanisme intégral,"* humanism with a "metaphysics of transcendence," was to embody for Eliot a genuine spiritual ally in the war against liberalism. Singleness of vision and not a choice of vision was what mattered in the end. Certainly, the humanists did proffer wisdom against the liberals' "gospel of mediocrity," words Eliot used in writing about Bertrand Russell's *The Conquest of Happiness* (1930). "But wisdom is one thing without Christian wisdom, and another thing with it," Eliot wrote in his essay "The Christian Conception of Education" (1941); "and there is a sense in which wisdom that is not Christian turns to folly." To repeat, Eliot insisted always on defining and ordering priorities. Humanism, under the circumstances, was a positive but secondary view of life. It was as admirable as it was effectual in combating liberal fallacies, particularly in education. In this same essay Eliot singled out for praise F. R. Leavis's statement that "the problem of producing the 'educated man'—the man of humane culture who is equipped to be intelligent and responsible about the problems of contemporary civilization—becomes that of realizing the Idea of a University in practical dispositions appropriate to the modern world." But Eliot was careful to pose questions about the thinking behind such a humane culture. That is to say, humane culture by itself is not enough, it becomes an anthropocentric cul-de-sac. The ideals of humanism can never be consummate insofar as humanist "alternatives" and "auxiliaries" to religion fail in the long run. As G.K. Chesterton was to observe: "Humanism may try to pick up the pieces; but can it stick them together? Where is the *cement* which made religion corporate and popular, which can prevent it falling to pieces in a débris of individualistic tastes and degrees?" To such questions Eliot gave unequivocal answer:

> It [humanism] can only appeal to a small number of superior individuals; it can help them to recognize what is wrong, but it cannot provide them with the power to influence the mass of mankind and to bring about what is right. It can appeal to those people who have already the humanists' feelings and desires: but it cannot change the will of those who worship false gods. It is powerless against the drifting desires or torrential passions which turn by turn provide the motive force for the mass of natural men.

Liberal critics will continue to dismiss Eliot's contribution to the critique of modern liberalism. The charge that Eliot's sociocultural views are "irrelevant" will continue to be broadcast. Nor does there seem to be any letup in the derision of Eliot's "elitist politics." (Nor at the same time is there any real attempt to grapple with the substance of Eliot's belief that "The pursuit of politics is incompatible with a strict attention to exact meanings on all occasions.") For the most part critics will continue to be curiously one-sided in their evaluation of Eliot's quarrel with liberalism, though such evaluation accords fully with the long-standing refusal of liberalism to see that man belongs to two planes of being and that man's rights cannot be separated from his responsibilities. Philip Rahv, the founding coeditor of *Partisan Review*, reflected this one-sided critical reaction (which too often sets a party-line judgment) when he wrote of Eliot: "His commitment to orthodox beliefs must have answered an irresistible inner demand of his nature for a discipline to shore him up against chaos. . . . In this sense it was no more than an anodyne." There is nothing wrong with society, we are told by such pundits, that the "organizational impulse" will not solve. John Dewey, in his ninetieth year, uttered a common liberal sentiment when he declared, "the one thing of prime importance today is development of methods of scientific inquiry to supply us with the humane or moral knowledge now conspicuously lacking." Yet, Dewey's valedictory, no less than Rahv's clinical judgment, is as one-sided as the Benthamism that, as John Stuart Mill wrote, "can teach the means of organizing and regulating the merely *business* part of the social arrangements."

The events of time must render the final verdict. But it is clear by now that in his social criticism Eliot has become one of the great modern prophets. He saw not only into but beyond liberalism. Eliot, it has been said, "has the 'uncynical disillusion' of a tempered religious sensibility." This constitutes no shortcoming in his vision. What makes Eliot's thought so forceful is his ability to size up the human situation with a prophetic sensibility that is missing in the liberal mentality. "If liberalism," Lionel Trilling reminds us, "has a single desperate weakness, it is an inadequacy of imagination: liberalism is always being surprised." Eliot's was a vision of unromanticized compassion, and in this compassion lay that endurance and serenity of ordered thought leading to the kind of thinking that informs the following observation in "The Aims of Education":

> And so long as we are capable of resenting control, and of being shocked by other people's private lives, we are still human. We are, at least, recognizing that man is something more than merely a social animal: that there should be limitations to social control. And by being shocked (when it is something more than a prejudice that is shocked) we are recognizing, however dimly, that there is some law of behaviour which is something more than a duty to the State.

Toughness of thought is a characteristic of Eliot's social criticism. This toughness was a quintessential principle of order needed to resist some of the consequences of liberalism that Eliot detected especially in the nineteenth century, some of which he identified in his essay "Arnold and Pater" (1930): "The dissolution of thought in that age, the isolation of art, philosophy, religion, ethics and literature, is interrupted by various chimerical attempts to effect imperfect syntheses." This "dissolution," Eliot saw, remained unchecked, the enemy as combative as ever. Sir Arthur Quiller-Couch, lecturing at Cambridge University in 1934, exhibited the kind of scorn that has greeted Eliot's views. Eliot's concept of liberalism, he said, "is anything which questions dogma: which dogma, to be right dogma, is the priestly utterance of a particular offset of a particular branch of a historically fissiparous Church." Sir Arthur went on to give his own estimate of liberalism, which, he claimed, "reveals itself rather as Tradition itself, throughout Literature (which is Thought worth setting down and recording) the organic spirit persisting, aërating, preserving, the liberties our ancestors won and we inherit." But surely the voice of liberalism heard here is the sentimental voice of the world. And the world, Eliot stated, "The world insists upon being right. It insists upon being virtuous. It is right, it is virtuous, it is damned."

"It seems to me," Eliot wrote to Herbert Read in 1924, "that at the present time we need more dogma, and that one ought to have as precise and clear a creed as possible, when one thinks at all. . . ." If, in time, Eliot did change his mind about some of his literary valuations, he did not alter his social views. To the end he remained critical of the process of de-Christianization, as well as of dehumanization, that he connected with liberalism. And to the end he believed that history, despite the deep contradictions and mysteries of human existence, has spiritual meaning. His social criticism marks him essentially as a man of wisdom, not, like John Dewey, a man of influence. "To be understood by a few intelligent people," Eliot said, "is all the influence a man requires." His quarrel with liberalism was moral; it must be seen as a creative quarrel that raised disturbing conceptual questions. Only a few liberals have been willing to read Eliot and to answer his questions with the sense of responsibility demanded of any scrutiny of ultimate issues that affect not only the structure of life but, more important, man's inner life. Certainly it is true that Eliot spoke as a conservative in his social criticism; yet he endowed his conservatism with a creativeness exceptional in its discriminations. Even if this conservatism, to use here John Stuart Mill's words regarding Samuel Taylor Coleridge, "were an absurdity, it is well calculated to drive out a hundred absurdities worse than itself."

Part II

THE RELIGIOUS IDEA

•

Commitment offers to those who accept it legitimate grounds for the affirmation of personal convictions with universal intent.

—Michael Polanyi

4

A Note on Religion and Literature

ALTHOUGH RENÉ WELLEK COMPLAINS that recent literary criticism has tended to abandon its central concern with the art, theory, and interpretation of literature by seeking to become sociology, politics, philosophy, or even mystical illumination, he nevertheless does not fail to stress that "criticism needs constantly to draw on [these] neighboring disciplines."

In a society that is dominated by science and technology, it is essential to effect a dialogue between literary and other scholarly disciplines. In this connection, the emphasis being given by critics to the organic relationship between literature and religion and to such special aspects as the "theological imagination" and the "religious meaning and dimensions" of literature gives cause for definite satisfaction—and hope. For the fact remains that any cessation of interdisciplinary dialogue in the world of letters would inevitably signal the triumph of the mechanical mind, belonging to the spirit of time, over the creative mind, belonging to the spirit of eternity.

Of course, the fear is sometimes voiced that the attempt to explore the connections between literature and religion will lead to the conversion of criticism into theology. Those who express this fear contend that to judge literature according to whether it adequately illustrates religious doctrine, or whether it correctly captures the essential mood of a particular faith, would constitute an abrogation of the functions and the responsibilities of literary criticism. Critics as different in their approaches—and indeed in their religious backgrounds and positions—as F.R. Leavis and Joseph H. Summers have indicated strong assent to the view that art must not serve a specific religion. Some years ago, Leavis clearly delineated his feelings in an essay "The Logic of Christian Discrimination." "As for Christian Discrimination," he noted, "it needs to be said that there can be no substitute for the scrupulous and disinterested approach of the literary critic. If Christian belief and Christian attitudes have really affected the critic's sensibility, then they will play their due part in his perceptions and judgments, without his summoning his creeds and doctrines, to the job of discriminating and pronouncing." Sum-

111

mers, addressing himself to his fellow "Christian literary scholars," warned that, "concerned with our particular vision of orthodoxy, we may forget that our first duty as scholars is the discovery and communication of truth, and, instead, spend our chief energies as religious and moral cops and judges, rapping knuckles and heads, assigning sentences."

All the while, it is becoming increasingly apparent that the problems of the modern age will be solved neither by the doctrinaire man of letters nor by the doctrinaire man of faith. Understanding, not manifestos is what we need at present. If, moreover, we must be wary of those who would confuse literature with religion, we must also be wary of those who insist that criticism must concentrate solely on art form and that literary values preclude religious values. D.H. Lawrence's well-known observation that "one has to be so terribly religious, to be an artist" would indicate certainly that there are levels of meanings and relationships existing between art and religion that can be neither escaped nor ignored. These thoughts should in no way imply that the strictly formalistic approach to literature is unimportant. They simply underscore its inadequacy. In fact, Nathan A. Scott, Jr., rejecting the notion that a work of literature should be treated "as a linguistic artifact that exists in complete detachment from any other independent existent reality," has declared that criticism today is "in something like a situation of crisis."

Now the qualities and the complexities of artistic vision are such that they cannot be contained by critical (or theological) dogmas. The truth of this statement has been singularly dramatized in the twentieth century, especially since the end of World War I, when, to quote Rainer Maria Rilke, "the world . . . passed out of the hands of God into the hands of men." As a result, in much of modern literature it is precisely the experience and consequences of the displacement that are recreated. Critics who are willing to examine this factor recognize the possibilities of extending our understanding of what is often spoken of as contemporary man's "cultural fragmentation and incommunicability" in a "desacralized world." That is to say, such critics—by rising above the obviously parochial limitations often imposed by schools of literary criticism and by remaining ever cognizant of artistic form, which is expressive of meaning—are attuned to the cultural actualities and the temper of the times and to the ever-changing patterns of modern human experience. It is in the nature of this critical and synoptic awareness, then, to be able to "take account of secular man in all his dynamics," to quote a phrase of Amos Wilder.

Any preoccupation with the relations of literature and religion must not be construed as a development or a requirement of a point of view or of what might be called religious criticism: the kind of criticism, for instance, that chooses to view literature within the framework of Boris Pasternak's contention that "art has two constant, two unending concerns: it always meditates on death and thus always creates life. All great, genuine art resembles and continues the Revelation of St. John." No, it is not the religious critic who is needed but the critic who can discern spiritual sources of art and can communicate religious essences of art that are applicable and complementary to human existence. For such a critic there are no literary confines. His assessments of art are not dictated by adherence to tests of orthodoxy; nor are they restricted to the region peculiar to structural analysis, to matters of technique, style, and form. Concurrently, his sensitivity to language encompasses a sensitivity to other energies that consciously or unconsciously give shape and value to the creative imagination—the social, the historical, the ideological, and the moral elements that are continually at work in the thinking and creative processes.

Doubtless the growing awareness of significant relationships between literature and religion is symptomatic of the discontent some literary scholars are showing with criticism that is too professional, specialist, or academic. Literary scholarship that limits itself to categories, criteria, and methodologies—always in the name of "objective" truths, so we are told—may, to be sure, reveal a disciplined critical intelligence. But it does not have the breadth and the acuteness of vision that inhere in a critical sensibility: the sensibility that transcends the mastery of so-called methods and aims of criticism so as to embrace what Erich Heller has described as a concern "with the communication of quality rather than measurable quantity, and of meaning rather than explanation." In essence, then, literary theoreticians who very tidily dismiss a critical work dealing with literature and religion as, say, a mere religious-metaphysical study (we need not be bothered by the tone of the dismissal: it is a tone we have learned to bear with in pundits) deny that the artistic imagination has important things to relate not only to the critic but also to the philosopher, the educator, and the priest. Critics who refuse to accept or to evaluate the place and the meaning of religious consciousness and convictions when they impinge on and inform the artistic imagination as a whole reveal a deficiency that impairs their study and appreciation of literature. (The study of literature, like the problem of education, must, as T.S. Eliot has declared, "be something more than the acquisition of information, technical competence, or superficial culture.")

The basic issue in the relationship of literature and religion, therefore, is whether or not a critic is prepared to admit the relevance, aesthetically and intellectually, of religious elements in art and to elucidate these in his interpretations. That literature and religion are not discrete entities, and that there is a living relation between them: these are truths that must be fully affirmed by a critic who in any way believes that criticism is the "pursuit of true judgment." Such an affirmation, on the other hand, in no way requires a critic to subscribe to an authoritative view, to a religious doctrine, or to particular theological tenets, comprising an outlook on life. Orthodoxies and neo-orthodoxies have done damage enough in literary studies.

In religion one of the most welcome developments in recent years has been the willingness shown by different denominations to exchange views leading to harmony, even to unity. Above all, the ecumenical movement has indicated a realistic comprehension of both the momentous changes and the dangers that grip the modern world. The challenges of new ways to old have prompted a continuing exploration of religious issues, and more and more the theologian recognizes the secular realities of human experience and the need to cope with them. Thus dialogue has replaced the disputation that characterized religious discussions in the past. Both the beginning and the end of this dialogue rest in the realization that, as Martin Buber wrote, "religions are mansions into which the spirit of man is fit in order that it might not break forth and burst open its world." To be sure, this is not the place for a discourse on ecumenism. These remarks are made only to point out that modern man is displaying a new readiness for finding understanding among people of conflicting religious beliefs. There is no reason the literary critic should not also participate in the dialogue by directing his attention to art that contemplates and identifies itself with those universals in human life that are religious in origin: the meaning of the human predicament, the nature of evil, the fact of death, the concept of redemption.

5

Without One False Note

EDMUND WILSON ON ONE OCCASION dismissed Leo Tolstoy's "cult of love and God" as "an arid self-directed exercise that simply raises the worshipper in his own esteem."[1] He chose, instead, to praise Tolstoy's efforts in saving lives during a time of famine in Russia (1891–93) and his compromises in his difficult relations with his wife and children. A chilling and shallow judgment, it tells us more about Wilson's pragmatic Western outlook than about Tolstoy's inner spiritual life. More trustworthy is the judgment of the German lyric poet Rainer Maria Rilke, who had made Russia one of his "elective homelands" and who visited Tolstoy in Moscow in 1899 and in Yasnaya Polyana in 1900. Speaking specifically of *The Letters of Tolstoy and his Cousin Countess Alexandra Tolstoy*, Rilke wrote:

> This correspondence is one of the most sincere and hence purest testimonies of inner intercourse with others and with oneself, the figure of Tolstoy emerges from these pages more direct, more moving than I ever realized; what the personal contact with him conveyed, his not being able to do otherwise, his being right behind all error, all this, which moved me so utterly that time, streams over to one from these pages, not overheated, just with the natural warmth of a man toilingly and joyfully alive. . . .[2]

Rilke's words can serve as a summarizing critical statement with respect to Tolstoy's letters, of which he wrote thousands. Six hundred of the most significant of these are included in two volumes, under the title *Tolstoy's Letters*, the only comprehensive selection in English translation.[3] This collection gives us the kind of source material needed to see Tolstoy's life as something far more (and far greater) than, as Edmund Wilson presumed, "some effort of spiritual

---

1. See "Notes on Tolstoy," *A Window on Russia: For the Use of Foreign Readers* (New York, 1972).
2. *Letters of Rainer Maria Rilke*, II, trans. Jane Bannard Greene and M.D. Herter Norton (New York, 1945–48), 95.
3. *Volume I: 1828–1879; Volume II: 1880–1910*, selected, ed., and trans. R.F. Christian (New York, 1978).

self-ennoblement." It provides, as does, for example, the correspondence of John Keats, Vincent van Gogh, or D.H. Lawrence, a psychograph of a writer who was great precisely because he was a great man.

No less than those two other Russian masters, Nikolai Gogol and Fyodor Dostoevsky, Tolstoy cannot be neatly categorized as a man, a thinker, or an artist. To attempt to do so leads to problems, as Sir Isaiah Berlin, in his celebrated study, *The Hedgehog and the Fox* (1953), discovered. Using a line from the fragments of the Greek poet Archilochus—"The fox knows many things, but the hedgehog knows one thing"—Sir Isaiah proceeded to count, among others, Plato, Lucretius, Dante, Pascal, and Dostoevsky as hedgehogs, and Herodotus, Aristotle, Montaigne, and Joyce as foxes. Placing Tolstoy in either of the two categories, however, was impossible. Tolstoy, Sir Isaiah found, was by nature a fox but also believed in being a hedgehog. The difference between what Tolstoy was and what he professed defied categorization. "I am only a weak man of evil habits," he said of himself, "who desires to serve the God of truth, but continually goes astray." If to some persons, like Maxim Gorky, who did not believe in God, Tolstoy was godlike, he was to himself a paradox. If to the Russian Orthodox hierarchs he was a heretic, to be excommunicated in 1901, he was to others a sage and saint, to whom homage was to be paid and from whom blessings were to be asked. If for some Tolstoy was, as Irving Babbitt claimed, an eleutheromaniac, to others he was, like the Dukhobors whom he befriended, a "spirit-wrestler" of unparalleled strength. If, in the words of the distinguished church historian Georges Florovsky, Tolstoy's was "a long life of gropings and ramblings," to Tolstoy himself "life is a trial . . . it is more than a trial, it is also an expiation of my faults."

Tolstoy has been many things to as many people, and it is the measure of his greatness that he has always excited an unending intensity of response and interpretation. Inseparable in their unity of vision, his art and life prescribe reflection. "Genius does not create; it reflects," Tolstoy declared, his own words here containing the secret of his genius and alerting one to its true aim. However much Tolstoy tantalizes his interpreters insofar as he never ceased to take sides on issues, to the extent that his genius has been termed devastatingly destructive, the fact remains that, as George Orwell observed of Tolstoy's fictive characters, Tolstoy struggled to make his own soul. In the end, as the letters disclose with terrifying honesty, Tolstoy's achievement must be examined in terms of its spiritual content: that is, in terms of the religious questions with which he never stopped grappling. Much has been made of the Tolstoy before and after his "conversion," as signaled by the most important of his autobiographical writings, *A Confession* (1879). Such a view is symptomatic of the desire to set off Tolstoy the primitivist from Tolstoy the Christian socialist, or, in D.H. Lawrence's words, Tolstoy the "true artist" from Tolstoy the "perverse moralist." Any careful study of Tolstoy's letters, from the earliest written in 1844 to those written in his last year of life, 1910, makes such bifurcation untenable. Not yet thirty years of age, Tolstoy was to write to his prospective fiancée, Valeriya Arsenyeva—their relationship actually ended by the beginning of 1857: "The main thing is—live in such a way that when you go to bed you can say to yourself: today (1) I did good to someone and (2) I became a little better myself." Less than a week before his death at the age of eighty-two, on November 7, 1910, he wrote to one of his children: ". . . you should think about your own life, who you are, what you are, what is the meaning of man's life and how every reasonable man should live it." Tolstoy's concerns revolved continuously around one fundamental religious question: "how to live one's life in the best and most moral way."

II

It is by now a commonplace to speak of Tolstoy as a "seer of the flesh" or as a "prophet of dissent," epithets that fail to convey fully the consuming earnestness of his religious search. If there is one description that both identifies and contains the whole of Tolstoy, in all of his contending parts and passions, with all of his inner and outer crises, and in spite of his ambivalences, it is that of Religious Seeker. Tolstoy's religious search was a search for the absolutes of perfection, moral and personal. His search was, in fact, a relentless act of confession; a test, and testament, of honesty. One of its supreme qualities is its candor. Self-presentation, self-examination, and self-renunciation are paradigms of the moral imperative that Tolstoy pursued, when, as he wrote, "Everything will find a true echo, without one false note." The letters corroborate the nature of Tolstoy's search, in the course of which he sought to strip himself of everything he believed to be false and corruptive. Indeed, that "huge and gratuitous act of renunciation," when, in the last days of his life, Tolstoy was to abandon his wife and family—"on my way to the place where I wished to be alone," as he said in his very last and unfinished letter—was to instance the most agonizing demand of his religious search: the need to triumph over "the discrepancy between my way of life and the truths which I profess"; the final answer to "what then must I do?," when Tolstoy could no longer reproach himself "because it hasn't been granted to me, if only just before I die, if only for a year, if only for a month, to live the life that is natural to me, away from this falsehood in which I not only live, but take part and drown."

"How should one live?" "What is it for?" "What does it lead to?" These life-questions tortured Tolstoy, and in his search for answers he found himself increasingly isolated: "My friends, even my family turn away from me. Some people—liberals and aesthetes—think me mad or feeble-minded like Gogol; others—revolutionaries and radicals—think me a mystic or a gas bag; government people think me a pernicious revolutionary; Orthodox people think me the devil." Religious understanding rather than transcendent belief was to become Tolstoy's criterion of judgment. He wanted a life that was simple, less perplexing, above all, less vulnerable to the accursed questions. A living piety and a reverence for life, "a religion that corresponds to the development of mankind, the religion of Christ, but purified of faith and mystery" (as he wrote)—these were for Tolstoy religious tenets that he came to associate with the "unlettered folk," the pilgrims, monks, peasants. His religious search was in essence a search for the confirmation of the possibilities of life in a world of straightforward facts. "It's possible to live perfectly on earth if one is able to work and to love," Tolstoy said, "to work for what one loves, and to love what one is working at." His search was characterized by a pious materialism—molding what he termed a religious union of all living things, "the brotherhood of men, [and] their service to each other." Tolstoy's search was one with his world view: rational rather than intuitive; material rather than metaphysical; horizontal rather than vertical. In this he never lost the spirit of the Enlightenment. Even when defining religion he spoke very much as a Russian *philosophe:* "Religion is the awareness of those truths which are common and comprehensible to all people in all situations at all times, and are as indisputable as $2 \times 2 = 4$. The business of religion is to find and express these truths, and when the truth has been expressed, it inevitably changes people's lives." As a religious seeker, it can be said, Tolstoy wanted not so much to possess truth as to be possessed by it.

The object of Tolstoy's religious search was syncretistic. The teachings of Confucius, Mencius, Lao-tzu, of the Stoics, Marcus Aurelius, Epictetus, and Seneca, of the Hebrew prophets, especially Isaiah, and of the Gospels were for him necessary to laying the stable foundation of a true education and faith. With respect to the four Gospels, he advised a young student, asking his opinion on "what to read and how to read," to strike out passages in which Christ is spoken about, leaving only those in which Christ speaks. Christ's words themselves should then be sifted in order to separate all that is incomprehensible from what is absolutely clear. One should meditate carefully on the expurgated passages, "trying to unite them into one whole." "The religious books of other peoples should be read in the same way," he concluded. "From all this a single whole outlook on the world will be evolved. This is the foundation of everything." The main ingredient that, according to Tolstoy, informs such an outlook, that actually makes it possible, is that of reason, since "reason is the divine power of the soul which reveals to it its attitude to the world and to God." Reason and religion became, for Tolstoy, consubstantial: a true sacramental union; an ultimate confession of belief; an infallible doctrine. Only reason, he insisted, makes faith comprehensible and enables one to get rid of the "superfluous" encumbrances of miracle and mystery and "to strive after complete consciousness." For Tolstoy what was miraculous and superhuman violated the immutable "laws of reason." It is necessary, he said, to choose one of two things: "I chose belief in reason, not miracles, long ago, and I chose it because reason is the same for all people, while miracles are different for all people, and reason is necessary to me for living, while miracles aren't necessary to me for anything."

III

Unlike Dostoevsky, who remained a "prisoner of Christ," declaring that if anyone proved to him that Christ was outside the truth, "then I should prefer to remain with Christ than with the truth," Tolstoy approached Christ from a severely rational perspective. Christ's divinity, crucifixion, and resurrection were for Tolstoy violations of reason. In Christ he revered a great religious teacher, not a savior: "I won't believe for anything that He was resurrected in the body, but I shall never lose the belief that He will be resurrected in His teaching." His perception of Christ was one of rational admiration, as is clearly confirmed by Gorky's remarkable reminiscence of Tolstoy: "When he speaks about Christ, it is always peculiarly poor, no enthusiasm, no feeling in his words, and no spark of real fire."[4] Tolstoy, as an enlightened moralist, allocated his fervency to Jean-Jacques Rousseau. To the founder of the "Société Jean-Jacques Rousseau," he wrote in 1905: "Rousseau a été mon maître depuis l'âge de 15 ans. Rousseau et l'évangile ont été les deux grandes et bienfaisantes influ-

4. *Reminiscences of Tolstoy, Chekhov, and Andreev* (London, 1968), 16.

ences de ma vie." Indeed, as a young adolescent, Tolstoy chose to wear round his neck not a cross but rather a medallion with the portrait of Rousseau on it! Tolstoy had not only read Rousseau's complete works, "L'ami des hommes," but also said that the influence on him of *La Nouvelle Héloïse* had been "very great" and that of *Émile* and of *Confessions* "enormous." Visiting Clarens in 1857, in the neighborhood of Geneva, where Rousseau wrote his *Nouvelle Héloïse*, Tolstoy wrote rapturously: ". . . I will only say that it's literally impossible to tear oneself away from this lake and its shores, and that I spend most of my time gazing and admiring while I walk or simply sit at the window of my room."

Like Rousseau, Tolstoy has been called a supreme religious thinker and moralist, an authentic saint, a mahatma. And pilgrims continue, despite obstacles instigated by Red commissars, to visit Yasnaya Polyana, no less than pilgrims earlier trudged their way to Rousseau's various rural retreats while he lived and, after his death, hastened, as J.M. Lalley noted in a remarkable essay on Rousseau's political philosophy, "to the shrine at Eremonville in search of holy relics, such as a snuff box or an old shoe."[5] Such adulation must be viewed as symptomatic of the "modern temper" that is characterized by doubts, insecurity, and dissatisfaction; by the lack of certitudes; by, above all, the formulation of those pitiless questions that continue to repeat themselves to a point of impotent despair, which is in itself capitulation to the chaos of values that grips modern man and that becomes *la condition humaine.* The Tolstoy who cried "I myself am nature" affirmed the doctrine of naturalism rather than the lessons of history, believing that answers to human problems are to be found in man's own experience. His "antihistoricism"—*War and Peace* has been called a "nihilistic epic"—has been radically, and blasphemously, accelerated by successive modernists, as "the eclipse of God" has accompanied "the eclipse of history." Historical Christianity, which Tolstoy rejected, has been increasingly replaced by the religion of behaviorism and now by the synthetic theology of the sociologists. Tolstoy steadfastly contended that the problem of religion is the problem of life. But if the religious questions he asked were central, his answers were sentimental. Plagued by doubt and dissatisfaction, he appealed to and glorified the modernist doctrine of "demystification." The penetration and the fathomability of the unfathomable became a goal of his religious searches. It brought him into that zero zone described by one Russian commentator as a "nihilism of common sense." He who explored so profoundly sexual passions (as

5. "The Solipsistic Saint," *Modern Age* (Spring 1977), 197.

in *The Kreutzer Sonata*) lacked Dostoevsky's spiritual capacity for depth soundings. His answers comfortably transformed into a "religion of syllogisms," as it has been remarked. "There must be some explanation" was Tolstoy's recurrent cry.

Significantly, Tolstoy's view of evil alerts one to the Rousseauistic limitations of his moral vision, and of his (and our) modernism as a whole, and is nowhere better crystallized than in this passage from a letter written in 1881 to N.N. Strakhov: "Man is always good, and if he acts badly it is necessary to look for the source of the evil in the temptations which lure him into evil, and not in the qualities of pride or ignorance." It is a statement that, at least in part, explains Tolstoy's muddled criticisms of the tragic vision of Dante, of Shakespeare, and of Milton—"I read them with great difficulty and then immediately forgot everything I had read," he noted. The limitations of Tolstoy's view of evil instance the absence of a metaphysical dimension in Tolstoy's thought. He saw evil in categorically ethical terms, in its materializing contexts, as when he wrote, "A man on his own can do no evil. Evil is lack of communication between people." Tolstoy was to discount metaphysical roots of evil, those labyrinthine ways and inscrutable energies that come under the heading of Satanism, which he equated with obscurantism. His conception of evil borders on the simplistic and the reductionist and accents the shortcomings of a statement like this: "I firmly believe that people are punished, *not for their sins but by their sins.* And the mitigation of any sin, if not escape from punishment, is only achieved by one means—by repentance and by stopping sinning, and not by the imagined legalisation of it, i.e. by making the sin worse." Intelligible solutions to the problem of evil can always be obtained, he claimed, since there are rules and regulations "fulfilling the law," those "Rules of Life" that Tolstoy talked about in *Youth* (1857). Nonresistance to evil became for him a principle of life, as he centered on Christ's Sermon on the Mount, which, as he wrote in a long letter on the subject, "expounds the simplest, easiest, most understandable rules for loving God, one's neighbour, and life, without the recognition and fulfillment of which it is impossible to speak of Christianity." Only when one understands (a word that is Tolstoy's equivalent of grace) these five rules does one understand the significance of Christ's teachings: "(1) Do not be angry. (2) Do not fornicate. (3) Do not swear. (4) Do not judge. (5) Do not make war."

Effecting what is good and reasonable—"Do God's work, carry out the will of the Father and you will then see the light and understand"—constituted for Tolstoy a spiritual value of successful human relations. Only the fulfillment of this value, central to the

Tolstoyan "theology," will lead to the Kingdom of Truth on earth. Yet Tolstoy's is not so much a theology as it is a modern sociology of religion, with its identifying emphasis on the idea of brotherhood and service: "Only that teaching contains the truth which points to activity—life—which satisfies the needs of the soul, and which at the same time is constant activity for the good of others." At times his "message" is akin to and no less inane than "the power of positive thinking," even as at other times it brings to mind the advice of the contemporary apostles of equivalence. No less than these latter-day apostles (and their therapeutics), Tolstoy was not aware either of the inadequacy of his doctrine or his own spiritual incapacity. Father Florovsky is to the point here: "There was a paradoxical disproportion in his moral teaching between the aggressive maximalism of his invectives and the striking poverty of his positive program."[6] Again and again we are reminded in reading his letters that the religion of Tolstoy is not too far from the religion of Rousseau. The same urge to deal with evil socially rather than at its source in the individual, the same vague longing for equality, the same emphasis on the humanitarian view of life, the same sentimental formulas are at work in Tolstoy. He remained to the end a moral didactician. His religion, an enlightened version of Christianity, kerygmatic but hardly kenotic, was concentrated in the love and deification of life in time rather than in eternity. Of this chronolatry he remained unwaveringly clear: "I think that in this life internal experience shows us that the less we live our personal life, the more we feel sure of immortality, and the reverse, so that by analogy we must think that immortality must coincide with complete renunciation of self."

IV

But, for Tolstoy, the question "What is death" invariably compelled still another question, "How can I save myself?" In this connection there is no more moving of Tolstoy's letters than that of October 17, 1860, written to his friend, the poet A.A. Fet, describing the death of his consumptive eldest brother, Nikolay Tolstoy (1823–60). This

6. "Three Masters: The Quest for Religion in Nineteenth-Century Russian Literature," *Mansions of the Spirit: Essays in Literature and Religion,* ed. George A. Panichas (New York, 1967), 177. The following are also valuable critical studies: Dmitri Merejkowski, *Tolstoi as Man and Artist, with an Essay on Dostoïevski* (New York, 1902); V.V. Zenkovsky, *A History of Russian Philosophy,* trans. George L. Kline (New York, 1953), especially I, 386–99; and Stefan Zweig, *Master Builders: A Typology of the Spirit,* trans. Eden and Cedar Paul (New York, 1939), 757–905.

letter, read as a prologue to Tolstoy's aspirations as religious seeker, should alert one to the materialistic nature of Tolstoy's religious seekings and questions. It reveals Tolstoy's mind and heart, as he describes Nikolay's death: "Nothing in life has made such an impression on me. He was telling the truth when he said that there is nothing worse than death. And if you really think that death is after all the end of everything, then there's nothing worse than life either." Simply, starkly, sparingly, Tolstoy etches the dire details of death with, as the Russian critic Dmitri Merejkowski was to express it, "a soulless callousness": "He didn't say that he felt death approaching, but I know he followed its every step, and surely knew what still remained to him of life. A few minutes before he died, he dozed off, then suddenly came to and whispered with horror: 'What does it all mean?' He had seen it—this absorption of the self in nothingness." That the end is nothingness was for Tolstoy an irreversible fact of life: ". . . as soon as man reaches a higher stage of development and ceases to be stupid, it becomes clear to him that everything is rubbish and a fraud, and that the truth that he nevertheless loves more than anything else is a terrible truth."

If for Dostoevsky the life struggle finally was with the "dreadful freedom," for Tolstoy it was with the "terrible truth." Out of this savage tension Tolstoy shaped his artistic vision and wrote works that, appropriately enough, he designated "letters to the public." The artist's aim, he declared, is "to make people love life in all its countless inexhaustible manifestations." His art emerged from, thrived in, his "earthbound imagination," in Stefan Zweig's phrase. (Tolstoy once described himself as "a plant louse" and "an indefatigable whoremonger.") The artistic values of clarity, honesty, livingness, comprehensibility, the confluence of which makes his achievement such an astonishing experience, are also the transposed religious values that he considered essential and viable. His art, no less than his religious seekings, had one central, ascertainable goal: a passage to spiritual understanding—here not there, today not tomorrow. Father Sergius, in the short novel of that title, is a study of spiritual pride and carnal desire, as well as a saintly man who discovers that "the kingdom of God is within you." When placing Father Sergius beside Dostoevsky's iconographic Father Zossima (in *The Brothers Karamazov*), one can easily distinguish Tolstoy's immanentist earthly vision from Dostoevsky's metaphysics of art. The difference is telling between artist as religious seeker and artist as religious visionary. In certain ways the crisis of modernism finds in Tolstoy its most gifted temporal representative, if not its best artistic spokesman. His modernism, like his secularism, was pious, loyal to an attitude toward life that exudes with belief in man's phenomenalizing renewal. What more revealing, or marvelous, sentence, underlining Tolstoy's naturalistic religious outlook, can be found than this in *War and Peace*: "O God, let me lie down like a stone and rise up like new bread." But ultimately Tolstoy's "theological rationalism," at war with both the world and the Church, was at war with itself. His attempt to synthesize Rousseau and Christ was as much doomed to failure as is the radical theologian's attempt to synthesize Marx and Christ today! Tolstoy's romantic Christianity, if it can be called that, comes to a dead end.

As "man and artist" and as "man and thinker" Tolstoy discloses a heroic though not, like Dostoevsky, a tragic magnitude. (Curiously, Tolstoy did not start to read *The Brothers Karamazov*, first published in 1879–80, until the very last days of his life. And with his flight from family and home, followed almost immediately by his illness and death in the train station at Astapovo, he never did complete the reading of the novel that Gorky called "a fifth Gospel.") Tolstoy tended to see too much of "the meaning of life" on the level of the same solubility that made his educational "primers" so famous. But the meaning of life must always remain far more difficult and complex, far more tragic, than that proffered by Tolstoy when, patriarchally, he counseled: "Live seeking God, and then you will not live without God." It is right to say that Tolstoy did finally break out of "the cage of secularism"; his spiritual effort was truly titanic, making his example an impossibility for others. Yet his effort lacked *transcensus* and returned to its original starting point of struggle. He did not aspire for that "enthusiasm for the distant." In Tolstoy religious belief and religious understanding were in constant conflict. He was never able to unify them. He could not, hence, hear the deeper, tragic notes of life, which perhaps explains his dismissal (in *What is Art?*) of Shakespeare's plays and of Beethoven's music as "meaningless twaddle." But, surely, anyone who listens to the Andante in Beethoven's *Fifth Symphony* must inevitably hear notes of "panic and emptiness" as the never-ending goblins walk over the universe, from end to end.[7] Is it not possible to believe that, in Beethoven's great symphony, Tolstoy ("I, being very susceptible to music") heard his own soul speaking his darkest fears? and that, in *King Lear*, he, too, "bound upon a wheel of fire," glimpsed the inflamed regions of his torments, rendering everything purposeless and unreasonable?

7. See the opening paragraphs of Chapter V in E.M. Forster's novel *Howards End* (1910).

6

Voyage of Oblivion

*No one can leap over his shadow, but poets leap
over death.*
—SAMUEL TAYLOR COLERIDGE

D.H. LAWRENCE'S PREOCCUPATION with the meaning of death is nowhere
more powerfully and memorably seen than in his volume of poetry
published posthumously under the title *Last Poems.* "Their appearance," Horace Gregory has written, "is melodramatic, like the
flowering of a great tree sprung overnight out of the dungheap of
modern civilization."[1] There can be little doubt that these poems
embody Lawrence's most fervent religious expression as well as the
final significance of his religious quest and message. As a profound
and indispensable part of a spiritual autobiography, moreover, they
become all the more meaningful when one recalls that they were
written in the last years of Lawrence's life, in the midst of his own
severe and fatal illness, the harsh outcries following the publication
of *Lady Chatterley's Lover* in July 1928, the seizure by British authorities of the manuscript copies of his *Pansies* as they came through the
mails in January 1929, and the police raid on Lawrence's paintings in
London in July.

Still, Earl Brewster has recalled that during the last year of his life,
when death was drawing nearer and nearer, Lawrence seemed to have
gained a greater tranquillity. He was now turning many of his
thoughts to the ancient Greeks, to God, and to death itself. We know,
likewise, that during the last days, when he was in southern France,
he was reading the Bible in James Moffatt's translation, W.R. Inge's
The Philosophy of Plotinus, and Gilbert Murray's *Five Stages of
Greek Religion.*[2] His concern with the Greeks was not at all an
inconsequential or passing interest, for in another of his great crises,
during the Cornwall period (1915–17), he had read Thucydides in

1. *D.H. Lawrence: Pilgrim of the Apocalypse* (New York, 1957), 113.
2. Earl and Achsah Brewster, *D.H. Lawrence: Reminiscences and Correspondence*
(London, 1934), 305.

translation, and later on he was to read John Burnet's *Early Greek Philosophy*.[3] And now, in his Villa Beau Soleil in Bandol, Lawrence used "to lie in bed and look at the islands out to sea, and think of the Greeks, and cough, and wish either that I was different or the world was different," as he wrote to Brewster Ghiselin.[4]

It must be stressed that Lawrence's interest in the Greeks, as seen in some of the *Last Poems*, was not in the Hellenism of classical civilization, but in the ancient world before Socrates and Aristotle—"Before Plato told the great lie of ideals"("For the Heroes Are Dipped in Scarlet").[5] He admired this period of ancient Greek life because, like that of the Etruscans, it was a way of life that was based on the "logic of action" and not reason, on "cult-lore" and not culture. The latter Lawrence particularly disliked, as he wrote in *Apocalypse*, "Because culture is chiefly an activity of the mind, and cult-lore is an activity of the senses."[6] In this connection, his earlier comments, as found at the beginning of the chapter entitled "Christianity" in *Movements in European History*, are quite pertinent. Here Lawrence voices his admiration for the pagan Greeks and Romans, especially the natural, living forms of their religion, in which he saw not prescribed and conventional modes of worship and belief, but the spontaneous, intuitive attempts of man to secure a "living relationship" with the creative and natural rhythm of life. "But it was all part," he says, "of the active, actual everyday, normal life—not something apart."[7] He observes, in addition, that in pagan times "there was no preaching, no praying, no talk about sin or salvation, no service at all," that "there was no sacred profession, no special beings were set apart, like our clergy," that "since everything that was wonderful had its god, the Greeks and Romans were not jealous of strange Gods."[8]

It is in the light of this that one can understand Lawrence's interest, as found in the *Last Poems*, in the voyagers from Cnossos. In "The Greeks Are Coming!" he describes them as follows:

> And every time, it is ships, it is ships
> it is ships of Cnossos coming, out of the
> morning and the sea,

---

3. *D.H. Lawrence: A Composite Biography*, ed. Edward Nehls (Madison, Wis., 1957), I, 402, 587 n. 346. See also Richard Aldington, *D.H. Lawrence: Portrait of a Genius, but . . .* (London, 1950), 168.

4. *Ibid.*, III, 408.

5. *Last Poems*, ed. Richard Aldington and Giusèppe Orioli (New York, 1933), 6. Unless otherwise indicated, all quotations are from this edition of Lawrence's poems.

6. *Apocalypse* (Florence, Italy, 1931), Ch. VII.

7. Oxford, Eng., 1921, Ch. III.

8. *Ibid.*

> it is Aegean ships, and men with archaic
>   pointed beards
> coming out of the Eastern end.

In "The Argonauts" he recalls Odysseus:

> Now the sea is the Argonaut's sea, and
>   in the dawn
> Odysseus calls the commands, as he steers
>   past those foamy islands.

In "Middle of the World" it is Dionysos and the gods of Crete and Tiryns who come to his mind, for

> This sea will never die, neither will it
>   ever grow old
> nor cease to be blue, nor in the dawn
> cease to lift up its hills
> and let the slim black ships of Dionysos
>   come sailing in
> with grape-vines up the mast, and
>   dolphins leaping.
>
> And the Minoan Gods, and the Gods of Tiryns
> are heard softly laughing and chatting, as ever;
> and Dionysos, young, and a stranger
> leans listening on the gate, in all respect.

Always his thought is of men who bravely adventure into life ("For the Heroes Are Dipped in Scarlet"):

> So now they come back! Hark!
> Hark! the low and shattering laughter of
>   bearded men
> with the slim waists of warriors, and
>   the long feet
> of moon-lit dancers.

In the interrelationship of Lawrence's death poems with those on his concept of God and the pagan Greeks, there can be readily seen the full religious significance of his vision of life and of death. Above all, the feelings of a healthy vitality and optimism predominate in these poems, and the poetic form and language are in complete harmony with these feelings. The poetry here is not poetry of sentiment expressed in Tennysonian "moods of misery unutterable"; nor is it characterized by a pessimistic sensibility in which pathos and melancholy are the chief qualities. Lawrence's death poems radiate a calm feeling of vigor and a sustained belief detached from sentimental self-absorption or elegiac rapture. Whenever any trace of bitterness and sadness appears, it is the result of passional regret and indignation with those who have denied life. The poems speak from the depths of the poet's feelings: there is nothing artificial or forced or insincere about them. For, as Lawrence himself remarked: "We can get rid of the stereotyped movements and the old hackneyed association of sound or sense. We can break down those artificial conduits and canals through which we do so love to force our utterance. We can break the stiff neck of habit. We can be in ourselves spontaneous and flexible as flame, we can see that utterance rushes out without artificial form or artificial smoothness."[9] In these *Last Poems* he wrote from what he termed "pure passionate experience" or "the immediate, instant self." Or, to put it another way, it is the voice of his "demon" that is speaking here, not the "voice of commonplace me." "The demon, when he's really there," he notes in his preface to *The Collected Poems*, "makes his own form willy-nilly, and is unchangeable."[10]

In the first of Lawrence's death poems, "Bavarian Gentians," originally entitled "Glory of Darkness" and written in Baden-Baden in 1929, not only the quality of reverence but also that of tranquillity becomes quite evident. The poem, with its mythological framework, is one of Lawrence's finest. Entirely free of any kind of intellectualized deliberateness, it arises from the deepest part of the soul, from "simple, sensuous, passionate life." In it the poet shows that death is a continuing part of a great mystery, transcending limitations of formal definition and academic explanation. Here it should be recalled that Lawrence's dislike for absolute definitions is apparent throughout his work, and it accounts as well for his admiration for the Etruscans, who, he believed, sought to live life amidst all its creative wonder. "But the white man," he exclaims in one of his charming essays in *Mornings in Mexico*, "has a horrible, truly horrible, monkey-like passion for invisible exactitudes."[11]

In "Bavarian Gentians" we see the lonely but resolute figure of the religious seeker continuing his way into "that sightless realm where darkness is awake upon the dark."

> Not every man has gentians in his house
> In Soft September, at slow, sad Michaelmas,

the poem begins with masterful and majestic restraint. The reference to Michaelmas (the feast day of the archangel Michael) is an interesting one, since along with references to Pluto and Demeter and Persephone, it again shows Lawrence's characteristic synthesis of

9. *Phoenix: The Posthumous Papers of D.H. Lawrence*, ed. Edward D. McDonald (London, 1936), 221.
10. *Ibid.*, 252.
11. "The Mozo" (London, 1927).

Christian and pagan symbols. (For Lawrence, of course, religion was not a matter of evolution or of distinction between the old and the new—for instance, paganism versus Christianity—but rather of a continuation of the old into the new.) As the poem continues, the religious seeker's impassioned appeal found in the line "lead me then, lead me the way" becomes symbolic of his journey into the dark and unknown realm of death, represented here by the lower world ("Pluto's gloom") of pagan times, and strikingly reiterated in words associated with darkness and blueness:

> Bavarian gentians, big and dark, only dark
> darkening the day-time torch-like with the
>   smoking blueness of Pluto's gloom,
> ribbed and torch-like, with their blaze of
>   darkness spread blue
> down flattening into points, flattened
>   under the sweep of white day
> torch-flower of the blue-smoking darkness,
>   Pluto's dark-blue daze,
> black lamps from the halls of Dio, burning
>   dark blue,
> giving off darkness, blue darkness, as
>   Demeter's pale lamps give off light,
> lead me then, lead me the way.

Here, as throughout the *Last Poems*, death is represented as some great "journey" from "the entanglements of life," as Lawrence puts it in "So Let Me Live,"

> to the adventure of death, in eagerness
> turning to death as I turn to beauty
> to the breath, that is, of new beauty
>   unfolding in death.

"Bavarian Gentians" sets the theme of all his death poetry:

> Reach me a gentian, give me a torch!
> let me guide myself with the blue,
>   forked torch of this flower
> down the darker and darker stairs,
> where blue is darkened on blueness
> even where Persephone goes, just now,
>   from the frosted September
> to the sightless realm where darkness
>   is awake upon the dark
> and Persephone herself is but a voice
> or a darkness invisible enfolded in
>   the deeper dark
> of the arms Plutonic, and pierced with
>   the passion of dense gloom,
> among the splendour of torches of

> darkness, shedding darkness on
> the lost bride and her groom.

Death, Lawrence maintains, is not easy—"O it is not easy to die the death," he says in his poem "Difficult Death." In this poem he characteristically refers to death as a journey to a "dark oblivion." But there is no feeling of futility or irremediable grief.

> So build your ship of death, and let the
>   soul drift
> to dark oblivion.
> Maybe life is still our portion
> after the bitter passage of oblivion.

In "All Souls' Day," the same thought is expressed again. The poem contains a deep sense of tender compassion; the first line pleads with the living to

> Be careful, then, and be gentle about
>   death.
> For it is hard to die, it is difficult
>   to go through
> the door, even when it opens.

The poem then goes on to describe the dead who have departed from "the walled and silvery city of the now hopeless body," lingering for a time "in the shadow of the earth":

> For the soul has a long, long journey
>   after death
> to the sweet home of pure oblivion.
> Each needs a little ship, a little ship
> and the proper store of meal for the
>   longest journey.
>
> Oh, from out of your heart
> provide for your dead once more, equip them
> like departing mariners, lovingly.

In the course of these poems Lawrence clearly differentiates between the dead who depart for the new journey with a feeling of quiet contentment and those "unhappy dead" who in actual life failed to affirm the creative meaning of being. Concerning the latter, he wrote with some indignation in the poem "Death":

> They dare not die, because they know
> in death they cannot any more escape
> the retribution for their obstinacy.
> Old men, old obstinate men and women
> dare not die, because in death
> their hardened souls are washed with

fire, and washed and seared
till they are softened back to life-
stuff again, against which they
hardened themselves.

Or again, as he wrote in "Two Ways of Living and Dying":

But when people are only self-conscious
and self-willed
they cannot die, their corpse still runs on,
while nothing comes from the open heaven,
from earth, from the sun and moon
to them, nothing, nothing.

The latter are unhappy precisely because they have not lived and have denied creative life all along, a denial that to Lawrence is the greatest of evils. In this connection the concluding lines of "Cypresses," found earlier in *Birds, Beasts and Flowers*, are quite relevant:

Evil, what is evil?
There is only one evil, to deny life.
As Rome denied Etruria
And mechanical America Montezuma still.[12]

Here, too, Lawrence's words in a letter to Miss M.L. Skinner, "Death's not sad, when one has lived," come to mind.[13] This feeling is registered in the poem "The Houseless Dead," which describes the inability of those who have denied life to continue the mysterious and wondrous journey into the realm of death:

Oh pity the dead that were ousted out
of life
all unequipped to take the long, long
voyage.
Gaunt, gaunt they crowd the gray mud-
beaches of shadow
that intervene between the final sea
and the white shores of life.

Such life-deniers, Lawrence continues, are really incapable of dying, for they have always been dead:

The poor gaunt dead that cannot die
into the distance with receding oars,
but must roam like outcast dogs on
the margins of life!

In another poem, "Beware the Unhappy Dead!," he draws a close

12. *The Collected Poems of D.H. Lawrence* (London, 1932), 377.
13. *The Letters of D.H. Lawrence*, ed. Aldous Huxley (New York, 1932), 646. Dated August 28, 1925.

connection between the "houseless," "uneasy" dead and death-in-life. The poem starts with a warning:

> Beware the unhappy dead thrust out of life
> unready, unprepared, unwilling, unable
> to continue on the longest journey.

Lawrence then seeks to show that the "lost souls" and "angry dead" who crowd "the long mean marginal stretches of our existence" are in reality those living dead who never really died because they never really lived. Their presence disturbs the atmosphere and they haunt life with "disembodied rage." (This brings to mind that memorable scene in "St. Mawr" in which Mrs. Rachel Witt says to her daughter: "And you know, Louise, I've come to the conclusion that hardly anybody in the world really lives, and so hardly anybody really dies. They may well say *Oh Death, where is thy sting-a-ling-a-ling!* Even Death can't sting those that have never really lived.")[14] The result is the perpetuity of a condition of living death ("Oh, now they moan and throng in anger") in the stagnancy of human existence:

> Oh, but beware, beware the angry dead.
> Who knows, who knows how much our
>   modern woe
> is due to the angry unappeased dead
> that were thrust out of life, and now
>   come back at us
> malignant, malignant, for we will not
>   succour them.

Yet, it is on a confident note that Lawrence's poems often end. For, as he wrote in his essay "On Human Destiny," "The exquisite delicate light of ever-renewed human consciousness is never blown out."[15] And in the lines that directly follow those quoted above, he shows that the human condition is not beyond hope of change:

> Oh on this day for the dead, now November
>   is here
> set a place for the dead, with a cushion
>   and soft seat
> and put a plate, and put a wine-glass out
> and serve the best food, the fondest wine
> for your dead, your unseen dead, and with
>   your hearts
> speak with them and give them peace and
>   do them honour.

Nevertheless, Lawrence does not attempt to speculate in absolute

---

14. *The Tales of D.H. Lawrence* (London, 1934), 626.
15. *Assorted Articles* (London, 1930), 211.

terms about the nature of life after death, and this accounts for his repeated use of such words as "darkness" and "oblivion" throughout the death poems. His approach to death and the afterlife can be seen, for example, in the poem "Song of Death," in which he speaks of the "utter peace" that is gained in the "oblivion where the soul at last is lost." The mystery of death, like the mystery of life, cannot be explained away or defined in any absolute terms. As he wrote in "The End, the Beginning":

> If there were not an utter and absolute dark
> of silence and sheer oblivion
> at the core of everything,
> how terrible the sun would be,
> how ghastly it would be to strike a match,
> and make a light.

Death, consequently, is not only a kind of "utter and absolute dark," a "silence," a "sheer oblivion," "a silent sheer cessation of all aware-ness," but also a form of sleep in which there is "a hint of lovely oblivion" ("Sleep"), the "sleep of God," in which "the world is created afresh" ("Sleep and Waking"). (This recalls a related thought of Lawrence's, uttered earlier in *Fantasia of the Unconscious*, that "For each time we lie down to sleep we have within us a body of death which dies with the day that is spent.")[16] In these poems, he thus conceives of death with a sense of vitalistic wonder, and in his choice of language he seeks to avoid giving to the experience of death any rigid finality of feeling and description, since "all description is a blasphemy," as he claims in the poem "Tabernacle."

Although Lawrence was not at all a mystic in the accepted sense of the word, he nonetheless shared the mystic's difficulty in choosing words to describe ultimate human experiences. (In *Women in Love*, for example, he notes "that words themselves do not convey mean-ing, that they are but a gesture we make, a dumb show like any other.")[17] Death, therefore, is the point at which one is freed from all knowledge and the ego ("Know-All"); it is a time for cleansing and forgetting as well, a cathartic period when the ego-tainted conscious-ness is supplanted by a new one. In "Forget" he says,

> To be able to forget is to be able to yield
> to God who dwells in deep oblivion.
> Only in sheer oblivion are we with God.
> For when we know in full, we have left off
> knowing.

16. *Fantasia of the Unconscious* (New York, 1922), Ch. XIV.
17. *Women in Love* (New York, 1920), Ch. XIV.

In the process of death, hence, Lawrence sees the death of the old, knowing self, and the birth of a new man. In "Gladness of Death" he puts it this way:

> I can feel myself unfolding in the dark
> sunshine of death
> to something flowery and fulfilled, and with
> a strange sweet perfume.
> Men prevent one another from being men
> but in the great spaces of death
> the winds of the afterwards kiss us
> into blossom of manhood.

Lawrence's concept of decay and corruption, followed by rebirth and renewal, can be seen especially in the beautiful poem "Shadows," which begins with a longing for peace in the sleep of death and in "the hands of God":

> And if tonight my soul may find her peace
> in sleep, and sink in good oblivion,
> and in the morning wake like a new-opened
> flower
> then I have been dipped again in God, and
> new-created.

The feelings then recounted are those in which the poet recognizes the ultimate meaning of the experience of death and rebirth:

> And if, as weeks go round, in the dark of
> the moon
> my spirit darkens and goes out, and soft
> strange gloom
> pervades my movements and my thoughts
> and words
> then I shall know that I am walking still
> with God, we are close together now the
> moon's in shadow.

The lines that follow are endemic to most of Lawrence's death poetry, with references to autumn, to "the pain of falling leaves," to "dissolution and distress." Death is not some new experience in remote isolation, but one that is closely associated with Lawrence's "vital and magnificent God," whose presence is a crucial one in the process of death:

> And if, as autumn deepens and darkens
> I feel the pain of falling leaves, and
> stems that break in storms
> and trouble and dissolution and distress
> and then the softness of deep shadows
> folding, folding

around my soul and spirit, around my lips
so sweet, like a swoon, or more like the
   drowse of a low, sad song
singing darker than the nightingale, on,
   on to the solstice
and the silence of short days, the silence
   of the year, the shadow,
then I shall know that my life is moving
   still
with the dark earth, and drenched
with the deep oblivion of earth's lapse and
   renewal.

And if, in the changing phases of man's life
I fall in sickness and in misery
my wrists seem broken and my heart seems dead
and strength is gone, and my life
is only the leavings of a life:

and still, among it all, snatches of lovely
   oblivion, and snatches of renewal
odd, wintry flowers upon the withered stem,
   yet new, strange flowers
such as my life has not brought forth before,
   new blossoms of me—

then I must know that still
I am in the hands of the unknown God,
he is breaking me down to his oblivion
to send me forth on a new morning, a new man.

Without doubt, the most memorable and remarkable of Lawrence's death poems is "The Ship of Death." It is a poem that nullifies R.P. Blackmur's critical judgment that Lawrence in his poetry left only "the ruins of great intentions; ruins which we may admire and contemplate, but as they are ruins of life merely, cannot restore poetry."[18] This poem, it should be remembered, was written by a dying man, and in it Lawrence shows the great skill of a true craftsman in harmonizing form and experience. It will be seen, too, that the "discipline of craft" that Blackmur accuses Lawrence of lacking in his poetry is as pervasive here as is the intensity of the visionary experience itself. The poem is the outgrowth of Lawrence's deepest religious feelings, and its spiritual integrity embraces its artistic expression as well. The discipline, for the lack of which Blackmur uses the word "hysteria," can be seen throughout, as, in fact, it can be seen in the ultimate and transcendent meaning and efficacy of the poem: in its tranquillity, its moderation, its reverence and piety, and

18. "D.H. Lawrence and Expressive Form," *Language as Gesture* (London, 1954), 300.

not least, its integrity. Moreover, in its form, which is of no less importance, the "discipline of craft" cannot be escaped: the "voyage of oblivion" that is described is both a symbolized experience and an artistic achievement of undeniable brilliance.

In his essay Blackmur refers to "The Ship of Death" as a poem in which the hysteric mode carries the pathetic fallacy and the confusion of symbols beyond any resolution. He makes this indictment within the whole context of his belief not only that Lawrence wrote from a "tortured Protestant sensibility" but also that he was a victim of "the plague of expressive form." Even when he admits that Lawrence was a religious poet, with a pious and honest recognition of life, he stresses that "Only with Lawrence the piety was tortured—the torture of incomplete affirmation."[19] A close examination of "The Ship of Death" will show, however, the indefensibility of this entire thesis. The intensity of the expression of this poem produces not the effect and prevalence of disorder and despair, as Blackmur concludes, but a deep religious intensity arising from the poet's integrity of affirmation. The very fact that such integrity is constantly evident is indicative, at the same time, of the extent of the poet's sense of control and order, of a poetic inspiration that does not surrender to sentimental banalities and vain and empty feelings. Blackmur's concern is with the need for a rational application of the "discipline of craft," as opposed to Lawrence's "demon of inspiration." Furthermore, his belief that there must be an "external criterion to show whether the demon is working or not" would diminish or discard the power of full and unfettered expression that a poet must be capable of in the poetry of truth-seeking. Blackmur, thus, would impose external criteria, on a rational and aesthetic basis, even to the extent of including and coloring that which is, presumably, inviolable—the integrity of the artist's experience as it affects his art.

Blackmur is concerned, then, not with the unalloyed truthfulness of one's expression of feelings but with some sort of an "orderly" dialectical imposition of form and craft, that is to say, external poetic elements and technique superimposed on a spontaneous expression of the meaning and truth of life experience. This, at least, is the major inference to be drawn from his overall discussion of Lawrence's poetry. His concern, consequently, is with the formalistic and technical essentials of discipline and order, and he distrusts any kind of vision (in this case Lawrence's) in which there is, as he claims, a lack of orderly insight. He even hearkens back, rather vaguely, to the great mystics (who they are we are not told), for "in them, reason was

19. *Ibid.*, 299.

stretched to include disorder and achieved mystery. In Lawrence the reader is left to supply the reason and the form; for Lawrence only expresses the substance."[20] If by this vague generalization, Blackmur means that "these" mystics often fashioned their feelings according to a particular theology, or that they embraced, arbitrarily, "the reason and the form" of some specific religious way, he is perhaps not far from the truth. Moreover, to "stretch" reason, as Blackmur would have it, necessarily implies a blasphemy against the whole mystery of life, for real mystery is not a forced achievement but an organic process of human experience and awareness. The fact remains that Lawrence was not at all content with any external and contrived disciplines interfering with the natural living relatedness and movement of life. Nor did he seek to "achieve" some ecstatic and beatific state, or what the mystic terms *enosis* with the One.

What Blackmur attacks in Lawrence's poetry is in some ways analogous to what T.S. Eliot attacks in Lawrence's prose. Blackmur sees in Lawrence's poems a disorderliness of vision and insight, a lack of rational imagination and form, a "heightening fire of hysteria." "But in his poetry," he claims, "the very intensity of his self-expression overwhelmed all other considerations, and the disorder alone prevailed." Similarly, Eliot, in his foreword to Father Tiverton's study on Lawrence, describes Lawrence as an "impatient" and "impulsive" man, "a man of fitful and profound insights." Eliot also notes Lawrence's religious importance and sensitivity but believes Lawrence's findings are too often "ill-formed" and the outgrowth of "ignorance": "Lawrence was an ignorant man in the sense that he was unaware of how much he did not know."[21] It was in his earlier book *After Strange Gods* that Eliot's assessment of Lawrence was definitively stated. To Eliot, Lawrence is "an almost perfect example of the heretic" and lacks the capacity for "self-criticism": "The point is that Lawrence started life wholly free from any restriction of tradition or institution, that he had no guidance except the Inner Light, the most untrustworthy and deceitful guide that ever offered itself to wandering humanity."[22] Blackmur and Eliot see in Lawrence's art a religious sensitivity, piety, and honesty. But both conclude that his religious vision is disorderly and unstable, ultimately untrustworthy and unreliable. "The man's vision is spiritual, but spiritually sick."[23] This is Eliot's conclusion regarding Lawrence's

20. *Ibid.*, 299.
21. See T.S. Eliot's foreword to Father William Tiverton (pseud. of Father Martin Jarrett-Kerr, C.R.), *D.H. Lawrence and Human Existence* (London, 1951), vii, viii.
22. T.S. Eliot, *After Strange Gods* (London, 1934), 59.
23. *Ibid.*, 60.

art and thought, and it is more or less the same as that uttered by Blackmur.

Both critics commit the serious critical fallacy of confusing and impugning the meaning of integrity and its place in art. With Lawrence it is precisely this integrity, or what A. Alvarez has termed "a complete truth to feeling,"[24] that gives to his art the greatness of its vision and meaning. Within this integrity, both disorder and order must be included, for life is an unmitigated expression of both. How clearly Lawrence recognized this can be seen in the words of the poem "The Breath of Life":

> The breath of life and the sharp winds of
> change are the same thing.
> But people who are fallen from the organic
> connection with the cosmos
> feel the winds of change grind them down.

At this point, likewise, one can better comprehend Lawrence's own observation on the value of free verse, as stated in his preface to the American edition of his *New Poems*. Free verse, according to him, "is, or should be the direct utterance from the instant, whole man. It is the soul and the mind and body surging at once, nothing left out. They speak all together. There is some confusion, some discord. But the confusion and discord only belong to the reality, as noise belongs to the plunge of water."[25] What he has to say about free verse is true of his total approach to his poetry. And it is particularly true of his poems on death.

Integrity is to be found not in the remoteness of the artist's attempts to achieve a sort of superhuman excellence, but in the unisolated, unviolated reality of the living moments of life. Lawrence's art does not ultimately stand or fall on the basis of any exoteric discipline and the support of "rational" imagination and aesthetic form, or on the basis of some sort of acquired theological orthodoxy, but rather on the spontaneous intensity of his integrity and feeling, wrought from the reality of life. He does not approach the meaning of life from a position outside of it, but rather from within, and it is this process of living, naked experience—one in which purpose and "passionate inspiration" are not divorced—that he invariably depicts in his poetry. Indeed, back in 1913, when he was breaking away from Georgian influences, Lawrence, in a letter to Edward Marsh, clearly defined his position in words that were, through the years, to become increasingly paramount in his approach

24. *The Shaping Spirit: Studies in Modern English and American Poets* (London, 1958), 141.
25. *Phoenix*, 200–21.

to poetry: "I think I read my poetry more by length than by stress—as a matter of movements in space than footsteps hitting the earth . . . it is the hidden *emotional* pattern that makes poetry, not the obvious form. . . . It doesn't depend on the ear, particularly, but on the sensitive soul."[26]

Whether one terms Lawrence's poetry the result of "pure passionate experience" or of "the sensitive soul," it cannot be denied that he combined emotional reality and a visionary insight that gave to his work a uniqueness and a meaningfulness of perception. To have regulated the inner meaning of Lawrence's vision would have vitiated the power of its integrity and perception. Then, it could not have been a vision at all, but an externalized and passive mode of feeling and experience, planned, defined, and regulated. This process would have subjected and reduced Lawrence's art and thought to a kind of theory and thesis—the very kind of falseness and formalism (of "the rule and measure mathematical folk") that he struggled against all along. "They want me to have form," he once wrote; "that means, they want me to have *their* pernicious ossiferous skin-and-grief form, and I won't."[27]

With the preceding in mind, one can approach Lawrence's poem "The Ship of Death" with a more sympathetic and appreciative understanding. As one of the last pieces of work of a poet of mature genius, it should be read in conjunction with such writings as *The Man Who Died, Apocalypse,* and *Etruscan Places,* all of which were written in Lawrence's final years of life. Like *The Man Who Died* it shows the direction of Lawrence's thought, especially his belief that the resurrection of life is not a matter of sin and salvation. Like *Apocalypse,* above all, it shows a decided distrust of doctrinal promises of afterlife: "But by the time of Christ all religion and all thought seemed to turn from the old worship and study of vitality, potency, power, to the study of death and death-rewards, death-penalties, and morals. All religion, instead of being religion of *life,* here and now, became religion of postponed destiny, death, and reward *afterwards,* 'if you are good.' "[28]

However, it is with his travel book *Etruscan Places,* published after Lawrence's death, that "The Ship of Death" has a much closer thematic affinity, as well as a structural relationship. During the last part of March and the first week of April 1927, Lawrence and Earl Brewster toured the buried cities and cemeteries of Etruria in central

---

26. *The Letters of D.H. Lawrence,* 155–57. Dated November 19, 1913.
27. *Ibid.,* 89. Dated December 24, 1912.
28. *Apocalypse,* Ch. VI.

Italy. Lawrence had been impressed by what he had seen earlier, during the spring of 1926, in the museums of Perugia, Florence, and Rome, and it was this that influenced him, a year later, to begin his systematic tours of the Etruscan sites from Cerveteri to Volterra. This Etruscan pilgrimage was for Lawrence an inspiring and revealing experience. Brewster recalled that even "the symbolism, as he explained it, seemed so convincing that I could but wonder at the variety of explanations archaeologists give to it."[29] What especially impressed Lawrence was the living religious feeling and sensitivity that he believed to be inherent in the ancient Etruscan civilization: its "delicate sensitiveness," simplicity, naturalness, and spontaneity:

> For oh, I know, in the dust where we have
>   buried
> The silenced races and all their abominations,
> We have buried so much of the delicate
>   magic of life.[30]

In and around the tombs, Lawrence saw and admired the Etruscan symbols of the phallic stone and *arx*, which to him suggested the continuance of life in the mystery of death. His interpretation of the carved stone house, or chest, over the doorway of some of the tombs is especially interesting: "The stone house . . . suggests the Noah's Ark box we had as children, full of animals. And that is what it is, the Ark, the *arx*, the womb. The womb of all the world, that brought forth all creatures. The womb, the *arx*, where life retreats in the last refuge. The womb, the ark of the covenant, in which lies the mystery of eternal life, the manna and the mysteries."[31] There is no doubt that the Etruscan concept and depiction of death provided him with the imagery and symbolism for which he was always searching: "In the

29. Brewster, *D.H. Lawrence*, 123. See Harry T. Moore, *The Life and Works of D.H. Lawrence* (New York, 1951), 288–89. See also Frieda Lawrence, *Not I, but the Wind . . .* (New York, 1934), 208, for Lawrence's letter of April 14, 1927, to Frau Baronin von Richthofen: "I am home again—I returned Monday evening from Volterra. I had a very beautiful week with Brewster. We went to Cerveteri, Tarquinia, and Vulci, Grosseto and Volterra, not far from the sea, north of Rome. The Etruscan tombs are very interesting and so nice and lovable. They were a living, fresh, jolly people, lived their own lives without wanting to dominate the lives of others. I am fond of my Etruscans— they had life in themselves, so they had no need to govern others. I want to write some sketches of these Etruscan places, not scientifically, but only as they are now and the impression they make."

30. *Collected Poems*, 377.

31. *Etruscan Places* (London, 1932), Ch. I. "*Etruscan Places* is the record of a spiritual act of excavation. Among the treasures he exhumed there was something of his own essential being. The Etruscans provided him with a group of symbols," writes Christopher Hassall in his "D.H. Lawrence and the Etruscans," in *Essays by Divers Hands*, ed. Peter Green (Oxford, 1962), XXXI, 71.

tombs we see it; throes of wonder and vivid feeling throbbing over death. Man moves naked and glowing through the universe. Then comes death: he dives into the sea, he departs into the underworld."[32] And it was the depiction of death as a further sojourn in the "living continuum" that primarily attracted him: "But one radical thing the Etruscan people never forgot, because it was in their blood as well as in the blood of their masters: and that was the mystery of the journey out of life, and into death; the death-journey, and the sojourn in the after-life. The wonder of their soul continued to play round the mystery of this journey and this sojourn."[33] The Etruscan concept of death as a sojourn in the afterlife so impressed Lawrence that in "The Ship of Death" he was to think of death almost exactly in these terms. The actual Etruscan death scene, which is reembodied in and even made the central *motif* in the poem, is clearly described by Lawrence in his essay "Cerveteri":

> Through the inner doorway is the last chamber, small and dark and culminative. Facing the door goes the stone bed on which was laid, presumably, the Lucumo and the sacred treasures of the dead, the little bronze ship of death that should bear him over to the other world, the vases of jewels for his arraying, the vases of small dishes, the little bronze statuettes and tools, the weapons, the armour: all the amazing impedimenta of the important dead.[34]

Written in free verse, "The Ship of Death" is divided into ten sections. The tone throughout is one of reverence and affirmation, expressed in a language of lyrical beauty, a vibrant rhythm, and a vigorous diction. The "journey of the soul" is described here, but the poem is free of any pervasive sense of despair or stoic abnegation, or the kind of moving but extreme, almost uncontrollable pathos encountered in some of the early poems relating to the death of his mother, such as these lines of "The Virgin Mother":

> Is the last word now uttered?
> Is the farewell said?
> Spare me the strength to leave you
> Now you are dead.
> I must go, but my soul lies helpless
> Beside your bed.[35]

Certainly, it is a death poetry that is singularly free of the enervating remorsefulness that is found, for example, in Baudelaire:

> —Et de longs corbillards, sans tambours

32. *Ibid.*, Ch. III.
33. *Ibid.*, Ch. III.
34. *Ibid.*, Ch. I.
35. *Collected Poems*, 119.

> ni musique,
> Défilent lentement dans mon âme; l'Espoir,
> Vaincu, pleure, et l'angoisse atroce,
>   despotique,
> Sur mon crâne incliné plante son drapeau noir.[36]

Indeed, in contrast with Gerard Manley Hopkins's "terrible post-humous sonnets," "The Ship of Death" is not in any way desolate or despairing, in the sense that Hopkins speaks of in such lines as "With this tormented mind tormenting yet," "I wake and feel the fell of dark, not day":

> Here! creep,
> Wretch, under a comfort serves in a
>   whirlwind; all
> Life death does end and each day dies
>   with sleep.[37]

Death is not to be approached as some sort of inevitable surrender to a greater retributive power, for judgment and punishment in some realm outside of time, but simply as a phase of one's life-journey. Lawrence avoids thinking of death as limited in some time sequence, with a beginning and an end, as "a continuity in an eternal line." His whole approach to death in this poem must be seen in direct relation to what he says in *Apocalypse:* "The pagan conception of time as moving in cycles is much freer, it allows movement upwards and downwards, and allows for a complete change of the state of mind, at any moment. One cycle finished, we can drop or rise to another level, and be in a new world at once. But by our time-continuum method, we have to trail wearily on over another ridge."[38]

From the very beginning of "The Ship of Death," there is a tranquillity of feeling and acceptance arising from a positive belief that marks the start of a long journey. In the first section an autumnal mood prevails, for "Now it is autumn and the falling fruit." It is a time "to go, to bid farewell," a time when the apples are "falling like great drops of dew." Yet, even in the midst of this serene feeling, there is no surrender to despair. It is time, simply time, Lawrence says, when one must move on into a new world and accept the reality of the flux of life:

> And it is time to go, to bid farewell
> to one's own self, and find an exit
> from the fallen self.

---

36. "Spleen" (iv), *Flowers of Evil*, trans. Edna St. Vincent Millay (New York, 1936), 158. With the original French texts and with a preface by Millay.

37. See *Poems of Gerard Manley Hopkins*, ed. W.H. Gardner (London, 1949), 106, 107, 109.

38. Ch. IX.

In the second section, the distinct figure of the ship of death, which Lawrence had first seen in his Etruscan travels, appears in the first line:

> Have you built your ship of death, O
> have you?
> O build your ship of death, for you
> will need it.

He goes on to point out that "the grim frost is at hand, when the apples will fall." The analogy of human death with the apples that will fall "on the hardened earth" is a striking one and fits in quite well with the consistent Lawrentian pattern of the living interdependence of the whole of nature and human life that was first to appear at the beginning of *The Rainbow* (1914), where the Brangwen family is seen in relation to the "pulse and body of the soil." In the lines that follow there is, understandably, a feeling of uncertain expectation, for the smell of death is in the air, and the "bruised body," like "the apples falling like great drops of dew," now awaits its turn for the journey to a new realm:

> And death is on the air like a smell of
> ashes!
> Ah! can't you smell it?
> And in the bruised body, the frightened
> soul
> finds itself shrinking, wincing from
> the cold
> that blows upon it through the orifices.

The third section presents the difficult question of how one can make his own quietus in the presence of death:

> With daggers, bodkins, bullets, man can make
> a bruise or break of exit for his life;
> but is that a quietus, O tell me, is it quietus?

Lawrence is completely aware of the temptation and fatalism that sometimes arise in an unhappy contemplation of death. But his rejection of suicide is a categorical one:

> Surely not so! for how could murder, even
> self-murder ever a quietus make?

His reverence for life is too great to give way to despair; and the acceptance of one's departure from the known into the unknown is too sacred to be sacrificed in a fit of disillusionment. Here, too, it might be noted that when Lawrence was informed of the death by suicide of his friend the American poet and publisher Harry Crosby in 1929, he cried: "That's all he could do with life, throw it away. How could he betray the great privilege of life?"[39] If there is anything to be sacrificed, Lawrence says in the poem "Self-Sacrifice," it should *not* be the "good, healthy, natural feelings, instincts, passions or desires," but "all the obstructions to life, self-importance, self-conceit, egoistic self-will," all the ugly impediments "to the free motion of life."

The momentary questioning of the third section soon gives way to a gathering tranquillity and reverence:

> O let us talk of quiet that we know,
> that we can know, the deep and lovely quiet
> of a strong heart at peace!

Following this, sections five and six go on to describe the "long and painful death / that lies between the old self and the new." Nonetheless, there is an absence of any feeling of panic or paralyzing fear. There is the realization of one's need, painful as it may be, to cleanse himself of an old, debilitated consciousness and to build "the ship of death" for the long journey to oblivion:

> Already our bodies are fallen, bruised,
>   badly bruised,
> already our souls are oozing through
>   the exit
> of the cruel bruise.
>
> Already the dark and endless ocean
>   of the end
> is washing in through the breaches of
>   our wounds,
> already the flood is upon us.
>
> Oh build your ship of death, your
>   little ark
> and furnish it with food, with little
>   cakes, and wine
> for the dark flight down oblivion.

In the meantime, a momentary feeling of fear arises and the poet appears to be adrift and isolated. The body is now dying piecemeal, and "the timid soul / has her footing washed away, as the dark flood rises":

> We are dying, we are dying, piecemeal our
>   bodies are dying
> and our strength leaves us,
> and our soul cowers naked in the dark rain
>   over the flood,
> cowering in the last branches of the tree
>   of our life.

39. Quoted by Brewster, *D.H. Lawrence*, 308.

The seventh section reads almost like a religious hymnal or chant. The poet realizes the certainty of death, yet he also realizes the certainty of a new journey into the unknown:

> We are dying, we are dying, so all we can do
> is now to be willing to die, and to build
>   the ship
> of death to carry the soul on the longest
>   journey
>
> A little ship, with oars and food
> and little dishes, and all accoutrements
> fitting and ready for the departing soul.

The painful process of physical death itself now comes to a climax as the body dies and the soul departs. But death is characterized by an acceptance of a new challenge and by a steadfast resolution to move on:

> Now launch the small ship, now as the body dies
> and life departs, launch out, the fragile soul
> in the fragile ship of courage, the ark of faith
> with its store of foods and little cooking pans
> and change of clothes,
> upon the flood's black waste
> upon the waters of the end
> upon the sea of death, where still we sail
> darkly, for we cannot steer, and have no port.

In the remainder of this section there is also a recognition that

> There is no port, there is nowhere to go
> only the deepening blackness darkening still
> blacker upon the soundless, ungurgling flood.

"The deepening blackness darkening still," so that "there is no direction any more," is not an implication of nothingness or purposelessness, but rather the understandably awkward attempt to depict verbally the magnitude of the infinite mystery and wonder of the death journey. The ship of death has departed, and its voyage is now a part of a greater mystery and wonder:

> and the little ship is there; yet she is gone.
> She is not seen, for there is nothing to see
>   her by.
> She is gone! gone! and yet
> somewhere she is there.
> Nowhere!

In death, Lawrence says in the next section (eight), "everything is gone, the body is gone":

> The upper darkness is heavy as the lower,
> between them the little ship
> is gone.

> It is the end, it is oblivion.

Yet, what he means by "oblivion" and "darkness" is clarified in the last two sections (nine and ten). Certainly, the terms do not signify doom and annihilation. The first four lines of the ninth section depict metaphorically a continuing connection between life and death:

> And yet out of eternity a thread
> separates itself on the blackness,
> a horizontal thread
> that fumes a little with pallor upon the dark.

There is here, and in the next and final section of the poem, a very definite sense of brave endurance and hope. The fuming pallor of the thread that comes out from eternity is not at all an illusionary one:

> Ah wait, wait, for there's the dawn,
> the cruel dawn of coming back to life
> out of oblivion.

The ship of death, now "drifting, beneath the deathly ashy-grey / of a flood-dawn," is no longer engulfed in the blackness and darkness of the "soundless, ungurgling flood," described earlier in section seven. Significantly, there is now a flush of yellow and rose:

> Wait, wait! even so, a flush of yellow
> and strangely, O chilled wan soul, a
> flush of rose.

> A flush of rose, and the whole thing
> starts again.

It remains for the concluding section of the poem to give complete, unerring expression to Lawrence's religious vision. It is a case in which, as Kenneth Rexroth has observed, "The craft is the vision and the vision is the craft."[40] It is a vision that is expressed in a language that is simple and direct, arising from both a realized strength of conviction and an undoubting intuitiveness and inspiration. Not only in its dignity and hope, but also in its piety and humility, his vision echoes an unqualified message of rebirth and renewal, when "the little ship wings home" and the "frail soul steps out," "filling the heart with peace" at the end of the "voyage of oblivion":

> The flood subsides, and the body, like a worn

---

40. *D.H. Lawrence: Selected Poems*, with an introduction by Kenneth Rexroth (New York, 1947), 15.

sea-shell
emerges strange and lovely.
And the little ship wings home, faltering and
   lapsing
on the pink flood,
and the frail soul steps out, into the house
   again
filling the heart with peace.

Swings the heart renewed with peace
even of oblivion.

Oh build your ship of death. Oh build it!
for you will need it.
For the voyage of oblivion awaits you.

7

The New Logos

I

DALE VREE IS A POLITICAL SCIENTIST who conceives his task to be that of
"conceptual analysis." Examining "the subject of synthetic Marxist-
Christian dialogue," Vree weighs the intellectual consequences of
efforts to Christianize Marxism or communize Christianity. In his
book *On Synthesizing Marxism and Christianity*,[1] he advances the
thesis that Marxism and Christianity are discrete systems of belief,
intellectually and spiritually antithetical and incompatible. His book
is written in the tradition of analytic philosophy, treating "Marxism
and Christianity as social facts, as the conceptual systems which
they are." Exegesis and apologetics are outside his special purview, as
he attempts to show how syntheses of Marxism and Christianity
"violate the living boundaries of the living linguistic traditions" of
each. His approach is critically dispassionate and discriminating; and
it is invariably provocative. He focuses on hard and central issues
with a relentlessness and seriousness rarely met in an age addicted to
the habits of relativism and revisionism. The word "dialogue," which
for many defies any incongruity between aspiration and reality, has
become a sacred word that it is perilous to question or doubt. Vree
addresses himself to the pitfalls of dialogue in the belief that there is a
Christian orthodoxy and a Marxist orthodoxy. The pull of sentiment,
of empty idealism, or of muddled rhetoric has no distorting place in
Vree's vindicating demonstration of his paramount goal: to "show
how dialogical Christians and dialogical Marxists, in departing from
their respective orthodoxies, place more weight on the concept of
human freedom than their respective belief systems can sustain, and
hence fall into philosophical confusion."

Also stressing, though from another perspective, the aim of synthesis, Jerrold Seigel in a "psychological biography," *Marx's Fate:
The Shape of a Life*,[2] employs a psychohistorical approach that

1. New York, 1976.
2. Princeton, N.J., 1978.

148

strives to interrelate Marx's public and private behavior and his thinking. "The shape of a life" is indicated by the titles of the three main parts of Seigel's book, "Becoming Marx," "Involvement and Isolation," "Economics: Marx's Fate." Seigel's purpose is summarized by Marx's own words, which Seigel uses as one of the epigraphs to the book: "In the general relationship which the philosopher establishes between the world and thought, he merely makes objective the relation between his particular consciousness and the real world." The delineation of Marx's "exemplary presence in the development of modern consciousness" is competent and illuminating. At its worst psychoanalytic literature can lead to strange and perverse interpretations; even in the psychoanalytic community it is admitted that psychoanalysis has "landed itself in a morass of reified concepts." Seigel's book does not suffer from those clinical animadversions that one has learned to expect to find (sometimes to one's horror) in books dealing with "literature and psychology." Here, Marx's "inward terrain"—that is, the psychological themes and patterns, as well as the determinants, of his life—is examined sympathetically and responsibly. Seigel is careful to insist that "the overall configuration of Marx's life was formed as much by the general shape of historical change in the nineteenth century as by his particular manner of experiencing it." (In terms of style, however, *Marx's Fate* has faults: throughout, the writing is tedious, dull, prolix. One feels mercilessly exposed to those stylistic liabilities associated with the writings of many American academics.)

Seigel helps one to understand how "Marx's fate" is reflected in Marx's doctrine; how and why (when one considers Vree's findings) the synthesis of Marxism and Christianity is problematic. The picture of Marx is entirely pertinent to making a psychohistorical connection with the individuating sociotheological implications that Vree presents. The Marx we see before us is a man who, in conveying his vision of an "unmediated humanism," discloses commitment, single-mindedness, and sincerity. Marx possessed an intrinsic religious fervor that enabled him to arrive at a social morality that he identified with an exclusively material life and, beyond that, with the absolute good. But whatever the religious earnestness behind his ideas, he did not deviate from his major idea that the "Criticism of religion is the foundation of all criticism." Seigel's book reminds one of the depth of Marx's hostility to religious life, and also makes one of his celebrated observations, in *A Contribution to the Critique of Political Economy* (1859), more revealing: "It is not the consciousness of men that determines their existence, but, on the contrary, their social existence determines their consciousness." Even a cursory look at Marx's life discloses a lack of any spiritual essence. One looks in vain for the slightest sympathy for the spiritual. Marx's obsession with "critiquing" the social universe precluded such sympathy, or understanding. Yet one could not expect much more from a social and economic theorist who has been revered as a "philosopher of action"—and whom his father called a "demonic genius." As one of his Young Hegelian friends said of him: "Imagine Rousseau, Voltaire, Holbach, Lessing, Heine, and Hegel fused into one person—I say fused, not juxtaposed—and you have Dr. Marx."

The fact is that Marx, like Freud, as Robert L. Heilbroner has suggested in citing the homology between the tasks of the social theorist and the psychoanalytical theorist, had therapeutic aims in mind in his diagnosis of the social mystery. One of Marx's most interweaving ideas relates to the irreducible importance of the "materialist" element in any view of the social universe or any judgment of life as it is lived, or not lived, in the world of social facts and statistics. For Marx, as for the Marxist doctrine, the materialist component is the equivalent of the spiritual component found in religious faith. Marx's vision constitutes a repudiation of any *recognition* of supernaturalist realities. "Either everything in man can be traced as a development from below, or something must come from above," wrote T.S. Eliot. "There is no avoiding that dilemma: you must be either a naturalist or a supernaturalist." Eliot's words alert one to the kind of dialogue that, as exponents from both sides suggest, should start from a sociomoral level rather than from a religious one. In other words, dialogue should start from a naturalist premise: "from below." Marx's own words speak volumes: "Communism as completed naturalism is humanism and as completed humanism is naturalism." If, then, Marx and the Marxists refuse any recognition to the supernatural reality, they also fail to recognize the existence of "Original Sin." Marx's conception of morality must be seen, in these contexts, as a utopian theology, which Albert Camus rightly labeled a "horizontal transcendence." The Feuerbachian influence on Marx— "we all became Feuerbachians," Engels exclaimed—cannot be underestimated: Feuerbach's contention that religion was a "mystified" knowledge of man, its secret was "anthropological," found its apogee in Marx and in his method of analysis.

II

Karl Marx remains inescapable, if many-sided, particularly for those ideologues who, sharing his desire to change the world rather than to interpret it, endorse his contention that "not criticism but revolution is the driving force of history." That "Marx's fate" is tied up with modern man's fate accents the continuing drama of this inescapability. Charles Darwin and Sigmund Freud pale in significance in comparison with Marx. Only Christ poses any formidable challenge to Marx's position of primacy, though such an admission hardly diminishes the ascendant role of Marx in modern society. In the secular city Marx, not Christ, determines man's fate. Twentieth-century life, examined in terms of the state of the soul, makes temptation and blasphemy quintessential: the appeal of Marx grows as that of Christ lessens; the cult of science and utopian socialism exerts a fascination that transforms into the illusion and the delusion determining man's destiny and thought. The appeal of Marxism is best gauged by Simone Weil: "If you do not believe in the remote, silent, secret omnipotence of a spirit, there remains only the manifest omnipotence of matter." The socioeconomic situation increasingly confirms the bleak and terrifying truth of these words. Strange new gods—whether as Marx's god of social matter or as the technologico-Benthamite god of the machine—abound; millions worship at their altars. Social necessity, as posited by Marx in both his political criticism and his economic theory, points to the "pure" truth of materialist solutions. Marxism has become, in its own right, a form of religion with its own ultimates and its own answer to ultimate questions: an answer that Simone Weil described, in all of its dark and dreadful ramifications, as what "ultimately regard[s] matter as a machine for manufacturing the good."

A concern with the common good often brings together movements that are antipodal. This concern has led Marxist and Christian to retreat from a historical position of confrontation to one of ideological encounter. What once actuated a crisis of separability has been transformed into a demand for dialogue and synthesis. And what has been hitherto accepted as unbridgeable in terms of first principles has been metastasized into a process of transcendence and reconciliation. The desire to "reformulate" older positions and "modernize" basic doctrines has been a powerful one among increasing numbers of Marxists and Christians. For some Marxists the political leap over Christian eschatology has been no insuperable problem. And for some Christians the religious leap over that materialistic value that Simone Weil pointed to has been relatively conscienceless. The quest for dialogue has tended to blur established definitions and to topple standards of discrimination. Where economic theory ends and where theology begins are matters of little importance. Enlightenment is now the overarching word, the new Logos: increasingly and incessantly, the eminences of enlightenment legislate an affirming "pluralism, compassion and social hope." A postmodern and post-Christian civilization, we are told, needs to adjust to the dynamic conditions of a new and radicalizing vision of man. The modern gospel of sociology, preaching as it does an orthodoxy of messianic materialism, and now allying itself to nuclear power, cybernetics, and computers, is everywhere commanding and pervasive.

If "liberation" theologians like the American Harvey Cox and the German Juergen Moltmann have their way, the chronolatry that Jacques Maritain warned against in his *Le paysan de la Garonne* (1966) will have become a grim prophecy of our destiny. The attempts to synthesize Marxism and Christianity can be dated, among Catholics, from the papacy of John XXIII and the Second Vatican Council and, among (de-Stalinizing) Communists, from the Twentieth Party Congress of the Soviet Communist Party. Among the Protestants the roots of this dialogue go back to Moltmann's "theology of hope" born in the sixties. Cox's main contribution goes back to 1965, when his most significant and influential book, *The Secular City*, was published. The antisupernaturalist example of Marx gradually turning from philosophy to empirical data is being reinforced by Christians turning from a biblical God to what Cox calls the God who is in and of the "social matrix"; the God who is subordinated to the zeitgeist. The often passionate pleas for dialogue and synthesis can also be placed against a concurrent yearning for "the demystification of authority." The Marxist-Christian dialogue is itself a portent of the politicizing process that grips modern life and thought, an offshoot of the liberalism and the radicalism that have become unquestioned power centers of twentieth-century civilization. Indeed, the Marxist-Christian dialogue must be seen as the religious manifestation of the reigning ethos of enlightenment. Yet to speak of it as a "religious manifestation" is to describe what is, in reality, a politicized and reified religiosity. *On Synthesizing Marxism and Christianity* serves as a warning against the gradual triumph of what Vree terms "the sin of messianic atheism." The Christian-Marxist encounter, to employ the euphemism, concretizes, in its most contemporary development, Marx's demand, posited in "On the Jewish Question" (1843): "We do not change secular questions into theological ones. We change theological questions into secular ones."

The Marxist-Christian dialogue is an additional and a prescient sign of "the end of the modern world," to quote the late Romano Guardini, the final desacralization of the world, the triumph of Mass Man. It signifies capitulation to "the materialist conception of history," as the symbolic value of existence, pointing to the divine and the eternal, is further subordinated to what Heinrich Heine spoke of as the need for "the rehabilitation of matter" and thus ultimately to the science of economics. It is Dostoevsky's "poem" of the Grand Inquisitor being written anew, with a vengeance. Marxist-Christian dialogue becomes another vehicle for giving modern man the polity he wants: the "normal satisfaction of all desires," as Marx put it, but for which there is another and truer term: Earthly Paradise. Marxist theories can be dispensed with in terms of their transitoriness. But the Marxist system of values, as Ignazio Silone insisted, remains monolithic, the basis on which one constructs a culture, a civilization—the faith of a new Logos and the faith in the new age. In opposition to the rogue political theorists (e.g., the Marxist Roger Garaudy) and the sham theologians, Vree focuses precisely on Marxist values as they are distinguished from Christian values. Marxist and Christian dialogists may yearn desperately for a "theology of joy," for what Heinrich Böll, the German recipient of the Nobel Prize for literature in 1973, called "a new tenderness in theology," but in the end a theory of theological (and political) tenderness prevails. This bridging of idealistic aspirations and materialistic conceptions constitutes yet another theory of liberation and desire: delusive, escapist, comforting, idealizing. (Stubborn facts, Irving Babbitt maintained, are as nothing compared with stubborn theory.) Marx's great idea, and undoubtedly his overriding value, lies in his belief that in human society any change must occur through material transformations. No true Christian can accept the hegemony of this Marxist value.

Dialogists who point to similarities between Christ and Marx; who, like the Brazilian archbishop Dom Helder Camara, encourage us to "try to do with Karl Marx today what in his day St. Thomas did with Aristotle"; who believe, with one energumen, that Marxists and Christians, if they can only start their dialogue from agreement, will be better able "to realize a unity of praxis," become the slaves of their own theories. The fundamental clash between Marxist and Christian, pace the dialogical sophists, is between the natural and supernatural. No amount of word-spinning regarding Marx's "methodological atheism," which, it is too glibly claimed, transforms into "the secular complement of Christianity," can ignore this clash. This clash instances a steady yielding of the theological to the sociological and to the economic view of life. Religious tradition, as Incarnation and Revelation, is in retreat; the "spirit of religion," as Edmund Burke termed it, is thwarted by pseudoreligious arguments. To claim that there is an "equivalence" between Marxism and Christianity is a gross violation of their intellectual structures, root presuppositions, and internal language norms. To claim, further, that a religion that cannot survive enlightenment is inauthentic is the kind of specious argument that surrenders to the Marxist dogma of "the truth of this world." This truth is a loaded truth that solidifies the tyranny of "the secular city." The dialogue itself is not a "dialogue of adversaries" but rather a dialogue of equivocators. It is no longer a matter of reexamination or reevaluation or of political or religious expectations. It is a matter of "transhistorical" values: of values that return ultimately to a conception of man: to, for instance, the Marxist view of man's temporal "estrangement" and the Christian view of the Fall in its universal framework. The most decisive contrast between Marxism and Christianity, as Paul Tillich declared, is "the realization between two possibilities of life." Neither dialogue nor any degree of synthesis can reconcile the Marxist value of life in time and the Christian value of life in eternity. "The decision between these two life possibilities," Tillich asserted, "is neither economic nor political; it is religious."

III

It is precisely the "religious" decision in its informing and identifying tensions that the Marxist-Christian encounter ultimately spurns. To believe with Cox and his chiliastic confreres that (as Vree says) "politics must replace metaphysics as the language about God" is to espouse a "theology of fantasy and hope" that is of a piece with Marx's vision of "the end of the quarrel between essence and existence, between freedom and necessity." We live in an age when solutions have absolute categories. A new generation of managers, technicians, and reformist ideologues thrives in all spheres of life. There is no crisis (including the crisis of faith, which, as Tillich noted, comprises both itself and the doubt of itself) that cannot be transformed. Theologians and ecclesiastics now rush to join sociopolitical theorists in heralding the secular gospel of transformation. The consequences of this transformational syndrome are everywhere in bleak evidence as prophecies become conspiracies, proportions become disproportions, order becomes disorder. The imperative need, then, is not for a "dialogue with the modern world" but rather for a review of the table of widespread human values in their astounding incorrectness, as Aleksandr Solzhenitsyn has demanded. Definitions, standards, judgments, in short the hierarchy of values, are now the truly oppressed minority. The new masters of transformation prod us on to the kingdom of depersonalizing ends, when, as even Herbert Marcuse feared, there is a glossing over of real differences. Vree helps us to assess the metaprophetic and metahistorical dimensions of the progressive transformations that characterize the totality of the technicalization of human existence. We have gone beyond Marx and beyond Christ to a stage of history that Vree discerns in words of frightening import: "A genuine synthesis of Marxism and Christianity only takes place after both orthodox Marxism and orthodox Christianity have been dismembered—at which point dialogue turns into monologue."

Enough has been said of dialogue. Its end is that of synthesis, in which it attains its consummation and in which the dialogist theory is verified. The achievement of secular syntheses does have its celebrated examples, and its warnings. Marcuse's *Eros and Civilization* (1955) evidences a form of synthetic progress toward a future of reconciliation. His aim, motivated by a synthesis of Marx and Freud, is "to develop the political and sociological substance of the psychological notions." Marcuse performs a marriage rite of materialisms: the marriage of Freud's sexual materialism and Marx's dialectical and economic materialism. We are given Marcuse's updated and reconstructed psychopolitical version of Marx's desideratum, the point at which man is "author and actor of his own history." Consciousness and action synthesize to create a praxis that affirms, in a Marxist sense, a dialectical ontology and a dialectical epistemology. For Marcuse such a praxis underlines the need "to learn the gay science (*gaya sciencia*) of how to use the social wealth for shaping man's world in accordance with his Life Instincts." The demand for a synthesis of Marx and Christ epitomizes the religious concomitant of what Marcuse speaks of as "the price of progress," in the context of his assertion that "Today the fight for life, the fight for Eros, is the *political* fight." Attempts to synthesize Marxism and Christianity are symptomatic of the obsession with political action that makes an idol of material value. The religious value of life, no less than the religious meaning of man, inevitably becomes a casualty of this reductive process. Man's search for the new Logos may indeed be a noble one. It can also be fatal.

Part III

METAPHYSICS OF POLITICS

·

*There is a center which commands all things,
and this center is open to imaginative but
not logical discovery. It is a focus of value, a
law of relationships, an inspiring vision. By
its very nature it sets up rankings and orders;
to be near it is to be higher; to be far from it
in the sense of not feeling its attraction
is to be lower.*

—RICHARD M. WEAVER

8

Politics and Literature

POLITICS AND LITERATURE, far from being mutually exclusive, give sustenance to each other. Creative vision is shaped and sharpened by the political world, forming as it does a continuous network of historical events, social conditions, political happenings, figures, and decisions. In his own special way the imaginative artist, as novelist or as poet, defines his political identity in his awareness of man as a political animal and of the world as a political situation. For the artist historical consciousness and political consciousness are convergent manifestations of man in society. The artist can, of course, reject history and politics, but he cannot banish their reality; he cannot escape their power, which brushes him wherever he may be, even in his isolation. Belief in the purity of art, an art that is somehow protectively concealed or separated from sociopolitical intrusion and conflict, is an indefensible belief. If the artist's concern is with man, in all of his possibilities, then that concern is in itself a political concern. If the artist is aware of the outer world, then that awareness in itself contains and ultimately discloses a political value. Life in the world prescribes a political existence, even when that existence is not necessarily understood or defined as such. One's existence inevitably means contact with political forces and movements. Each day of one's existence is not without lightning contact with some form of political energy. Even one's life at its earliest and most formative stage in the family has its political ramifications in terms of recognizing authority, relating to others, reacting to governance, rules, responsibilities, standards, and judgments. One's political existence begins with birth and becomes more complex in its progressive assimilation: in a growing comprehension of what lies outside of it, in that great network of interpersonal relationships, of intercourse with others and with institutions, in short, with the world as it is found and as it is developed in time and space. The true artist captures and renders the reaches and the depths of this unfolding existence, in all of its inescapable complexity.

It is not the artist's governing task to define or to criticize politics; nor is he concerned with measuring the nature of man's role in a political framework. The artist leaves it to the political theorist to speculate as to what politics is, that is to say, what it promises both as the art of the possible and as the art of human relations. Awareness, rather than participation, best characterizes the extent of the artist's political involvement. For the artist the goal is ultimately that of charting and communicating as precisely as he can, simultaneously catching the intervening subtleties, man's changing political fate rather than his political action. The novelist, of course, does dramatize actions, all those events in which his characters find themselves and with which they are variously grappling. These events are a character's stuff of life. They pinpoint his immediacy. They constitute an irrevocable dimension of his life stuff and his life rhythm. They are the existentializing occasions of experience that contain his works and days. In a sense these actions, as experience, attain a particularizing cumulativeness that the artist transforms essentially into a chronicle that awakens insight. To record these details of daily experience is for the artist to respond to the world in which human transactions occur. There is no end to these transactions, whether in their external makeup or their internal impact. Whether large or small in importance they make their political impression on life. They register, even if only infinitesimally, the making and the molding of life in the contexts of evolving attitudes, feelings, emotions, and patterns. Insofar as all existence is political, in the sense that one must live in and relate to the world (affirmatively or negatively, or both), inescapable and unremitting in its presentness, its consciousness, man remains a citizen, if also a slave, of the world as polis. There is not a day that passes that he does not receive the world unto death. Even when he does not want to be such a receiver, even when he doesn't seem, or want, to understand the nature of his receptiveness, he phenomenalizes the intrinsic connection between himself and his world. This connection is necessarily political. The artist who truly seeks to portray man in the world must portray this connection in its multiplicity.

Man's existence is a political fact. Whatever his moral, metaphysical, or religious essences—all those abstractions that he comes, in time, to recognize and define, thus also recognizing and defining himself—whatever the spiritual meaning of these may be in their vulnerability and tenuousness, the political aspect of man's being is incontrovertible. Indeed, it can be said that man's political reality is second only to his biological reality. This is another way of instancing man's societal instinct. Man's physical and political selves attain their unity in the encounter. Though this encounter discloses anthropological and sociological emphases, to the artist it is always alive with possibility, with the drama and the dialogue that the anthropologist and the sociologist, no less than the political scientist, see and understand and state statistically, even abjectly. Thus, though Plato is a political philosopher he is also (in this special quality far outshining Aristotle) our earliest novelist with a heightened sense of drama and dialogue. In this respect, the creator penetrates more deeply the meaning of man's political place in that he captures its force of rhythm, its interrelations, the totality of its ebb and flow. The pressures and tensions of man's political situation, where he stands (or hides) in society, and his view of and activities within (or outside) that society come alive in the attainment of the literary imagination. The artist gives to the world its true form and colors; he sees it on both a vertical and a horizontal plane. He gives us more than the names of streets, or the addresses of citizens, or the political identifications of areas or of men and women, of peoples collectively and individually. More than anything else he ventures deep into the political psyche of man and his world, as political actions and emotions are recorded in their pregnant convergences and conflicts. No political rhythm remains undetected; no political attitude is ignored. Man's political dimension ultimately becomes, in the hands of the creative artist, dimensionless. Political boundaries vanish in great art, or, better, are subsumed by the magnitude of man's political destiny as it is being made and experienced: as it is being rendered in its shimmer.

Though the artist, if his vision is to have a pointed authenticity, cannot escape the political world of facts, he can endow it with poetry. No matter how anguished and despairing a political situation happens to be, the artist helps one to enter that situation poetically. Through language as a form of life, he creates and captures political reality at a heightened degree. He attains an amazing confluence of sociopolitical reality, poetic expression, and communication with creative insight. There is also an added dimension that sharpens the poet's political sensibility: his compassion, or sympathy. Whether in verse or prose the creative artist conveys his vision of existence, in its specifically political essences, comprehensively. He sees beneath and beyond the outer life. The human psyche is as much the object of his concern as is the outer life. For the artist, political phenomena constitute a totality of phenomena. He discovers and shows, ever so much more deeply, a political entity that is not isolated. He detects innermost heartbeats. It is the artist's poetic comprehensiveness, as it might be called, that makes it possible for him to communicate the full political consciousness of man and his world. As such the poet does not impose on his political vision—one thinks here of William Blake—defining limitations. He does not separate and delineate the meaning of political life and experience. For him there is no rectilinear compartmentalizing, no barriers to seeing and establishing connections between political and emotional facets, between one's political existence and one's spiritual self, between the outer and the inner life. What distinguishes most the task of the creative artist is his conception of the burden of his vision, his own sense of the poetic expansiveness of his view of life. For him perception is a key word as well as an identifying mission. In him, through the word, the Logos, the political voice finds its speaker, its tone and timbre, is placed and orchestrated. Politics becomes music into words, as it were. The historical moment, in all its antinomies, contingencies, and conundrums, attains its true horizontality. But, at the same time, the artist becomes its depth recorder.

What makes the mission of the artist so unique is that his rendering of life penetrates deeply and relentlessly into the soil of life. For him an aspect of human existence, whether political or personal or both, is no mere statistical unit of experience, or mere statement of fact or opinion, or mere measurement of particular relations, consequences, or values. A creative intensity of insight characterizes the artist's—the poet's—capturing of man's experience of the world. He captures, that is, tensions of living and communicates explosions of consciousness. An event that is, politically speaking, a matter of statistical reportage, to be factually defined, expressed, weighed, and presented, becomes, in the process of the artist's communicated vision, radiant with meaning. This meaning reconciles the passion of an event transcribed and dramatized with the passion of language itself: that language employed by the artist in his expression of substance. If, in the historical purview, an event of importance unfolds and extends in all its social and political mobility and pressures, whether of an individual or collective character, in the creative, in the visionary, process, that event attains, or bodies forth, pregnantly, what can be termed its unfolding mystery, its numen. The artist has the power both to catch and to identify that mystery, with all of its inner and sometimes hidden networks. He seduces, so to speak, the encounter of political man and political history. The artist's creation ultimately becomes the reader's reflection, in short, a trap for meditation. In a great work of art, man confronts himself, his history, his destiny. In it he becomes (again) the actor of his epoch, as well as his own (and the work's) judge. He is forced, *in continuum*, to relive and reenact his experience of himself and of his time and place, through the medium of the artist's words. But this is more than a reenactment of conditions of experience. It is man's dramatic, and finally moral, valuation of what he has done and been and seen, of what has happened to him, of what he has felt and suffered. The creative process becomes a vehicle for man's self-recognition and self-examination. Art of such magnitude crystallizes an expedition for truth. Art-truth creates the unifying dimension.

A political event, in its making, testifies to some particular reaction as it is generated and to some particular energy as it is expended. Man is thus a witness to an aspect of his and his world's destiny. He is, so to speak, at the center of things, a centrifugal force, in whom action incites, impinges, crystallizes; he is also a sufferer, one who receives and contains a historical and a political happening. A direct and present part of the political vortex, he is its living witness, its actor and messenger, its vulnerable focus, its victim and victimizer—its consciousness, temporality, epochalness; its sinner, sage, and saint. In man political existence etches its history. Even when he is a nameless unit of a political event, in peace or in war, in a small skirmish or a major battle, in a town or a city, in the hands of God or in the jaws of Satan, man is nonetheless its indispensable and irreplaceable center. Without man there is no history. Man is his own uniqueness, and history's. History itself, in its unending political ramifications, is man's first and last, his real, name, and his telos. It is man's final synthesis. By no means should these observations signify an equivalence between political man and historical man. Interrelations do not necessarily dictate parity. But one cannot survive without the other, even as history without man is no history. If history is man's totality, politics is man's most viable constituent. Man's political self, or selves, is the choice he makes to make himself and his society, the decision that he reaches, or grasps, as to *how* to make himself in society: the physiognomy by which he is placed and identified, whether as Medieval Man, or European Man, or Modern Man, or Soviet Man. His political dimension adverts to his special conditions of quality defining precisely the ultimate content and form of his political choices and decisions. If history is the concretization of man's consummate achievement, his irrevocable verdict, politics is man's immediate struggle, and delineation, in all its gradations, gravity, compromises, transits, in short, his human plasticity. History is the judgment of man (and of nations) and his ultimate point of control and order. Man's political realm is where he lives and exerts his passions, sometimes rationally and at other times irrationally; where he, consciously or unconsciously, constructs, positively or destructively, his history as his legacy to others. Man's political realm is his crisis, if not his inferno (when one thinks, for example, of the French Revolution).

To infer that politics and crisis are intrinsically related, perhaps even interchangeable, is no dangerous or excessive generalization, if one has followed the argument of the preceding reflections. History, these reflections have intended to show, becomes a nethermost stasis, the historical equivalent of the theological *kairos*, that frozen moment of eternity subsuming all human experience, man's personal and common fate, when God arrests history and then garbs it with his mantle, once and for all time, when time itself is sanctified against all assaults of time. Politics, on the other hand, never ceases movement on the clock of time; its fate is as processive as the uninterrupted striking of bells at each hour of the day, day in and day out. With and within these passing hours, days, months, and years, man's political actions unfold. The purposes of his political actions may be order and stability (or the reverse of these), but these latter elements are ultimately long-term goals rather than the more immediate attainments, or meanings. Political life, even as it does not cease evolving, is the frenzy of day-to-day business. It vibrates with each passing reverberation. It gestures and salutes, or laments and weeps, or doubts and rejects, or affirms and accepts, always in relation to the constantly changing and exerting pressures of the moment. It beats to the rhythm and pattern of daily events, as these announce themselves, predictably or not, bringing with them a momentum of consequences of varying durations and intensities. One cannot help noticing that political life is itself a cumulative and, above all, an immanent emotionalism, endlessly framing and responding to announcements and proclamations, to new laws and to old laws, to ambitions achieved and schemes aborted; it is very much a part and symptom of the passing scene; of rhetoric that becomes action, or of action that remains stillborn in rhetoric. Yet, whatever the elemental strength and significance of man's political existence, it is his perception of it that is invariably in evidence. That perception, within whatever span of its existence, signifies a crisis of reality that one cannot escape in life and that never fails to present itself, relentlessly and even mercilessly. In facing that crisis of reality man actively defines his political self, even in his failure and disappointment, even in his folly and madness. His definition of this self may be abstract, to be sure, but it is simultaneously active and dynamic, insofar as he enacts it, experiences politically the history that in time underlies meditation.

Bringing all these things to consciousness, fusing beginnings and endings, remains the mission of the artist. In a sense, what the artist does is give intuitive order to men and events, to the inclusive political realm and all that it contains and shows within its boundaries. The artist fathoms human and natural energies in their commingling; he arrests crisis, reveals its development, captures its mystery, penetrates its paradox. He converts intuitive order into moral order—interconnects life in time and life by values—and provides, at the same time, a dramatic sense of things in their ebb and flow. He gives to kinesis the accent of Logos; is the creator who transforms flesh into word and word into flesh. He renders the seraphic revelation. Thesis, antithesis, synthesis: these for the artist constitute the network of revelation to be discovered, explored, understood, centralized, expressed, and presented. Creation and reflection are the marks of imaginative genius that overcome the implacable and the inscrutable. More than anything else the artist sees and lifts human meaning from behind the political veil. He defies the changeable, with which element politics is paired. The political phenomenon becomes the raw material and then the projected image of his vision. The artist's ability to reconcile the consciousness of the moment and a consciousness of history attests to his imaginative interpretation of man's existential situation. To put it in another way, the artist who succeeds in this aesthetic form of reconciliation enters a third realm, that of metapolitics, in which he (as, say, Dostoevsky or Kafka) expresses, and interprets, and contemplates, in terms of the authority of his imaginative genius, the metaphysics of politics. This does not, and should not, mean that the artist surrenders to politics, as some insistent fact to be pursued and reported, as questions to be answered, or as power, and power networks, to be enshrined. Surrender to such a noisome, drab process is for the genuine artist the surrender of intimate truths that emerge from the depths and singleness of his contemplation. His metaphysics of art can be simultaneously his metaphysics of politics, in the total process of which he differentiates the contemplative vision from the sham vision, the permanent things from the impermanent things, the true artist from the false artist. How closely and yet courageously the artist expresses and distinguishes his creative loyalty, how he devotes himself to shaping and presenting his vision, discloses the sincerity, the authenticity, and the transcendence of his achievement.

How does political fact transform into believable political image; how is the political metaphor extracted from the precarious world of sense (in the manner of Joseph Conrad); how are fleeting passions, whatever their individuating forms and impulses, captured, to be patiently and luminously re-created through the poetry of language? These are major occupying questions that confront the artist especially responsive to man's role in society and to society's effect on man. Questions of art intertwine with questions of life. Unraveling these inexorable questions, focusing on and dramatizing their threatening demands, is for the artist an impelling task, his ultimate political challenge. But it is not only a matter of unraveling these questions as they batter and tantalize the imagination. The artist must somehow descend into their very depths, navigate and discover their boundaries, measure their terrain, listen to their sounds, perceive their distances and shadows, absorb and re-present experience with all its subtleties and mystery. He absorbs and interprets, that is to say, what can be termed political boundary conditions in the contexts of a higher universal meaning; his vision, as it is rendered, re-presents a higher operative principle of control and makes the political function more comprehensible. In the creative mind tangible and external facts, as they vibrate in the political zeitgeist, attain their moral and social validity, their true organic consciousness and integration. The artist, in his own creative freedom, liberates a political phenomenon from its sentience. He sees it beyond the level of a particular conflict, or advocacy, or politicizing identity. He gives it its subtilizing purity of experience, presents its significance, registers its symbolic value. Through the imagination life escapes its political captivity; in the imagination life finds its transcendent analogues. If in the political life the search is for a solution to or a program of governance, in the imaginative life it is for the poetic truth of credible things. In both the yearning for fulfillment is a strong one: in the first, fulfillment points to some modality of form in the whirlpool of time; in the second, it points to an experienced metamorphosis. Politics, as a science and an art, seeks to guide, manage, and satisfy the body's longings for work, security, ethical imperatives, and order. Art helps make these longings, these conceptual feelings, more meaningful, as it also seeks to excite and creatively inspire the experience of judgment and the meaning of moral struggle.

Relativism, it is often heard, is the authentic experience of political man. It remains to the artist to touch the reality of this experience, to enhance, heighten, and intensify it. His primary function, and it is ultimately a moral function, is to make man contemplate and understand himself, his time, and his world. As such the artist calls upon man to be greater than himself, his time, and his world. He assists man to look at the face of the crisis of consciousness on all levels, to examine the structure of reality, to enter the drama of discrimination, even to uncover the power of evil and to fathom all that is relative and profane. The components of this reality are incontrovertible, since no one who lives lives without contact with what is. But one may also rightly ask, What is what is? There is no lack of answers to this question, for the full and unremitting force of political actuality points to the emerging political fate, in terms of means and goals. Politics and history validate and refine substantively the evidence that overarches the meaning of all human experience. This evidence inevitably manifests itself as power that tells the difference between life and death, between civilization and barbarism, between hope and despair. One may want perhaps to challenge the either/or framework of these dichotomies; nuances both in human sensibility and in society are a living, tensive witness to the legitimacy of this challenge. Yet, in the end, beyond political action and historical retrospect, the moral consequences of action and fact disclose a unilateral significance and truth, an absolute idea of the world. The interdisciplinary relations between politics and literature (as also, for instance, between religion and literature) underline the immense possibilities and the glories of the written arts. Not only does the literary artist help us to live our lives, with greater understanding and sensitivity, but also he enables us to grasp the moral real as it is rendered and revealed. The very coupling of politics and literature leads to the artist's impelling conception of his own function and calling: that of expressing and communicating his vision as an aesthetic infinitude. Politics cannot permanently command the imagination, however violent and oppressive the edicts of führer or of commissar. To claim, on the other hand, that the imagination can solve the political problem is to indulge in a claim that easily falls into the pit of illusion. But that the imagination, in its freedom, mystery, and wisdom, can help apply the value of arts and letters to the problems of political life, is a central value of redemption for which there can be no end to man's gratefulness.

II

A theory of modern politics without a text is as meaningless as history without politics. Beyond a theory and a text, meditations on the text, and their disclosures, constitute a total critical experience. D.H. Lawrence's *Women in Love* provides a text in the area of politics and literature that no other text since 1920 has yet supplanted and that no other writer, whether as creative genius or as political commentator, has yet equaled. In it the great modern historical world and modern political society have their moment of mutual recognition and revelation. Crisis and prophecy congeal in this novel. The crisis is the prophecy; the prophecy is the crisis. Here we have a novel that has permanence and universality; that holds vindicating lessons and paradigms that no student of politics and literature can ignore. No study or understanding of the modern social and political world of the West can be complete, or intelligent, without *Women in Love* serving as the required text. The whole of modern man's political conscious-ness is diagnosed in this masterpiece. Lawrence's novel arises from the ashes of the Great War of 1914–18. Not the actual conditions of war itself but rather the psychic and civilizational detonations caused by the war are the subject of *Women in Love*. It is a novel that provides us with a text of life since 1914. All the urgent questions of the modern age are asked in this novel—all the political, educational, religious, economic, sociological, and cultural questions with which modern man is preoccupied but which elicit no final answers or solutions. From beginning to end, from one's reading of the novel to one's meditations on the text, the image of a void, of a terrifying chasm, over the edge of which one gazes, presents itself forcefully. The opening of the novel itself (a marriage is taking place) serves as an entry into the modern world. Both the dominating images of a threat-ening darkness and the life feelings of fear and terror that Lawrence creates are apocalyptic. The reader, along with some of Lawrence's central figures here, wants to escape from a hostile world, wants not to confront its annihilative power, yet must go forward to encounter its underworld faces and forms.

The people who inhabit this world reflect a profound weariness, a wolflike furtiveness; one gets the impression immediately of a people lost, abandoned, neutralized, and repulsive (even in their beauty). Though it is rich in dialogue, the novel's silences are sometimes overwhelming, as if coiled in darkness. The ecology and the topogra-phy are those of England, particularly of the English Midlands, the heart of England. That is, *Women in Love* revolves around English civilization during the years 1914–18. This English ambience, in its significance, should not mislead or circumscribe the reader. England represents the reader's encounter with the world. This encounter, like the dialogue, has a universal value, and validity, of experience; Lawrence, as poet, penetrates to basic images and basic emotions, composes a fundamental poetry, a supreme vision, that goes beyond all national boundaries and yet also connects them. *Women in Love* can be termed Lawrence's metapolitical novel, which communicates a full-scale problematic modernism and dramatizes a modern polity in all of its challenging (and chilling) paradoxes. Human relations and possibilities, as they are immediately evoked, are observed in steady decline. A sickness unto death characterizes the fate of man and his civilization in the novel. Alienation, even within a family (the Criches), is a pervasive human condition; the accompanying feeling that nothing matters or materializes is inclusive. In the war the old humanistic ethos, as personified in the old father and the owner of the mines, the dying Thomas Crich, has heard its death knell. In a sense, whatever is being said now is after the fact; throughout, the endless discussions that go on are thick and unctuous in texture. The dialogists themselves seem to be in quest of certitudes and inner satisfaction, which remain stubbornly elusive. Nothing materializes, nothing matters: against such negatives the novel's characters seem repeatedly to beat their wings in vain. Major life questions are repeatedly asked: What does one live for? What is the aim and object of one's life? What does one do once the material things have been attained? But the answers, with time, convey a distinct hopelessness, that mood and feeling which the city of London crystallizes in the novel. (Lawrence's wife wanted to call this novel *Dies Irae.*)

This hopelessness is stressed by the element of decadence and of boredom that one finds in London's café society and intelligentsia. A disintegrative consciousness comes into prominent view. Outer dissemblance and inner emptiness reinforce each other, darkly. Breakdown on personal and civilizational levels is in indisputable evidence. The death of the heart is no less terrifying than the death of humanistic civilization. The references, in the early part of the novel, to several negro statues, wood carvings from West Africa, with the carved negroes looking almost like the fetus of a human being, underscore, in an epiphanal sense, a feeling of decay and degeneration. The sickness, grayness, nausea, and bestiality that Lawrence associates with physical and emotional malaise inevitably relate to and objectify the new reality: an age of uncertainty and brutality. During long intellectual discussions, major social, educational, and political issues, among others, are examined in the tenuous contexts of very clever talk, often colored by a positivist skepticism. It is interesting to note that, in this novel, so startlingly unlike Lawrence's earlier novels, even the flowers are not seen by the characters. (Rather, the characters' clothes, in resplendent, if garish, colors, are endowed with a brilliant visual appeal and value.) Human sensibility seems transmogrified: it is the world after 1914 that comes into focus here. The eddies of a sinister violence move treacherously in the undercurrents of human relations and actions. Hard and vindictive, the combatants, and they are that rather than conversationalists, in the course of their discussions, seek to annihilate each other. Battlefield conditions, it seems, now extend to the areas behind the lines. No one is safe from anyone or anything. A destructive spirit reigns, epitomized at one point by the dance of death, with three of Lawrence's female characters dancing the parts of Naomi, Ruth, Orpah. This dance, occurring in the early part of the novel, magnifies, ominously, the events that follow. Sickness of dissolution, death of life and of civilization, harrowing fear and dread constitute a funereal drama done in a dumb show. Even the manorial houses (first at Shortlands and then at Breadalby), in which some key actions take place, have the appearance of a hall of kings in an Egyptian tomb. On the other hand, when the informing images are not of a deathly malevolence, they are of a primeval slime. The human figures in a swimming scene, for instance, are suggestive of saurians, water rats, slithering sea lions, great lizards, a shoal of seals. Early on in the novel the motif of dehumanization takes hold.

But the discursive orientation of the novel is never far off. Lawrence's characters are preoccupied with the great political question as to how a new world of man is to be created from chaos. One (Sir Joshua Malleson, modeled after Bertrand Russell) suggests that the great social idea is the social equality of man. Another (Gerald Crich, soldier, explorer, and industrial magnate) suggests that the unifying principle is the work in hand, the business of production, insofar as society itself is a mechanism. Still another (Rupert Birkin, Lawrence's own spokesman) insists that a state must first be founded on the idea that between people, spiritually, there is an inherent difference that defies both equality and inequality. The overarching political question, and its special solutions, returns to and (re)emphasizes the desperate difficulty of confronting a world in which the old ways and values are no longer relevant, discarded with so much other refuse in the dead man's dumps dotting the Western Front. Indeed, this political question is so urgent, and its solution so remote, that it borders on what is violent, perverse, misanthropic. The responses to the great political question that is posed prophesy the various ideological extremisms that would, in the years after the Armistice of 1918, lead to some of the totalitarian methodologies that have made this century the terrible twentieth. In its political, that is in both its metaphysical and metapolitical, dimension, *Women in Love* explores extremism in its various modern guises. At the center of this extremism, as Lawrence clearly demonstrates, is the infatuation with and application of power, *Wille zur Macht;* of power over men and machines, animals and nature. In the process the virtues of human decency and dignity are particularly (and pitilessly) scorned. Even when there is an instinctive exchange of passional feeling, this gradually transforms into a matter of will and nerves, callous and oppressive. Under the circumstances, then, it is not difficult to see that when one attempts to cultivate a relationship with another, it is done in terms of incipient suspicion, unease, mistrust, danger, tantamount to making a foray into no-man's-land. Lawrence likens mankind to a dead tree of lies, and human beings to apples of Sodom, Dead Sea Fruit, ichthyosaurs. His employment of extreme images fits the extreme moods and events of the time. History sanctions his vision: *Women in Love* is a vision of modern political history, of a cruel history.

The novel is both the story and the rejection of the dying forms of social mankind in the wake of deaths in belief. The old reverences, like the old words (e.g., glory, loyalty, patriotism), which Ernest Hemingway later spoke of as having been debased in the Great War, are irrelevant. An impatient anger and scorn inform the characters' feelings about the existing state of things. Obscenity and madness seem to lurk in the shadows of the characters' movements and to tinge the words they speak to each other, even the words of love. Continuously we are made aware of imaging negations by the characters. Dissolution, debasement, corruption, nothingness are associated with a world that has come to an end. That men and women are now *fleurs du mal:* this is a recurring observation in the novel. Accordingly, the world of *Women in Love* assumes grotesque shapes and shadows, produces fantastic amalgams of color, and echoes strange and unreal sounds. It is as if some terrible mystery is speaking and gesturing, with apparitions and demons swaying ominously in the background. A sense of imminent fatality is ever present; the death of life and the death of civilization are the real dramatis personae of this tragic modern novel. A stern and terrible history is the antagonist. How can one resist or escape its mechanistic cruelty and terror? This is an intrinsic question that absorbs Lawrence's characters, preoccupied as they are in salvaging their inner meaning, or at least in protecting it against the brutal force of an outer, mechanical nullity, which Lawrence registers with a Dantesque and Blakean poetic vision. Not infrequently, Lawrence's characters seem to welcome death as a voyage of oblivion coming at the end of the struggle against a modern world that they see shrouded in ignominy and sordidness, whether experienced in London or in Nottingham and the mining countryside, where the largest part of the novel occurs. Within *this* world the feeling that they are prisoners gains as the novel progresses to a dead end. At the same time, this feeling is intensified by symptoms of sickness, about which characters voice repeated complaints. The theme of destruction is everywhere in evidence, both in private human relationships and in the external world. As such this novel is not so much about the modern world as about the death and the end of the modern world.

Some of the profoundest and most prophetic pages of the novel are devoted to the portrayal of an ascendant industrial civilization. Lawrence lays bare the consequences of this ascendancy in relation to what goes by the name of modernism. The instrumentality of life, the functional qualities of man, scientific expertise and experimentation, the absolutism of the laws of physics and chemistry, the technical mastery of all existence, the arrogant questioning and dismissal of the intangible: these are the new gods who constitute a modernism that gradually leads to an all-inclusive absurdity, on which desperate and drastic note the novel ends. Particularly relevant is Lawrence's insight into the structural and operational principles that are employed to modernize the old mines (and the old miners). What matters now is the great social productive machine, which contains and supplies the main criterion of harmony. We are reminded in dramatic terms of a positivistic empiricism challenging the old humanism. Beyond this, or, better, along with this, Lawrence also helps us to comprehend the rise of modern totalitarianism, whether in a fascistic or a Marxist mold, in both of which systems we detect a morality of truth embodied in the perfect, inhuman machine and in the machine principle. One of the major metapolitical functions of *Women in Love* is found precisely in its recognition of the emerging political myths and creeds and disasters of the modern age as these are tied more and more to the ambition to translate the Godhead into a pure mechanism. What Lawrence does, with so much implicit intuition and diagnostic understanding, is expose the roots of our disorders. With the reform of the mines the beautiful candles of belief burn no more; mechanicalness is the order of the day. In delineating this process, the seventeenth chapter is of unparalleled help to anyone who gives thought to political and social matters. The lessons to be derived from this chapter, and from the novel as a whole, are not merely sociological; the conditions of mind and of sensibility are rendered in their deepest, subtlest meanings, so that convictions and passions, abstract thought and concrete human experience are viewed in their total sociopolitical intercourse.

This novel, Lawrence's greatest, appears to be also his most pessimistic. In it he paints much more than a political catastrophe of a particular people and nation. Recurring references to the African fetishes accentuate Lawrence's vision of the breakdown of an entire civilization. If the beetlelike statuettes signify for the West Africans a phallic disintegration and dissolution, for the white races the African process has also another message: that of a cerebral and abstract annihilation. Lawrence makes no direct comments, as he does in his letters and in the novel *Kangaroo* (1923) regarding, say, David Lloyd George, whom he saw as a portent of political ruthlessness and opportunism. Instead, the concentration is on the wider metapolitical ramifications and consequences; Lawrence takes his reader beyond the time of war, beyond personality and political breakdown. A moral and symbolic metapolitics, as it might be termed, is at the impelling center of *Women in Love*. The political issues that Lawrence poses have a universal significance; how one reads and responds to them constitutes the transcending tests of discrimination that enable one to view the world apart from its parochial frontiers. Much more is at stake, in the symbolic contexts and demands of the novel, than an immediate event or crisis. Repeatedly Lawrence emphasizes—renders his preoccupation with—that which follows an event or crisis, that which comes beyond everydayness and culminates in the authentic. It is these metapolitical considerations that, in a sense, pull the novel to its astonishing conclusion; that, in fact, help it to reach above and beyond its particular historical limits, in social history, by demanding of the reader a discriminating reaction to what ultimately constitutes the recognition of finitude in the perspective of possibility. *Women in Love* was to take shape in the historical moment: a moment of shipwreck, when one thinks of the total impact of the years 1914–18. The despair and negation, the terrifying sense of lostness, that inform the dialogue and the actions arise from the phenomena of these years of crisis with which the modern age began. But history for Lawrence has to do not with the past but rather with a movement toward the future, toward the authentic possibilities of man's future. *Women in Love* discloses the human condition in its most dangerous and vulnerable hour, which accounts for the pessimism. Yet, at the same time, in this novel Lawrence wrestles with himself (and with his reader) in order to escape the old and dead metaphysical categories that he sees in the wake of war and destruction. He is a spiritual gladiator; the remarkable wrestling scene (in the twentieth chapter) has its relevance here.

The conflict between the outer world and the possibility of strong essential life is unceasing in the novel. For Lawrence the outer world signifies a circling nullity of fallenness and death. It is the reigning *What is* that Lawrence challenges as a composite of dead forms. The sick, dying figure of the paternalistic mine owner and Christian philanthropist, Thomas Crich, hovers wearily but dreadfully throughout the greater part of the novel; his figure epiphanizes misery and dissolution, and yet also a willful denial of death. He represents the past that was to expire murderously in 1918. What happens when he and it die? This is the question that Lawrence parades before the reader and whose answer contains the metapolitical thrust of the novel's intrinsic concerns. Endings and beginnings are curiously intermixed in Mr. Crich's life and death. He marks both a phenomenological and an epochal stasis in the novel. His dead stillness in the novel is to be measured in introspective, as well as apocalyptic, terms. In him one comes up against the ultimate degree of decay. Is it possible to liberate one's self from this decay? This, too, is a question that comes into view, particularly in the final pages of the novel. Some of the intense (and unwarrantably criticized) sexual scenes in the novel are frantic attempts to defy the power that nihilates; to attain some moment of permanence, some viable experience of otherness that resists the finality of ending. Lawrence's juxtaposition of the sexual scenes with the death agony of Mr. Crich points to the indwelling complexity of the critical problems facing those who are survivors in a world in which the dread of nothingness prevails. Of all of Lawrence's novels *Women in Love* is the one in which the feeling of terror erupts and lingers almost preternaturally. For somehow the strange and haunting questions that echo in the novel, always pleading for answers and resolutions, seem to culminate recurringly in grim words and sounds, the linguistic counterpart of a war-torn world in disarray: *No . . . Not . . . Nothing . . . Nowhere . . . Never.* These words boom like the rhythmic discharges of small cannon. To the existence and power of these post-1914 negatives, which no armistice could ever quiet, *Women in Love* testifies with brooding insistence and paradoxicalness.

The concluding three chapters of *Women in Love* take place in the winter, in the Tirolese Alps. The four main figures of the novel, Gerald Crich and Gudrun, Rupert Birkin and Ursula, have fled from England. Yet even their perception of the need to withdraw from one world, to live, if possible, in the chinks of another, does not fully squelch the fear that they are living in the final stage of civilization. Particularly painful is Lawrence's picture of their departures from families, homes, friends, careers, and familiar surroundings. Sometimes too deep for tears or words, the scenes of departure, accented by feelings of emptiness and futility, instance sharp, irreparable breaks with the past. The pernicious negatives rapidly enlarge in these latter scenes, made even more forbidding by the background of a perfect whiteness and silence. Lawrence's description of the snow-and-ice world and its mountain peaks is exhilarating; one thinks of Goethe's primal phenomenon (*Urphänomen*). A poetry of genius, of a Shakespearian magnitude, triumphs, as the dance of death, begun much earlier in the novel, now reaches its eerie but inevitable conclusion. Now, however, it is the *Schuhplatteln,* the highly animate and boisterous Tirolese dance, that takes place in a kind of space-time and almost in a frenzy. The novel's prophetic questions attain their final dramatization, their unconsoling thingness. Impossibility and possibility are, in the larger contexts, fierce antagonists here. The metapolitical debate, in short, is enacted in a world that seems to be situated at a point, cold and eternal, between light and darkness, both beneath and above the heaven. Lawrence paints a spectacle of heaven and hell being completed by the other two *eschata,* death and judgment. Concomitantly the biblical (and sermonic) pulse of Lawrence's language quickens memorably at this point. The dazzling world of snow and ice serves as a frozen backdrop, its immense, awesome silence punctuated by the frantic words and gestures of Lawrence's four characters as each awaits a fateful verdict. The feeling of loneliness is for each unbearable. Their world below, as they have known it, has come to an end; it is his own personal ending that each sinner and sufferer approaches. Lawrence not only refines his metapolitics but also contemplates his theology of politics in these last pages.

Ultimately he gives us his metapolitical vision of the modern industrial world formed by technology and science. One of Lawrence's most astonishing underground creations, Herr Loerke, an insectlike German master sculptor, appears here as the prophetic personification of the last phase of civilization, the phase announcing man's cybernetic function. Loerke is precisely that future of nothingness that is all that now remains of a decayed and devalued world; he is the mechanistic executioner of *homo humanus.* Even his sculptures epitomize the nonorganic and soulless, the unconnected and disconnected: the new programmatic reality. In him one hears the whirl of the world, as metaphysics gives way to cybernetics, homecoming to homelessness, and the sacred to the profane. Loerke induces in the other characters violent incertitude, conflict, and alienation. He dictates choices that are categorical. One must accept and join Loerke, or reject and flee him, or flee him and die. Loerke is a modern-day Satan; the Alpine world of snow and ice, of peaks and ridges, is his City of Dis. Whenever he refers to the future it is perceived as a dream of destruction, of the world blown into two halves by a catastrophic explosive invented by man. Loerke incarnates the negation and the horror that lie at the heart of Lawrence's prophetic vision of evil. These last pages dramatize a period of waiting and watching in the midst of a feeling of eternal unrelief. The desperate questions asked in the novel, having attained no resolution, are now submerged in words of cynicism and gestures of mockery. As on the clock face of time so too in the snow the mute reminder of death is inescapable and is nowhere better evoked than in a half-buried crucifix, of a little Christ under a little sloping hood, at the top of a pole, that stands out, silently and menacingly, in the snow. Indeed, for the visionary poet of *Women in Love* there could now be no new answer to the old and accursed questions about life and death. Had the answer not been given on Calvary, by the man hanging on the middle wooden cross, in suffering and death, in death—but life, nearly two thousand years earlier: *Consummatum est!*

9

Dostoevsky's Political Apocalypse

The Prince is another name for the world. The
Master is a metaphor for reality. There is no
ontology that is not a politics.
                                        —BERNARD-HENRY LÉVY

"PART OF THE TRUTH about Dostoevsky is that this extraordinarily
sensitive man who trembles for the slightest creature can also be a
coarse and brutal reactionary." So wrote Irving Howe in his influential study *Politics and the Novel* (1957). These condemning words,
particularly as they are repeated by liberal (and nonliberal) critics,
comprise a critical commonplace with respect to any appraisal of
Fyodor Dostoevsky's political views. A reader must look hard to find
a volume that rejects such a misconception and misrepresentation
and sees Dostoevsky's political thought in a more sympathetic light,
untainted by liberal presuppositions and dogmas. One such book is
Ellis Sandoz's *Political Apocalypse: A Study of Dostoevsky's Grand
Inquisitor*, which repays frequentation, if only to provide a dissenting
and more balanced point of view.[1]

Sandoz's essential judgments can be summarized as follows: Dostoevsky's Legend is a carefully structured political apocalypse, an
unveiling, a revelation. It contains an urgent message in times of
crises, the crisis of consciousness and the crisis of Christian culture
and of civilization. It envisions history, particularly in connective
terms of present and future, as a constant battleground between the
power of good and the power of evil. It is prophetic and eschatological
in content, temporal and spatial in range, as well as both ultimate in
human consequences and historical in its dynamics. The encounter
between Dostoevsky's Grand Inquisitor and Christ dramatizes apocalypse to the extent that drama itself is "pushed into the theatre of
the mind." And we are once again reminded that in Dostoevsky's
major works the problem of man in particular and of the human

1. Baton Rouge, La., 1971.

condition in general is delineated, or, better, creatively rendered. Sandoz asserts:

> The Legend of the Grand Inquisitor articulates an apocalyptic vision of the present age considered as the penultimate phase of history in the Christian tradition: the reign of the Antichrist. In taking biblical apocalypse as its form, it employs a conception of history as a present under God which moves from genesis through the Incarnation irreversibly toward the *parousia* and the Kingdom of God, an extension of time suspended in the Sabbath of eternity made meaningful through the self-disclosure of the divine Realissimum Who is the sovereign Lord of being.

The informing concern of Sandoz is with the penultimate and the Christological—in a word, with the kenotic. His thesis is rooted in his conception (and Dostoevsky's) of man pitted against the anthropology of atheistic humanism. It is as an apologist that Sandoz presents his views. Apologetics, needless to say, can never replace disciplined literary criticism and speculation. If the apologist justifies, the critic, it is well to remember, seeks (just as the artist finds). Criticism is not, and cannot be, a final vindication. There is ever implicit in the critical process an inescapable "yes-but" dialectic of search. The critic must be initially concerned with the words on the page, with their structure as meaning. He cannot proceed on an a priori act of faith. Yet the critic cannot avoid an awareness of extrinsic matters that may relate to his overall evaluation of a work of art, its religious *and* political implications, for instance—its extended social meanings. Whatever the critical validity of the specific positions that Sandoz assumes here, his conclusions (in their religious foundation) have the value of recalling for us the fact that a work of art is essentially "a calculated trap for meditation." In his development of his main thesis, Sandoz recalls for us the immense mystery of his meditative process in its attendant critical contexts. Criticism, if it cannot be apologia, can nevertheless show an awareness of what the latter presents for absolute acceptance. The critical process cannot ignore derived and asserted answers, if these in any way serve the cause of a deeper illumination of the text and a judgment of its attainment and meaning.

Certainly Dostoevsky's meaning, which is ever so rich and profound, and of which the subtleties are fathomless, needs to be extricated with whatever help the critic can be given. This attempt helps to distinguish great art from inferior art and true creative vision from the second-rate. Perhaps, too, it is this that should constitute a main criterion for what is today called relevance. An artist's vision that conveys wisdom is not only sapiential but also relevant in a permanent, a classic, sense. Dostoevsky's higher and, as it were, prophetic relevance is precisely the relevance that emerges from an unquestioned ability to realize the quintessence of all things human. In the political realm, in his probing and understanding of the outer order of life, its constituents and its governance, Dostoevsky is a novelist who has insights of universal significance, superior to those of the political scientist, the sociologist, the psychologist, or the social theorist. The truths of great art are not only universal in import, but also transcendent in their diagnosis and application. They are creatively rendered truths and as such are both experiential and existential. Dostoevsky's greatness in this respect is, as André Gide well observed, "that he never reduced the world to a theory, that he never let himself be reduced by a theory." This irreducibility in creative art is tantamount to the final freedom that gives birth to and informs Dostoevsky's work and to what Thomas Mann called its "surging fullness of visions and passions."

Dostoevsky's "political apocalypse" is directly related to what critics have termed a "metaphysics of rebellion." "The Legend itself is," Sandoz declares, "in one of its aspects, a myth of paradigmatic disorder [psychic, pneumatic, and social]. The anthropology of disorder is the dominant stratum in his work, the level of thought which pulls together the great existential issues of ethics, politics, and metaphysics." Hence, as "the discoverer of political apocalypse as a mode of apprehending existentially decisive experiences in the modern age of ideology," Dostoevsky's prophetic relevance to the "modern experience," to "the idea of the modern," to the "modern temper," to the "modern tradition," or to "modern culture" is what stands out above all. Dostoevsky can be called the father of modern novelists, and that is to say that with his great novels modern literature began and established that from which it has yet never really escaped. It would be difficult to define absolutely modern literature, let alone the modern age. But it is not difficult to pinpoint some of the characteristics of the modern writer: his concern with the problematic, his tendency to raise disturbing questions, his exploration and sifting of value systems, his awareness of cultural dissociation and discontinuity and disinheritance, his perplexity in face of the cultivation of the "relative spirit" in place of the "absolute," his gravitation toward moral and spiritual renovation, his preoccupation with the subject of damnation and salvation, his increasing reaction to, as Matthew Arnold once expressed it, "this strange disease of modern life / With its sick hurry, its divided aims." Paul Tillich in *The Courage To Be* helps us to comprehend the first estate of modern literature, even as he helps us to trace back to Dostoevsky the very essences that modernism and modern literature are all about: "The anxiety of doubt and meaninglessness is . . . the anxiety of our period. . . . The great art, literature, and philosophy . . . [of the modern age] reveal the courage to face things as they are and to express the anxiety of meaninglessness. It is creative courage which appears in the creative expressions of despair."[2]

It is almost unnecessary to say that Dostoevsky, as a novelist "eavesdropping upon destiny" and as the father of modern literature in the contexts defined above, is not unlike all fathers in all ages: He was to beget children who were not "children of spirit." Dostoevsky, in the midst of an age of disbelief, when foundations shook and walls crumbled and edifices rotted, rendered his political apocalypse without at the same time surrendering to it. If his politics was apocalyptic, his faith was biblical. In this capacity, "he simultaneously showed apocalypse in the ancient sense not to be dead," for, as Sandoz rightly stresses, "he performed the revelation of the Russian Christ of his meditations." Dostoevsky was a spiritual artist, and his art evolved as an unbroken meditation, even as it revolved around two poles: "life as it is, the world as it goes its way, is one; and the beyond, 'resurrection,' eternity, is the other. Here is man, there God," to quote Eduard Thurneysen, the Swiss theologian. These facts comprise the ground of Dostoevsky's vision, the ontological conditions of his art. What sets off Dostoevsky from his progeny in modern literature—from his inspired but rebellious and often heretical successors in an age in which, according to Graham Greene, modern literature has lost the religious sense ("and with the religious sense went the sense of the importance of the human act")[3]—is a spiritual awareness of living in a "tragic age" but rejecting the culs-de-sac of its modernism and its defiant absorption of the liberalizing ethos inherited from the Philosophes and from the Romantics. We have come, particularly since the time of David Hume, "master-builder of the naturalistic view" of life, to understand just how dominant the world view of modern positivistic empiricists is in the dismissal of the moral meaning of suffering and of the problem of evil.

Dostoevsky's spiritual courage (to return here to Tillich's rubric) is the redeeming difference that arises out of what might be termed "a sense of history." His rebellious successors in modern literature, embracing teleological doctrine and rejecting metaphysics once they had pressed and exhausted its essences in their technical innovativeness (in this the true representatives of the modern empirical spirit),

2. New Haven, Conn., 1952, 139–41.
3. *Collected Essays* (New York, 1969), 115.

could merely instance a deficient secular courage that arises out of and necessarily dies in "a sense of the moment." Temporal apocalyptists live and create in the waning shadow of a day. Spiritual apocalyptists like Dostoevsky belong to the eons.

Dostoevsky's novels are transfigurations not only of his political apocalypse but also of his "artistic thoughts," or, better, his images of the empire of power as the innermost substance of politics. The politics of power, and of power in its various problematic levels, outer and inner, social and psychic, collective and individual, is at the center of Dostoevsky's thought. No other novelist in modern times has better penetrated or grasped the meanings of the power of power. For Dostoevsky power is the paramount image of man and his modern world; man's "Crystal Palace," his "ant-heap," as well as his ongoing dramatic debate between *pro* and *contra*, render Dostoevsky's awareness of this problem. The search for power, the uses to which it can be put, the gains that it can earn for its wielders, are concepts that Dostoevsky sensualizes. It is the distortion and the perversion of such power that command Dostoevsky's most fervent visionary insights. This empire of power, as it is transfigured in his novels, is at its lowest but most widespread levels secular and profane; it entails manipulations of the worst sort—"empires as pure power constellations without ulterior significance."

Dostoevsky's "titans," his "man-Gods," represent the mastery of power, and in consequence they assert a master's freedom. The Grand Inquisitor is the modern novel's heresiarch of power, just as Father Zossima is its purest saint. In the former there are great and terrifying deceptions of power through "miracle, mystery and authority." In the latter power is absent from his teleology, insofar as spiritual power informs beatitude and is, therefore, the most refined and spiritualized essence. Between barbarism and beatitude, between naturalism and supernaturalism, as Dostoevsky shows again and again, the qualities and range are immense. At the same time Dostoevsky recalls for us the infuriating paradoxes of power, for power insures existence and makes a telling difference between order and disorder. It is not that power is to be scorned, Dostoevsky implies, but that it is necessarily subject to limitations, to the limitation above all that power must not be "mistaken for the end of action in an absolute sense." Or, as he warns in *The Idiot* (1868–69), "from the right of force it is not far to the right of tigers and crocodiles."

The despiritualizing and dehumanizing aspects of power in the cause of ideology: it is this perversion that finally leads to irrationalism and to terror, of which in its practical aspects there is no more vivid example in modern literature than what happens as the result of the irrevocable corruption of power and the death of all human dignity in Dostoevsky's *The Devils* (1871–72), indeed the end of life itself. In *The Brothers Karamazov* (1879–80) the Grand Inquisitor is the archetype of the theorists of power who have sought to give a façade of dignity to the perversions of power. Such theorists include Voltaire, Rousseau, Marx, and, surely, a contemporary "nihilist heresiarch" like Herbert Marcuse. The results of their theories are nothing but "negations" and diabolism. Diabolism is best portrayed in the character of Peter Verkhovensky, in *The Devils*, in whom the savagery of power attains—artistically, metaphysically, prophetically—pure, cynical, brutal, demonic, and irrational force. Perhaps in no other figure in the halls of fiction do we have a more revealing case study of power as a pathological phenomenon.

What the Grand Inquisitor enunciates as a new gospel of life, as a kind of "algebra of revolution" (in Vissarion G. Belinsky's phrase), becomes in *The Devils* (in Eric Voegelin's phrase) a "metastatic faith" of power that reduces, devastates, in short undeifies and reifies man. ("The critique of religion," to recall Marx's formula, "is the presupposition of all critique.") Peter Verkhovensky embodies political apocalypse, he is the agent of the applied powers of destruction—totalitarian reductionism ad infinitum, the fire that, Dostoevsky insists in *The Devils*, "is in the minds of men, and not in the roofs of the houses." Madness, "delirium," "incendiarism," and murder are the overarching images of this novel, even as they are the intrinsic elements of Peter Verkhovensky's conception of power, which parallels in its rawest aspects the more sophisticated but equally insidious and annihilative theories of the Grand Inquisitor, though much younger and without a cardinal's robes, yet whose common God is negation. Verkhovensky screams,

> "We will proclaim destruction. . . . We'll set fires going. . . . We'll set legends going. Every scurvy 'group' will be of use. Out of those very groups I'll pick you out fellows so keen they'll not shrink from shooting, and be grateful for the honour of a job, too. Well, and there will be an upheaval: There's going to be such an upset as the world has never seen before. . . . Russia will be overwhelmed with darkness, the earth will weep for its old gods. . . ."

Here Peter Verkhovensky's words embody the empire of power, of brutal might. "And as pitilessly as might crushes," that passionate Christian Platonist Simone Weil tells us, "so pitilessly it maddens whoever possesses, or believes he possesses it."

Dostoevsky's novels do not progressively expand in terms of theme or problem. That is to say, a progressive development or the graduated buildup of a special issue is not what impels his work as it does the work of some novelists. Not progressive growth of concern, structural and thematic, but rather a progressive intensity of vision occurs in Dostoevsky's novels. The world of *The Idiot*, for instance, is darker, more terrible, and more tragic than the world of *Crime and Punishment* (1866). In this respect his art is inclusive, it has a vertical in-depth quality, and it ultimately constitutes a meditation on the problem of man in historical actuality and on the meaning of historical life. Dostoevsky's fictional world is in effect, as Father Georges Florovsky has noted, "situation-conditioned" and requires "historical commentary."[4] His political apocalypse must be viewed precisely against this background, for his vision of man in society and of society in the cosmos is steadfast and, above all, inclusive. At the heart of his political apocalypse is his understanding of power, of might, and indeed of violence, in the problematic contexts of existence—of existing. Dostoevsky's comprehension of the subtleties and the components of power contains in it those profound levels of intensity that give to his art and thought an intensity of illumination "that falls upon his page . . . like the glare of a furnace-mouth." Power expressed as might and as violence is for Dostoevsky an "emblem" and a "warning sign," as he himself phrases it. Dostoevsky's realpolitik is inescapable. He is totally, transcendently, aware of how men walk and act in "the corridors of power," and his awareness has a universality of insight. There is nothing merely transient or local in his awareness: Power is a pivotal condition of existence. It is unanswerable in its applicability and lessons. Lying as it must between historical actuality and human paradox, between necessity and freedom, power is a phenomenon that Dostoevsky sees into and measures as a dynamic presence and energy in human relations.

Certainly here one can gauge what Dostoevsky meant when he described himself as a "realist in the higher sense." He had looked into the empire of power as into the abyss itself. And he had seen there the terrifying truths that great seers alone are able to see and to reveal. His novels are re-creations of these truths. At the root of this visionary insight is Dostoevsky's apprehension of the capacity, of the possibilities of power in various forms. It was still early in his life that he understood this fact, as shown in the following passage from *The Diary of a Writer* (January 1876, Chap. III, 1). The incident that Dostoevsky describes occurred in May 1837, when his father was taking his two elder sons to St. Petersburg for matriculation in the

---

4. "Three Master: The Quest for Religion in Nineteenth-Century Russian Literature," in *Mansions of the Spirit: Essays in Literature and Religion*, ed. George A. Panichas (New York, 1967), 160.

Chief Engineering School. One evening, while stopping at a wayside inn, Dostoevsky saw the following:

[From the post-coach station there rushed out an official courier], a very hefty thickset fellow purple of face, who sat down in the small carriage, then half rose and silently, without any words whatsoever, lifted his enormous right fist and from above let it fall with a mighty blow onto the back of the coachman's neck. The man collapsed forward, lifted the whip and with all his might lashed out at the middle horse. The horses strained forward, but this in no way reduced the courier's fury. Here was a method, not irritation, but something pre-conceived and tested in long experience. The fearful fist flew up once more and once more hit into the neck. Then again and again, and this went on until the troika was lost to view.

Dostoevsky's novels are enlargements of this passage, this ground of experience to which the artist recurringly comes back and from which he cannot escape, and which establishes the difference between sacred and profane or, more correctly, the ceaseless battle between the power of good and the power of evil—that "invisible warfare" that rages in the hearts and in the minds and in the bodies of men and from which no one is spared as long as power itself informs human action in both its physical and its spiritual properties: "This revolting picture," Dostoevsky concluded, "remained in my memory for life . . . this picture was like an emblem, like something which clearly demonstrated the connection between cause and effect. Here, every blow that hit the animals sprang forth as though by itself from every blow that fell on the man." Any study of Dostoevsky's recollection of this experience will not fail to underline its correlation with the passage already cited from The Devils. For in essence Peter Verkhovensky's worship of power is an elaboration of "the connection between cause and effect."

The executioner, it has been often said, exists in embryo in every man. Dostoevsky's art is a prophecy of this truth; is a prophecy, above all, when one thinks of the course of European history since 1881, the year of Dostoevsky's death. The lust for power in direct relation to madness and death has been, since 1881, increasingly "emblematic" of the executioner in "all of us," even as the presence of men such as Stalin and Hitler has determined the destiny of civilization in terms of "the terrible plague" that ravages the world and that Dostoevsky apocalyptically described at the end of Crime and Punishment. Dostoevsky's is not only a vision of evil but also a vision of power—of power that smashes and kills life: the "emblem" of what has been the history of modern civilization that Karl Jaspers has imaged as an endless "moment of shipwreck." In his comprehension of the relation between victimizer and victim, Dostoevsky saw into a world of breakdown and failure. "A man who has once experienced power," he wrote in *The House of the Dead* (1861–62), "and the possibility of humiliating another creature with the deepest kind of humiliation, somehow loses control over his own sensations. Tyranny is a habit; it can develop, and it does develop, ultimately, into illness. . . . The best man can become crude and callous through habit to the point of bestiality." These are irrevocable words that summarize the fate of modern civilization. If they are our prophecy they are also our temptation and our condemnation.

Here, once again, it is Simone Weil who can help us to understand Dostoevsky's "political apocalypse" and, specifically, his view and treatment of power. Her essay "The *Iliad*, Poem of Might" contains in it the reflections of a philosophical genius who, by comparative projection and correspondences, can make more meaningful the work of an imaginative genius who, as Robert Louis Jackson has stressed in his book on *Dostoevsky's Quest for Form*, viewed himself as poet and as philosopher and seer, "weaving all and everything of philosophy into the canvas of his artistic consciousness."[5] Simone Weil's essay, especially her insights into the empire and properties of power in Homer's epic, does more than define aesthetic and philosophical similarities that join ancient bard and modern prophet. The essence of Dostoevsky's concept and even image of power is crystallized in Simone Weil's opening statement: "That might which is wielded by men rules over them, and before it man's flesh cringes. The human soul never ceases to be modified by its encounter with might, swept on, blinded by that which it believes itself able to handle, bowed beneath the power of that which it suffers."[6] The encounters and the confrontations of Dostoevsky's people invariably accentuate the truth of precisely this relationship, for in Dostoevsky's world the human soul never fails to respond to and be transformed by the encounter with a greater or a different might. The encounter with the intellectual might of an Ivan Karamazov poisons, imprisons, and kills the soul. The encounter with the physical might of a Peter Verkhovensky makes a thing of man—"makes him a corpse." Yet, as Simone Weil emphasizes, the nature of might is such that "Its power to transform man into a thing is double and it cuts both ways; it petrifies differently but equally the souls of those who suffer it, and of those who wield it." Any examination of the interior condition of Dostoevsky's characters corroborates this observation concerning the reciprocal transmutations that the element of power

5. New Haven, Conn., 1966, 185.
6. See *Intimations of Christianity among the Ancient Greeks*, ed. and trans. Elisabeth Chase Geissbuhler (Boston, 1958), 24–55.

brings about. In his sin and fate, Rodion Raskolnikov of *Crime and Punishment* is a classic example of the terrible impact that enactment of power brings about. His crime is impelled by the drive for power; it embodies a merciless imperialistic assault on life around him. But in the course of violating the souls of others, he himself suffers a schism of soul that denies him the absolute imperialism for which he seeks so desperately.

No one is spared and no one escapes contact with power. Both Homer, as seen by Simone Weil, and Dostoevsky recognize this as an ineradicable fact of the human condition, and both recognize human misery. This common revelation is in the end apocalyptic, is indeed tantamount to Christ's Passion, or as Simone Weil states: "The accounts of the Passion show that a divine spirit united to the flesh is altered by affliction, trembles before suffering and death, feels himself, at the moment of deepest agony, separated from men and from God. . . . Only he who knows the empire of might and knows how not to respect it is capable of love and justice." To compare this statement with the following quotation from Dostoevsky's *The Diary of a Writer* (December 1876, Chap. I, 3) is to understand the metaphysical depth of experience and of truth that ultimately unites the epic genius of Homer and the imaginative genius of Dostoevsky, there being in both the urge (in Simone Weil's words) to "learn how to accept the fact that nothing is sheltered from fate, how never to admire might, or hate the enemy, or to despise sufferers." "In the end," wrote Dostoevsky, "the triumph belongs not to material forces, frightful and unshakeable as they may seem, not to wealth, not to the sword, not to power, but to some at first unnoticeable thought often deriving from the apparently humblest of men."

That there are spiritual affinities between a religious philosopher like Simone Weil and a metaphysical novelist like Dostoevsky, that her thought can help us penetrate his thought, beyond the achievements of other modern critics, should not be difficult to understand. A common love of Plato, an obsessive fear of a collectivized morality as imaged in Plato's "Great Beast," an unyielding protest against secularization, a recognition of the power of love and yet of affliction and of the paradoxes of power, an immanent awareness of Christ and a preaching of Crucified Love: these are aspects of a vision that gives Simone Weil a capacity for perception denied to others. But that Dostoevsky, in his treatment of power, should be connected through Simone Weil to Homer, and to one of the great epics of all time, will sound strange to some ears. Is it possible—is it legitimate—for a novelist whose so-called "monstrous" novels and "cruel talent" are characterized by awesome darkness and distorted shadows, so that one never really knows "what there is at the end of a street, [or] what lies round the next corner" of his scenery,[7] to be related to an epic poet whose vision is rendered in fierce daylight and wrought "far on the ringing plains of windy Troy"?

Tolstoy, not Dostoevsky, it is said repeatedly, is the novelist who, in temper and in vision, is most truly Homeric. We need only consider Tolstoy's pastoral settings, his stress on the sensuous energies of life and on the strength of the body, his "humanness," in short his anthropomorphic world, to be able to pinpoint the epic roots of his work.[8] Yet it is perhaps easily forgotten that Dostoevsky admired and no doubt learned much from Homer, in whose poems he surely saw "the religious idea of the European spirit." To his brother Michael he wrote that Homer was "sent to us by God, as Christ was . . . [and] in the *Iliad*, gave to the ancient world the same organization in spiritual and earthly matters as the world owes to Christ."[9] In Tolstoy the epic element is structurally expansive. In Dostoevsky the epic element must be approached in terms of epic psychology. At the center of this is Dostoevsky's view of power, of the moral and spiritual warfare of symbolic figures engaged in symbolic actions amid symbolic objects, of man struggling in himself, in his soul, to comprehend the greater meaning of his nature and of his destiny.

Dostoevsky's world view, like that of Homer and that of the Greek tragedians, is essentially one of reverence, and his art and thought are sapiential. He continues the ancient Greek spirit through his sacramental view of man's unending moral struggle and of his suffering, as well as in a minute examination of conscience. His political apocalypse indicts the theory of the subjectivity of moral values and protests against the destructive cynicism of a Thomas Hobbes, for example, whose materialistic philosophy has pervaded Western civilization and glorified man's "perpetual and restless desire of power after power." A reading of Dostoevsky's *Winter Notes on Summer Impressions* (1863) clearly underscores his indictment. In more directly Russian contexts, Dostoevsky's political apocalypse answers the therapy of socialism, "the idea of ideas, the being of beings, the questions of questions," proposed by Belinsky. The Legend of the Grand Inquisitor is in the end a prophetic warning against proposals that could lead only to the "man-brute," or as Belinsky himself announced in desacralizing terms that Dostoevsky could never forget

7. Percy Lubbock, *The Craft of Fiction* (New York, 1957 [1921]), 47.
8. See George Steiner, *Tolstoy or Dostoevsky: An Essay in the Old Criticism* (New York, 1959), 71–83.
9. *Letters of Fyodor Michailovitch Dostoevsky to His Family and Friends*, trans. Ethel Colburn Mayne (New York, n.d.), 13.

once he had passed through "the crucible of doubt": "My God is negation! In history my heroes are the destroyers of old—Luther, Voltaire, the Encyclopaedists, the Terrorists, Byron. . . . I prefer the blasphemies of Voltaire to acknowledging the authority of religion, society, or anything or anybody."[10]

What connects Dostoevsky and Homer is precisely an awareness of the magnitude of the outer and inner struggle of man, of man ever contending with the spirit and power of negation. Under Dostoevsky's pen, as Vyacheslav Ivanov shows, "the novel becomes a tragedy in epic dress, like the *Iliad*."[11] His is an "epic-narrative style": epic in form and tragic in its presentation of inner antagonism. The war of might in Homer becomes the war of the soul in Dostoevsky. The ethical design and heroic ideal of the *Iliad* become the spiritual design and tragic vision of Dostoevsky's oeuvre. Spiritual war rages on a tremendous scale as God and the Devil, to use Dostoevsky's words, do battle over the fate of man, their battlefield being the hearts of men. The war here is no less heroic, no less total, and no less furious and portentous than that fought on the plains of Troy:

> As inhuman fire sweeps on in fury through the deep angles
> of a drywood mountain and sets ablaze the depth of the timber
> and the blustering wind lashes the flame along, so Achilleus
> swept everywhere with his spear like something more than a mortal
> harrying them as they died, and the black earth ran blood.[12]

But there is a crucial difference in that the epic idea of an immediate heroism in Homer becomes the transcending idea of the Holy Spirit in Dostoevsky. This epic transcendence is what crystallizes Dostoevsky's religious imagination, which secular critics have steadily ignored or, worse, distorted. In his "epic-tragedy" Dostoevsky sees new vistas, even as in it epic is transformed into an arrested, metaphysical moment of crisis in the labyrinth of the soul. At stake is the soul's finality of damnation or promise of redemption.

Homer and Christ come together in Dostoevsky. Novelists, like philosophers, to paraphrase Clement of Alexandria, are children unless they have been made men by Christ.

10. See *Selected Philosophical Works* (Moscow, 1956), 170, 175–77.
11. See *Freedom and the Tragic Life. A Study in Dostoevsky*, trans. Norman Cameron (New York, 1957), 6, 49.
12. Book XX, lines 490–94, *The Iliad of Homer*, trans. Richmond Lattimore (Chicago, 1951).

10

The Modernist Impasse

A MORE ACCURATE TITLE for *An Inquiry into the Human Prospect*,[1] one of Robert L. Heilbroner's most significant and provocative books, would have been "an inquiry into the socioeconomic prospect of man." For though he is concerned with the human predicament, his concern is essentially technical and secular in its roots and orientation. That is to say, Heilbroner's main concern is with the social organization of life or, better, with the technical prospects of that organization at a time when life is increasingly in the process of transformation, indeed of dehumanization, a process that the author accepts as a fait accompli and that he seeks to arrest and to restructure, or at least to find a way of living with and enduring. What must be said about *An Inquiry into the Human Prospect* is that its basic thesis and informing spirit are overtly and ideologically empirical in nature. It is, in short, an explicit example of the modern mind that, in Michael Polanyi's words, "distrusts intangible things and looks behind them for tangible matters on which it relies for understanding the world. We are a tough-minded generation." As such this book illustrates an intellectual's static reaction, and solution, to the besetting problems of contemporary civilization. "Static" is, in fact, the best word to describe the ethos of this book, inasmuch as Heilbroner addresses himself completely to the visible world in its present, continuing plight. Thus, what his "inquiry" ultimately lacks is spiritual centrality.

These criticisms should not be construed as objections to Heilbroner's rigorous examination of the modern human condition. It is an examination that is sincere, serious, responsible, discriminating, sometimes profound. What he says is both troubling and frightening in its honesty of observation and insight. Intellectually, then, his findings have a respectable significance. Few would, or could, want to argue with Heilbroner's contentions as he delineates these with a sobering clarity that is, in the end, devastating in its scrupulosity and impact: The future of civilization is bleak, one in which "the dark-

1. New York, 1974.

ness, cruelty, and disorder of the past" continue and accumulate to a dangerous point. The quality of the surroundings of life deteriorates; "civilizational malaise" reflects man's inability to satisfy the human spirit, despite immense and innumerable material attainments. The values of our industrial civilization are now "losing their self-evident justification." The human prospect itself becomes more problematic when one considers certain objectifying phenomena that multiply and constitute direct threats to man's future: burgeoning demographic changes; widespread possession and use of nuclear weapons; sharp competition for dwindling resources that can lead to various acts of aggression through "nuclear terrorism" and blackmail; and finally, but by no means least important, environmental deterioration as seen, for instance, in global thermal pollution.

Heilbroner is also careful to point out that both industrial capitalism and industrial socialism, despite unprecedented economic growth, have been unable to produce affirmative results in terms of human contentment, or happiness, or satisfaction. Scientific technology, in a word, has not been able to overcome the intrinsic metaphysical complex of life, as that prophetic novelist D.H. Lawrence saw back in 1920 in his novel *Women in Love*, when he wrote: "And when we've got all the coal we want, and all the plush furniture, and pianofortes, and the rabbits are all stewed and eaten, and we're all warm and our bellies are filled and we're listening to the young lady performing on the pianoforte—what then? What then when you've made a real fair start with your material things?" The response to this question is, of course, crucial. But while Lawrence was searching for some deeply metaphysical, or religious, answer to the eternal question he posed, Heilbroner assays what he labels as "socioeconomic capabilities for response." And he concludes that the present orientation of society must change radically: "In place of the long-established encouragement of industrial production must come its careful restriction and long-term diminution within society. In place of prodigalities of consumption must come new frugal attitudes." The dangers of the human prospect, he further emphasizes, are now nonideological in their origins and effect, since the causes of social and economic pressures impose common problems on capitalism and on Western socialism. (The impasse, it seems, that Lawrence foresaw has now crystallized with a perverse, mocking vengeance.)

With special reference to a capitalist society, Heilbroner addresses himself to what he terms the prospect of a stationary economy. He foresees inevitable transformations leading to the adoption of the authoritarian measures: "For the majority of capitalist nations, however, I do not see how one can avoid the conclusion that the required transformation will be likely to exceed the capabilities of representative democracy." He is careful to note, as well, that the convergence of problems will be severe enough to prevent an industrial socialist society, whether democratic or authoritarian, from sustaining any social, economic, or political transformation. "The resolution of the crises thrust upon us by the social and natural environment can only be found through political action," he declares. Here, as he also stresses, the matter of political behavior and the uses (and abuses) of political power must be realistically confronted. "I have tried to take the measure of man as a creature of his socioeconomic arrangements and his political bonds," he notes. Hence, for Heilbroner, any "reconstruction of the material basis of civilization" must have its beginning and its ending in human capacities that have a measurable and verifiable dimension. Moral, metaphysical, and religious essences, and contingencies, it is made amply clear, are irrelevant.

The full challenge to human survival still lies in the future, for, as Heilbroner argues, no modern industrial nation wants any systematic economic retrenchment at this point. Nevertheless, as he insists, "the outlook is for what we call 'convulsive change'—change forced upon us by external events rather than by conscious choice, by catastrophe rather than by calculation." The prophetic note here, and throughout the book, is a compelling one, though it arises, again, not from religious roots but rather from a pessimistic utilitarianism. Heilbroner's intellectual preoccupation, no matter how much moderation he counsels, is with the material meaning of life, with man's getting, having, spending, and keeping of the material goods. But, surely, the struggle is something more than a mechanicomaterial struggle, and something more than man's socioeconomic prospect. Heilbroner fails to go beyond the raw fabric of such a struggle and consequently fails to make his prophetic arguments and speculations satisfactory. The question is whether man, even if and when he meets the challenges or effects the transformations that Heilbroner posits, will have no more faith or hope or contentment than he has now. This ultimate question draws no sustaining response from Heilbroner. His argument, with all its prophetic percipience, is limited by a surrender to those selfsame secular conditions with which he is wrestling.

Heilbroner is an example not only of the modern mind at work, at its intellectual best to be sure, but also of a positivistic empiricism in its intellectual judgments and sympathies. It is a mind that deals almost exclusively with the known, the tangible, the external. As such it is a portent and a symptom of our technologico-Benthamite world. His approach to the human condition, his recommendations and solutions, his diagnosis: these are all clearly signs of an ascendant if not victorious pragmatism and rationalism that have spawned many of the very problems that the book surveys. As a result, even if he wants to liberate himself, and life, from these problems, Heilbroner is unable to do so. He remains a prisoner of precisely that deified abject spirit of fact that during the last four hundred years has led to our present predicament. What is so sad is that such a mind recognizes its predicament and dilemma and seeks to modify—to reformulate and to reconstruct—it in those same positivistic, empirical ways that make for self-destruction. This phenomenon is dangerous as well as pathetic, for it shows how much modern man is a slave of materialist illusion, what Simone Weil, and Plato long before her, imaged as "the Great Beast." Even when civilization is tottering at its roots, faith in social organization per se remains the religion of the new order. Even when intellectuals like Heilbroner see what has gone wrong, they still insist on sustaining their illusion of progress, no matter how limited or modified.

In the final struggle against the terrible epochal happenings that he traces in the future of man, Heilbroner calls for help from "the intellectual elements of Western nations whose privileged role as sentries for society takes on a special importance in the face of things as we now see them." This is an astounding statement! Anyone who has read Irving Babbitt's *Rousseau and Romanticism* (1919) or Julien Benda's *La Trahison des clercs* (1927) should by now know the full and continuing extent of betrayal and the high rate of desertion among intellectuals in the modern age. But this is another instance, really, of the alarming limitations of Heilbroner's general premises and approach. If he had any understanding of the roots of the crisis of spirit in our time he could hardly appeal to those "sentries for society" who have steadily, even ruthlessly, and with an imposed uniformity of thought in all cultural spheres, preached the new gospel of power, the new Logos, that rejects those lessons in piety which must contain first and last principles. But Heilbroner's remarks here are, if astounding, not surprising. Wisdom is not something we have come to expect from our enlightened intellectuals. Heilbroner's thesis, in spite of all the intelligence of its sociological "reflections," dissolves (like our "dissolving society," in Lord Radcliffe's phrase) into nothingness insofar as it ultimately ignores the truth of what Edmund Burke expressed in words that progressivist ideologues scorn: "There is no qualification for government but virtue or wisdom, actual or presumptive."

11

Presenting Mr. Marx

FOR MARXISTS, *The Letters of Karl Marx*,[1] containing in translation 366 of the 1,523 preserved letters in the *Marx-Engels Werke*, is something of an embarrassment. In a discussion of *The Letters of Karl Marx*, Amiri Baraka (Leroi Jones) accuses Saul K. Padover of trying to "De-Marx" the letters by excising their political meaning and angrily concludes that "This 'collection' is merely a bourgeois comment on Marx, extremely unfortunate since it interferes with our understanding of Marx himself."[2] The Marx who should be remembered, he thinks, is the Marx who constructed "a basic scientific Communist philosophy as a method of analysis and a means of action, in real life!" Only then, Baraka seems to be saying, will Marx be properly presented as a martyr and savior, as a modern dialectical equal to the Socrates of Hellenism and the Jesus of Christianity. And only then will we have the kind of icon appropriate to a revolutionary prophet, a genius who made simultaneously "a critique of heaven" and a "critique of earth." Obviously what Baraka is demanding is that Marx be presented as more than a hero, or a fighter, or a saint (without God): that, in fact, he be presented in a form that accords with hagiographic scripture. One is reminded by such complaining remarks that the intellectual left, seeking incessantly to "demythologize" whatever opposes its dialectics, cannot tolerate any challenge to the myth of Marxism, even when, as it happens, Karl Marx damns himself in himself. In concluding, therefore, that an understanding of the real Marx will emerge only when a collection in English of the Marx–Engels correspondence is made by a Marxist, Baraka also reveals why it is fortunate, for a change, that a radical doctrinaire is not the editor of these letters.

The personal side of Marx disclosed in this collection is not especially sympathetic. The softer, gentler elements that lend themselves to hagiography are precisely those that in Marx transpose into rancor, abrasiveness, pugnacity, self-righteousness; into a consuming aggres-

1. Selected and trans. with Explanatory Notes and an introduction by Saul K. Padover (Englewood Cliffs, N.J., 1979).
2. "The Domesticated Marx," *Book World* (January 13, 1980), 8.

siveness that helps to explain why, for their books, biographers of Marx have used such subtitles as "a study in fanaticism," "the passionate logician," and "man and fighter." Here it is worth noting that Marx was an admiring student of Epicurus, the materialist Greek philosopher; his doctoral thesis sought to show the differences between Democritus and Epicurus. Yet, even the little we know of Epicurus's life, as reported by a third-century Greek biographer, Diogenes Laertius, gives a picture of a man of "unsurpassed good will," gentleness, reasonableness. For these qualities one will look in vain in Marx's letters, most of them written to his intimate friend and collaborator, Friedrich Engels (1820–1895), from whom, as Marx said, he kept no secrets. These letters help to delineate Marx's outer and inner terrain; the public man and the private man emerge monogenically, despite some scholars' insistence that there are "many Marxes." Such insistence tends not only to rationalize the flaws in Marx's character but also to disregard his brutal intellectuality. No matter how eclectic or protective his apologists may be, the Marx who reveals himself in these letters is precisely the Marx perceived with astonishing insight by Carl Schurz (1829–1906), the German-American statesman and writer. In his autobiography Schurz recalled being present at a congress of democratic associations, held in Cologne in the summer of 1848, and went on to pen this memorable sketch of Marx, one of the participants:

> The somewhat thick-set man, with his broad forehead, his very black hair and beard and his dark sparkling eyes, at once attracted general attention. He enjoyed the reputation of having acquired great learning, and as I knew very little of his discoveries and theories, I was all the more eager to gather words of wisdom from the lips of that famous man. This expectation was disappointed in a peculiar way. Marx's utterances were indeed full of meaning, logical and clear, but I have never seen a man whose bearing was so provoking and intolerable. To no opinion, which differed from his, he accorded the honor of even a condescending consideration. Everyone who contradicted him he treated with abject contempt; every argument that he did not like he answered either with biting scorn at the unfathomable ignorance that had prompted it, or with opprobrious aspersions upon the motives of him who had advanced it. I remember most distinctly the cutting disdain with which he pronounced the word "bourgeois"; and as a "bourgeois," that is as a detestable example of the deepest mental and moral degeneracy he denounced everyone that dared to oppose his opinion.[3]

Schurz's impression of Marx correlates with the overall impression of the letters in this volume. Neither apologetics, nor critical or biographical eclecticism, nor a psychohistorical approach can alter

3. *The Autobiography of Carl Schurz*, an abridgement in one volume by Wayne Andrews, with an introduction by Allan Nevins (New York, 1961 [1906–1908]), 20.

the traits that shaped Marx's character and defined his sensibility. Engels himself, in a short eulogy delivered at Marx's burial in unconsecrated ground at Highgate Cemetery, London, on March 17, 1883, helps us to penetrate that character and to measure that sensibility when he asserts that fighting was Marx's element (*Der Kampf war sein Element*).[4] Any perusal of his letters corroborates this belligerent aspect of Marx's life. Marx's was a life without felicity or refining grace, without *humanitas*; a life that lacked appreciation of music, sun, beauty, poetry. To be sure, in a letter dated November 10, 1837, which has been preserved from his youth and which begins this collection, a nineteen-year-old Marx, then studying at Berlin University, writes at length to his father of his ambition to be a poet who wants to find "the dances of the Muses and the music of Satyrs." But he goes on to explain in this remarkable letter of self-examination and self-advertisement that his ambition "was purely idealistic," poetry "to be merely a companion." Marx gave up writing poetry after 1837, having written three volumes in all, most of the poems of a romantic and uneven quality, disconcerting to his disciples. In April 1841 Marx received the Ph.D. degree from Jena University. From early July till mid-October he lived in Bonn in expectation of securing a university appointment. But neither the vocation of a poet nor that of a teacher was to be Marx's. He began to turn his attention to journalism as a career, even as he now found the proximity of the Bonn professors intolerable: "Who wants forever to converse with intellectual stink animals, with people who study only for the purpose of finding new boards in all the corners of the world!"

Cocksureness marks even his earliest letters, as does also a condescending and a choleric attitude. During his stay in Bonn he particularly vented his disdain on the theologians of Bonn University, singling out Friedrich Rudolf Hasse for special abuse: "... I never saw anything more in him than a big, booted provincial parson ... [who] speaks of religiosity as a product of life experience, by which he probably means his flourishing pedagogy and his fat belly, for fat bellies undergo all kinds of experiences and, as Kant says, when it's behind it's an *F.*, and if above, a religious inspiration. The pious Hasse with his religious constipations!" Early on in these letters, in fact, Marx's scatological orientation takes hold and becomes at times as embarrassing as his anti-semitism: "Many Jews and bedbugs hereabouts," he remarked at one point, completely forgetting the fact that he was descended from rabbis on both sides of his family.[5] Indeed, as

---

4. Quoted in full by Robert Payne, *Marx* (New York, 1968), 500–501.
5. See Nathaniel Weyl, *Karl Marx: Racist* (New Rochelle, N.Y., 1979).

one repeatedly encounters mean attitudes in Marx's letters, the reasons why he did not become a lyric poet or a *Dozent* ("rotten and rotting others") explain themselves without much difficulty. In Marx some, like Amiri Baraka, hear the voice of "the new Moses." But the voice of Marx is unvaryingly grim, oppressive, unyielding, harsh. The so-called "many Marxes" speak in one voice, homogenous rather than resilient, strident rather than compassionate. To read Marx's letters is to be reminded of how far he is removed from, how much he is antagonistic to, the serene counsel of a Baruch Spinoza: "With regard to human affairs, not to laugh, not to cry, not to become indignant, but to understand." It is not understanding that one finds in Marx's letters; nor is it the virtue of equanimity, what Marx's "worthy Epicurus" spoke of as imperturbability, that informs his thought.[6] Rather, it is the voice of a driven and possessed man that speaks with shrill intransigence, the voice of one who delighted in struggle. "It is bad to perform menial services even for freedom and to fight with needles instead of clubs," we hear Marx screaming in one letter. And again we recall the words in Engels's funeral oration: "Battle was his element."

The early 1840s were to signal the beginning of Marx's lifelong journalistic efforts, invariably revolving around his radical social criticism of political questions. His letters during this period provide an ardent revolutionary view of "the old world [which] belongs to the philistines." In a letter written in September 1843, while he still lived in Cologne, Marx spoke of the need to discover the new world from a critique of the old one, pleading for a "ruthless criticism of all that exists, ruthless also in the sense that criticism does not fear its results and even less so a struggle with the existing powers." The chief function of the critic should be the creation of a criticism of and a participation in politics, "in *real* conflicts, and in identifying with them." "The reform of consciousness consists *only* in making the world aware of its perception, waking up from its own dream, *explaining* its own actions," he wrote with a Promethean defiance that anticipated *The Manifesto of the Communist Party* (1848). From late October 1843 till mid-January 1845 Marx lived in Paris. These were decisive years which saw him associating with Communistic societies and calling for an "uprising of the proletariat." During his Gallic years, too, he began his long friendship and collaboration with Engels and developed and defined his political and economic ideas. Following his departure from Paris, Marx went to Brussels. One of his most important letters of his Brussels years is that of December 28,

6. See George A. Panichas, *Epicurus* (New York, 1967).

1846, in which he discussed Pierre-Joseph Proudhon's book *The Philosophy of Poverty*. This long letter speaks volumes in communicating Marx's violent polemical manners, as well as showing his materialist concept of history; it also looks ahead to Marx's destructive criticism of Proudhon, a libertarian socialist, in *La Misère de la philosophie* (1847). Contempt and controlled rage are evident throughout this letter; Marx, as Engels so well described his friend's intellectual weaponry, "battled with a passion and a tenacity which few could rival."

Marx judged Proudhon's book as being "on the whole bad, very bad." He accuses his socialist contemporary of failing to understand "the present social conditions in their concatenation" and of being incapable of comprehending economic development. Emphasizing that man's material relationships form the basis of all his relationships, Marx charges that Proudhon confuses ideas with things and that, "incapable of following the real movement of history, gives you a phantasmagoria which has the presumption of being a dialectical phantasmagoria." As such Proudhon's is "Hegelian rubbish." The letter, as it goes on page after page, with increasing ferocity and abuse—"Mr. Proudhon has very well understood that men produce cloth, linen, silks, and it is a great merit that he has understood that little!"—underscores Schurz's belief that Marx was intolerably dogmatic and condescending. Proudhon, as an unforgiving Marx knew, distrusted the latter's authoritarian and centralist ideas, no less than he distrusted the Communism that destroys freedom by taking away from the individual control over his means of production.[7] Marx posits his arguments with savage force in order to paint Proudhon as a socialist political theorist who sought to equilibrate his radical, realist, and moralist orientations. For Marx, then, Proudhon accepts and even deifies economic categories which, as motive forces, express bourgeois relationships in the form of thought. That is, he believes that Proudhon operates with bourgeois ideas, that he supposes them to be eternal verities, and that he seeks a synthesis of these ideas. The error, or heresy, of Proudhon and his followers, according to Marx, "arises from the fact that the bourgeois man is to them the only possible basis of every society, and that they cannot imagine a state of society in which man has ceased to be bourgeois." That Proudhon is blind to the empirical fact that it is necessary to overthrow the categories in order to transform the practical life of society; that, in short, "you find in him from the beginning a *dualism*

---

7. Two important studies are Alan Ritter's *The Political Thought of Pierre-Joseph Proudhon* (Princeton, N.J., 1969) and Edward Hyams's *Pierre-Joseph Proudhon: His Revolutionary Life, Mind, and Works* (New York, 1979).

between life and ideas, soul and body . . . ," are incapacities, social contradictions put in action, that make Proudhon "from head to foot the philosopher and economist of the *petite bourgeoisie.*" In his biography, which so angered the intellectual left, Robert Payne discerns the confrontation between Marx and Proudhon as an instance of the "first purge," and he goes on to observe: "The purges were not invented in Soviet Russia. They appeared at the very beginning of Marxist communism, and were part of the system."[8]

Expelled from Germany, Belgium, and France for his revolutionary activities, Marx finally departed in August 1849 for London, where he spent the rest of his life. The early years in England were for Marx, his wife, and his children squalid and distressing. "My situation is now such that I must under any circumstance raise some money in order to be able to continue working," he wrote of his besetting financial problems, which he likened to a small war that always threatened to defeat him. That "one is stuck in the muck up to one's neck" becomes a common complaint in his letters. Illnesses were to join economic debilities in plaguing Marx and his family. The death of his eight-year-old son Edgar, on April 6, 1855, was a heavy blow. "It is indescribable how we miss the child everywhere," he wrote to Engels. "I have already experienced all kinds of ill luck, but only now do I know what real misfortune is. I feel myself broken down. . . . I have had such wild headaches since the burial that I have lost the power of thinking, hearing, and seeing." Despite deprivations and heartache during his first twenty years in London, Marx worked on tenaciously: "I spend mostly from nine in the morning to seven in the evening in the British Museum." Withal, too, Marx had to live with the "secret" that the bastard son born in 1851 to Lenchen Demuth, the family's faithful servant, was his, whether by rape or seduction, though Engels, a womanizer, willingly assumed the paternity. (For Marx's aristocratic wife, Jenny, this event, as she wrote in her memoirs, was one "which I shall not dwell upon further, although it brought about a great increase in our private and public sorrows.") Personal anxieties, however, did not keep Marx from his work as the European political writer for the *New York Daily Tribune,* in 1851–62, or from his systematic economic research. His first major book on the subject, *Critique of Political Economy,* was published in Berlin in 1859. Nor did adversity diminish an acerbic, arrogant temperament. His attacks on political enemies and deviators remained vicious, as just one sentence from a letter of commination to an anti-Marx German journalist confirms: "I await you on a different field, in order to tear

8. Payne, *Marx,* 138.

off the hypocritical mask of revolutionary fanaticism, behind which you had known how to conceal cleverly your petty interests, your envy, your unsatisfied vanity and your malcontent over the world's oversight in recognizing your great genius—an oversight that began when you failed your examination."

Marx perceived himself as a modern Prometheus: ". . . I who am engaged in the most bitter conflict with the world (the official one)," we find him writing in 1867. Yet, in the midst of continuing conflict, indeed, even in the midst of his active involvement in the International Working Men's Association, known as the First International and founded in 1864, Marx was not above adopting roles in life which he singled out for attack in the bourgeoisie. He invested in the stock market. He worried that expenses incurred during a prolonged illness would cause disastrous complications. (". . . I am faced with a financial crisis in the *immediate* future, a matter which, apart from the direct effect on me and my family, would also be ruinous for me politically, especially here in London, where one must keep up *appearances*.") He considered becoming a British citizen, though his aim was other than patriotic or grateful. ("I am thinking of becoming *naturalized* as an Englishman for the purpose of being able to travel to Paris in safety. Without such a trip, the French edition of my book [*Das Kapital*] will never come to pass.") He felt that Paul Lafargue's attentions to his daughter Laura were "inappropriate," the unfortunate product of a "Creole temperament." (Marx called Lafargue, who had French, Jewish, Carib Indian, and Negro ancestry, "Gorilla" and "Negrillo.") "In my opinion," he wrote Lafargue on August 13, 1866, just before the latter's engagement to Laura, "true love is expressed in reserve, modesty, and even shyness of the lover toward his idol, and never in temperamental excesses or too premature intimacy." Ten days later, in a letter to Engels, Marx stressed that Lafargue's engagement to his daughter "is arranged to the extent that the Old Man [François Lafargue, Paul's father] wrote me from Bordeaux, asking me for the title of *promesso sposo* for his son and stating his very favorable economic situation."

Undoubtedly there are those who prefer to explain away the paradoxes in Marx's personal attitudes as being the derivatives of a normative-Victorian character or as the manifestations of a day-to-day struggle with, in Baraka's words, "deadly capitalism and its supporters, even with those who count themselves 'Communists.'" But that Marx could also be at once a bourgeois and a revolutionary prophet is corroborated by some of the letters. He speaks, for instance, of his need for the "absolute quiet" that he finds in family life: "Under 'quiet,' I understand 'family life,' the 'noise of children'—this 'microscopic world' that is much more interesting than the 'macroscopic' one." At the very same time he thrills to the severe consequences of the economic crisis which began in Europe in 1857. To Ferdinand Lassalle (1825–1864), the leading spokesman for German socialism, whom Marx distrusted and repeatedly mocked as a "Nigger-Jew," he wrote on May 31, 1858: "On the whole, the present period is agreeable. History has patently in mind to take again a new start, and the signs of dissolution everywhere are delightful for every mind not bent upon the conservation of things as they are." Marx's words here support Baraka's belief that picturing Marx as "the domesticated Marx" is an untruth. They also remind us that Marx was first, last, and always a professional revolutionary, pitilessly preoccupied with the collectivist society of the future. His was a materialist sensibility, rooted in the cult of science and utopian socialism, that makes so devastatingly pertinent Albert Camus' charge that Marx "found any form of beauty under the sun completely alien." In essence, then, Marx affirmed a system that is mechanistic and ruthless: a philosophical destructiveness. Whatever generosity of spirit he may have had was to be readily sacrificed to the laws of social necessity and to the phenomenon of Marx himself. As Simone Weil declares: "Like the feudal magnates of old, like the business men of his own day, he had built for himself a morality which placed above good and evil the activity of the social group to which he belonged, that of professional revolutionaries."[9]

Not unexpectedly the letters underline the absence of an aesthetic sense. Neither paintings nor music appealed to Marx. And though he admired Aeschylus, Shakespeare, and Goethe, his admiration was unremarkable in enthusiasm and ultimately subordinated to *primum vivere* as his first principle of determination. (In Marx's "Paris Manuscripts," in a short section on money, he quotes extensively from Goethe's *Faust* and Shakespeare's *Timon of Athens* in order to stress that money, as the "bond of all bonds," destroys society.) "Bookworming" was, as he said, his most enjoyable occupation, but he lacked any aesthetic response to books or fondness for them, as he was the first to admit: "I am a machine, condemned to devour them and then, throw them, in a changed form, on the dunghill of history." During a walking tour to Canterbury, a city famous from ancient times as the see of the Primate of all England and as the site of the shrine of Thomas à Becket, Marx failed to see Canterbury Cathedral: "Happily, I was too tired, and it was too late, to look out for the

9. *Oppression and Liberty*, trans. Arthur Wills and John Petrie, with an introduction by F. C. Ellert (Amherst, Mass., 1973), 193.

celebrated cathedral." This reaction is equivalent to a double sin of omission and of commission in a man who, disdainful of pilgrimages and illuminations, just managed to spare Christianity from full condemnation on only one count: "After all, we can forgive Christianity much because it taught us to love children." (One can also recall, in this connection, Marx's remark in "On the Jewish Question": "Christianity is the sublime thought of Judaism and Judaism is the vulgar application of Christianity.") In the end Marx's own explanations of himself, given in the Victorian parlor game of "Confessions," serve as the best way of presenting a man who sometimes signed his letters as the "Moor."[10] His favorite virtue, he said, was Strength; his favorite characteristic, Singleness of Purpose; his idea of happiness, To Fight; his favorite heroes, Spartacus and Kepler; his favorite color, Red; his favorite motto: *De omnibus dubitandum* (You must have doubts about everything).

During his last years Marx was sick and unable to work, suffering from carbuncles, toothaches, hemorrhoids, liver disorders, bronchitis, insomnia, coughing—and "God knows what else," as Mrs. Marx exclaimed. His family circumstances were equally depressing: his wife was to die of cancer in 1881; his oldest daughter, Jenny, was to die of the same disease shortly before Marx's own death on March 14, 1883. (Two other daughters, Laura and Eleanor, committed suicide, one in 1898 and the other in 1911.) For him the most cheering news in the final phase of his life came from Russia. To a supporter in the United States, he wrote on November 5, 1880: "In Russia, where *Das Kapital* is more read and appreciated than anywhere else, our success is even greater. . . . Russia is to leap by somersault into the anarchist-communist-atheist millennium!" And to his daughter Laura he wrote on December 14, 1882: "Some recent Russian publications, printed in Holy Russia, not abroad, show the great run of my theories in that country. Nowhere my success is to me more delightful; it gives me the satisfaction that I damage a power, which besides England, is the true bulwark of the old society." No words could have been more aptly written as Leon Trotsky shows in his biography of *The Young Lenin*. Nikolai Lenin (1870–1924), towards the end of the 1880s, was carefully reading and annotating *Das Kapital*, having just a few years earlier turned against religion, when, according to one Bolshevik, he denied the existence of God, tore the cross from his neck, spit on it, and then threw it to the ground (or in the garbage, as one variant of the story has it). Trotsky writes: "Vladimir studied *Das*

10. Quoted by David McLellan, *Karl Marx: His Life and Thought* (New York, 1973), 456–57.

Kapital so thoroughly that everytime he looked at it again he was able to discover new ideas in it. Even during his Samara period he learned, as he himself said later, to 'confer' with Marx."[11]

Whether one is presenting or conferring with Marx, he remains inescapable. "His name will live through the centuries and so also will his work." Engels was absolutely right in the last sentence of his eulogy at Marx's gravesite. No less right is Robert L. Heilbroner, Marx's American interpreter in the present day, who declares in his most recent book, "In our times and henceforth, change is upon the world, in large part inspired and guided by Marxism itself."[12] But neither in eulogy nor in interpretation is the full truth of Marx and Marxism to be fathomed. For *that* truth one needs to hear from those who are witnesses to the destructive change that Marx caused. One of these witnesses, the press agency Tass reported, "has been conducting subversive activities against the Soviet state for a number of years" and has been repeatedly warned about their "impermissibility." His crime was that, in "alarm and hope," he was decrying the phenomena of decomposition in "a sick society": "the most refined form of totalitarian-socialist society [which] exists in the USSR." That witness is Andrei D. Sakharov, who only the other day, en route to exile in the Volga River city, sent this message to his wife—and to the world: "Apparently I'm being sent to Gorky."

11. Leon Trotsky, *The Young Lenin,* trans. Max Eastman, and ed. and annotated by Maurice Friedberg (New York, 1972), 187.
12. *Marxism: For and Against* (New York, 1980), 174.

12

Conservative Expositors

THE SPECTRUM, TONE, AND DIRECTION, as well as the idiom, aim, and emphasis of Richard L. Cutler's *The Liberal Middle Class: Makers of Radicals*[1] are aptly and adequately summarized in this paragraph from the dust jacket:

> Dr. Cutler reviews the influences that helped sire these [American] radicals: the glorification of sex, permissiveness in our courts and schools and homes, tolerance of drugs, the welfare mentality, double-minded politicians—but he digs deeper, too. To the equation he adds Mom's and Dad's nights out and weekend vacations "to get away from the kids"; their easy acceptance of everything the *Times* and TV had to say; their failure ("We're just too busy") to check out Johnny's teachers and textbooks, to attend church with him (where they might have been shocked at the preacher's latest exhortation); the dozens of other "little" things that shape today's radical.

Cutler enumerates the most overt problems of the contemporary cultural situation that some Americans have been complaining about with various degrees of severity, or success, or sincerity since the late 1960s. Such a book is essentially, therefore, a chronicle of historical and cultural happenings in their special American contexts. As a protest against an aspect of the ethos of modern liberalism, this book is one for which we have need if we are ever to comprehend the total liberalizing process that contributes to the political radicalization that, at its worst, must culminate in nihilism. A special form of our American malaise is hence focused on through episodic reminders of and references to the radical movement.

The main value of Cutler's book is in its descriptive rather than in its investigative and critical powers. For it is in the medium of reenactment of what has transpired that it underlines its purpose. The approach is usually exclamatory and rhetorical; the bitterness of the ideological confrontations of the sixties and the early seventies still lingers in these pages, chiefly because the overview is polemical, at times as sanctimonious and dully didactic in its conservative dialectic as is that in the liberal dialectic with its by now all too

1. New Rochelle, N.Y., 1973.

familiar neurasthenic symbology and crude vocabulary. In presenting the drama of contemporary American social and political history as it has developed furiously—barbarously—Cutler captures a sense of the immediate moment. To say this is to say that *The Liberal Middle Class* is limited in scope: limited in its content and in its exposition of the conservative viewpoint. The impersonal, the dispassionate, the disinterested and transcendent qualities required of the critical spirit do not inform Cutler's effort. His is not so much a critique of the "liberal middle class" as it is a commination. If we are to discover the problematic significance of the matters that Cutler portrays, and if the conservative critique of liberalism is to have enduring influence, it will need to be based on rigorous critical discriminations and judgments. In any discouraging period, when the crisis of civilization reaches fearful proportions, the need for a highly disciplined critical spirit is indispensable to any conservative critique.

What has always been wrong with the liberal doctrine is its expansive, orgiastic emotionality, its shallowness, its sullied romanticism and sickly sentimentality. But these fallacies cannot be explained away by conservative ideologues who posit rhetorical animadversions. The dissimulating liberal habit of mind should not be echoed in the conservative. It easily becomes cant, of which the liberals have been such celebrated purveyors. The critical spirit, and the critical method, by which man analyzes and discriminates and traces causes and effects, was never one that enlightened liberals adopted or favored. Discipline is not, after all a sustaining strength of the liberal creed. "At the bottom of man's heart," T.S. Eliot wrote back in 1916 in the course of discussing Paul Elmer More's *Aristocracy and Justice,* "there is always the beast, resentful of restraints of civilized society, ready to spring out at the instant this restraint relaxes. . . . The human soul . . . in order to be human, requires discipline." This element of discipline, and that of definite standards, is one that no genuine intellectual conservatism can ever overlook and is, or should be, the moral mainstay of the conservative critique. In any metaphysic of the conservative doctrine the discipline, or askesis, to which Eliot refers is what ultimately creates insight and wisdom. No conservative, no conservatism, can be either transcendent or consummate if it fails to fulfill such a metaphysic. The drama of liberalism—and it is to the cruder and more obvious aspects of this drama that Cutler largely confines himself—requires diagnostic, critical evaluation if cultural order, permanence, and truth are to be grasped. Merely to decry liberalism's chaos of sensibility does not legitimatize any conservative critique, particularly when that critique amounts to no more than journalistic or political platitudes, as the case may be.

Unfortunately, contemporary American conservatism, like American liberalism, does not seem to have great expositors (or statesmen) equipped to see beyond today's headline and crisis with that moral and metaphysical vision that is pregnant with discipline, distinctions, and standards. Cutler's book is another example of such a deficiency. He, too, views our present and general plight from a journalistic rather than from a metaphysical outlook. Such a conservative view is incomplete insofar as it cannot move beyond the edge of the dramatic. Conservative pundits, no less than their adversary liberal pundits, are captives of the immediate moment. The cumulative effect of such a captivity is one of mediocrity.

We need much more critical diligence than that displayed in *The Liberal Middle Class*. We continue to need, and we must demand, a conservative critique that, to repeat, analyzes and discriminates and traces causes and effects. When we have it, either in part or in whole, we shall only then be able to threaten the liberal bastion, which in Western society has been steadily fortifying itself for at least two hundred years now. The enemy is entrenched and powerful, if one is to judge by the pervasive disorder and indiscipline of twentieth-century civilization. Any attempt to defy such a situation requires the most strenuous effort of thought commensurate with a total outlook on life. Journalistic, simplistic, uncritical values abound on both sides of the liberal-conservative debate, as any glance at multiplying opinions and publications will confirm. We know, or should know, the sad truths of what Cutler re-creates for us here. But in what direction must we go? How are we to deal with cultural breakdown beyond some of the threadbare solutions that Cutler and others mechanically supply? How is the critical spirit really to be implemented in the momentous confrontation between two opposing outlooks on life? These questions are deeper and more troubling, and certainly more philosophical than political, than anything seen in this book, in which symptoms are duly indicated but in which the disease of liberalism is hardly gauged in its multidimensional consequences.

Indeed, Cutler reveals a peculiarly conservative form of self-indulgence. No reader who subscribes to the critical spirit will be easily convinced by a statement like the following: "On the actions of the great majority of Middle Americans, then, rests our future." Such words merely stress the faulty thinking found in Cutler's work. Minority culture, to which conservatism traditionally gives support and ideological guidance, is certainly not understood by any writer who can appeal to "the great majority of Middle Americans." No reasoning and reasonable conservative, whatever his views of the "rapid evolution of collectivisim," would declare in such a callous way, as does Cutler, that "Under the Social Security concept, the central government has assumed the responsibility of providing basic care to elderly, disabled, or retired people." Once more Cutler speaks like some ancient conservative mandarin, a true-blue Tory, who refuses to affirm the ultimate and redeeming virtues of a compassionate and humanistic conservatism. Here he helps to recall the serious nature of the charge directed against William Buckley's "heartless" conservatism. Finally, but not least, there is this statement that must bring into question the worth, even the integrity, of Cutler's judgmental power: "They [the radicals] are revolted by Spiro Agnew because he is not intimidated by them and is tough enough to take them on directly." Such a mindless statement, by itself, is enough to discredit Cutler's basic conservative aims. Conservatism without heart and without mind and without metaphysical anguish is depressingly evidenced in such statements. We must necessarily conclude that a conservatism that disintegrates into reactionaryism is no less acceptable than a pluralistic liberalism that breeds radicalism.

In its deficiencies and in its negativeness, however, *The Liberal Middle Class* has the virtue of forcing one to reexamine both the essences and the exposition of true critical conservatism, which is at once in a great tradition that goes back to Edmund Burke and yet alert and adaptable to our modern dilemma. Cutler, of course, is in the end impervious to the intellectual tradition of modern conservatism in which the writings of Irving Babbitt, Paul Elmer More, or T.S. Eliot, for example, comprise monuments of critical excellence. It is in the writings of these masters of modern conservatism that one will find precisely those ideas and beliefs that elude Cutler, except in his rhetorical perversities. Curiously enough he provides neither a single footnote nor a selected bibliography, even though much of what he is trying to say here has been said in the recent past, and said with much critical perspicacity, in John W. Aldridge's *In the Country of the Young* (1970). One repeated problem with *The Liberal Middle Class* is that it is permeated by the tantrums of a provincial conservatism that neglects the great tradition in favor of the dreary sayings of a Spiro Agnew. Clearly this is conservative Americanization at a low ebb: a superficial, misused conservatism that, intellectually and critically, has no shock—the "philosophical shock [which] is the beginning of wisdom," as Paul Tillich put it.

It is the ills of our age, particularly since 1945, as much an apocalyptic date as 1918 in terms of civilizational breakdown, that undoubtedly concern Cutler. But his book lacks not only the critical acuteness of Aldridge's study but also the philosophical shock that exemplifies, for instance, the late Richard M. Weaver's *Ideas Have Consequences*, which was published in 1948 as a reaction to World War II and specifically to the modern cultural dissolution and the decline of belief in standards and values. This is not the place to eulogize Weaver's book, to which neither eulogy nor summary can do justice. It is the kind of book that must be read and assimilated. At all events, *Ideas Have Consequences* has enormous value in a comparative critical relation to *The Liberal Middle Class*. Weaver's book satisfies, as Cutler's does not, the criteria that place it in the great conservative tradition that alone is worthy of intellectual respect. The judging mind of a conservative expositor can be seen at work in *Ideas Have Consequences* as we fathom in it vigorous and subtle handling of conservative ideas, moral seriousness, and judicial courage and poise. It is the kind of exposition of a pure philosophical conservatism that synthesizes conservative convictions and critical standards. In it, above all, we recognize the conservative point of view as a total disciplined view of life.

Invariably standards require definition, that is to say the support of discriminating judgment and maturity of thought. No view of life can be sustained without such a careful process. In the end what is so wrong with *The Liberal Middle Class* is that the critical process is marred by a violence and excess that make any critique of liberalism suspect and even meaningless. Because of its inherent weaknesses, Cutler's contribution neither refines nor strengthens the conservative idea. This failure is all the more apparent when we consider what Weaver writes in his book. Even a random sampling of statements like the following from *Ideas Have Consequences* is enough to remind us what standard of judgment the critique of liberalism ideally requires; what, in short, challenges in the most compelling way the dominant liberal faith governing the desecration of American, of Western civilization:

> The practical result of nominalist philosophy is to banish the reality which is perceived by the intellect and to posit as reality that which is perceived by the senses. With this change in the affirmation of what is real, the whole orientation of culture takes a turn, and we are on the road to modern empiricism.

> A frank facing of the past is unpleasant to the tenderminded, teaching as it does sharp lessons of limitation and retribution.

> Egotism in work and art is the flowering, after long growth, of a heresy about human destiny. Its abhorrence of discipline and form is usually grouped with the signs of "progress."

What has happened to the one world of meaning? It has been lost for want of definers. Teachers of the present order have not enough courage to be definers; lawmakers have not enough insight.

. . . the world is now more than ever dominated by the gods of mass and speed and that the worship of these can lead only to the lowering of standards, the adulteration of quality, and, in general, to the loss of those things which are essential to the life of civility and culture. The tendency to look with suspicion upon excellence, both intellectual and moral, as "undemocratic" shows no signs of diminishing.

Conservatism has, in Richard Cutler, its ranter, but it also has, in Richard Weaver, its seeker.

Part IV

MODES OF SENSIBILITY

.

Only the living heart and the creative spirit matters—nothing else.

—D.H.LAWRENCE

13

The Jamesian Mirror

I

THE LETTERS OF AN IMAGINATIVE ARTIST can help to explain the birth and the growth of his artistic consciousness. They can reveal the undisguised workings of his mind, the reaches of his intellectual comprehension, the interior realm of his psyche. Letters can communicate the elemental immediacy of an artist's thought and art. They can help in discovering a writer's impelling pattern of thinking and working; in providing hints, that is to say, as to the ways in which his vision first manifests itself and progresses. Letters of men of genius give clues, record reactions, clarify and amplify the process of vision. They also disclose a writer's critical process, which plays no small part in the maturation of his creative vision. The force of insight, the intuitive perception of human meaning and truths, the enduring formative power of overwhelming impressions, the discriminations of a fertile mind and a creative imagination: these intrinsic facets, indispensable to a writer's rendered vision of man and his world, can be identified, even in their rawest forms and fragments of enunciation, in his letters. A writer's letters thus contain a running commentary with regard to his immediate personal situation, whereby he comments existentially and, above all, spontaneously on his world, on his time, on himself and others, on his public and most private concerns. Such letters contain the infinite reverberations of internal dialogue.

Henry James's letters, written during the years 1856–83,[1] should remind readers of a literary genre that, in the modern world of technics and electronics when, it is proclaimed, a computer can write a poem, is becoming a lost art. A major symptom of this loss, as we can see from any number of examples, is the breakdown of the written word. The English language, particularly in its American form, has become the "language of hurry," to use E.M. Forster's phrase. Too,

---

1. *Henry James: Letters, Volume I: 1843–1875*, ed. Leon Edel (Cambridge, Mass., 1975).

the barbarization of language is generally concomitant with the barbarization of civilization. One can only begin to wonder, then, what a volume of letters by a contemporary novelist, say Norman Mailer, will be like if and when published a half century hence. It is fairly predictable that it will not be in the class of great letter-writing like that of John Keats in the nineteenth century or of D. H. Lawrence in the twentieth. It most certainly will not have the refining graces, the informing sensibility, the beauty and sensitivity, the opulence and quiet vigor—in short, the character and integrity—that distinguish James's use and command of the English language in his correspondence (and ultimately in all his writings). In a deep sense these letters portray the substantive development of James's sensibility, its education and its discipline, as well as his search for standards of order. Throughout one finds a reverence for civilization, a quality eminently characterizing our most civilized of novelists.

James's letters can be exemplarily approached within these contexts of epistolary criteria. He was convinced that only his finest letters should be published. A rigorous selectivity is invariably precedent to standards of excellence in all literary forms. What is most impressive about James's early letters is the extent of his connections, his wide range of interests, his intellectual curiosity and depth. "The love of art and letters," he wrote, "grows steadily with any growth." An undemonstrative but always discriminatingly powerful vitality is evident in these letters as they describe the people James came to know, the places in Europe to which he traveled and in which he lived for varying periods of time, the books he read and wrote about, the serious matters of civilization to which he gave pious and concentrated attention. The most evident quality that James discloses is that of a full and consecrated seriousness. Again and again he shows a prescient awareness of his future tasks, as his judgmental power, his exploration and measurement of character, his growing recognition of the life of value are viewed in steady development. With enviable and exceptional maturity of critical reflection a twenty-four-year-old James wrote: "It is by this constant exchange and comparison, by the wear and tear of living and talking and observing that works of art shape themselves into completeness; and as artists and workers, we owe most to those who bring to us most of human life."

Repeatedly we find a young and privileged James brushing shoulders with people of talent and achievement—Dante Gabriel Rossetti, Leslie Stephen, William Morris, John Ruskin, George Eliot, Matthew Arnold, Henry Adams. His reactions to his encounters with the great show the independence and acute percipience that belong to genius. Of his meeting with Ruskin he wrote:

> In face, in manner, in talk, in mind, he is weakness pure and simple. I use the word, not invidiously but scientifically. He has the beauties of his defects; but to see him only confirms the impression given by his writing; that he has been scared back by the grim face of reality into the world of unreason and illusion, and that he wanders there without a compass or a guide—or any light save the fitful flashes of his beautiful genius.

James's reaction to George Eliot is equally compelling for its visual and analytical powers of observation:

> To begin with she is magnificently ugly—deliciously hideous. She has a low forehead, a dull grey eye, a vast pendulous nose, a huge mouth, full of uneven teeth and a chin and jaw-bone *qui n'en finessent pas*. . . . Now in this vast ugliness resides a most powerful beauty which, in a very few minutes, steals forth and charms the mind, so that you end as I ended, in falling in love with her. . . . An admirable physiognomy—a delightful expression, a voice soft and rich as that of a counselling angel—a mingled sagacity and sweetness—a broad hint of a great underlying world of reserve, knowledge, pride and power—a hundred conflicting shades of consciousness and simpleness—shyness and frankness—graciousness and remote indifference—these are some of the more definite elements of her personality.

But whether it is on an individual or a collective basis, James displays strength of insight and comprehension, as instanced in his view of the American travelers who are incapable of "possessing" Europe:

> There is but one word to use in regard to them—vulgar; vulgar, vulgar. Their ignorance—their stingy, grudging, defiant attitude towards everything European—their perpetual reference of all things to some American standard or precedent which exists only in their own unscrupulous wind-bags—and then our unhappy poverty of voice, of speech and of physiognomy—these things glare at you hideously.

Order, proportion, and control are virtues that James especially revered in art as in life. Yet his affirmation of humanizing restraints is not without the firm support of an underlying compassion and sympathy, which appear in this passage of a letter to Charles Eliot Norton, James's first mentor, whose wife had recently died:

> One thing however by this time you know a good deal about—the mysteries of sorrow and what the soul finds in it for support as well as for oppression. The human soul is mighty, and it seems to me we hardly know what it may achieve (as well as suffer) until it has been plunged deep into trouble. Then indeed, there seems something infinite in pain and it opens out before us, door within door, and we seem doomed to tread its whole infinitude; but there seems also something infinite in

effort and something supremely strong by its own right in the grim residuum of conscious manhood with which we stand face to face to the hard reality of things.

A reticent romanticism often appears beneath the surface, particularly in James's evocation of spirit of place, in this respect prefiguring one of the most enchanting features of his novels. Unlike his brother William, who preferred Germany, he was profoundly attracted by Italy, as he shows in this portentous passage:

> But the atmosphere is nevertheless weighted—to infinitude—with something that forever stirs and feeds and fills the mind and makes the sentient being feel that on the whole he can lead as complete a life here as elsewhere.—Then there is the something—the myriad some-things—that one grows irresistibly and tenderly fond of —the unanalysable *loveableness* of Italy. This fills my spirit mightily on occasions and seems a sort of intimation of my learning how to be and do something, here.

Nobility and generosity are qualities that one inescapably meets in the letters. One does not detect any sense of that impoverishing malaise—the hysteria, the anger, the despair, the dread, the hatred—that some modern novelists have suffered from and enshrined in their art, overcoming James. Evenness of temperament, fully comprehending but not surrendering to the "modern temper," informs the education of James's sensibility. Steadiness, honesty, dignity, a refining conception of right and wrong: these attributes are there in the early letters. Nowhere are these better or more cogently seen than in his (relevant) appraisal of critics: "There is such a flood of precepts and so few examples—so much preaching, advising, rebuking and reviling, and so little *doing:* so many gentlemen sitting down to dispose in half an hour of what a few have spent months and years in producing. A single positive attempt, even with great faults, is worth generally most of the comments and amendments on it."

Dedication to craft and to excellence is explicit in James's letters. "To write a series of good little tales," he declares, "I deem ample work for a life-time." There is no easy formula for finding one's best form of expression; writing requires hard, steady work, as James informed William Dean Howells: "I know I'm too ponderous. But the art of making *substance* light is hard." The need for standards cannot be compromised by an artist who is genuinely committed to a great moral responsibility and who, in the end, writes not only in a "great tradition," with an undeviating emphasis on cultural continuity, but also for a minority culture. "The multitude, I am more and more convinced," he stated, "has absolutely no taste—none at least that a thinking man is bound to defer to. To write for the few who have is doubtless to lose money—but I am not afraid of starving." In a letter dated November 1, 1875, James announced his retreat from the "American scene." The "passionate pilgrim" returned to England. "I take possession of the world—I inhale it—I appropriate it."

II

During the years between 1875 and 1883, James confronted his imagination, exploring, disciplining, and determining its genius. What is most observable in his correspondence of this particular period[2] is the assertion of self-confidence, which he disclosed with commanding consistency. His dedication to the novelist's craft, to the application of his vision, presages the indomitable allegiance that was to become the hallmark of a lifetime's labors. Indeed, though he showed himself to be very much a man of the world—during the winter of 1879 in London he dined out, as he almost triumphantly announced, 107 times!—he invariably knew and indicated that his first loyalty belonged to his art. If there is any phrase that captures the communicated quality of these letters, it is disciplined control. The mind that is ever at play here is one that practices a constancy of discipline. Though he makes no great (or complaining) issue of it, it is implicitly evident that he is continuously, relentlessly involved in the creative effort, the great fruition of which is to be measured in the published writings of this period: *The American* (1877), *The Europeans* (1878), *Daisy Miller* (1879), *Confidence* (1880), *Washington Square* (1881), and *The Portrait of a Lady* (1881).

The letters make it plain that his creative tasks proceeded with a powerful vigor and an unbroken pattern informed by a profoundly moral purposiveness. It is character, a word our crass modernity brutally dismisses, that pervades James's sense of life and molds and supports his achievement in its permanence of meaning. The constituents of the character of his life and work are identifiable everywhere here: in his tone of seriousness, in his feelings of reverence, in his brave decisions and convictions, in his perception of what is right, in his view of civilization, in his refined and refining manner of presentation, in his acute judgments and discriminations. These letters are wonderful and bracing in their manliness, that is, in the absence, whatever the adversities and paradoxes and difficulties of the human

2. *Henry James: Letters, Volume II: 1875–1883,* ed. Leon Edel (Cambridge, Mass., 1976).

situation, of the kind of whining, cowardice, decay, trivializing, perversion, shamelessness, self-pity, debasement, in a word, the rot that modernity increasingly expresses and ennobles. James permits no undue sentimentality, no crude excessiveness or excrescence to impede or distort the process of his rendered thought. His letters bring us into contact with a civilized vitality and ultimately a civilized toughness.

The discriminating levels of this toughness are apparent throughout. And each level is of major proportions and of fateful consequences. There are always, for James, decisions to make and directions to take. He can be seen weighing his decisions judiciously, responsibly—courageously. Each decision, implicit in the discriminating process, portends a gesture of destiny. A moral courage, surely derivative of and consonant with character, dominates his choices. Undoubtedly, his most crucial decision, and the one having the greatest effect on his life's work, was his decision to "appropriate" England. Though James was to call himself an "observant stranger," he was much more than that when one considers the roots that he planted in and the loving allegiance he gave England. Earlier his Parisian domicile excited in him a deep admiration for Gallic life and letters. But his *déménagement* from the rue de Luxembourg to Bolton Street, in London, was to impress upon him a distinctly different and impelling understanding of things, as he made clear in this passage from a letter to his mother, written on Christmas eve, 1876:

> I take very kindly indeed to London, and am immensely contented at having come here. I must be a born Londoner, for the place to withstand the very severe test to which I am putting it: leaving Paris and its brilliancies and familiarities, the easy resources and abundant society I had there, to plunge into darkness, solitude and sleet, in mid-winter— to say nothing of the sooty, woolsy desolation of a London lodging—to do this, and to like this murky Babylon really all the better, is to feel that one is likely to get on here. I like the place, I like feeling in the midst of the English world, however lost in it I may be; I find it interesting, inspiring, even exhilarating.

We have in these words a typifying reaction that is repeated in other letters concerning James's choice of place; of a place where he could locate a center of values and attain a vantage point: "I am, as I say, more and more attached to this great rotundity of London: doubtless because I find that such an attachment is an excellent condition for work." To his brother William he wrote: "I positively *suck* the atmosphere of its intimations and edifications." And to Charles Eliot Norton he stressed: "I attached myself to its mighty variety and immensity, so interesting do I find the spectacle of English life, so well do I get on, on the whole, with people and things, so successfully, on the whole, do I seem to myself to assimilate the total affair." His vision, no less than his destiny, was dependent on the values of an old world, as he made clear to William Dean Howells: "It is on manners, customs, usages, habits, forms, upon all these things matured and established, that a novelist lives—they are the very stuff his work is made of. . . ." England was to constitute for James what modern existentialists term an "entity encountered": a creative opportunity that he felt he could not find in his native America, which lacked, as he noted in his little book of criticism, *Hawthorne* (1879), "a higher civilization." "My dream," he asserted, "is to arrive at the ability to be, in some degree, its [England's] moral portrait-painter!"

Glimpses of James's commitment to his art recur in these letters, revealing a singleness of purpose and a brave perception of the refining virtues of civilization. ("I am interminably supersensitive and analytic," he wrote.) To the discipline of his art he gave himself fully and selflessly; he provided in this respect supreme lessons and examples, the comprehensive value of which is inestimable. It is the inspiration of genius that prevails in his resilient recognition of his mission. "I suspect it is the tragedies in life," he wrote in his thirty-fourth year, "that arrest my attention more than the other things and say more to my imagination; but, on the other hand, if I fix my eyes on a sun-spot I think I am able to see the prismatic colors in it." The tone of the letters is invariably balanced, honest, dignified (another great word that modernity has desecrated). At the same time it is a tone of firmness, doubtlessly arising from an implicit sureness of his own strengths, the enormously reciprocating strengths of character and of vision, that one encounters here. In a letter to William, for example, he defended *The Europeans* against some of his brother's criticisms: "I think you take these things too rigidly and unimaginatively—too much as if an artistic experiment were a piece of conduct, to which one's life were somehow committed. . . ." He also made it clear that he was receptive to disinterested criticism, without which the creator is hindered in striving for excellence: "It is a great thing to have one write to one of one's things as if one were a third person, and you are the only individual who will do this." Hard, steady work is the creative artist's central obligation, he told his brother, even as he went on to formulate this diagnostic insight: "It is something to have learned how to write, and when I look round me and see how few people (doing my sort of work) know how (to my sense,) I don't regret my step by step evolution."

With the death of both his parents in the same year, 1882, deep anguish possessed James. To read his letters relating to their deaths, particularly his mother's, is to fathom the magnitude of his "acute pain." His control of his emotions was, of course, dominant in the face of deep personal loss; a reverential element helped to assuage his grief. "I have *felt* my dear mother's death very deeply—I was passionately attached to her," he wrote to one of his correspondents. "She was sweet, gentle, wise, patient, precious—a pure and exquisite soul. But now she is a memory as beneficent as her presence; and I thank heaven that one can lose a mother but *once* in one's life. The loss of the love, however, is a suffering absolutely apart—for it is the most absolutely unselfish affection any of us can know." And in a letter to his brother, in London when their father died, he described his visit to the graves: "He lies extraordinarily close to Mother, and as I stood there and looked at this last expression of so many years of mortal union, it was difficult not to believe that they were not united again in some consciousness of my belief." More than twenty years later, James was again to describe, this time in his notebooks, another visit to "that unspeakable group of graves" at the Cambridge Cemetery. The following notebook entry, read in the earlier light of his letters on his parents' deaths, affords an inner view of the fine sensibility of a "singular and specialized person" (as Edmund Wilson has described him):

> It was late, in November; the trees all bare, the dusk to fall early, the air all still (at Cambridge, in general, *so* still), with the western sky more and more turning to that terrible, deadly, pure polar pink that shows behind American winter woods. But I can't go over this—I can only, oh, so gently, so tenderly, brush it and breathe upon it—breathe upon it and brush it. It was the moment; it was the hour; it was the blessed flood of emotion that broke out at the touch of one's sudden *vision* and carried me away. . . . Everything was there, everything *came*; the recognition, stillness, the strangeness, the pity and the sanctity and the terror, the death-catching passion and the divine relief of tears.[3]

But James refused to accede to what he called "the grim view"; to Grace Norton he thus wrote: "All one can say is that life brings with it the better as well as the worse, and that while we suffer and talk and call out in vain, we do still live and profit to some extent by the chances of life." Yet he himself never availed of one of those "chances": marriage. For him not to marry, but instead to remain one of the most exceptional of celibates (irreversibly dedicated to the chaste life of the word), excited no paradox. In 1880, in another letter to Grace Norton, he wrote:

> I am unlikely ever to marry. If I were to tell you the grounds of this

3. *The Notebooks of Henry James*, ed. F. O. Matthiessen and Kenneth B. Murdock (New York, 1947), 320–21.

conviction you would think me dismally theoretic. One's attitude toward marriage is a part—the most characteristic part, doubtless—of one's general attitude toward life. Now I don't want to calumniate my attitude toward life; but I am bound to say that if I were to marry I should be guilty in my own eyes of an inconsistency—I should pretend to think just a little better of life than I really do.

In this decision, as in others, he was to display "the courage and the resistance" that are of a piece with his vision; that, like his writings, according to T.S. Eliot, form a complete whole with an interlocking unity and progression.

Repeatedly James disclosed a creative awareness of his life's destiny. This awareness was strictly in character, *and* characteristic of a purer loyalty to imagination and aspiration, which neither adversity nor calamity could extinguish, and which gave him the strength to confront, in himself and in his art, the world that is unrelenting in its glory and affliction. No one who reads the following excerpt, from a letter written on July 28, 1883, to Grace Norton, can fail to be touched by James's acceptance of life, always and heroically, as Ezra Pound wrote in 1918, "on the side of civilization—civilization against barbarism":

I don't know *why* we live—the gift of life comes to us from I don't know what source or for what purpose; but I believe we can go on living for the reason that (always of course up to a certain point) life is the most valuable thing we know anything about and it is therefore presumptively a great mistake to surrender it while there is any yet left in the cup. In other words consciousness is an illimitable power, and though at times it may seem to be all consciousness of misery, yet in the way it propagates itself from wave to wave, so that we never cease to feel, though at moments we appear to, try to, pray to, there is something that holds one in one's place, makes it a standpoint in the universe which it is probably good not to forsake. . . . We all live together, and those of us who love and know, live so most. We help each other—even unconsciously, each in our own effort, we lighten the effort of others, we contribute to the sum of success, make it possible for others to live. Sorrow comes in great waves—no one can know that better than you—but it rolls over us, and though it may almost smother us it leaves us on the spot and we know that if it is strong we are stronger, inasmuch as it passes and we remain. It wears us, uses us, but we wear it and use it in return; and it is blind, whereas we after a manner see. . . . Don't think, don't feel, any more than you can help, don't conclude or decide—don't do anything but *wait*. Everything will pass, and serenity and *accepted* mysteries and disillusionments, and the tenderness of a few good people, and new opportunities and ever so much of life, in a word, will remain.

14

D.H. Lawrence's War Letters

AT THE TIME that World War I was declared D. H. Lawrence and three male companions were on a walking tour in Westmorland in the Lake District of England. Their mood, as Lawrence later recalled in a letter to Lady Cynthia Asquith, dated January 31, 1915, radiated much merriment, and the four travelers felt that they were dwelling in a world of genuine happiness. In this same autobiographical letter he also recollected how he wore a hat round which were twisted water lilies, how they shouted songs, he imitating music-hall twins, and his friend S.S. Koteliansky groaning the Hebrew song *Ranani Sadekim Badanoi* (based on the words of the Thirty-third Psalm, "Rejoice in the Lord, O ye righteous"). Later, but only after they had come down to Barrow-in-Furness, did they realize that "The Great War for Civilization" had begun. Then all the preceding happiness became hushed in an experience that was dramatically transposed into an "electric suspense" as the "amazing, vivid, visionary beauty" of the Lake District was heightened by an "immense pain everywhere."

For Lawrence the early days of the war struck a hard and crushing blow: "The War finished me: it was the spear through the side of all sorrows and hopes." Indeed, so staggered was he that for months following his return to Barrow-in-Furness he felt "as if I had spent those five months in the tomb . . . having the smell of the grave in my nostrils, and a feel of grave clothes about me." In a very deep sense he believed that the war had nearly destroyed his will to live, literally violating and canceling his very being and meaning. He lamented:

> And since then, since I came back, things have not existed for me. I have spoken to no one, I have touched no one, I have seen no one. All the while, I swear, my soul lay in the tomb—not dead, but with a flat stone over it, a corpse, become corpse-cold. And nobody existed, because I did not exist myself. Yet I was not dead—only passed over—trespassed—and all the time I knew I should have to rise again.[1]

This picture of Lawrence at the beginning of World War I, at once

---

1. *The Collected Letters of D. H. Lawrence*, ed. Harry T. Moore (New York, 1962), I, 309–10. All references to Lawrence's letters are from Volume I.

beautiful and terrible, was to remain largely unchanged until the cessation of hostilities and well into the postwar era of the 1920s. When we read through his correspondence written in the period of 1914–18 we are able to see more completely, and with an astonishing intensity, the full range of Lawrence's response to World War I. Likewise, these letters bring to the forefront the figure of a creative artist whose suffering in the course of the war, as J. Middleton Murry wrote in his last work on Lawrence, "was absolutely different, and of an altogether higher order. He suffered under a prophetic vision of the war as a portent of the imminent doom of modern civilization and modern man."[2] Lawrence's response was so direct and unequivocal, so real and unvarnished, that to dismiss or to misinterpret it as being exaggerated, selfish, egotistical, and hysterical is to deprecate an honesty and seriousness inhering in a consciousness undergoing profound travail.

As personal and immediate commentary on a catastrophic event, Lawrence's war letters, as they may very well be called, offer in their own special way as much "truth about the war" as does Siegfried Sassoon in his *Memoirs of an Infantry Officer* (1930), or Edmund Blunden in *Undertones of War* (1928), or Robert Graves in *Goodbye to All That* (1929). It will be seen, too, that the letters are often complemented by Lawrence's artistic achievements. Taken and appraised together they dramatize a basically nonconformist reaction to war that finds its keynote, so to speak, in Lawrence's own statement: "One should stick by one's own soul, and by nothing else. In one's soul, one knows the truth from the untruth, and life from death. And if one betrays one's own soul-knowledge one is the worst of traitors."

Lawrence's immediate reactions to the war must be assessed in an altogether different light from the optimistic faith voiced by many of his contemporaries who, like Rupert Brooke, Julian Grenfell, and even, at first, Isaac Rosenberg, responded to the conflict with an almost religious enthusiasm and sense of relief. (E.B. Osborn in the introduction of his edition of *The Muse in Arms*, published in New York in 1917, glowingly characterized this mood as one of "infinite cheerfulness.")[3] To be sure, Lawrence was not to be counted among

2. J. Middleton Murry, *Love, Freedom, and Society* (London, 1957), 30. See also Paul Delany, *D.H. Lawrence's Nightmare: The Writer and His Circle in the Years of the Great War* (New York, 1978).

3. With an efflorescence of cliché equaled only by a pitiable naïveness, Osborn wrote: "They were not merely unafraid; they all gloried in the thought of the great ordeal to come. And so they went up in sunshine and with singing to win undying fame and deathless gratitude in the valleys of decision where 'The thundering line of battle stands / And in the air Death moans and sings.' "

those "good squires" who were drawn from the demands of polo, roses, croquet, cricket, and fox hunting to become "good soldiers" in The Great War. Undoubtedly, he could appreciate the yearnings of many of his countrymen to escape from a stifling Victorian dullness, "from a world grown old and cold and weary," as Brooke phrased it in his sonnet sequence *1914*. But World War I did not denote for Lawrence the end of the old order, nor the termination of a commercialized society that was steadily and unconscionably throttling life with its impositions of drabness and monotony.

To Lawrence the war was, from the very beginning, a "colossal idiocy," a "disintegrating autumnal process," sheer "decomposition" portending the crumbling of "the whole of England, of the Christian era." It epitomized the brutal triumph of "a decadent life" when "all is destruction and dying and corruption," when "a collapsing civilization" is finally revealed in "so much hate and destruction and disintegration." It signified a blasphemy against life, a cruel and unreasonable struggle that would rend each man's "conscious, proud, self-responsible soul" by "the annulling of all one stands for," "the nipping of the very germ of one's being." It was born essentially out of hopelessness and the loathing of conscious life in its most creative sense. It was the direct outcome of "these personal times" when human relations, as Lawrence wrote to Katherine Mansfield, failed to be "based upon some unanimous accord in truth or belief, and a harmony of *purpose,* rather than of personality." The war announced the end of any vital aspiration for human connection and tenderness: it was like "a plague, a fire, God knows what," like a "bad spirit" that now shrouded life in a "general state of ugliness and base foulness" and "destroyed the unifying force from among us."

In short, Lawrence felt that the war marked the inception of a "killing process" by which "massive creeping hell is let loose," and cruelty and violence dispossessed the living of body and spirit. Despair and rage seemed to hover over him during these years; his soul, he declared, was "charged and surcharged with the blackest and most monstrous 'temper,' a sort of hellish electricity," and he became "a walking phenomenon of suspended fury." Ultimately all this not only led to Lawrence's irrevocable rejection of modern civilization but also witnessed those strangely desperate attempts on his part to seek for that "ultima, ultima, ultima Thule." "It is impossible to believe in any existing body," we hear him saying, "they are all part of the same evil game, labour, capital, aristocrat, they are the trunk, limbs, and head of one body of destructive evil."

In these war letters the extraordinary diversity of Lawrence's temperament and attitudes is closely interlinked with a powerful integrity and sensibility. Impulsive, domineering, inconsistent, curt, preachy, impatient, he unhesitatingly pronounced judgment on all sorts of matters and persons. At times one gets the feeling of a brash young man who simply could not check his tongue or respond to difficult problems in a more sober and orderly way. After meeting E.M. Forster, for example, Lawrence found that he did not altogether like him, since "his life is so ridiculously inane, the man is dying of inanition." He was perhaps at his silliest in his relationship with Bertrand Russell, whom he knew fairly well in 1914–15, and with whom he planned to achieve "the great and happy revolution" inaugurating a new social order "when each man shall seek joy and understanding rather than getting and having." The friendship of these two fiery geniuses was short-lived and ended with bad feelings and clumsiness, especially intensified when Lawrence came into contact with "Cambridge civilization" ("I cannot bear its smell of rottenness, marsh-stagnancy. I get a melancholic malaria. How can so sick people rise up? They must die first.") His description of Russell in the following passage from a letter to Lady Ottoline Morrell could hardly be conducive to what Lawrence pleaded for earlier as their need to "build all words together into a great new utterance": "What ails Russell is, in matters of life and emotion, the inexperience of youth. He is vitally, emotionally, much too inexperienced in personal contact and conflict, for a man of his age and calibre. It isn't that life has been too much for him, but too little."

At the same time, harsh, shrill tones echo in Lawrence's reactions to the gathering crises of the war. No one was spared from the venom of his feelings. "I spit on your London and your government and your armies," he wrote to one correspondent. "Pah, what are they, Lloyd Georges and Haigs and such-like canaille? Canaille, canaille all the lot of them—also Balfour, old poodle that he is."[4] His hatred and contempt for humanity were unmitigated: "I have never come so near to hating mankind as I am now"; "one is happy in the thoughts only that transcend humanity"; really, he doesn't "even mind if they're [all] killed." "Everything that is done, *nationally*, in any sense," he further said, "is now vile and stinking, whether it is England or Germany. One wants to be left alone, only that. . . . I hate the whole concern of the nation. Bloody false fools, I don't care what they do, so long as I can avoid them, the mass of my countrymen: or any other countrymen." The sight of the people of London in the

---

4. It is interesting to compare this with the following quotation from Lawrence's *Fantasia of the Unconscious*: "Our leaders have not loved men: they have loved ideas, and have been willing to sacrifice passionate men on the altars of the blood-drinking ever-ash-thirsty ideal" (Ch. IX).

early days of the war struck him into "a dumb fury," and "the persistent nothingness of war makes me feel like a paralytic convulsed with rage." His fury and rage became, on occasion, so overwhelming that he could kill every one of the Germans who "goad us to this frenzy of hatred." "I would like to kill a million Germans—two millions."

It should be noted, however, that the intransigent tone of Lawrence's war letters was an aspect of a most immediate and naked response, which at its depths was inherently compassionate and humane. Much of the cruder, shriller element in these letters should be judged as the distillation of an excessive moral impatience and of a passionate protest against and condemnation of war (*Bella, horrida bella!*). It reveals, too, Lawrence's own intuitive apprehension of a condition that contaminated and crippled the whole of human existence with which he was to identify himself in these memorable lines of his poem "New Heaven and Earth," written in the early part of the war:

> War came, and every hand raised to murder;
> Very good, very good, every hand raised to murder!
> Very good, very good, I am a murderer!
> It is good, I can murder and murder, and see them fall,
> the mutilated, horror-struck youths, a multitude
> one on another, and then in clusters together
> smashed, all oozing with blood, and burned in heaps
> going up in foetid smoke to get rid of them,
> and murdered bodies of youths and men in heaps
> the heaps and heaps and horrible reeking heaps
> till it is almost enough, till I am reduced perhaps;
> thousands and thousands of gaping, hideous foul death
> that are youths and men and me
> being burned with oil, and consumed in corrupt thick smoke, that rolls
> and taints and blackens the sky, till at last it is dark, dark as night, or
>   death, or hell.[5]

Lawrence himself was to be aware of his "monstrous temper." To his publishing agent, J.B. Pinker, he was to write with a disarming candor and humility: "Please don't mind me when I am stupid or impertinent. It is all so difficult for us each to be his intrinsic self, each one of us to be the angel of himself in a big cause." A careful probing of the letters discloses an impelling and piercing honesty, which enabled Lawrence to see the war in all of its dreariness and to follow it home to the heart of its causes: that is to say, to that spirit and condition of destruction that he equated with *"doing dirt"* on life. His feelings must be viewed, finally, within the context of an

5. See *The Collected Poems of D.H. Lawrence*, 325–30.

unwavering denunciation of a debased spirit of life, of which war was the consummate and most painful manifestation.

The violence of his repudiation of the war reflects, concurrently, the degree of his attempts to stay apart from the evil that engulfed life. "As far as I possibly can," he wrote, "I will stand outside this time, I will live my life, and, if possible, be happy, though the whole world slides in horror down into the bottomless pit. There is a greater truth than the truth of the present, there is a God beyond these gods of today." This statement is an important testament of faith and defines the intrinsic nature of his position, as well as the main source of those rare gifts of a creative genius that, in the words of F.R. Leavis, are characterized by a "transcendent impersonalizing intelligence" and "a fulness of imaginative responsibility." The war letters indicate the baffling difficulties and temptations encountered in the operative development and defense of this talent—a talent that is all the more amazing when we stop to think that a novel like *Women in Love* was entirely rewritten and finished in Cornwall in 1917, at the height of wartime grief and derangement.

What Lawrence especially opposed in the war was the obscene process of its blasphemous translation of ideas into engines of death and destruction. He believed that the war resulted "from the necessity of money and the production of money" and was interrelated with what Gerald Crich (a former army officer!), in *Women in Love*, spoke of as the "subordination of every organic unit to the great mechanical purpose." In turn, the war led to a willed death-courage and "death-passion," and to Robert Nichols Lawrence wrote in this connection: "The courage of death is *no courage* any more: *the courage to die has become a vice*. Show me the courage to live, to live in spirit with the proud, serene angels."

In these letters, he spelled out very clearly his feelings against the military spirit and equated it with automatism and dehumanization. "The soldier spirit," he wrote, "is fatal, fatal: it means an endless process of death." And there is this characteristic outcry: "The military authorities are in the filthiest state of bloodthirstiness, it is all a just hopeless mess." Lawrence's antimilitarism should come as no surprise to readers of *The Rainbow*, in which the young subaltern Anton Skrebensky personifies a devitalized spirit of life and lacks any positive understanding of the values of responsible participation in the changing rainbow of living relationships ("I hate soldiers," Ursula Brangwen says to Anton, "they are stiff and wooden"). In his earlier novel *Sons and Lovers*, too, antimilitarism is evident in the scene where Paul Morel's brother, Arthur, enlists in the army. The scene is unforgettable, as the stunned reactions of Mrs. Morel indicate: "A *soldier!*—a common soldier!—nothing but a body that makes movements when it hears a shout!" Her husband, in fact, on hearing of his son's enlistment, "was almost ashamed to go to his public-house that evening."[6]

Another fatal result of the war, Lawrence believed, was its imposition of false ideals in a process that was insidious and unhealthy. True, some of the positive outer features of the war—male comradeship, bravery, and common purpose—could not be too easily discarded. But beneath such an enthusiastic endeavor, he detected a threatening disillusionment and emptiness. "And even this terrible glamour of camaraderie, which is the glamour of Homer and of all militarism, is a decadence, a degradation, a losing of individual form and distinction, a merging in a sticky male mass." So he observed in a letter to Dollie Radford following a physical examination for military service at Bodmin, Cornwall, on June 28, 1916, and his insight could hardly be less revealing. Lawrence refused to become assimilated in this "merging," for he felt that it signified a diluted form of living experience, the kind of "empty Allness," "this merging, *en masse,* One Identity, Myself monomania," that he so vigorously took issue with in his essay on Walt Whitman in *Studies in Classic American Literature,* which he began to write in 1915, though the book was not published until 1922. On the contrary, Lawrence insisted, "Every man has his own times and his own destiny apart and single. It only remains for us to fulfil that which is *really* in us." The war vitiated the nature of this potentiality and enjoined on each man a choice that committed him to defend a form of life that was devoid of "that which is *really* in us." Lawrence's own position was to be summed up in these words: "To fight for possessions, goods, is what my soul *will not do.* Therefore it will not fight for the neighbour who fights for his own goods." This attitude should not imply that Lawrence was indifferent or uncharitable, rather it underlines a categorical rejection of the assent to the war. He made this explicit in the following passage of a letter to Catherine Carswell describing his reaction to the men with whom he was examined for military service:

> Yet I liked the men. They all seemed so *decent.* And yet they all seemed as if they had *chosen wrong.* It was the underlying sense of disaster that overwhelmed me. They are all so brave, to suffer, but none of them brave enough, to reject suffering. They are all so noble, to accept sorrow and hurt, but they can none of them demand happiness. Their manliness all lies in accepting calmly this death, their loss of integrity. They must stand by their fellow man: that is the motto. . . . This is what the

6. See *The Rainbow* (1915), Ch. XI; *Sons and Lovers* (1913), Ch. VIII.

love of our neighbour has brought us to, that, because one man dies, we all die.

Lawrence himself did not experience the actual perils and pains of the front lines. (He was examined thrice for military service and turned down because of his consumptive condition.) While the war went on, he and Frieda lived in various sections of England, particularly in Cornwall, where they remained nearly two years until the authorities expelled them on ridiculous spying charges (one reason for their expulsion doubtless being Frieda's German ancestry and her kinship to the German war ace Manfred von Richthofen). "When we were turned out of Cornwall," Frieda later recalled in her memoir, "something changed in Lawrence for ever."[7] To comprehend the terrible anguish of this change in Lawrence, we need only to read "The Nightmare" chapter in *Kangaroo* (written, it should be noted, in 1923), in which Richard Lovat Somers (i.e., Lawrence) recalls what he underwent at the time: "He had always believed so in everything—society, love, friends. This was one of his serious deaths in belief." The extent and depth of Lawrence's loss of faith in modern civilization can be gauged by the collation of two passages. The first is from "The Nightmare":

> From 1916 to 1919 a wave of criminal lust rose and possessed England, there was a reign of terror, under a set of indecent bullies like Bottomley of *John Bull* and other bottom-dog members of the House of Commons. Then Somers had known what it was to live in a perpetual state of semi-fear: the fear of the criminal public and the criminal government. The torture was steadily applied, during those years after Asquith fell, to break the independent soul in any man who would not hunt with the criminal mob.

The second is from a letter written on October 17, 1917: "But oh, the sickness that is in my belly. London is really very bad: gone mad, in fact. It thinks and breathes and lives air-raids, nothing else. People are not people any more: they are factors, really ghastly, like lemures, evil spirits of the dead." In the midst of this debasement the Lawrences were "horribly poor," and he found it increasingly difficult to publish his work, particularly after the official suppression of *The Rainbow* in November, 1915. "For months and months, now, we have lived from shilling to shilling," Lawrence depressingly wrote of their plight. For a prophetic writer like Lawrence, insisting that he had an important message to convey in such times, these factors further contributed to bringing on fitful moods of irritability and

7. *Not I, But the Wind* . . . (New York, 1934), 90.

misery, to the extent that, as Frieda recorded, "It was torture to live, and to live with him."[8]

Some commentators will no doubt suggest that Lawrence's own instability reveals the effects of a gnawing inferiority on the part of a man who did not participate in a critical conflict; that Lawrence, in all his utterances relating to the war, was trying very hard to convince himself and others that he was right in refusing to condone the war and take any part in the war effort. Thus, he was merely bolstering his own defense against any impugning, real or imaginary, of his courage, integrity, or manhood. It may even be pointed out that his recurrent use of military figures in his short stories (e.g., "The Prussian Officer," "The Thorn in the Flesh," "The Blind Man," "The Ladybird," "The Fox," and "The Captain's Doll") reflected a subconscious admiration of the soldier. It may also be claimed that behind Lawrence's open repudiation and dislike of the military lay a suppressed but latent respect for the soldier. Even in his final novel, *Lady Chatterley's Lover*, we find that Oliver Mellors had once been a soldier, having joined the army in the spring of 1915, with service in India, Egypt, and India again. He was eventually made a lieutenant. He had been very close to his colonel, a man twenty years his senior: "He was a very intelligent man: and alone in the army, as such a man is: a passionate man in his way: and a very clever officer. I lived under his spell while I was with him. I sort of let him run my life. And I never regret it."[9] After the colonel died of pneumonia, Mellors became very ill himself, his health was damaged, and he underwent a profound restlessness that finally led to his departure from the army and his return to England.

But in his portrayals of the soldier Lawrence generally evidenced an admiration and respect *not* for the "heroic villain," to use a Blakean term, but rather for one who has rich, generous, human qualities and is able to contribute to and induce the cultivation of tender human relationships. Lawrence's ideal, and idealized, soldier can best be imaged, then, as a man with kingly qualities, a modern David, as it were, who wields power and leadership for the purpose of securing a "natural warm flow of common sympathy." In the main, such a figure tends to be strongly paternal and sincere in his reverence for and response to a "vital consciousness": he is passionate and kind, but not sentimental, commanding and even domineering, but not cruel or insensate, and never the victim of an "insistent will." His goal is not to wage battle in a brutal contest of strength and cunning,

---

8. *Ibid.*, 91.
9. *Lady Chatterley's Lover* (1928), Ch. XV.

but rather to lead others in a vital, nonmilitary sense, inspiring by example and achieving his aims by strength of conviction and devotion. As such, Lawrence's soldier seeks a constructive solution to life issues: he is a type of "strong man," in reality, who steadily labors to create, as Lawrence characteristically put it, "a new bond between men." Here, too, the significant comment regarding Mellors's relationship to Constance, namely that "He had that curious kind of protective authority she obeyed at once," comes into proper and normative focus. This "protective authority" encompasses the main quality of a true Lawrentian warrior. When this trait is lacking, or when it is present in a distorted and perverted sense, as it is with the German captain in "The Prussian Officer," then the soldier is portrayed as a callous and overweening human being who has no understanding at all of a "delicate sensitiveness." By the same token, he is also a mere automaton, barren of the more creative and healthy human elements—like "a body that makes movements when it hears a shout!" to recall Mrs. Morel's description in *Sons and Lovers*.

In addition it may be remarked that in a deep sense Lawrence's concept of the soldier can be traced back to his early days in the English Midlands, among the working class of his father's generation. It may be safely assumed that his soldiers are a projected image of the colliers whom Lawrence nostalgically pictured in his essay "Nottingham and the Mining Countryside": men alive with an instinct of beauty, without a willed ambition, free of the yearning for material wealth and acquisition, happy to respond to life's situations instinctively and intuitively, talking always more "of wonders and marvels, even in politics, than of facts." His soldiers are very much like Midlanders who have merely exchanged the work clothes of the collier for the uniform of the soldier; they are better at catching poachers than at killing the enemy, at caring for horses than at riding them into battle, at living in a hut than at burrowing trenches. His soldiers, the fact remains, never mastered either the language or the art of war. Though they had the task of facing common dangers and perils, it was in the realm of life that the real "battlefield" was to be found, where the conditions and setting, as well as the "contact" established between men, were akin to those that Lawrence pictured as existing in the pit:

> Under the butty system, the miners worked underground as a sort of intimate community, they knew each other practically naked, and with curious close intimacy, and the darkness and the underground remoteness of the pit "stall," and the continual presence of danger, made the physical, instinctive and intuitional contact between men very highly developed, a contact almost as close as touch, very real and

very powerful. The physical and intimate *togetherness* was at its *strongest* down pit.[10]

No one, of course, can deny that there was much anger in Lawrence's response to the war. Granted, the anger did not arise from the more dispassionate impulse, peculiar to great war poets, to convey the truth and horrors of conflict to those not directly engaged in it; but neither did it arise from any self-pity or self-concern. The anger that he did express was occasioned by what he believed was happening to the capacity for creative life. As the outgrowth of a violated conscience, then, his anger registered the impact of the permanency of the damage and violence being inflicted on life. "But I do mind," Lawrence wrote to Gordon Campbell at the outset of the war, "those who, being sensitive, will receive such a blow from the ghastliness and mechanical, obsolete, hideous stupidity of war, that they will be crippled beings further burdening our sick society. Those that die, let them die. But those that live afterwards—the thought of them makes me sick." The truth and consistency of his feelings relating to the mutilation of the human psyche can be correlated with his discerning characterization of a returned war hero, Captain Herbertson, found in the chapter entitled "The War Again" in *Aaron's Rod* (1922). Lawrence's portrayal of this officer sustains the meaning of what, eight years before, he had prophetically described as "further burdening our sick society": "In this officer, of course, there was a lightness and an appearance of bright diffidence and humour. But underneath it all was the same as in the common men of all the combatant nations: the hot, seared burn of unbearable experience, which did not heal nor cool, and whose irritation was not to be relieved. The experience gradually cooled on top: but only with a surface crust. The soul did not heal, did not recover."

Throughout the letters Lawrence's response to the war is not something that has merely reached "the pitch of extreme consciousness." He was genuinely appalled by what he saw transpiring around him, and he decried the ugliness and baseness of the modern industrial society which the war had now unmasked with a greater ferocity. Thus, while on a wartime visit to his sister's home in Ripley, Derbyshire, he observed: "These men, whom I love so much—and the life has such a power over me—they *understand* mentally so horribly: only industrialism, only wages and money and machinery. They can't think anything else." The war, in effect, revealed the increasing power of a demonic spirit, and if was from this that he longed to escape to "a little Hesperides of the soul and body," to be

10. *Phoenix*, 135–36.

located at one time or another in Florida, in Mexico, or in the eastern slopes of the Andes. The fact is that from the very beginning Lawrence felt that he was being slowly enveloped by emptiness and desolation, which are candidly and strikingly evoked in his reaction to the news of the death of Rupert Brooke in the early period of the war:

> The death of Rupert Brooke fills me more and more with the sense of the fatuity of it all. He was slain by bright Phoebus' shaft—it was in keeping with his general sunniness—it was the real climax of his pose. I first heard of him as a Greek god under a Japanese sunshade, reading poetry in his pyjamas, at Grantchester,—at Grantchester upon the lawns where the river goes. But Phoebus smote him down. It is all in the saga.
> O God, O God, it is all too much of a piece: it is like madness.

Still, underneath all his embitterment and imprecations, and despite his desperate longings to "curse, damn, and blast," Lawrence was able to reveal an almost persistent lyrical faith in the future of life. "The war," he insisted, "doesn't alter my beliefs or visions," but is "a kind of interval in my life, like a sleep": a period of supreme anguish that tested to the full his belief that "Only the living heart and the creative spirit matters—*nothing else.*" When, finally, we consider his overall creative achievement after and in spite of World War I, even in spite of the despair found everywhere in the years following 1918, we must also remember the informing and positive meaning of Lawrence's words that "One must speak for life and growth, amid all this mass of destruction and disintegration."

15

In Retreat

We are an unfortunate generation; it has befallen
us to witness during our brief passage through life
these great and terrifying events whose
reverberations will fill the whole of our lives.
—PAUL VALÉRY

THE YEARS BETWEEN 1897 and 1917 belonged to another world, as the late Anthony Eden, Lord Avon, confirms in his reminiscences of these two decades.[1] Now, from the distance of well over half a century, we can look back at this period and see not only another world but also a world in irreversible transition. Stability and crisis; civilization and barbarism; peace and war; beauty and obscenity: these were the antitheses that were to collide in startling and tragic ways as the nineteenth century expired with the coming of the Great War in that "monstrous" August of 1914. "Everything good and nice and clean and fresh and sweet is far away—never to return," wrote Sir Edward Elgar. Peace, hope, certitude: "never to return," these were some of the accepted values of a way of life that many of the 1914 generation were never to forget and that made their permanent, identifying marks on Eden's generation. Private schools, great books and music, foreign travel, beautiful gardens, and magnificent houses were some of the forms and shapes of the life that Eden and his aristocratic contemporaries enjoyed "before the war." His recollection of Windlestone, his family's sandstone country manor in County Durham, with its chapel, its avenue of yews, its stable clock, its lake, its terraces and trees, is especially vivid. "Apart from pictures and furniture," he recalls, "the decoration, the curtains, the library kept up to date, all these taught, beguiled, even inspired any visitor in the least sensitive to beauty." Here he paints from memory a scene of a place in time that, as Eden notes, is "the only link one has with another world."

1. *Another World, 1897–1917* (New York, 1977).

Eden provides some very evocative vignettes of a life-style that can now be recaptured only through memoirs. It is sometimes tempting to romanticize the prewar years, and one must guard against such a sentimental pull. Yet when one considers these years, one can envision a way of life and a mode of thought that belonged to spacious days. Indeed, there is a certain plenitude that one connects with the years before "the fret, the hurry, the stir," as Virginia Woolf expressed it, were to prevail once the war had ended. The men and women of Eden's generation were destined to experience the rigors of thought-tormented days. Above all, the civilizing force of beauty, perhaps the single most informing word in Eden's pre-1914 reminiscences, would give way to the twin rhythms of debasement and disintegration that were to comprise the aftermath of the war years. And aftermaths, we know, can be crueler and uglier than the events that have impelled them. New tendencies, new movements, new ideas would begin their insidious prowls and assaults. To learn of Eden's experiences on the Western Front is to be reminded of the changes that war announced, and brought, mercilessly and vengefully. It is the destructive element, in fact, that Eden chose to dramatize as he recounted how, in his old age, he returned to his former home, Windlestone. What he saw epitomizes the aftermath of ruin, when the values of a settled civilization are no longer either affirmed or revered. Windlestone remained intact, "yet what had been spacious and elegant was now gaunt and recently lonely," he says. "The curved and squat outlines of some Nissen huts crowded up against the north front windows and the lake had lost its limpidity under a green mask."

These comments should in no way imply that Eden laments a vanished world. With controlled emotion and measured tone, he helps the reader to see an older civilization in retreat. What he records here, at times almost in the form of a *tableau vivant,* is an epochal crisis. A world at peace becomes a world at war, and beyond that, as a German writer later observed, "the first civil war of the West."[2] In their concentrated facility and economy, in their craftsmanship, his reminiscences compare favorably with those of other soldier-memoirists, e.g., Sir Herbert Read, Edmund Blunden, Siegfried Sassoon, Vivian de Sola Pinto, and Robert Graves. Eden, of course, stresses the English experience of conditions of existence that were to come into prominence after 1914. Yet by 1917 it was plain that neither in England nor on the continent would life ever be the same again. The nightmare of trench warfare on the Western Front would

---

2. See Edwin Erich Dwinger, "The First Civil War of the West," *Promise of Greatness: The War of 1914–1918,* ed. George A. Panichas (New York, 1968), 217–25.

be complemented by the explosion of the Russian Revolution. No-man's-land would extend into the heart of Russia, as death and rapacity stalked an entire continent. The tendency to remember the Great War but to forget the Russian Revolution is curious, to be explained perhaps by modern man's desire to avoid confronting not one but two cataclysmic events. Eden underlines the immensity of a tragic destiny; at the same time he reminds us of a world tragedy. Aleksandr Solzhenitsyn, in his *August 1914*, registered the shock resulting from this double tragedy, this double disaster, when he wrote that the world had moved "into a new era; that the entire atmosphere of the planet—its oxygen content, its rate of combustion, the mainspring pressure in all its clocks—had somehow changed."

This radical change receives graphic explication in Eden's reminiscences. Most evident after 1914 are the nihilistic assaults on sensibility; indeed, the Great War marked the dawn of an era of nihilism. European sensibility as rarifying consciousness, as the voice of awareness, as, in short, the ultimate perception of conscience, engaged both in defining the conditions of the universe and in responding to the limit-situation of culture and society that these conditions create, creating as they do criteria of value and human fate itself—European sensibility disclosed the impact of the ascending nihilism of twentieth-century life. Vision of order retreated before visions of disorder. War in the west and revolution in the east objectified a cruel history. For Eden, still in the flush of youth, what he was to experience on the Somme battlefield was a version of the Void: "The stench, the mud, the corpses, the destruction everywhere, the torn and twisted guns and limbers, the shattered wagons, the mutilated horses and mules created a scene of desolation beyond description." There could be no more obscene epiphany than this of a dead man's dump. Etched in Eden's words is the vulnerability of civilization. The downfall of Prime Minister Herbert Asquith in 1916, it is worth noting here, and the coming to power of David Lloyd George, would be, for those attuned to the subtleties of moral sensibility, emblematic of the emerging spirit of barbarism that would soon sweep like a deadly pestilence from the "sceptred isle" of England to "Holy Russia." Asquith, John Maynard Keynes later observed, "possessed most of the needed gifts of a great statesman except ruthlessness towards others and insensitiveness for himself," whereas Lloyd George disclosed "that flavour of final purposelessness, inner irresponsibility, existence outside of or away from our Saxon good and evil, mixed with cunning, remorselessness, love of power."[3]

3. *Essays in Biography* (New York, 1951 [1933]), 35–36, 45.

Interestingly, Nikolai Lenin regarded Lloyd George as the greatest political leader that Britain had produced—a regard symptomatic, surely, of the political mentality of the modern thug.

Eden was too young and too dangerously involved in the immediate necessity of conflict to worry over shifts in sensibility. At the front the soldier confronted death as a fact of existence. Herbert Read, who survived some of the bloodbaths on the Western Front and who, like Eden, received the Military Cross, has observed that "A future, from 1916 onward, did not exist for us. We learned how to live from day to day, from hour to hour, believing that the only future was death, a future to which we were indifferent."[4] Read's comment is pertinent to Eden's own experiences as a platoon leader in Flanders at the age of eighteen, an adjutant at nineteen, and a brigade major at twenty. Eden's descriptions of the battles in which he participated leave the overwhelming impression of mind and soul unable to escape the valley of death. In recalling the death from shrapnel wounds of a yeoman volunteer, Eden catches the violence of an experience from which the memory never recovers: ". . . a message came through that Spencer had died of his wound in hospital. This was our first contact with sudden death and we were utterly miserable. The passage of years has never blunted it. We had yet to learn that it was the chance deaths in the trenches which left a sharper imprint than the wholesale slaughter of a battle." In a very moving letter F.R. Leavis, a stretcher bearer during the entire conflict, speaks of his war experience as "a major presence in my life." What he goes on to write, especially when placed alongside Eden's and Read's recollections, has much to say about the permanent images of the Great War in subsequent life: "I see the faces of those boys who were with me at school as if it were last week and hear their voices. They began to appear in the 'Roll of Honour' within a few months: Festubert, Loos, and then the Somme, where they were reaped in swathes. They were shot down over Ypres, and, having survived from the days of Kitchener's first army to the 'victorious' battles of 1918, died of wounds—and of sickness after the Armistice."[5]

Eden's rendering of battle scenes, especially trench warfare with its raiding parties at night and forays into no-man's-land, shows an astonishing power of recall and underlines the truth of an incisive line in James Barrie's play *A Well-Remembered Voice* (1918): "When one has been at the Front for a bit, you can't think how thin the veil seems to get." Frontline conditions come alive as Eden shows how,

4. Foreword, *Promise of Greatness*, ed. George A. Panichas, vi.
5. Letter to George A. Panichas, January 12, 1967.

through their courage of innocence, "the men of 1914" endured a negative eternity, a continuous Now: "There was so much waiting in the trenches. Waiting through the hour before dawn for stand-down, waiting for the battalion which was to relieve us, waiting for rations and for letters, waiting for leave, or the blighty wound, or . . ." Paying tribute not only to his fellow officers but also to the men in the ranks, he shows how ties between the soldiers often constituted "the finest form of friendship." It was during these years that he learned "the irrelevance and unreality of class distinction." Particularly revealing is Eden's description of the famous hanging Virgin and Child atop the steeple of the ruined basilica at Albert, on the Somme, and of his own feelings at the time: "The town of Albert lay below us with the dislodged statue of the Virgin still precariously suspended from her church roof. All around us were the sights and sounds of war as I had never known it. Bivouacs everywhere, the roads choked with transport, troops, guns and ambulances. I was awed, but also not a little thrilled." A sense of the heroic still impelled Eden and his contemporaries, even as the conflict, especially after the Somme battles of 1916, hardened into more relentless, mechanical forms, breaking through to sinister levels of horror. Eden consistently affirms humanistic qualities that so many of his generation possessed: that loyalty, generosity, patience, honesty, bravery, dignity, and decency that R.C. Sherriff's famous play, *Journey's End* (1929), dramatizes "under fire." An intrinsic grace, it could be said, resided in Eden's generation.

In 1914 war embodied for many Englishmen a promise of greatness; a great heroic adventure; a great chance "To win Eternity / And claim God's kiss." By 1918, however, survivors were unable to wipe out the terrifying memory of a "murder war." Even after returning to civilian life, Robert Graves recalled, "shells used to come bursting on my bed at midnight . . . strangers in day-time would assume the faces of friends who had been killed."[6] For those who had not served in the armed forces, the war was no longer a "Great Interruption," as Henry James called it in 1914, but rather a Great Negation, as Leonard Woolf described it in the fourth volume of his autobiography, *Downhill All the Way:*

> . . . [the war] destroyed, I think, the bases of European civilization. We, like everyone who lived through those years, had been profoundly influenced by them. When the maroons boomed on November 11, 1918, we were no longer the same people who, on August 4, 1914, heard with amazed despair that the guns had begun to boom. In 1914 in the background of one's life and one's mind there were light and hope; by 1918 one had unconsciously accepted a perpetual public menace and

6. *Goodbye to All That* (London, 1960 [1929]), 235.

darkness and had admitted into the privacy of one's mind or soul an iron fatalistic acquiescence in insecurity and barbarity.

Less pessimistic is Eden's reaction: "I had entered the holocaust still childish, and I emerged tempered by my experience and bereft of many friends, but with my illusions intact, neither shattered nor cynical, to face a changed world." His words remind us of the contention that only literary men agonize about war. "Perhaps silence is the best," we are told. Or perhaps we cannot escape the irrevocable fact, with all its pang and complexity, that "We're all guilty—if guilt is the word." Or perhaps, and all too finally, we are asked to resign ourselves to the unconditional in life: "We desert those who desert us; we cannot afford to suffer; we must live how we can."

But, as always, final judgment belongs to history, insofar as the Great War was a judgment upon history and upon nations. The exhaustion of Russia gave the Bolsheviks their opportunity. The debasement of values and the death of beliefs in England and in France led to the imposition of a peace vindictive to Germany. This peace, in turn, gave Hitler his opportunity, which brought on a "Second Darkness" in our century. And it led to the lethal cynicism and madness of Stalin, which spurred him to institute forced labor camps, mass deportations, brainwashings, purges, and liquidations. The Armistice signaled modern man's retreat into an existential vacuum. The war of 1914–18 was the home of his youth and would never cease marking his works and days.

16

Testaments of Devotion

I

Devotion is a virtue that in both theory and practice is frequently absent from the contemporary situation. Devotion to family, or to friends, or to country, or to God, or to work, or to excellence has been replaced all too often and all too easily by mean tendencies, by the fanatical and sometimes by the fantastic. Modern life-styles, it seems, leave little room for devotion; and the media, it is very clear, praise everything that in the end deprecates devotion. There is no time and little use for a quality of character, indeed of civilization, that encourages reverence for and allegiance to something greater than one's own self. If devotion is not a forgotten word, it is certainly an abused one. In an age of extremes it is a word that has been much defiled by those who preach its necessity while never practicing it and misused by those who embrace it while searching "after strange gods."

As both a word and a concept devotion needs to be rehabilitated, so that it may again become part of life as a civilizing force and perspective. Devotion is an exceptional quality given to exceptional people. In fact the survival of civilization owes something to this exceptionalness. One has to be tough and patient and uncompromising in one's devotion to what transcends the mediocre and the transient. Although we may not recognize the power of devotion among ourselves, we may recognize it at least in the lives of men and women whose writings re-create it. In Harold Acton's *Memoirs of an Aesthete, 1939—1969*[1] and in *Carrington: Letters and Extracts from Her Diaries*,[2] we view devotion from different but interacting sides. In each book we see an act of consecration by two singularly dissimilar people. The degree of dedication to something or to someone else discloses a great strength of purpose, a selflessness, and a sacrifice

1. New York, 1971.
2. Chosen and with an introduction by David Garnett (New York, 1971).

that in turn have some lessons for all of us. In a slipshod age these lessons are urgent.

Acton, a poet, novelist, and historian, is devoted to beauty. In his first volume, *Memoirs of an Aesthete*, published in 1948 and "written in self-defense," he stated his creed in these words: "... I love beauty. For me beauty is the vital principle pervading the universe—glistening in stars, glowing in flowers, moving with clouds, flowing with water, permeating nature and mankind. By contemplating the myriad manifestations of this vital principle we expand into something greater than we were born. Art is the mirror that reflects these expansions, sometimes for a moment, sometimes for perpetuity."

Belonging to the branch of the Acton family that produced the great historical thinker, he was born of an English father and an American mother at Villa La Pietra in Florence, and he lives there today amid the art treasures collected by his father and amid magnificent gardens. In the volume dealing with events up to 1939, Acton described his education at Eton and at Oxford in the mid-1920s. He told of his travels and of his experiences as a "citizen of the world" (his description of himself) in Switzerland, France, Java, Bali, Cambodia, Africa, and particularly Peking, where he lived for eight years and taught English literature at Pei Ta, the Peking National University. His devotion to universal culture can be explained, of course, on the basis of his origins, his education, his travels, and his surroundings.

Acton's devotion to the writer's craft, it should be noted, is no less than his devotion to beauty. He is a fine stylist, and his writings are filled with exemplary passages, of which the following account of Gertrude Stein delivering her famous lecture "Composition as Explanation" (1926) to an Oxford audience is representative:

> Edith, Osbert and Sacheverell Sitwell accompanied Gertrude as well as Miss Alice Toklas, her inseparable companion, who looked like a Spanish gipsy and talked like a Bostonian. Gertrude had left all her nervousness at Cambridge: it was a fine summer day and she was ready to enjoy herself. . . . Owing to the critics, the popular conception of Gertrude Stein was of an eccentric visionary, a literary Madame Blavatsky in fabulous clothes, the triumph of the dream and escape from life personified, with bells on her fingers as well as on her toes, or a mermaid swathed in tinsel, smoking drugged cigarettes through an exaggerated cigarette holder, or a Gioconda who had her face lifted so often that it was fixed in a smile beyond the nightmare of Leonardo da Vinci. One was aware of the rapid deflation of these conceptions, as Gertrude surpassed them by her appearance, a squat Aztec figure in obsidian, growing more monumental as soon as she sat down. With her tall bodyguard of Sitwells and the gipsy acolyte, she made a memorable entry.

His second volume continues Acton's memoirs from 1939, "which seemed the end of an era when many Englishmen 'thought imperially.' After a prelude of ominous calm another dance of death began that autumn." In spite of the barbarism of this period, the fervor of Acton's devotion to beauty remained undiminished. The tone of his comments regarding others is less peevish than in the first volume, though Somerset Maugham is seen as the least likable among his close friends, who include Arthur Waley, Lady Cunard, Cecil Beaton, Norman Douglas, Evelyn Waugh, and Bernard Berenson. Especially of Berenson there are some fascinating vignettes. A neighbor of Acton's in Florence, Berenson is singled out for praise as "a humanistic sage" and "an illuminating beacon in my existence." Portraits of other friends and acquaintances—Picasso, Benedetto Croce, George Orwell, Jean Cocteau, Sinclair Lewis, among others—are also interesting. Throughout Acton is a perceptive human observer with an essentially aesthetic response to the scene. "Memoirs should concentrate on all that is vital," he insists, "and attempt to recapture the hours and moments of exaltation and delight, the friendships, colours, emotions that have intensified an existence and magnified it for the time being." "For me art is the highest truth and I have always lived more intensely through works of art. And art is silenced by mechanized modern warfare."

Such comments define the nature of Acton's devotion as well as the reasons that the cataclysmic events since 1939 are subordinated to the matters that instinctively matter most to Acton—his family and friends, his literary inclinations, his aesthetic pursuits and possessions, his Florentine villa:

> ... I believe, like Candide, that we ought to cultivate our garden. I consider myself lucky to have a garden to cultivate. I am aware that I am privileged, that I belong to a vanished period: entangled in the past as I am, I have no desire to belong to any other—unless it was the middle of the eighteenth century. In the constant flux of those fashions and systems which the impotent try to foist on us I have kept my independence: I have not attempted to force fresh flowers from the modish manure and twist myself into the latest trendy postures. We must be true to our own vision of this world. My own vision has been enhanced but also circumscribed by La Pietra.

Here, then, Acton discloses inevitably the limitations of his devotion. He is no social theorist, no moralist. He is content to stay within a realm of devotion that he knows intimately and loves, a fact that explains why, for example, the war years and his own wartime service in the RAF lack purpose. Besides its savagery, barbarism has its inconveniences. If Acton is repelled by the savagery of the modern world, he is all too understandably horrified by its ugliness, particularly the ugliness of contemporary American society, as expressed in this passage:

> Much as I appreciated American dynamism, I felt at a loose end among the Titans of American technology. Unduly susceptible to physical surroundings, I was horrified by the implications as well as the sheer ugliness of a sprawling city like Los Angeles, which seemed to be made for machines rather than for men. The implications were of spiritual and cultural starvation. Engineers were replacing architects, and new jungles of metal and concrete would continue to devour the world's surface, a nightmare prospect. Viewed from above, New York was a strident symphony of soaring towers, but from the street the effect was generally impersonal and drab: the very skyscrapers seemed vacant-minded when I compared them to the buildings of Florence, the miracle of Venice, the magnificence of Rome, the voluptuousness of Naples, and countless other Italian cities comparatively small but noble in conception, the harmonious creations of individual genius.

II

In Acton's memoirs devotion merges with a transcendent experience of beauty. In Dora Carrington's diaries and letters ("surely the best letters to have been published in English in this century," according to one critic), devotion is an immanent part of the complex experience of love. The object of her love was Lytton Strachey, "great anarch" (as Cyril Connolly called him) and author, whom she met in 1915 and with whom she lived, first at The Mill House, Tidmarsh, and later at Ham Spray House, Hungerford. They were lovers, but physical love between them was not possible: Strachey was a homosexual and Carrington (the name by which she was always called) was a bisexual painter who harbored an intense dislike of her femininity. In any event, her devotion to Strachey held steadfast until his death on January 21, 1932. Less than two months later she committed suicide, for she was unable to bear the loss of the man to whom she had dedicated her life.

Carrington's devotion to Strachey remained as unique as did their ménage. In 1922 she married Ralph Partridge, whom Strachey loved, and later she fell in love with Gerald Brenan. In 1926 Partridge fell in love with Frances Marshall, whom he married in 1933. But no matter what happened, Strachey, Carrington, and Partridge maintained to the end a "trinity of happiness" to which others were admitted as time and conditions or as temptation and opportunities allowed. This was in every way a Bloomsbury kind of situation in the 1920s, a "golden age" that, as Lord Annan has said, "reaffirmed the romantic principle of diversity."

Whatever the moral implications of such relationships, Carrington was always an enigmatic character who attracted, among many others, Aldous Huxley. In his letters Huxley described her as "enchanting"; and in his novel *Crome Yellow* (1922) he depicted her in the person of Mary Bracegirdle, the "moonlike innocence" of whose "face shone pink and childish. . . . Her short hair, clipped like a page's, hung in a bell of elastic gold about her cheeks. She had large blue china eyes, whose expression was one of ingenuous and often puzzled earnestness." Other critics were less impressed by Carrington, seeing in her symptoms of a malaise in the years between the two world wars—a malaise synonymous with the Bloomsbury ethos. Of these critics F.R. Leavis is the most commanding and uncompromising in his indictment of the values of the Bloomsbury sociointellectual milieu. Moral debilitation, snobbism, aesthetic flabbiness, inanition, irreverence: these are traits that critics of Bloomsbury have attacked. Indeed, no less a figure than Bertrand Russell has written in his *Autobiography* (vol. I): "The generation of [John Maynard] Keynes and Lytton [Strachey] . . . aimed . . . at a life of retirement among shades and nice feelings, and conceived of the good as consisting in the passionate admiration of the *élite.*" Moralists and puritans alike will share Russell's qualms in reading Carrington's letters and diaries. For the deficiencies of Bloomsbury are unmistakably there in the world that Carrington reveals.

But these deficiencies have been by now well enough publicized and their consequences well enough assessed. It would be wrong to dismiss completely some of the positive aspects of the Bloomsbury ethos: love of literature and the arts, respect for the inner life, passion for beauty, loyalty to friends. What Lytton Strachey's circle demonstrated was the need in the post-1918 "weed world" (as Wyndham Lewis has described it) for hanging on to something of value. Such a goal was difficult in a period in which, as Leonard Woolf believed, barbarism was ascendant. "The last moment of the greenwood," to quote E.M. Forster, had vanished. The relationship between Carrington and Strachey needs to be viewed, at least in part, against this background. Some life-value, in a word, needed to be grasped, if only to lessen the blows inflicted by history and physiological anomalies.

The relationship between Carrington and Strachey instances not only this need but also a profound psychological anomaly in each of two talented friends seeking a normalizing process. In Carrington a devotion to Strachey had to take the place of the more consummate emotions that lead to a career or to family and children or to other stabilized pleasures and advantages. "All these years," she wrote to Strachey in one of her most moving letters, "I have known all along that my life with you was limited. I could never hope for it to become permanent." She added in a postscript: "I only cried last night at realising I never could have my Moon, that some times I must pain you, and often bore you." No less moving or revealing is Strachey's reply, a reply that helps to rebut the charge that Strachey was never "wholly serious":

> . . . You *do* know very well that I love you as something more than a friend, you angelic creature, whose goodness to me has made me happy for years, and whose presence in my life has been, and always will be, one of the most important things in it. . . . Remember that I too have never had my moon! We are all helpless in these things—dreadfully helpless. I am lonely and I am all too truly growing old, and if there is a chance that your decision meant that I should somehow or other lose you, I don't think I could bear it.

Carrington's letters show simultaneously the paradoxes that assail life. Her correspondence in 1926 with Frances Marshall, pleading with the latter not to bring an end to the relations of Strachey, Ralph Partridge, and herself, gives a clue to great emotional complications:

> I . . . beg you to try, while these adjustments are being made, to see the position from my point of view and to try and see if it's not compatible with your happiness to still let me keep some of my friendship with Ralph. I can't get away from everything, because of Lytton. Even although the happiness of my relation with Lytton, ironically, is so bound up with Ralph, that that will be wrecked. I am obliged to accept this situation; you must see that. . . . You see, Frances, you can afford to be lenient because R[alph] is so completely yours in his affections. In spite of all your difficulties and unhappiness you are a gainer, we losers. And if you face it, the situation really is that *Ralph can only give me what you can spare to give.*

Frances Marshall's reply to Carrington is generous in its humanity and in its recognition of "this horrible knot in which our happinesses have got involved": "Because I love R. and want to live with him, and want him to share my life instead of being a visitor into it—I can't see how I could find this incompatible with his being fond of you and seeing you every day of his life." The ménage at Ham Spray thus remained intact—at least on weekends. During the rest of the week Frances Marshall and Partridge lived together in London.

One cannot help admiring the tenacity of Carrington's devotion. It was a quality of strength that gave meaning to life even in its absurdist forms and that also helped to salvage life from the destructive process. The relationship between Carrington and Strachey must not be lamented because of its barrenness. Given the special circumstances of each person, their physical and emotional idiosyncracies, it was a relationship that not only crystallized the saving powers of devotion (beyond the mere fulfillment of common needs) but also brought into their lives an element of grace: a certain emotional security based upon the bonds of loyalty and friendship. Above all Carrington's devotion provided a modicum of happiness and harmony in a world in which such states are often elusive. It no doubt helped to alleviate frustration and desperation. For Strachey and Carrington devotion was the vehicle of mercy, and in this there was something Dostoevskian in their relations. (It was not for nothing that Strachey admired the novels of the great Russian novelist. Dostoevsky would have *understood* the relationship between Carrington and Strachey.)

The selections from Carrington's letters and diaries concerning Strachey's death and her consequent despair are filled with pathos. Her devotion to him enabled her to endure everything except his death. An ultimate test of devotion, when irreparable personal loss occurs, is acceptance and patience, a "waiting for God." But Carrington could not endure the void, as this passage in her diaries shows:

> Nothing inside me felt the same. Ralph brought me some bay leaves, and I made a wreath. I tried it on my head, it was a little large. I went in and put it around Lytton's head. He looked so beautiful. The olive green leaves against his ivory skin. I kissed his eyes and his ice cold lips. The sun shone through the open window. . . . I asked . . . if I could go in again to Lytton. . . . and then I went in for the last time and kissed his lips, and his forehead and the tears dropped from my eyes on his face.

Her own end, only weeks later, was "indescribably sad," to quote Gerald Brenan. Neither Voltaire nor Hume, the all too human gods of Strachey and of Bloomsbury, could possibly ease her burden of grief. Indeed, she confessed that she could not refute Hume's *Essay on Suicide,* which she now reread. At one time Strachey had read it to her, she recalled, and "both agreed on the sense and truth of the arguments." On March 11, 1932, she shot herself. When Virginia Woolf heard of her friend's death, she felt "terror at night of things generally wrong in the universe" and "saw all the violence and unreason crossing in the air: ourselves small; a tumult outside; something terrifying: unreason."

17

A Family Matter

My Father and Myself[1] is the title of the posthumous memoir by J.R. Ackerley (1896–1967), who for more than twenty years served with distinction as editor of *The Listener*, the much respected magazine published by the British Broadcasting Corporation. "The book is *not*," the author insists, "an autobiography, its intention is narrower and is stated in the title and the text, it is no more than an investigation of the relationship between my father and myself and should be confined as strictly as possible to that theme." Within these limits of aim and execution this volume recalls an earlier "biographical recollection," Edmund Gosse's *Father and Son* (1908). Both books examine the relations of a father and his son, the nature of the differences in their personalities, public and private, their psychological orientations, their idiosyncrasies, their outlooks. Both books portray in subtle, often profound, ways the failure of father and son to communicate and the suffering that results from this failure. This theme, of course, is as old as civilization and is there in the Old Testament, which in itself is *the* unfolding drama of fathers and sons. It is a theme, also, that fascinates, in some cases to extremes of psychoanalytical overstatement and bias, as is demonstrated, for instance, by *Thomas Woodrow Wilson: A Psychological Study* (1967), by Sigmund Freud and William C. Bullitt.

Neither in *Father and Son* nor in *My Father and Myself* is there that romantic tendency to which some biographers and memoirists surrender—the play on psychic theory, the belaboring of contradictions of character and of inner conflicts, the rooting out of neuroses "on the jangling Freudian battlefield of the id," as one writer puts it. In both books there is a distinguishing constraint and a simplicity and honesty of expression, conveyed in a son's search to understand the father and, in the final analysis, to understand himself. Of the two, Gosse's *Father and Son* is the more classically executed in its dignity, its *pudeur*, its organic discipline of language, feeling, and attitude, its discovery of human truths without recourse to a display of

1. New York, 1969.

emotionalism. Offered as "a document, as a record of educational and religious conditions," and as a "diagnosis of a dying Puritanism," it describes "the struggle between two temperaments, two consciences and almost two epochs," and concludes on a note of "disruption."

Rigid in his adherence to the Calvinist doctrines of his religious sect, the "Plymouth Brethren," the elder Gosse defended the old Puritan ways. This "honest hodman of science," as Huxley described him, opposed the Darwinism and the discoveries of an age that hammered against traditional religious foundations. He lived his life in an atmosphere of faith, distrusting anything that contributed to spiritual levity—e.g., imaginative literature and the theater. Occasionally he would sing Dorsetshire songs of his early days, in a strange, broad Wessex dialect. Once, however, his singing was overheard by two workers nearby. "In a pause, one of them said to his fellow: 'He can zing a zong, zo well's another, though he be a minister.'" Mr. Gosse, his son reports, never again sang a secular song. Such was the delicacy of his conscience. The son, Edmund Gosse, represents the spirit of the new cosmology as he turns against the "untruth . . . that evangelical religion, or any religion in violent form, is a wholesome or valuable or desirable adjunct to human life." In the end, no compromise being offered, alienated from his father's faith and judged a victim of "the infidelity of the age," "he took a human being's privilege to fashion his inner life for himself."

Gosse's memoir conveys, in the midst of a son's protestation and rebellion in a universe increasingly revealed by science, deep moral anguish. To a large extent he is exploring the moral ramifications of "the clash of two temperaments." It is in this important respect that Ackerley's memoir differs from Gosse's. For Ackerley's attempts to reveal and, when possible, to explain his father's life, and his own relation to him, can perhaps best be described as psychophysiological, but by no means clinical. A practicing homosexual for most of his life, he hunts for some explanation of his own dissonance in his father's life. How he goes about this, in technique and style, discloses genuine artistic skill. Always anxious to track down some clue that will shed light on his own predicament, he does not allow his writing to become overcharged and passional in self-pity. The narrative, which moves with quiet momentum, is not, it should be noted, chronological, since the author felt he would be unable to tell his story "straightforwardly." Hence, he adopted "the method of ploughing to and fro over my father's life and my own, turning up a little more sub-soil each time as the plough turned."

Especially vivid are the human portraits rendered by Ackerley. The most interesting figure to appear in these pages is the father, Alfred

Roger Ackerley. The first sentence in the memoir evokes the mystery as well as the paradox of the relation between father and son: "I was born in 1896 and my parents were married in 1919." The picture of the father that evolves is characterized by deftness and balance, the writing always kept on a low key, without sentimentality or idealization, the author exerting a singularly Joycean impersonality. Even where scatological details appear with respect to the father's habits of life (he was a prosperous supporter of two households, a fact known only to himself, and to his son only after the father's death in 1929), and with respect to the author's own sexual confessions, these are kept under control. What startles and scandalizes is not the informing purpose of this book. This is not to say that four-letter words and elaborate details of sexual experience are missing from the text, which synthesizes orthodox and unorthodox writing methods. Thus, the human characterizations are brilliantly but conventionally drawn, whereas the sensual episodes are handled amorally, as it were. Whether he is describing his father's liaisons or his own, Ackerley does so with remarkable candor. (Inevitably he brings to mind André Gide's words: ". . . I have a horror of lies. . . . I would rather be hated than loved for what I am not.") It is precisely the absence of any moral reticence or anguish that separates *My Father and Myself* from *Father and Son*: what, in a word, also designates a "modern temper" marking a general *exeunt omnes* of spiritual struggle, in art as in life.

Yet, if this memoir skirts moral struggle, it compensates by its artistic power to disturb. Here, too, Ackerley can be compared with his earlier confrere, Gide, though he lacks the latter's lyrical and reflective bent. Where Gide achieves his effectiveness through atmosphere, with an artistic confluence of shadows, relief, and chiaroscuro, and through movement, with the evocation of the flux of life ("a past empty of surprise"), Ackerley does so on the basis of the men and women whose emotional states he presents with creative power and insight. (Throughout, he puts into practice Joseph Conrad's advice to John Galsworthy: "A creator must be indifferent; because directly the 'Fiat!' has issued from his lips, there are the creatures made in his image that'll try to drag him down from his eminence,—and belittle him by their worship.") How human lives interpenetrate, at times in enigmatic ways, provides the basis for the story. Inevitably, the concentration is on emotional ambivalence, with historical exigencies like the Great War of 1914–18, in which Ackerley served and to which he devotes a chapter, subordinated to his primary aim of relating the story of his father's and his own life, and that of the people and episodes that in one way or another touched their lives.

Ackerley shows the talents of the dramatic artist in various ways. He was also a successful playwright, author of *The Prisoners of War* (1925), which for Siegfried Sassoon was "the most painful play I have ever seen and one of the most impressive." There is the way in which he creates dramatic tensions, especially in his treatment of the furtive techniques he developed in his sexual adventures. Awkward situations; chance and fateful meetings; "the thrill of the risk"; the yearning for the "Ideal Friend"; the phenomena of sexual obsession, secretiveness, disappointment, suspense, and surprise; the pervasive feelings of anxiety and degradation: it is with acute dramatic skill that Ackerley endows these manifestations of life with their peculiar energies. There are, too, the dramatic questions that are shrouded in the awful mystery of silence: Does the father ever fully discern the truth about his son's life? What would have been the consequences if, only once, the son had been able to talk over his problems with his father? Indeed, as Ackerley's story of his father and of himself evolves in its irremediably anomalous pattern—the father ever desirous of amorous delights with "plump little partridges," the son experiencing fleeting infatuations, first with one young man and then with another—it also assumes (hopefully?) a humane shape in an implicit comprehension that all men have touched pitch. Nevertheless, readers will not detect here what, in a critic's words, was Oscar Wilde's "wistful hankering for the dignity of damnation."

In the sixties we saw a rich harvest of memoirs by English writers. Gerald Brenan's *A Life of One's Own* (1962), Basil Willey's *Spots of Time* (1965), Sir Maurice Bowra's *Memories, 1898–1936* (1966), V.S. Pritchett's *A Cab at the Door* (1968), and Vivian de Sola Pinto's *The City That Shone* (1969) clearly stand out. But none of these has dramatized the condition nor achieved the consummate artistry of Ackerley's "examining and self-examining book." None has managed, as has *My Father and Myself*, to approach in its developed problematic theme Gosse's *Father and Son* and, concurrently, to maintain the aesthetic capacity to disturb that infuses Gide's work. Rendering emotional consciousness, Ackerley's memoir goes beyond statement of fact, beyond mere reportage, seeking at all times "to be perfectly sincere," to use here a Gidean phrase. As such, the self-analysis that comprises one of the main aims of the book transcends what is merely personal. Indeed, the immediate absence of a moral element in the lives and the human situations that the author recreates attains a greater relevance in the reader's own struggle to judge this book, and to judge it justly. Again, Gide is to the point when he observes: "Knowing how to free oneself is nothing; it's being free that is hard."

My Father and Myself helps one to fathom the more intricate levels of human experience, particularly of the personal condition, in the need to see passion incomplete when people themselves fail to connect. Life in its isolation and decay is, therefore, one of the focuses of this book. Denis de Rougemont reminds us that art is a "calculated trap for meditation."[2] Inevitably, as a memoir that is transposed into art itself, Ackerley's book leads to this, and to the moral judgments that must ensue. Its power in evoking a crisis of personal experience and purpose is such that sympathy of understanding will be aroused. But it is a book that also perhaps forces into the mind words bespeaking an ancient wisdom for all fathers and all sons: "Gird up thy loins like a man."

2. See "Religion and the Mission of the Artist," *The New Orpheus: Essays Toward a Christian Poetic*, ed. Nathan A. Scott, Jr. (New York, 1964), 63.

Part V

TEACHERS AND CRITICS

·

*This double quality of experiencing our own
time to the full and yet being able to weigh it
in relation to other times is what the critic
must strive for, if he is to be able to discern
and demand the works of art that we need
most. The most mature function of the critic
lies finally in that demand.*

—F.O. MATTHIESSEN

18

Creative Questioner

I

WHAT MOST CHARACTERIZES the magnitude of the achievement of Frank Raymond Leavis (1895–1978) is the insistence on standards so invariably strict in their conception and application that those who fail to satisfy them take violent offense. Standards, of course, endanger those who worship at the shrine of relativism. Indeed, it can be said that Dr. Leavis's lifework was directed at an enemy whose only absolute is the absolutism of the relative, which now pervades many areas of intellectual culture in Western society. No definition of standards will ever satisfy the relativist, even as the state of modern civilization confirms the consequences of the absence of standards and the power of the forces of relativism contributing to such an absence. And the enemy is aggressive, alert to any threat to his too often unchallenged authority. Leavis consistently and bravely presented such a challenge, and the reaction has been unforgiving and scornful, as these words, as symptom and portent, from John Gross's *The Rise and Fall of the Man of Letters* (1969) clearly show: "He [Leavis] asks to be judged as a moralist, and it is his whole moral stance which I find repugnant. . . . But it seems to me that ultimately he is preoccupied with the value of Value, that he makes the critical act an end in itself."

The misrepresentation of Leavis's position as well as the allied detestation of the value of moral criteria in relation to a view of life are implicit in Gross's words. No words could better crystallize the relativistic spirit of the times that Leavis was to quarrel with during a large part of the twentieth century. The titles of some of Leavis's books—*For Continuity* (1933), *Education and the University* (1943), *The Great Tradition* (1948), *The Common Pursuit* (1952), *Nor Shall My Sword: Discourses on Pluralism, Compassion and Social Hope* (1972), *The Living Principle: 'English' as a Discipline of Thought* (1975)—are significant here, for they underline precisely those interconnected and interdependent literary and cultural concerns that give his contribution its highest value. That is to say, even in the titles themselves one detects the basic concerns that, of their very nature, proclaim a civilizational need for standards that make for "tradition," "continuity," and "centrality." At the very heart of these preoccupations lie those moral essences that the relativists would proscribe, or at least transform into a spurious value system. In the end, then, the quarrel between Leavis and his opponents is much more than a quarrel. Its results are telling and of permanent consequence to how one sees the world and the way in which one lives his life in that world.

Leavis pursued this quarrel not only in his literary and cultural writings but also in his letters to newspapers and periodicals (e.g., *The Guardian, The Observer, The Times, The Criterion, The Spectator, The New Statesman*) in the years between 1932 and 1973.[1] In his letters, as in his other writings, there is abundant and abiding evidence of that strenuous honesty and independence of thought that inform Leavis's critical and cultural views. Throughout, the moral note is intransigent and uncompromising, no matter what the occasion for or the subject of the letter. It would not be excessive to say that in his letters there is that (nontheological) religious urgency that one repeatedly encounters in Leavis's oeuvre. This religious element is quintessentially and impellingly moral. Leavis's enunciations, in short, command a discipline of thought, of attitude, and of life that is not without its religious austerities, precedents, parallels, and principles, for his enunciations have ultimate concerns that are inherently religious in their arraignments, exhortations, warnings, protests, and strictures. Not untypically Leavis wrote in a letter to *The Times Literary Supplement:* "A creative work, when it is such as to challenge and engage us to the full, conveys the artist's basic allegiance, his sense of ultimates, his real beliefs, his completest sincerity, his profoundest feeling and thought about man in relation to the universe. When I say that a great work will inevitably have a profound moral significance I am thinking of such significance as will need to be described as religious, too." Such a judgmental statement shows why Gross and his fellow travelers can hardly accept Leavis's position, for in it there are standards that are delineated and prescribed. In its literary and cultural implications Leavis's work presents for the relativist, to apply a judicial term, a "clear and present danger."

His letters contain what is by now the familiar but by no means less relevant Leavis critical style. Any examination of this style is bound to discover the source of its power, those marks that stamp its

1. *F.R. Leavis: Letters in Criticism,* ed. John Tasker (London, 1974).

singular and undiminishing strengths. Here, too, the moral essences of Leavis's style stand out with stark clarity. It is an unembellished, an unconditional, an unequivocal style—fearless, straight, deliberate, determined, and tough; a moral style that is ever informed, indeed driven, both by a continuous search for value and by the demanding act of judging, of a "judging mind." "You cannot be intelligent about literature without judging. A judgment is a personal judgment or it is nothing—you cannot have your judging done for you," Leavis wrote. It is a style that is at once serious and preoccupied with fundamentals and significance. The difficulties ascribed to Leavis's style are not so much difficulties as they are the implicit requirement for the reader to confront the task of exacting and applying standards of discrimination that must finally evolve from "the interplay of thought and judgment." Such a style must grow out of rigorous thought, or as Leavis himself categorically described the entire process in one of his letters: ". . . one should be clear with oneself about one's judgments, and state them as clearly, responsibly and challengingly as possible." No style could be more antithetical to the relativistic "world of Lockean or technologico-Benthamite blankness," obsessed with the generalizing, aggregating, and averaging of *all* of life.

That there are definable and applicable critical and civilizational standards to be maintained: this is the governing principle behind Leavis's work and thought. In very reminding ways his letters variously and opportunely corroborate this principle. "Nor shall my sword": William Blake's words capture the specificity of the letters, as Leavis speaks out for the defense of those standards that he sees under attack from those who would have no standards. His defense, like his style, is combative in character, which is as it should be in a world in which relativistic values have led to an erosion of Value (pace Gross) and thus to the growing collapse of humane consciousness itself. Concern and vigilance provide the controlling spirit and the constituent tone of Leavis's letters; hence, his letters belong to his critique as an inclusive whole. They underline and complement the validity, the "living principle," of *the* critique and are an integral part of the entire record. Even a random glance at the letters will reveal a representative preoccupation with literary standards:

> I take Auden's as the type-career of the 1930s and a portent. The "arrival," the acceptance of the star-turn aplomb of an undergraduate-coterie hero as the creative brilliance of a major poet, the continued failure to mature—we have here, I point out, the clear manifestation of a portentous lapse of standards.

with sociopolitical standards:

> Today we have to fear that the country that in its time produced Shakespeare, George Eliot and Lawrence ("England my England!") has become, irretrievably, the country of the Welfare State, the Football Pools, and the literary culture of the *New Statesman* and the Third Programme.

and with educational standards:

> Neither democratic zeal nor egalitarian jealousies should be permitted to dismiss or discredit the fact that only a limited proportion of any adult age group is capable of profiting by, or enjoying university education. The proper standards can be maintained only if the students the university is required to deal with are—for the most part, at any rate—of university quality. If standards are not maintained somewhere the whole community is let down.

In these quoted extracts one hears the hard ring of Leavis's style. It is endemic to that total process in which he is, as a man of letters, so actively engaged: engaged, that is, in molding the full conception of criticism in its literary and cultural dimensions, arrived at through forceful valuations, discriminations, judgments, and scrutinies. This critical process, in which Leavis reveals an unshakable faith, has as and at its center a sensibility and energy that make his perception and judgment so emphatically arresting and impressive. The profound and lasting endurance of his worth as a critic, like that of Matthew Arnold, is directly manifested in the operative consistency and certainty, the authority and intellectual integrity of his responses to literary and social matters in their interrelationships. His critical panoply contains a fierce courage of judgment, the outgrowth of thought in its most demanding refinement and precision of forms. What makes Leavis a premier critic of our time, what gives him such a great worth (whatever the level of agreement or of disagreement he is bound to incite), is that he addresses himself to the greatest issues of life and literature with that sense of responsibility and conviction that must, in the end, question and disturb those sloppy sentimentalities and complacencies on which relativists too often and too easily confer certified respectability. When nothing matters and nothing has value, standards are subverted and civilization flounders. It is against this desperate, menacing situation that Leavis struggles; in this respect, his efforts are inspiring. Very much an implicit part of this struggle or, better, what Leavis himself calls "battle," his "letters to the press" give an added dimension to the province of criticism, even as they depict that continuous process of thought that, in Henry James's phrase, intensifies with the "wear and tear of discrimination."

II

Largely because of Leavis's efforts, English studies have become a discipline of literary and civilizational importance. His achievement constitutes something monumental and is characterized by a vigor and a consummateness of purpose and of meaning that will withstand the passage of time. His is a permanent contribution to the study and the judgment of literature: It now has classical standing and classical rightness and is classical in a most relevant and living sense. Just how relevant and living it is, and in what special ways it has significance for all of us, is best summed up in Leavis's own words concerning the critical function:

> Situations differ, opportunities vary, I know, but it will always be necessary to insist (and in a more than theoretical way) that criticism is a collaborative and creative interplay. It creates a community and is inseparable from the process that creates and keeps alive a living culture; that creates a civilization in so far as a civilization is something more than a matter of material conditions and externalities of social behaviour. If you believe that literature matters, you are committed to believing that.

It is within the province of literary critics, indeed, it is within the nature of prompting critical responsibility itself, as Leavis often points out, to respond to the great cultural problems of the world—of civilization at large. Arnold exemplified this critical dimension in the nineteenth century. In this century T.S. Eliot is often cited as the exemplar, for his critical writings are both literary and "sociological." The latter adjective is perhaps not the best to use, but it is the one most likely to suggest a writer's extraliterary (or is it interdisciplinary?) concern with cultural problems as a whole, with what is and what makes for civilization, its orientation, its directions, its values and essences. Eliot, in any event, spoke out courageously and consistently concerning political, economic, religious, educational, and social issues. His social criticism is generally labeled "conservative." He has even been attacked as a fascist by "enlightened" liberals, that is, by the liberal ideologues who object to any standards that may apply to themselves. But Eliot is now dead, and his fate at the hands of these spokesmen speaks for itself.

Leavis is the only other modern critic who shares with Eliot the honor of representing the critical discipline at its influential best. Together these two men provide a picture of great practicing critics writing in the English language, concerned with the formulation and the maintenance of "standards of discrimination," with specifying principles, and with adhering to a discipline in terms of constantly coalescing literary and cultural positions. Ultimately, it should be said, Eliot's profoundest strength appeared in his creative work, in his poems from *The Waste Land* to his greatest triumph, *Four Quartets.* Unlike his social criticism, his literary criticism was often divided and unsure of itself (with exceptions, no doubt, as the essays on the "Metaphysical Poets" and on the Elizabethan dramatists show)—the "cleft" Eliot, in other words, who irritated his friend Paul Elmer More. Eliot's essential heroism was not, in the end, critical but rather creative. As a literary critic he had his special loyalties and weaknesses (of inconstancy and of inconsistency), refined and purified only when the creative impulse took over as a total impersonalizing process of critical intelligence. The point is that Eliot lacked the vital inner strength to guard himself against compromise in essays like that on the parlor figure Charles Whibley, or even in plays like *The Cocktail Party*—and that made him, to the acquiescing social (and coterie) world of his time, the "Great Tom."

Eliot's greatness is not being questioned here. Rather, these necessarily qualifying references have their comparative force in establishing the critical place and worth of Leavis. For what Eliot lacked was a vigor, a critical heroism that would have enabled him to overcome the Bloomsbury ethos and, for instance, to see Virginia Woolf's limitations as an artist, or to measure the mediocrity of David Garnett's "novels," or, above all, to count D.H. Lawrence among the really great novelists of the age. It is precisely that sustaining power of conviction, of integrity, that Leavis disclosed. Eliot refused, or was emotionally unable, to pay the price that Leavis was willing to pay in order to uphold his critical function with the honest severity that empowers it. Leavis's literary criticism has that kind of completeness that Eliot's only erratically displays. There is in Leavis's work, in other words, a constant refusal to compromise, to be a party to the *trahison des clercs*, in which single phrase, incidentally, is summed up some of the most glaring and even perverse manifestations of the critical stance that George Orwell possibly had in mind (after his early failures to find a publisher for his *Animal Farm,* which Eliot's Faber and Faber rejected) when he complained that the liberal fears liberty and the intellectual strives to do dirt on the intellect.

There is, it will be seen, a correlation between Orwell's complaint and Leavis's continuing complaints, especially, for example, in *Nor Shall My Sword,* in that they both have a common enemy in the heralds of modern progressivist enlightenment who reduce life to sheer material measurement, whether as a "Great Society" or as a "New Deal." Ideologues of enlightenment, wielding mighty political power (and found, ironically enough, in *all* political camps), often formulate their schemes for human progress without concern for any cultural and moral consequences. They fail, as Leavis insists, to engage in the "creative questioning"—"What for, what ultimately for? What, ultimately, do men live by?"—that must define the limits of mere "social hope" and that should, in the end, inform its deepest values. "But," wrote Leavis, "life in the civilization of an age for which such creative questioning is not done and is not influential on general sensibility tends characteristically to lack dimension: it tends to have no depth—no depth against which it doesn't tacitly protect itself by the habit of unawareness. . . ." It is not material civilization in all its humane achievement that Leavis questions here. Rather, it is "the energy, the triumphant technology, the productivity, the high standard of living and the life-impoverishment—the human emptiness" that he seeks to focus on. He is questioning, then, the absence in modern life of the moral measure that provides a perspective, indeed a "religious depth of thought and feeling," which civilization must have if life is not to be enjoyed "in a vacuum of disinheritance."

The world of enlightenment is, for Leavis, a world in which standards and discipline are sacrificed to the technological spirit, to the spirit of permissiveness, to an attitude "that can see nothing to be quarrelled with in believing, or wanting to believe, that [for example] a computer can write a poem." It is a complacent and self-indulgent attitude that is dialectically negative, that must negate the critical spirit and "the creativeness that is responsibility." In his criticisms Leavis, of course, focuses on the permissive and the sloppy attitudes that get attention as distinguished critical and creative attitudes and on the kind of values that are accepted and even required in the whole of culture. These are the attitudes and the values that play a crucial role in the making of civilization, the civilization that in its totality is identified by an ethos, a way of thought, of intelligence, of discrimination—the ways that say and tell (or do *not* say and tell, as the case may be) about man's view of himself and of the life around him, about those matters that must count and that inform the higher value of cultural continuity, which, in Leavis's words, "has its life in time, and transcending 'present' and 'past,' gives time its meaning and humanity its grasp of a real."

Predictably, Leavis's assertions are sometimes greeted with derision. One academic dismissed *Nor Shall My Sword* for containing "a conspiratorial rhetoric for which no sufficient evidence has been produced." After all, few people, especially academics, want to be reminded of conditions they have made possible through their betrayal of moral, spiritual, and educational values. There is nothing that touches enlightened ideologues to the quick more than the charge (or reminder) that they have encouraged the disorder and the indiscipline that shake the foundations of civilization. Yet an enlightened orthodoxy that insidiously creates a permissive spirit and that sanctifies, for the wrong reasons, a *Lady Chatterley's Lover* poses the danger that Leavis seeks to overcome. The danger is one of *un*critical thought. Not Dickens but C.P. Snow is the model for emulation, the comprehender of what the modern world is, where it is going, how it can be saved. Surely Leavis emphasizes a timely truth in seeing Snow as a portent.

Leavis's main and ultimate critical concern is with "judgments about life." "What the critical discipline is concerned with," he insists, "is relevance and precision in making and developing them." The discipline of literary studies, then, is as genuine and as important as that of any of the sciences; without it "there can be no adequate attention paid to the problems of our civilization." In the study and the evaluation of literature in one's own language (in the first place), one comes to recognize the nature and the priority of what Leavis calls "the third realm," a realm "which is neither merely private and personal nor public in the sense that it can be brought into the laboratory or pointed to." It is English literature, he maintains, that, in its diversity and range, fully registers changing life and shows the continuity of mind, spirit, and sensibility. Indeed, it is only in "the third realm" that a "cultural community of consciousness" can be attained, or as Leavis says in *English Literature in Our Time and the University:* ". . . unless society . . . develops by dint of sustained intelligent purpose the habit and the means of fostering in itself this collaborative and creative renewal, the cultural consciousness and the power of response will fade into nullity, and technological development, together with administrative convenience, will *impose* the effective ends and values of life. . . ."

Leavis's lifetime work can be viewed as a reasoned and connected protest against those forces that would repress "the essential creativeness of life." Often, then, he points to William Blake as an inspiration for contemporary society. Blake serves as the antithesis to Locke and Newton, and he points forward to, even as he is corroborated and reinforced by, the Dickens of *Hard Times* and the Lawrence of *Women in Love.* "To emphasize creativity as Blake did,"Leavis states, "is to be committed to bringing home to the world, if in a world of Lockean or technologico-Benthamite blankness that can be done, that you can't generalize life, that individual lives can't be aggregated or averaged, and that only in individual lives is life 'there.'" Human creativity and human responsibility: these are the recurring, the affirming preoccupations of Leavis's work and thought. Unlike Snow, he refuses to accept the existence of "two cultures," the humanist and the scientific. There is only "one culture," Leavis asserts: "The world we live in is not the world that forms a tiny part of the distinguished chemist's—the scientific—universe. It is a world, a reality, of human values and significances which is created and maintained by continuous collaborative human creativity. Without it there would have been no science."

Like Arnold's, Leavis's best work is that of a literary critic, even when it is not literary criticism. This is so because it comes from an independent and disciplined intelligence, profoundly aware of humane values. How are humane values to be defended and to be passed on in our time? How are these values to be saved from the process of dehumanization that, in the technologico-Benthamite world, alters everything it comes into contact with? Leavis responds positively to these questions. If his view of contemporary developments is negative, his significance is not, for Leavis rises above negations. His work as a teacher-critic is a great plea for the affirmation of humane values and of humanistic culture. This plea has in it both latitude and depth, has centrality of unifying purpose and of relevance. Certainly it easily refutes the charge of provincialism that one hears used against him. But then, whenever it is a matter of maintaining standards and exercising discipline, an advocate of such a view is very apt to be charged with being "provincial" and "narrow." ("Puritano frenetico," for instance, is a description that has been applied to Leavis.) What has been happening in the universities—and one thinks here of the portent of the "free university," or of the "open university," or of the "university without walls"—discloses precisely the representative consequences of the power of "enlightened" (mis)direction.

It should be noted that Leavis addresses himself to "the condition of England" and to an English audience. His diagnostic insights, however, have a much wider and, above all, prophetic value, for they ultimately relate to the condition of both European and American civilization, to the human condition itself. In this respect the prophetic spirit is shown to be not limited to visionaries like Blake and Lawrence. It has (and should have) an equally appropriate and endemic place in the critical spirit that Leavis exemplifies. The prophetic spirit that a great man possesses, Paul Tillich remarks, "exposes him to a terrible anxiety within himself, to severe and often deadly attacks from others, and to the charge of pessimism and defeatism on the part of the majority of the people. Men desire to hear good tidings; and the masses listen to those who bring them." No words could better capture the difficulty of Leavis's labors nor better underline his burden of responsibility, as well as the heroic mission that he never surrendered.

III

In literary creativity abide significances and potencies that, discriminatingly analyzed, judged, ordered, and placed, contribute to intelligent critical thought and inevitably to a finer civilization. The creative act and the critical function meet in meaning and comprise a collaborative process. Life and literature attain a viable transaction; art and society assume a healthy interalliance. And human possibility is strengthened when this transaction is effected, and effected in the face of the technocultural power centers aggressively shaping man's faith. What can be called the "living principle," that is the qualitative power of creative-critical thought that resists negation, must be maintained in an era when, as Robert Lowell reminds us, "We feel the machine slipping from our hands." The "living principle" contains the spirit of a minority culture that defies modern mass civilization and creates discipline and standards. This "living principle" can be defined as the apprehended totality of what, as rendered in the English language, has been won and established in the development of civilization. Literary creativity entails the study of language, which in turn must demand and impose a discipline of thought. In this interaction purposiveness and opportunity present a conjoined specificity—that, in short, life matters and has value, if only its possibilities are responsibly explored and affirmed. But any apprehension of the possibility of value is impossible without recognizing that the criteria of intelligent thought are inseparable from intelligence about the nature of language itself. Unless modern man is alert to these fundamentals, and to the transcending fact that the critical discipline is itself a discipline of intelligence, then cultural malaise will triumph and the principle of life, of creation, will be thwarted. The dangers of this contingency can be resisted only as long as the "living principle" is recognized and asserted. Its diminution is something that must be actively opposed, if cynicism and apathy are not to become a frozen attitude, an axiomatic condition, of the human world. Insistence on human creativity must be simultaneously insistence on human responsibility.

The preceding paragraph can serve as, at best, a summary of Leavis's highly important and perhaps greatest book, *The Living Principle.*

The limiting "at best" needs stressing, for *The Living Principle,* in its profundity and distinction, requires reflection and will repay frequentation. For Leavis criticism is of supreme cultural importance. The drive behind his critical conception and practice is best suggested by D.H. Lawrence's words to a young novelist, "One writes out of one's moral sense—for the race, as it were." *The Living Principle* underlines the compelling nature of Leavis's responsibility as a critic whose practice of criticism is addressed to the deeper and greater—to the ultimate—problems of existence. Without seeking either to simplify or to reduce the uniqueness of Leavis's work, it can be said that his is a criticism that confronts human crisis actively, militantly—one could even say prophetically, "for the race, as it were." It seeks, above all, to keep alive the "living principle," despite those who would betray it and who would retreat into the abject despair that has "no exit."

To survive in a world addicted to the idols of social science, Leavis insists in the first part of the book, entitled "Thought, Language and Objectivity," the "living principle" depends on the kind of interrelation that exists between language and thought and between judgment and analysis. A vital relationship instances the potential form of cultural reciprocity that makes for an educated public conscious of its responsibility to maintain the language of creative thought and to integrate its standards into the social order. Cultural life cannot be divorced from the literary situation. The state of health of the one reflects the state of health of the other. That discrimination is life and indiscrimination is death, as Leavis has said elsewhere, is a statement that warrants relevance here. It is toward the attainment of the discriminating process that Leavis focuses his final attention. The true function of the university, he declares, is based on the idea of an educated public that needs to be trained in this process, that is to say, a training of sensibility. Where and when the process is vigorous, sociopolitical life itself cannot but feel the effects. In his adherence to and belief in this possibility Leavis depicts an optimistic faith that is now necessarily on the dangerous edge of things: "Change is certainly upon us, menacing and certainly drastic; to meet it, there must be opportunism—the opportunism that answers to a profound realization of the need."

The specifics of these literary-cultural concepts are found in the second and middle part of *The Living Principle,* "Judgment and Analysis." Synthesizing text and context, this part contains paradigms of criticism. Whether he is examining "'thought' and emotional quality" in particular poems (as in the discussion of Lawrence's "Piano"), or "imagery and movement" (as in the analysis of William

Wordsworth's "Upon Westminster Bridge"), or "reality and sincerity" (as in the appraisal of Thomas Hardy's "After a Journey"), Leavis discloses a critical process that exacts discriminating judgments. Such criticism is not an exercise for its own sake, not some passing academic interest. Nor is it a display of erudition or cleverness, or "the declaration of outlook," as one interpreter has sardonically described it. The underpinning of Leavis's criticism is incontrovertibly, and characteristically, moral. How does literary creativity play its due role in the "human world"? How can the study of it contribute to the life of man? These are some of the "creative questions" that Leavis keeps asking of himself and of the reader. The closeness of his reading; the precision and clarity of his thought; the organization and exposition, the force and economy of his arguments; the integrity and disinterestedness of his explication—the registered valuations of a "judging mind" (" 'This is so, isn't it?' . . . 'Yes, but'—the 'but' standing for corrections, refinements, precisions, amplifications"): these critical qualities, so unmistakable in their concentrated strengths, are more than criteria that Leavis proffers. They are exempla of civilized thought.

The final part, and nearly half, of *The Living Principle* is devoted to T.S. Eliot's *Four Quartets*, which Leavis examines within the contexts of his critical formulations. We have here a kind of coda that takes on considerable critical dimension. Eliot clearly fits in at this point since he has status as a major poet in whom "the creative nisus works impressively." In almost every way his poetry fulfills the criteria of the "living principle": "*almost,*" for there is "something in him too [that] makes him deny human creativity—he recoils from being responsible. The denial, which comes from the selfhood (for Eliot is in the 'placing' sense a 'case'), gravely affects the quality of his affirmation when he offers to affirm—and *Four Quartets* is dedicated to an offer of affirmation." The pivotal value of *The Living Principle* will be found in this part of the book; however, as any careful reading will verify, it is a part that can only be comprehended in relation to the full and developed force of critical thought that has been elaborated in the preceding parts. A profound and concluding critical passage is executed here and leaves an impression of finality. One's appreciation of the first two parts is heightened and renewed by this final one. The critical (and subtle) interplay of all three parts attains here a tour de force. One could almost say that this final part, as a movement of thinking quality, is inevitable.

Leavis's critical views are bound to disturb those who see *Four Quartets* as Eliot's supernal experience; as the recording of moments of mystic illumination; as Eliot's intuition of the supernatural involving "neither flesh nor fleshless" (*Burnt Norton,* II). Eliot's religious, that is to say his metaphysical and spiritual, essences are stripped away. A more naked Eliot appears, as Leavis sifts through and weighs the communicated values of Eliot's poetic vision in its full complexity. He never denies, he insists on, the fact that Eliot is a "creative master of the English language." The "living principle" of *Four Quartets* distinguishes itself in Eliot's creative resource in making language serve him as the exploration of experience and in offering thought that is "searching, basic and rigorous." But Leavis also reveals how Eliot's "desperate" preoccupation with establishing an apprehension of eternal reality ends in an "essential contradiction." (Yvor Winters has also severely attacked Eliot as being unaware of his contradictions: ". . . he is able to join at one and the same time the pleasures of indulgence and the dignity of disapproval.") In *Four Quartets* Leavis sees a basic attitude of antilife, an incomprehension of reality and of the human situation: an insistence, ultimately, "on the unreality, the unlivingness, of life in time." The upshot is one of self-contradiction. Eliot "registers his recoil from mechanistic determinism; but in doing so he denies life's essential creativity, though committed to vindicating by creative means his *ahnung* of a spiritual reality he posits as the only escape." In consequence he remains in the prison of selfhood.

If it can be claimed that Leavis has a critical system, then the apex-thought of his criticism quintessentializes at this point. This is not to be hyperbolic. Rather it is to emphasize what, in the totality of Leavis's achievement, stands as a vindication of the critical pursuit. Nor is it to ignore the critical disagreement that Leavis invites regarding the significance of *Four Quartets.* The reader who is being pushed to respond to Leavis's valuation will want, in the end, to consider whether or not Eliot's great poem is ever fully penetrated by a critical method that, in its uniqueness and power, as the critic's most formidable contribution to truth, deflects the meditativeness of a poem. At which point does the critical act, as it is exemplified by Leavis, fail to apprehend the (metaphysical) possibility of what can be called the mystery of meditative criticism, that criticism that is perhaps most commensurate with what Eliot is doing in *Four Quartets?* This is certainly a major question, however awkwardly phrased (or arrived at), that Leavis's critique will conduce among readers of *Four Quartets.* But, then, this is as it should be. The "living principle" and "creative questions" are interdependent entities, the divorce of which proves fatal to intelligent critical thought.

Exemplary, if not unequaled, in its intensity of concern and strength of commitment, Leavis's critique of *Four Quartets* is a process of reflection. It would seem, nonetheless, that Eliot's poem, itself a long sequential meditation on the conquest of time and the meaning of history, needs a transcendent criticism of meditation. Yet no better preparation for attaining such a transcendence can be gained than by being first disciplined by a great master of modern English criticism. In the larger critical view the difference between reflection and meditation is a significant corrective. That the difference is not bridged in *The Living Principle*, that Leavis makes no attempt to bridge it, is equally significant—and revealing. His conception of the "living principle" precludes the Eliotic stress on the "redemption of time." The basal nature of this stress is eschatological, possessing a Christian reference. Leavis's criticism of Eliot is analogous to Lawrence's criticism of Dostoevsky's "The Legend of the Grand Inquisitor": "The bread, the earthly bread, while it is being reaped and grown, it is life. But once it is harvested and stored, it becomes a commodity, it becomes riches. And then it becomes a danger. For men think, if they only possessed the hoard, they need not work; which means, really, they need not live. And that is the real blasphemy. For while we live we must live, we must not wither or rot inert." Whatever the critic's moral sense, Leavis has shown, it must halt at the frontier of theology. In this decision we can detect what, for Leavis, must always differentiate between criticism as thought and as meditation, and ultimately between morality and mysticism.

Still, if Leavis is skeptical about the eschatological pull of *Four Quartets*, he is not about the nature of the ultimate religious fact. *The Living Principle* is one of those rare enactments of a critical discipline that transforms into a spiritual exercise, the combination of which serves to redeem the spiritual from the sentimental, the illusionary, the ambivalent, the equivocal; from, to use words from Eliot's *The Cocktail Party*, "The kind of faith that issues from despair" and the "Dung and death" of *East Coker*. What some of Leavis's detractors fail to see is that his criticism, far from being imperious communiqués, facilitates a reader's passage in the paths of the critical dialectic, of that "'third realm' where values and meanings belong." The paradox that he finds in *Four Quartets* is not one that can be easily dismissed. In this paradox he detects the disintegration of the "living principle." But the disintegrative process, too, forces one to discover and present, to rethink, one's own position. Leavis's adverse criticisms of *Four Quartets* amount to "criticism [that] is at the same time a tribute." His critical precepts are clearly antithetical to the eschatological, to the predominantly theological distinctions of *Four Quartets*. Leavis has always been careful not to slide into the "orthodox generalities" of "Christian discrimination."

But this effort has never been generated by hostility. Scrutiny, not celebration, is at the center of his critical work. The real defense of spiritual values must begin with the recognition of this datum. In Leavis a reciprocating courage of life and courage of judgment constitute an enduring article of faith. Yet the effluence of his critical examples has a decidedly religious cast, which is best understood in Leavis's belief that "there is no acceptable religious position that is not a reinforcement of human responsibility."

This writer recalls a conversation with his old teacher at Nottingham University, England, the late Vivian de Sola Pinto, concerning the special endowments of Leavis's criticism. "Dr. Leavis is a genius," Pinto kept repeating in that inimitable way of his, as the discussion was concluding. His parting salute has always stayed with me. If there ever existed any question, even then in 1960, of bestowing such high honor, *The Living Principle*, even as it attests to genius, now confirms its legitimacy. For, in its cumulative power, Leavis's criticism belongs to a great critical vision, to a realized process that must be viewed in the light of Thomas Carlyle's contention that "genius . . . means transcendent capacity of taking trouble, first of all."

19

Voice in the Wilderness

DESPITE WHAT THE LIBERAL INTELLECTUALS write so superlatively for and about each other, in the learned journals as well as in the overlord press, our literary and cultural situation remains barren. Where, today, are our great teachers and critics, our great statesmen, philosophers, and religious thinkers, our great poets and novelists, our great men of letters? Any attempt to answer this question must end in a discouraging brevity of response. Malaise is a word that immediately presents itself here; and one thinks, too, of the frightening truth of Aleksandr Solzhenitsyn's assertion that a universal spiritual death touches us all. Standards of judgment and value, let alone of example and conduct; seriousness of the general critical intelligence and conscience; intellectual honesty and moral concern and commitment: everywhere these criteria of perspective are, along with excellence and discipline, in eclipse. Our liberal pundits, to be sure, dismiss such a protestation as the dying remnant of nonprogressive and unenlightened metaphysics. By now we are all too aware of this responding tactic and, worse, of the harm it brings relentlessly and irretrievably. The contemporary absolutism of liberalism, as is everywhere evident, exerts a thought control alarming in power; and a reductionist technologico-Benthamite conformity prevails. But, even in desperation and dismay, we must continue to believe in and to insist on the courage of judgment.

Obviously, the "we" of the previous sentence signifies not a horde but a minority whose voice, even if it is a voice out of the whirlwind, steadily weakens as the insanities and irreverences of the horde increase. At any rate, it suffices to say that the serious critic, who, as Irving Babbitt once observed by way of indicting H.L. Mencken, is "more concerned with achieving a correct scale of values and so seeing things proportionately than with self-expression," is fast disappearing from the cultural map. When, and if, the serious critic dares raise his voice, he is quickly silenced or ostracized. (One thinks here of what generally happens to Jacques Barzun or Lionel Trilling when he speaks out about the state of the American mind and soul and about the effects of liberal "progress.") Clearly, the generating mood and climate around us do not favor the critical spirit, that is to say, the discriminating mind and the judgments it renders. The result is lamentable and nowhere better underlined than in the decline, even the absence from the American (and European) scene, of the man of letters. A man of letters belongs to a great tradition of responsibility, as not only Babbitt but also T.S. Eliot reveals. He is concerned, quintessentially, with standards as these affect the prospect of man and the condition of civilization. "He must," as Allen Tate reminds us in a superb essay, "The Man of Letters in the Modern World" (1952), "recreate for his age the image of man, and he must propagate standards by which other men may test that image, and distinguish the false from the true." Indeed, as Tate further observes, "There would be no hell for modern man if our men of letters were not calling attention to it."[1]

Lewis Mumford (b. 1895) is our most distinguished surviving man of letters, whose warnings regarding the chaos of modern life are steadily receiving confirmation.[2] Mumford has devoted a whole lifetime, as a man of letters, to battling for the idea of a humane society against an onrushing specialist spirit, with its loss of proportion, its overemphasis, and ultimately its technical dehumanization of human existence, resulting finally in what Tate terms "the secularism of the swarm." In challenging this life-negating spirit Mumford has disclosed a constant and consistent dignity and sincerity of effort. What he calls the "miscarriages of 'civilization'" and the "transformations of man" are in the end his two most central preoccupations; and in the fearless exposure of these miscarriages and transformations, which he sees ultimately crystallizing into a new barbarism, he brings into view a prophetic energy of concern and response. In speaking out and speaking forth the felt truths of what he sees, and discriminates, Mumford further discloses that moral dimension of thought, of judgment above all, that characterizes the mission of the man of letters. Prognosis and diagnosis, in light of "the condition of man," become in this respect the major task of the man of letters, as Mumford's writings from over the last half century prove. In the pursuit of these tasks, he also discloses that creative, life-saving constituent that girds the prophetic critical spirit in all its offshoots: Vision. For the man of letters is also a man of vision who understands, on the deepest levels of sensibility, that "Where there is no vision, the people perish."

Of course, Mumford retains just enough of his optimistic faith not

1. In *Essays of Four Decades* (Chicago, 1968).
2. See his *Interpretations and Forecasts: 1922–1972* (New York, 1973).

to pronounce man's total collapse. But that modern man has come more and more to the outermost edge of civilizational dissolution and now approaches that zero zone of total nullification: against this hell of man's fate Mumford re-creates the full force of his message. This is by no means a happy task; the prophet's responsibility is, from the earliest of times, always a troubling one, both for himself and for his audience. Which again returns us to the essence of the main task of the man of letters: the refining maintenance of standards that distinguish human society, and humane civilization as a whole, from the kind of society in which spiritual servitude becomes the ultimate dehumanizing law. Even the roughest analysis of the evolving significance of Mumford's writings since 1922, whether in his choice of great figures, or of historical movements, trends, and directions, or of major themes and theses, will show a steady, undeviating line of concern with human possibility in a world of growing impossibility. Mumford is uncompromising not only in expressing his vision of life but also, and even more importantly, in affirming the meaning of life—and the meaning of man. He shows this affirmation in the highest humanistic terms, seeing the value of a spiritualizing love as an ultimate value in transcending the modern spirit of desacralization that impedes "the flowering of plants and men." "We need," says Mumford, "such a redeeming and all-embracing love at this moment to rescue the earth itself and all the creatures that inhabit it from the insensate forces of hate, violence, and destruction."

Yet, the possibility of a spiritualizing love remains a stubbornly remote one in the modern world. Everywhere the forces of antilife are ascendant, as what Mumford calls the "megamachine" and "megatechnics" become the new religion of our culture. Duty to humanity is replaced by duty to scientific truth, and this obscene process of transvaluation leads to the debasement of life that Mumford summarizes cogently in one sentence: "for the fact is that standardization, organization, automatism, which are the real and special triumphs of modern technics, tend with their very perfection to produce routineers: people whose vital interests and activities lie outside the system to which they have committed themselves." The imposed dogmas of this new religion of technics contain a frightening absolutism based on quantity and quantification, on bureaucracy, regimentation, mediocrity, and external (cybernetic) control. These are precisely those depersonalizing elements of both life and governance that, as we see to our horror, destroy the humanistic hierarchies that, as Mumford notes, "give authority to knowledge over ignorance, to goodness over malice and evil, to the rational over the irrational, to the universal and enduring over the time serving and particular." In the end nothing is more triumphant in the midst of the rise of the new religion than the specialist spirit that Mumford views as the most formidable enemy: the ultimate desecrator whose empire of might is almost impregnable. No field of human activity remains unchallenged or untouched by this presiding specialist spirit, as its "new" metaphysicians of disorder—our new reformers, scientists, educators, psychologists, artists, theologians, philosophers—remorselessly lead us to Armageddon.

There is another, even absolute, quality that the man of letters must possess and reveal with a kind of irradiating grace. This is the quality of wisdom, or better than just mere quality, the unexcelled capacity to communicate meaning and value as an interdependent entity. Intelligence of itself, we know, can convey meaning in its various interpretive levels of signification; and it is no doubt an important and respectable facet of the critical function. But beyond definition of meaning one needs, above all, also to discover the life essences of value. A critic, even a very good critic, can achieve only the first of these qualities, or criteria, of perception. A man of letters achieves both. In some ways, these greater, or higher, critical qualities that the man of letters has and discloses endow his vision with a special, innate religious quality, perfected in a communicated form of wisdom. Such wisdom has a generalist dimension, as it were, for it embraces the whole of existence. It speaks of and to the total human condition, in all of its immediacy and history, and the voice that is heard has a universal echo or tone. It contains and is contained by, in a word, "the idea of the holy." The view of life that is delineated is reverential; the counsel proffered, whether as pronouncement or announcement, prophecy, protest, precept, reflection, or warning, is sapiential. A wise man has acutely seen and discovered and said things ordinary mortals neglect or refuse to see. His revelation, thus, becomes his testament, his conveyed wisdom, the kind of wisdom that our modern civilization has too often, and often disastrously, rejected. Particularly in his style, in the manner of his writing that dictates the relation between form and moral content, the man of letters is very much an ancient teacher of wisdom in modern dress.

Of this ancient legacy of wisdom Mumford is both teacher and exemplar, eloquently synthesizing and unifying as he also does, and as any true man of letters must, the Hebraic element of conscience and the Hellenic element of consciousness. His portrayal and scrutiny of actual human existence and his way of addressing himself to his listeners underline the style of the wisdom writer. Exhortation and prophecy are conveyed in a vigorous language and style in which even the habit of repetitiousness intensifies the heavy burden of Mumford's teachings:

> To save technics itself we shall have to place limits on its heretofore unqualified expansion.

> We discarded the universal insights of Confucius and Buddha, of Mo Ti and St. Paul, at the very moment they were needed most to make technics a true agent of civilization.

> The test of maturity, for nations as for individuals, is not the increase of power, but the increase of self-understanding, self-control, self-direction, and self-transcendence. For in a mature society, man himself, not his machines or his organizations, is the chief work of art.

Throughout Mumford speaks as a wise man who, in his universalizing awareness and indictment of the decay of civilization, affirms ethical and moral precepts of life. One outstanding essay that especially corroborates this paradigmatic quality is Mumford's "Post-Historic Man," which in its terrifying truth of insight captures the very essence of a wise man's observation and consideration of a world in which the posthistoric is also the posthuman. The following passage from this essay gives a characteristic hint of what one encounters in the whole of Mumford's wisdom books:

> During the present era . . . man's nature has begun to undergo a decisive final change. With the invention of the scientific method and the depersonalized procedures of modern technics, cold intelligence, which has succeeded as never before in commanding the energies of nature, already dominates every human activity. To survive in this world, man must adapt himself completely to the machine. Nonadaptable types, like the artist and the poet, the saint and the peasant, will either be made over or be eliminated by social selection. All the creativities associated with Old World religion and culture will disappear. To become more human, to explore further into the depth of man's nature, to pursue the divine, are no longer proper goals for machine-made man.

At no other time in history have we had a more urgent need for the man of letters who is also a man of wisdom; for the wise man, that is, who is in accord with both priest and prophet, with the former speaking for reverence and the latter courageously warning against the transgressions of titans. If the twin tyrants of our modern world, Blasphemy and Barbarism, are ever to be resisted and contained, the sage pleas and admonitions of a Lewis Mumford can only be ignored or dismissed at one's peril. "They [who] sow the wind . . . shall reap the whirlwind."

20

A Constant Dimension

MODERATION AND BOLDNESS must inform the critic's attitude toward literature. Without moderation he is prone to the sin of hubris, and his critical prejudices move in extremes. Without boldness he cannot have a clear perspective or express a steadfast conviction. Moderation provides balance; boldness assures commitment. Their reconciliation creates a critical synthesis of values and standards. How to penetrate and arrest the artist's vision remains for the critic the highest challenge. Beyond this, how to distinguish permanent truths from temporary truths must finally test the critic's strength of judgment. This challenge and this judgment comprise the burden of criticism. One must not expect criticism to be an invincible force. The critic, even if he is militant, even if he is a warrior in his own right, can hardly issue victory proclamations. His raison d'être is ever so tenuous, and his work has no measurable destiny. When he refuses to believe this fact and fights against it, society, which knows where the real power lies, has the habit of telling him exactly where he stands. What, then, is the value of criticism as a literary art if, in its most empirical aspects, it seems so peripheral to the battle of life? Formulating an answer is far from simple, and perhaps there is no final answer. But this much is certain: The critical function in its innermost essences has prophetic power. Not that criticism predicts the future; rather it helps achieve the future or, better, it helps save the future by its quest for and its defense of excellence. Like the work of the best educator, criticism can never be weighed, even though one knows when it has done its work by enlarging one's perception of the quality of life—by making one see what hitherto remained unseen. As a constant dimension of the judging mind, criticism refines and completes the love of beauty. Criticism is a moral form of reflection that arises out of both the recognition of limitations and the affirmation of the possibilities of vision and individual talents. "For criticism that is critical," John Middleton Murry observes, "is the expression of a real spiritual energy and the satisfaction of a real spiritual need."

Of this critical spirit John W. Aldridge is a fine exemplar, as is impressively confirmed by the essays that he wrote between 1951 and 1971, collected under the title *The Devil in the Fire*.[1] "Retrospective," the first word in the subtitle, should serve as the informing word in an estimation of these critical essays. We need to recall what this word means, and we can do no better than to begin with the definition found in *The Oxford English Dictionary:* "Directed to, contemplative of, past time." This collection illuminates some of the conditions and the directions of American literary and cultural history during an eventful period. What happened in and to American literature and culture (for the two go together) during these twenty years? What was significant? What promises of greatness were kept? What disappointments occurred? These are questions that Aldridge confronts in his essays and review essays, the latter a genre of critical writing in which he excels. It is an added virtue of this collection of essays that it helps us to contemplate American literary culture in the light of postwar happenings. War and its aftermath have boundless literary-cultural implications, and the time has come to consider those of World War II as extensively as those of World War I are being assessed.

If "retrospective" and "past" describe the informing significance of the essays in *The Devil in the Fire*, it is the word "serious" that characterizes Aldridge's system of principles, his critical ethos. For he is a critic who cares deeply about the critical function and about the special standards of that function. For him criticism is neither an aspect of the "associational process" that Henry James decried nor a vested interest of self-seeking academics. Criticism for Aldridge is a serious civilizational pursuit, and his seriousness contains an implicit integrity. It is criticism, too, that belongs to a great tradition. Unfortunately no great tradition of criticism prevails in the present period. What Edmund Wilson wrote back in 1928 still holds true: "It is astonishing to observe, in America, in spite of our floods of literary journalism, to what extent the literary atmosphere is a nonconductor of criticism." We hear voices but no voice. Critical aridity is symptomatic of a cultural malaise that belongs to the technological spirit of modern civilization, when quantifiers become oracles of literary taste. Such are the trappings of what has become an insidious form of spiritual philistinism. In Aldridge we still hear the voice of the great tradition, and this voice is immensely responsible and keenly aware of the present without negating the sense of the past. Indeed, this is one way of describing a great critical tradition: a

---

1. *The Devil in the Fire: Retrospective Essays on American Literature and Culture, 1951–1971* (New York, 1972).

tradition that is aware of civilizational order and discipline and wisdom and yet sensitive to the demands and the changes of contemporaneousness, to which, nonetheless, order, discipline, and wisdom bequeath an ordonnance of standards. This critical tradition has saving qualities, and today we have very urgent need of it so as to resist the levelers and contain the intellectual diaspora.

Fugitive pieces do not usually attain an easy coherence. However, the value of genuine criticism, as found in a collection of essays, is not difficult to detect, for there are always unmistakable signs that enable one to "feel" its permanence of value. *The Devil in the Fire* is such a book, for one reads it not as a book of occasional essays but as a book containing a total and organic response: the ongoing response of a mature sensibility and a critical intelligence formulating and applying standards of discrimination. In Aldridge's volume the element of an impelling concern for excellence is so dominant, so clear in tone and so vigorous in range, that no difficulty occurs. Aldridge clearly knows what and where the literary-cultural centers of excellence are. He knows there can be no compromise with any condition or with any situation that makes for mediocrity. He is not afraid of viewing the critic as a monitor of taste. In a permissive and mediocre era such a critic is to be doubly valued, for literary-cultural standards once desiccated are difficult to restore. As Aldridge shows, commercialism and journalism are twin evils that break foundations and cause literary and cultural drift—and betrayal. The job of all critics is to be vigilant against this deteriorative process, even if such vigilance leads to unpopularity.

Aldridge is one of the few American critics writing today whose commitment to a hierarchy of values is unremitting. His treatment of American literary reputations contains no sacred cows; his evaluation of imaginative vision never surrenders to expediency. Greatness demands disciplined, selfless dedication; it also demands a stern critical sifting of imaginative materials in terms of their value of achievement. Slackness and carelessness can never be substitutes for excellence. Ernest Hemingway, F. Scott Fitzgerald, John Dos Passos, James T. Farrell, and Katherine Anne Porter are some of the established names that come under Aldridge's scrutiny and are seen at one time or in one way or another as exhibiting shortcomings not commensurate with imaginative vision at its best. The essay on "Art and Passion in Katherine Anne Porter" exemplifies his criticism in practice. Her reputation for excellence, he finds, does not fully stand up, or at least it pales. That Porter writes "such a pure English" is indisputable; at the same time, "all contradictions and discords appear to have been sacrificed to the purity of the English." Her

275

writing fails to be work of the first magnitude, for beneath the "surface effect of elegant and stylish finish," the full play of imaginative power and originality of vision are absent. Aldridge goes on to observe that she is best in the short novel rather than in the short story (e.g., "Flowering Judas" is criticized for its desperate straining for symbolic effect, a point anthologists and teachers might well try to keep in mind) and that she is a regionalist writer more at home in the American Southwest of her childhood—indeed, she is a Southern storyteller and memoirist in the Faulknerian and even Wolfean tradition. Yet "some perverse fastidiousness or shyness has always compelled her to turn away in the main body of her work from the Southern experience, to repress her feelings of intense personal connection with it, and to try to serve an ideal of complete artistic objectivity."

It would be inaccurate to interpret Aldridge's reverence for proven literary accomplishment as a frozen critical position. Modern literary classics in no way preclude the end of imagination. Here Aldridge's critical concern, moreover, is mostly contemporary, and when he hammers away at some of the contemporary problems (e.g., the American writer's continuing isolation in either a culturally hostile or an indifferent society, or the increasing institutionalization of the creative arts, or the dismal spectacle of the puff reviewers), he does so in a corrective sense. Aldridge can be an indefatigable deflater, but he is no callous debunker. His criticism, in theory and in practice, is always diagnostic and evaluative. In examining some of the causes of the problems interconnecting the state of American literature and the condition of American culture, he strives to separate the important from the unimportant, genuine artistic talent from the second-rate. He is never content with litterateurs who are unable or unwilling to go beyond the experience and the literary techniques of the twenties and the thirties; who cannot, in short, render the uniqueness of contemporary consciousness that that consciousness rightly demands:

> But for the genuinely perceptive and talented, the burden of writing in an age of hypersophistication is heavy indeed. And for the intellectual, who reads and judges their work, the problem of imaginative ennui, the nagging little foreknowledge that wherever the work may take him he will very probably have been there already, must constantly intrude, since it is inevitable that he will know as much and often far more about literature and experience than the majority of the writers he reads, and that he will bring to them expectations they can hardly hope to satisfy. He, after all, judges on the basis of critical standards formed by the best achievements of an exceptional past. They, on the other

hand, must try to *be* best while living in the shadow of that past and fighting not only against the fear that the best has already been done, but also against the knowledge that the established ways of being best are now blinders they must somehow throw off if they are to be any good at all.

Few contemporary writers have been able to *"be* best" while living in the shadow of an "exceptional past." Aldridge particularly helps to remind us that the contemporary American novel, not unlike the novel elsewhere, is in trouble, to the extent that it perhaps has no future. What E.M. Forster called "terrors of the imagination," and all that this phrase connotes, have not had an original or a felt impact on contemporary writers. Until 1945 it was possible to group together "ancients and moderns," as the phrase goes, because the problems Aldridge underlines had been met head-on. To speak of "moderns and contemporaries," on the other hand, is another matter. One can go from the Hebrew prophets and Homer to Dostoevsky to William Faulkner with a sense of intensifying relevance and comparative order of achievement. But one cannot, as Aldridge clearly shows, move with an equivalent ease of critical appreciation from the great moderns to contemporary writers like William Styron, John Cheever, John Updike, James Jones, Saul Bellow, and Mary McCarthy. Creative genius necessarily creates its own hierarchy and standards. Surely, there can be no line of continuity, except that of sharp decline, from Joyce's *Ulysses* (1922) to Updike's *The Centaur* (1963).

The contemporary scene is not all that bleak, however. Aldridge sees some hope in the novels of Wright Morris, Eudora Welty, and Norman Mailer. His assessment of Mailer's work is particularly illuminating. Even for readers who still cannot see in Mailer the excellence that Aldridge sees, his critical interpretations will be enlightening. Mailer is found to be an imaginative writer whose vision of contemporary American life is "the product of a devastatingly alive and original creative mind at work in a language capable of responding with seismographic sensitivity to an enormously wide range of impressions." Not since Faulkner has any other American writer brought to full development a prose idiom attuned to "the exact condition of contemporary consciousness," creating "an image of our time" that transcends the older and more comfortable modes of seeing and feeling. Aldridge's essay "From Vietnam to Obscenity" is, in this respect, an excellent example of a critic doing his work— concretely discerning, elucidating, comparing, judging, and persuading. Its insights into Mailer's scatological and fornicatory obscenity; its careful reading of his impelling purpose; its delineation and placing of the novel's American appropriateness: these are the components of Aldridge's critical method that even those who disagree with him will single out for praise.

Standards for Aldridge involve growth through ascent. He is unrelenting in scrutinizing writers who shirk greatness of vision, who are satisfied with second best, who are content, as in the case of Styron, to stay in a "dimension of irrelevance and unreality that is the dimension neither of life nor of literature but of something in between"; or, as in the case of Mary McCarthy, to ignore the gap between a novel's sophistication of style and tone and "the essential banalities of its perceptions of life"; or, as in the case of John Cheever, to express one's vision of contemporary horrors in stereotypes and platitudes and not in the perceived actualities of experience. The artist's striving for the ultimate discipline that differentiates excellence from mere satisfactoriness is for Aldridge a quintessential matter. Unfulfilled talent is something to be regretted, even as it no doubt reveals something about the cultural conditions in which this self-same talent is rewarded. The last twenty years are largely a history of the rewarding of minor talent. Major distinction, like that of Wright Morris's, is ignored while the potential of a Joseph Heller is made too much of. That which is fashionable is too often and too easily taken for excellence and originality.

In reflecting on his role as a critic Aldridge confesses: ". . . I seem always to have functioned best in an adversary position. . . . I never belonged to the New York literary family or the *Kenyon* or *Partisan* cadre or any of the fraternities that make it a business to protect and promote their members." His independent critical verdicts may appear to some readers to be hard, even as his concurrent cultural observations about the sloppiness of American culture, in its intellectual and physical properties, will appear to be rigidly moralistic. There is a nonconformist puritan strain in Aldridge's work that brings to mind the critical thought, in its English versions, of Leavis and of Orwell. For not unlike the former Aldridge can be severe; and not unlike the latter he can be a bit of a nagger. Such a critic is always discomforting. When, too, the temper of the age is sentimental and relativistic, critical valuations like Aldridge's are bound to be resented. But the truth is that so many critics have abdicated the adversary role that this abdication now constitutes something of an irreparable cultural defeat. As equalizers and popularizers solidify their power (in the name of "the politics of relevance") in almost all aspects of cultural life, the meaning of this defeat becomes more apparent.

Acknowledgments

"The Challenge of Simone Weil" was first published in six parts, the first appearing, under that title, in *The Reformed Journal* (November 1977); the remaining five, introductions to the five sections of the volume of essays I edited under the title *The Simone Weil Reader* (New York: David McKay, 1977), were captioned "A New Saintliness," "Prelude to Politics," "Language and Thought," "Criteria of Wisdom," and "Paths of Meditation," respectively.

"T.S. Eliot and the Critique of Liberalism" was first published in *Modern Age: A Quarterly Review* (Spring 1974); the following writings also first appeared in *Modern Age:* "Without One False Note" (Fall 1979); "The New Logos" (Spring 1979); "The Modernist Impasse" (Winter 1975); "Presenting Mr. Marx" (Fall 1980); "The Jamesian Mirror" (in two parts: "The Perspicacious Pilgrim," Spring 1976; "The Jamesian Mirror," Spring 1977); "In Retreat," originally entitled "An Historical Divide" (Summer 1978); "Testaments of Devotion" (Summer 1972); "A Family Matter" (Fall 1969); "Creative Questioner" (in three parts: "The Creative Questioner," Summer 1973; "The Courage of Judgment," Summer 1975; "The Living Principle," first published in *Comparative Literature Studies*, June 1977); and "Voice in the Wilderness" (Summer 1974).

"A Note on Religion and Literature" was written as the preface to the volume of essays I edited under the title *Mansions of the Spirit: Essays in Literature and Religion* (New York: Hawthorn Books, 1967).

"Voyage of Oblivion" was first published in *English Miscellany: A Symposium of History, Literature, and the Arts* (Rome, Italy, 1962).

"Dostoevsky's Political Apocalypse" was first published in *The Intercollegiate Review* (Winter 1976–77).

"Conservative Expositors" was first published in *The Michigan Academician* (Winter 1974).

"D.H. Lawrence's War Letters" was first published in *Texas Studies in Literature and Language: A Journal of the Humanities* (Autumn 1963).

ACKNOWLEDGMENTS

"A Constant Dimension" was first published in *Michigan Quarterly Review* (Fall 1972).

To the editors of the journals and to the publishers of the books in which the preceding writings first appeared, as cited, I want to extend my gratitude for giving me permission to reprint and, in some instances, for initially providing me with the necessary stimulus and even the ideational contexts of some of the essays. In the case of each essay, however, I have made revisions of varying degrees in style, in content, and particularly in organization, so that the form of each essay has been considerably altered to synthesize with and to support the unifying critical scheme and principles of this book.

"The Critical Mission of Irving Babbitt," written in the summer of 1978, and "Politics and Literature," written in the summer of 1979, are printed in this book for the first time. I have to thank the General Research Board of the University of Maryland for awarding me a grant that enabled me to give uninterrupted time and attention to composing the essay on Babbitt's critical work and thought.

Mary E. Slayton typed the original and the final versions of the entire manuscript and also prepared the index. I am indebted to her for her boundless and devoted assistance. Martha R. Seabrook edited the manuscript with enviable skill and diligence; her various corrections and suggestions were invariably helpful to me in avoiding errors both in thought and in expression.

To Carol Orr, Director of the University of Tennessee Press, I am grateful for her continuing interest in and encouragement of my work. I want, finally, to thank Professors John W. Aldridge and Norman Sanders for astute assessments of my original manuscript and for constructive suggestions designed to make the final version of my book a stronger, more cogent representation of my critical argument.

Index

Aaron's Rod (D.H. Lawrence), 230
Ackerley, Alfred Roger: liaisons of, 247–48; and his son, 245–49
—*My Father and Myself* (J.R. Ackerley), 245–49
Ackerley, J.R.: homosexuality of, 245–49; and his father, 245–49; parents' marriage, 247; and Siegfried Sassoon, 248; and World War I, 247
—*My Father and Myself*, 245–49
—*Prisoners of War*, 248
Acton, Sir Harold, 238; on art, 239, 240; devotion to beauty, xi, 239–41; and Somerset Maugham, 240; on memoirs, 240; and Gertrude Stein, 239
—*Memoirs of an Aesthete*, 238–41
Adams, Henry, 212
Aeschylus, 40; and Karl Marx, 200
Affliction: Simone Weil on, 26, 28, 42, 48, 50
"After a Journey" (Thomas Hardy), 264
After Strange Gods (T.S. Eliot), 88–96, 137
Agnew, Spiro, 206
Aids to Reflection (Samuel Taylor Coleridge), xii
"Aims of Education, The" (T.S. Eliot), 102, 104, 107
Aldington, Richard: *D.H. Lawrence: Portrait of a Genius, but . . .*, 126
Aldridge, John W., 206; and F.R. Leavis, 278; literary criticism of, 273–78; on Norman Mailer, 277–78; and George Orwell, 278; on Katherine Anne Porter, 275–76; and William Styron, 277–78
—*Devil in the Fire, The*, 274–78
—*In the Country of the Young*, 206
"All Souls' Day" (D.H. Lawrence), 130
Alvarez, A.: on D.H. Lawrence, 138
American, The (Henry James), 215
Animal Farm (George Orwell), 258
Annan, Noel, 242
Another World, 1897–1917 (Anthony Eden), 232
Antichrist: John Henry Newman on, 85

Apocalypse (D.H. Lawrence), 139, 142
Archilochus, 116
"Argonauts, The" (D.H. Lawrence), 127
Aristocracy and Justice (Paul Elmer More), 204
Aristotle, 116, 126, 153; and Irving Babbitt, 63, 68, 69, 80, 83; and Plato, 161
Arnold, Matthew, 59, 212; and Irving Babbitt, 66, 69–70, 72, 74; on culture, xi, xii; and T.S. Eliot, 105, 107; and F.R. Leavis, 256, 257, 261; on modern life, 179
—*Essays in Criticism*, xii
"Arnold and Pater" (T.S. Eliot), 107
Arsenyeva, Valeriya, 117
Art: Sir Harold Acton on, 239, 240; Boris Pasternak on, 113; Simone Weil on, 39, 40–41
Asquith, Lady Cynthia (*née* Charteris), 220
Asquith, H.H.: John Maynard Keynes on, 234; Liberal prime minister of England, 227, 234
Assorted Articles (D.H. Lawrence), 132
Atlantic Monthly, The, 64
Attention: Simone Weil on, 27, 31, 46–47
Auden, W.H., 98; and F.R. Leavis, 255
August 1914 (Aleksandr Solzhenitsyn), 234
Augustine, Saint, 53, 80
Aurelius, Marcus, 118
Autobiography. *See* Memoirs
Autobiography (Bertrand Russell), 242
Autobiography of Carl Schurz (abridged by Wayne Andrews), 194

Babbitt, Irving, ix, xi, 85, 89, 153, 206, 268, 269; and Aristotle, 63, 68, 69, 80, 83; and Matthew Arnold, 66, 69–70, 72, 74; on Buddhism, x, 61, 79–82; on classicism, 61–65, 68; on Samuel Taylor Coleridge, 70; on Confucius, 80, 82; detractors of, 56, 57, 59, 70, 72–73, 76, 79; and Jonathan Edwards, 80; on *élan vital*

Babbitt, Irving (*cont.*)
and *frein vital*, 60; and T.S. Eliot, 69, 76, 82–83, 93, 206, 269; and Ralph Waldo Emerson, 57, 65, 70, 71, 72; on the German scientific spirit, 64; and Johann Wolfgang von Goethe, 55, 68, 72, 79; and Homer, 67; humanism of, 54–84, 93; ideas of, 73–74; on Joseph Joubert, 70–71; and Wyndham Lewis, 79; on H.L. Mencken, 268; and Paul Elmer More, 65, 74, 82, 83, 85, 206; and New England, 56, 58; new humanism of, x, 93, 104–105; and Blaise Pascal, 80; and Plato, 66, 81; on romanticism, 61–65, 68; on Jean–Jacques Rousseau, 60, 61, 62, 63, 64, 68, 71, 72, 77, 84; and Friedrich Schlegel, 81; and Arthur Schopenhauer, 81; and Percy Bysshe Shelley, 62; and T.V. Smith, 76; and Socrates, 59, 72, 76; on the Spanish character, 78–79; and Theodore Spencer, 74; and J.E. Spingarn, 72; on Madame de Staël, 77; on standards, 74–77; on Leo Tolstoy, 116; and Voltaire, 54; on World War I, 78
—*Democracy and Leadership*, xii, 70, 75–77
—*Literature and the American College*, xii, 65
—*Masters of Modern French Criticism*, 70
—"Rational Study of the Classics, The," 64, 65
—*Rousseau and Romanticism*, 64, 77, 192
—*Spanish Character and Other Essays*, 78
Bacon, Sir Francis, 73
Baillie, John: *Revelation* (ed.), 94
Balfour, Arthur James, 223
Baraka, Amiri: on Karl Marx, 193, 196, 199, 200
—"Domesticated Marx, The," 193
Barrie, Sir James Matthew: *A Well–Remembered Voice*, 235
Barzun, Jacques, 268
Bate, Walter Jackson: *Criticism*, 56
Baudelaire, Charles: poetry of, 141–42
—*Flowers of Evil*, 141–42
—"Spleen," 141–42
"Bavarian Gentians" (D.H. Lawrence), 128, 129
Beaton, Cecil, 240
Beauty: Sir Harold Acton's devotion to,

Beauty (*cont.*)
xi, 239–41; "beauty of the world," 50–52; and criticism, 273; and Anthony Eden, 233; and Karl Marx, 200–201; Austin Warren on, xi; of Simone Weil, 23; Simone Weil on, 44, 50–52
—*Memoirs of an Aesthete* (Sir Harold Acton), 238–41
Beauvoir, Simone de: *Memoirs of a Dutiful Daughter*, 20
Becket, Saint Thomas à, 200
Beckett, Samuel, 39
Beethoven, Ludwig von: *Fifth Symphony*, 124
Belinsky, Vissarion G., 182; on negation, 187–88; and Voltaire, 188
—*Selected Philosophical Works*, 188
Bellow, Saul, 277
Benda, Julien, 85
—*Trahison des clercs, La*, 192
Bentham, Jeremy, 90; technologico–Benthamism, 87, 107, 191, 255, 260, 261, 268
Berdyaev, Nikolai, 85
Berenson, Bernard, 240
Bergson, Henri–Louis, 61
Berlin, Sir Isaiah: *The Hedgehog and the Fox*, 116
Bernanos, Georges, 28
"Beware the Unhappy Dead!" (D.H. Lawrence), 131–32
Bible, The Holy, 125. *See also* Old Testament, The
Birds, Beasts and Flowers (D.H. Lawrence), 131
Bisexuality: of Dora Carrington, 241–44; of Ralph Partridge, 241–44
Blackmur, R.P.: on D.H. Lawrence, 135–38
—*Language as Gesture*, 135–38
Blake, William, 162; and Charles Dickens, 260; and D.H. Lawrence, 28, 171, 228, 260, 261; and F.R. Leavis, 255, 260; and John Locke, 260; and Sir Isaac Newton, 260
Blavatsky, Elena Petrovna, 239
"Blind Man, The" (D.H. Lawrence), 228
Bloomsbury: and Dora Carrington, 241–44; and T.S. Eliot, 93, 258; and friendship, 241–44; and John Maynard Keynes, 242; and D.H. Lawrence, 93; and F.R. Leavis, 242; and Ralph Partridge, 241–44; and Bertrand Russell, 242; and Lytton Strachey, 241–44; and Voltaire, 244;

Bloomsbury (*cont.*)
and Leonard Woolf, 242
—*Carrington* (ed. David Garnett),
238–44
Blunden, Edmund, 233
—*Undertones of War*, 221
Böll, Heinrich, 153
Bottomley, Horatio, 227
Bousquet, Joë: and World War I, 27
Bowra, Sir Maurice: *Memories,
1898–1936*, 248
Bradley, Francis Herbert: T.S. Eliot on,
94
"Breath of Life, The" (D.H. Lawrence),
138
Brenan, Gerald: and Dora Carrington,
241, 244
—*Life of One's Own, A*, 248
Brewster, Achsah: *D.H. Lawrence:
Reminiscences and Correspondence*,
125, 140
Brewster, Earl, 144; with D.H.
Lawrence in Italy, 139–40
—*D.H. Lawrence: Reminiscences and
Correspondence*, 125, 140
Brooke, Rupert: death of, 231; and
World War I, 221, 222, 231
—*1914*, 222
Brothers Karamazov, The (F.M.
Dostoevsky), 40, 123, 124, 177–88
Brunetière, Ferdinand, 70
Buber, Martin: on mansions of the
spirit, 114
Buckley, William, 206
Buddha, 272
—*Dhammapada, The*, 61, 80
Buddhism: Irving Babbitt on, x, 61,
79–82; Friedrich Schlegel's romantic,
81; pessimistic Buddhism of Arthur
Schopenhauer, 81
Bullitt, William C.: *Thomas Woodrow
Wilson*, 245
Burke, Edmund, 153, 192, 206
Burnet, John: *Early Greek Philosophy*,
126
Burnt Norton (T.S. Eliot), 265
Byron, George Gordon, Lord, 188

Cab at the Door, A (V.S. Pritchett), 248
Camara, Dom Helder, 153
Cameron, Norman, 188
Campbell, Gordon, 230
Camus, Albert, 150, 200
Canterbury Cathedral: Karl Marx on,
200
Capitalism: stationary economy of,

Capitalism (*cont.*)
190–92; and Simone Weil, 32
—*Inquiry into the Human Prospect,
An* (Robert L. Heilbroner), 189–92
"Captain's Doll, The" (D.H. Lawrence),
228
Carlyle, Thomas, 72, 267
Carrington, Dora, 238; appearance of,
242; bisexuality of, 241–44; and
Bloomsbury, 241–44; and F.M.
Dostoevsky, 244; and David Hume,
244; and Aldous Huxley, 242; and
Frances Marshall, 241, 243; marriage
to Ralph Partridge, 241, 243–44; and
Lytton Strachey, 241–44; suicide of,
244; and Virginia Woolf, 244
—*Crome Yellow* (Aldous Huxley), 242
Carrington (ed. David Garnett), 238–44
Carswell, Catherine, 226
Catharism: Simone Weil on, 30
Catholic Faith, The (Paul Elmer More),
83
Catholicism. *See* Roman Catholicism
Centaur, The (John Updike), 277
"Cerveteri" (D.H. Lawrence), 141
Chamberlain, Neville, 95
Chateaubriand, Vicomte Francois–René
de, 70
Cheever, John, 277, 278
Chesterton,G.K.: on humanism, 106
Children: and Karl Marx, 198, 201
Christ, Jesus the, 21, 24, 29, 42, 46, 82,
92, 99, 176, 187; Antichrist, 178;
Cross of, 46–49; and F.M.
Dostoevsky, 119; and T.S. Eliot, 99;
and Homer, 188; D.H. Lawrence on,
139; and Karl Marx, 124, 151–55,
172, 193; Passion of, 186; Leo
Tolstoy on, 118–22, 124; and Simone
Weil, 46–49, 53; Christian socialism
of Leo Tolstoy, 117
—"Concerning the Our Father," 52–53
—*Man Who Died, The* (D.H.
Lawrence), 139
Christ the Word (Paul Elmer More), 83
Christian, R.F., 115
"Christian Conception of Education,
The" (T.S. Eliot), 105
Christianity, 79, 81, 82, 83, 95, 104,
105, 108; Christian discrimination,
111; and F.M. Dostoevsky's Grand
Inquisitor, 177–88; and T.S. Eliot,
95–101; and Hellenism, 20; historical
Christianity, 120; of D.H. Lawrence,
x; Christian literary scholars, 112;
and Marxism, 148–55; and Paul

Christianity (cont.)
Elmer More, 83; and paganism, 129; and Platonism, 43–44, 81, 83, 182; and Paul Tillich, 154; and Simone Weil, 23, 24, 25, 29–30, 43–44, 46, 47, 51, 53, 182. See also Roman Catholicism
—Idea of a Christian Society, The (T.S. Eliot), 95–101
—Intimations of Christianity among the Ancient Greeks (Simone Weil), 185
—Letter to a Priest (Simone Weil), 24
—"Logic of Christian Discrimination, The" (F.R. Leavis), 111
—On Synthesizing Marxism and Christianity (Dale Vree), 148–55
—Secular City, The (Harvey Cox), 152
—Simone Weil Reader, The (ed. George A. Panichas), 19–53
Churchill, Sir Winston, 95
City That Shone, The (Vivian de Sola Pinto), 248
Civilization: and barbarism, 219; breakdown of modern, 167–76, 189–92; death of modern, 173–76, 220–37; E.M. Forster on "the greenwood," 242; Leonard Woolf on, 236; post-World War I in England, 167–76, 232–37
—Interpretations and Forecasts (Lewis Mumford), 269–72
—Women in Love (D.H. Lawrence), 133, 167–76, 190, 225, 260
Classicism: Irving Babbitt on, 61–63, 65; and T.S. Eliot, 101–104
—"Modern Education and the Classics" (T.S. Eliot), 101–104
—"Rational Study of the Classics, The" (Irving Babbitt), 64–65
Clement of Alexandria, 188
Cocktail Party, The (T.S. Eliot), 258, 266
Cocteau, Jean, 240
Coleridge, Samuel Taylor, xii, 108; Irving Babbitt on, 70; on death, 125
—Aids to Reflection, xii
Collected Essays (Graham Greene), 180
Collected Letters of D.H. Lawrence, The (ed. Harry T. Moore), 220
Collected Poems of D.H. Lawrence, The, 128, 131, 140, 141, 224
Colombe, Sister, 21
Common Pursuit, The (F.R. Leavis), 253
Communism: and Karl Marx, 148–55, 193–202

"Composition as Explanation" (Gertrude Stein), 239
"Concerning the Our Father" (Simone Weil), 52–53
Confession, A (Leo Tolstoy), 117
Confessions (Jean–Jacques Rousseau), 120
Confidence (Henry James), 215
Confucius, 118, 272; Irving Babbitt on, 80, 82
Connolly, Cyril, 241
Conquest of Happiness, The (Bertrand Russell), 105
Conrad, Joseph, 165, 247
Conservatism: conservative criticism, ix–xiii; and Richard L. Cutler, 203–208; of T.S. Eliot, 85–108, 257; of D.H. Lawrence, ix, x; and liberalism, 85–108, 203–208, 257; Austin Warren on, ix–xiii; and Richard M. Weaver, 99, 157, 207–208; of Simone Weil, ix
Contribution to the Critique of Political Economy, A (Karl Marx), 149, 198
Courage of judgment: defined, xi–xiii, 3–15
—Reverent Discipline, The (George A. Panichas), x
Courage To Be, The (Paul Tillich), 179–80
Cox, Harvey, 152, 154
—Secular City, The, 152
Craft of Fiction, The (Percy Lubbock), 187
Crime and Punishment (F.M. Dostoevsky), 183, 184, 186
Crisis: of criticism, 112; of faith, 154; and prophecy, 167–68
Criterion, The, 254
Criticism: academic, 7–8; of John W. Aldridge, 273–78; of Irving Babbitt, 54–84; and beauty, 273; conservative criticism, ix–xiii; crisis of, 112; of Richard L. Cutler, 203–208; as discrimination, xi, 111, 256, 263; and education, 7–8, 11; failures of, 15; of Robert L. Heilbroner, 189–92; critical humanism, 3–15; of F.R. Leavis, 253–67: his critical style, 254–55, 278; of liberalism, 85–108; F.O. Matthiessen on, 251; of Lewis Mumford, 268–72; J. Middleton Murry on, 273; nature of, 3–15, 178, 273; of George Orwell, 278; of Saul K. Padover, 193–202; of George A. Panichas, ix–xiii; and religion,

Criticism (*cont.*)
111–14, 149; reverent discipline of, x–xi, 4, 36; of Ellis Sandoz, 177–88; of Jerrold Seigel, 148–55; standards of, ix–xiii, 3–15, 113, 204, 214, 253–69, 278; values of critical thought, ix–xiii, 3–15; of Dale Vree, 148–55; and Austin Warren, ix–xiii; and Simone Weil, 36–37; and René Wellek, 111; Edmund Wilson on, 274
Criticism (Walter Jackson Bate), 56
Critique of Political Economy (Karl Marx), 149, 198
Croce, Benedetto, 240
Crome Yellow (Aldous Huxley), 242
Crosby, Harry: D.H. Lawrence on his suicide, 143–44
Culture: and Matthew Arnold, xi, xii; definition of, 98–103; John Dewey on, 98–104; D.H. Lawrence on, 126; Austin Warren on, xi; and Richard M. Weaver, 99
—*Democracy and Education* (John Dewey), 103
—*Democracy and Leadership* (Irving Babbitt), xii, 70, 75–77
—*Devil in the Fire, The* (John W. Aldridge), 274–78
—*Freedom and Culture* (John Dewey), 98–104
—*Inquiry into the Human Prospect, An* (Robert L. Heilbroner), 189–92
—*Liberal Middle Class, The* (Richard L. Cutler), 203–208
—"Man of Letters and the Future of Europe, The" (T.S. Eliot), 87
—*Notes towards the Definition of Culture* (T.S. Eliot), 99–103
—*Spanish Character and Other Essays* (Irving Babbitt), 78
—*Waste Land, The* (T.S. Eliot), 258
Cutler, Richard L.: conservatism of, 203–208; and Richard M. Weaver, 207–208
—*Liberal Middle Class, The*, 203–208
"Cypresses" (D.H. Lawrence), 131

D.H. Lawrence: A Composite Biography (ed. Edward Nehls), 126
"D.H. Lawrence and the Etruscans" (Christopher Hassall), 140
D.H. Lawrence and Human Existence (Martin Jarrett–Kerr), 137
D.H. Lawrence: Pilgrim of the Apocalypse (Horace Gregory), 125
D.H. Lawrence: Portrait of a Genius, but . . .(Richard Aldington), 126

D.H. Lawrence: Reminiscences and Correspondence (Earl and Achsah Brewster), 125, 140
D.H. Lawrence: Selected Poems (ed. Kenneth Rexroth), 146
D.H. Lawrence's Nightmare (Paul Delany), 221
Daisy Miller (Henry James), 215
Daladier, Edouard, 95
Dante Alighieri, 116; and D.H. Lawrence, 171; and Leo Tolstoy, 121
Das Kapital (Karl Marx), 199, 201–202
Dawson, Christopher, 85
Death, 114; and art, 113; of belief, 237; of Rupert Brooke, 231; Samuel Taylor Coleridge on, 125; Etruscan concept of, 126, 128, 140–44; Gerard Manley Hopkins on, 142; of Henry James's parents, 217–18; D.H. Lawrence's poetry of, 125–47; of Edgar Marx, 198; of Jenny Marx (Marx's daughter), 201; of Karl Marx, 195, 196; of modern civilization, 173–76, 220–37, 268; of Mrs. Karl Marx, 201; of Grace Norton, 213–14; of Lytton Strachey, 244; of Leo Tolstoy, 117–18, 124; Leo Tolstoy on, 122–24; of Nikolay Tolstoy, 122–23; of Simone Weil, 25; Simone Weil on, 35, 41. *See also* Suicide
"Death" (D.H. Lawrence), 130
De Beauvoir, Simone. *See* Beauvoir, Simone de
De Gaulle, General Charles André: on Simone Weil, 33
De Rougemont, Denis: "Religion and the Mission of the Artist," 249
Decreation: and Simone Weil, 22, 46, 48
Delany, Paul: *D.H. Lawrence's Nightmare*, 221
Demeter: D.H. Lawrence on, 128, 129
Democracy and Education (John Dewey), 103
Democracy and Leadership (Irving Babbitt), xii, 70, 75–77
Democritus, and Karl Marx, 194
Demuth, Lenchen: and Karl Marx, 198
Devil in the Fire, The (John W. Aldridge), 274–78
Devils, The (F.M. Dostoevsky), 182, 184, 185
Devotion: of Sir Harold Acton to beauty, xi, 239–41; of Dora Carrington to Lytton Strachey, 241–44; defined, 238
Dewey, John: on culture, 98–104; and

Dewey, John (cont.)
  education, 102–104; and T.S. Eliot,
  86, 88–90, 92, 98–104, 107, 108; on
  freedom, 98–104; and liberalism, 86,
  88–90, 92, 107, 108
—Democracy and Education, 103
—Freedom and Culture, 98–104
—Liberalism and Social Action, 88–90,
  91
—"My Pedagogic Creed," 103
Dhammapada, The, 61, 80
Dialogue: religious, 114;
  Marxist–Christian, 148–55
Diary of a Writer, The (F.M.
  Dostoevsky), 183, 186
Dickens, Charles: and William Blake,
  260
—Hard Times, 260
"Difficult Death" (D.H. Lawrence), 130
Diogenes Laertius, 194
Dionysos, 127, 129
"Domesticated Marx, The" (Amiri
  Baraka), 193
Dos Passos, John, 275
Dostoevsky, Fyodor M., ix, 116, 277;
  and Dora Carrington, 244; and
  Christ, 119; and André Gide, 179;
  and God, 180, 182, 187, 188; Grand
  Inquisitor of, 177–88, 266; on history,
  180; and Homer, 187, 188; and D.H.
  Lawrence, 266; Thomas Mann on,
  179; his metaphysics of art, 123–24;
  modernism of, 179–80; politics of,
  165, 177–88; and power, 181–88; and
  Lytton Strachey, 244; and Leo
  Tolstoy, 122–24; and Simone Weil,
  28, 40
—Brothers Karamazov, The (F.M.
  Dostoevsky), 40, 123, 124, 177–88
—Crime and Punishment, 183, 184, 186
—Devils, The, 182, 184, 185
—Diary of a Writer, The, 183, 186
—Freedom and the Tragic Life
  (Vyacheslav Ivanov), 188
—House of the Dead, The, 185
—Idiot, The, 181, 183
—"Iliad, Poem of Might, The" (Simone
  Weil), 34–35, 185–86
—"Legend of the Grand Inquisitor,
  The," 266
—Political Apocalypse (Ellis Sandoz),
  177–88
—"Three Masters" (Georges Florovsky),
  122, 183
—Tolstoi as Man and Artist (Dmitri
  Merejkowski), 122

—Tolstoy or Dostoevsky (George
  Steiner), 187
—Winter Notes on Summer
  Impressions, 187
Dostoevsky, Michael, 187
Douglas, Norman, 240
Downhill All the Way (Leonard Woolf),
  236
Dwinger, Edwin Erich, 233

Early Greek Philosophy (John Burnet),
  126
East Coker (T.S. Eliot), 266
Eastman, Max, 202
Economic theory: of Karl Marx,
  148–55, 193–202; stationary
  economy, 190–92
Edel, Leon, 211, 215
Eden, Anthony (Earl of Avon): on
  beauty, 233; on his country manor,
  Windlestone, 232–33; memoirs of,
  232–37; and World War I, 232–37
—Another World, 1897–1917, 232
Education: and Irving Babbitt, xii,
  54–84; and criticism, 7–8, 11; and
  John Dewey, 102–104; and T.S. Eliot,
  101–105, 107, 113; F.R. Leavis on,
  106, 256; and Simone Weil, 27
—"Aims of Education, The" (T.S.
  Eliot), 102, 104, 107
—"Christian Conception of Education,
  The" (T.S. Eliot), 105
—Democracy and Education (John
  Dewey), 103
—English Literature in Our Time and
  the University (F.R. Leavis), 260
—In the Country of the Young (John W.
  Aldridge), 206
—Literature and the American College
  (Irving Babbitt), xii, 65
—"Modern Education and the Classics"
  (T.S. Eliot), 101–104
—"My Pedagogic Creed" (John Dewey),
  103
—"Reflections on the Right Use of
  School Studies with a View to the
  Love of God" (Simone Weil), 27
Education and the University (F.R.
  Leavis), 253
Edwards, Jonathan: and Irving Babbitt,
  80
Elgar, Sir Edward, 232
Eliot, Charles Norton, xii
Eliot, George, 256; and Henry James,
  212, 213
Eliot, T.S.: and Matthew Arnold, 105,

Eliot, T.S. (*cont.*)
107; and Irving Babbitt, 69, 76,
82–83, 93, 206, 269; and Bloomsbury,
93, 258; on Francis Herbert Bradley,
94; and Christ, 99; and classicism,
101–104; conservative social
criticism of, 108, 257; and John
Dewey, 86, 88–90, 92, 98–104, 107,
108; and education, 101–105, 107,
113; and Thomas Hardy, 91, 92, 93;
humanism of, 85–108; and Henry
James, 219; on Judaism, 92; and D.H.
Lawrence, 92–93, 137–38; and F.R.
Leavis, 257–58, 264–67; and
liberalism, 85–108, 257; on literature,
113; on lost causes, 1; on Niccolò
Machiavelli, 86; and Paul Elmer
More, 258; on naturalism and
supernaturalism, 150; and Walter J.
Ong, 99; and Sir Arthur
Quiller–Couch, 107–108; and Philip
Rahv, 106–107; and Sir Herbert Read,
108; and Bertrand Russell, 105;
anti–Semitism of, 92; and standards,
204; and Vergil, 85; and Peter
Viereck, 87; and Simone Weil, x, 21,
35, 40, 102; and Yvor Winters, 265;
and World War II, 95–100
—*After Strange Gods*, 88–96, 137
—"Aims of Education, The," 102, 104,
107
—"Arnold and Pater," 107
—*Burnt Norton*, 265
—"Christian Conception of Education,
The," 105
—*Cocktail Party, The*, 258, 266
—*East Coker*, 266
—*Four Quartets*, 258
—"Humanism of Irving Babbitt, The,"
105
—*Idea of a Christian Society, The*,
95–101
—"Literature of Politics, The," 86
—"Man of Letters and the Future of
Europe, The," 87
—"Metaphysical Poets," 258
—"Modern Education and the
Classics," 101–104
—*Notes towards the Definition of
Culture*, 99–103
—*Points of View*, 91, 93
—"Religion and Literature," 95
—"Religion Without Humanism," 105
—"Second Thoughts about
Humanism," 105
—*T.S. Eliot: A Bibliography* (Donald

T.S. Eliot: A Bibliography (cont.)
Gallup), 86
—*Waste Land, The*, 258
Emerson, Ralph Waldo: and Irving
Babbitt, 57, 65, 70, 71, 72
Émile (Jean–Jacques Rousseau), 120
"End, the Beginning, The" (D.H.
Lawrence), 133
Engels, Friedrich: and Karl Marx, 150,
193–202
"England my England" (D.H.
Lawrence), 256
*English Literature in Our Time and the
University* (F.R. Leavis), 260
Epictetus, 118
Epicurus: and Karl Marx, 194, 196
Epicurus (George A. Panichas), 196
Eros and Civilization (Herbert
Marcuse), 155
Essay on Suicide (David Hume), 244
Essays by Divers Hands (ed. Peter
Green), 140
Essays in Biography (John Maynard
Keynes), 234
Essays in Criticism (Matthew Arnold),
xii
Essays of Four Decades (Allen Tate),
269
Etruscan Places (D.H. Lawrence), 139,
140
Etruscans: D.H. Lawrence on their
concept of death, 126, 128, 140–44
—"D.H. Lawrence and the Etruscans"
(Christopher Hassall), 140
Europeans, The (Henry James), 215, 217
Evil, 114; and good, 39–40; D.H.
Lawrence on, 131, 175–76; Leo
Tolstoy on, 121; and Simone Weil,
26, 34, 39–40, 44–45, 52, 53, 151
—*Flowers of Evil* (Charles Baudelaire),
141–42

F.R. Leavis: Letters in Criticism (ed.
John Tasker), 254–56
"Factory Work" (Simone Weil), 27, 28
Fantasia of the Unconscious (D.H.
Lawrence), 133, 223
Farrell, James T., 275
Father Sergius (Leo Tolstoy), 123
Faulkner, William, 276
Faust (Johann Wolfgang von Goethe),
200
Fet, A.A., 122
Feuerbach, Ludwig: influence on Karl
Marx, 150
Fitzgerald, F. Scott, 275

Five Stages of Greek Religion (Gilbert Murray), 125
Florovsky, Georges: on Leo Tolstoy, 116, 122
—"Three Masters," 122, 183
"Flowering Judas" (Katherine Anne Porter), 276
Flowers of Evil (Charles Baudelaire), 141–42
Foerster, Norman: and Hellenism, 104–105; on humanism and religion, 104–105
—*Humanism and America*, 105
—"Humanism and Religion," 104
For Continuity (F.R. Leavis), 253
"For the Heroes Are Dipped in Scarlet" (D.H. Lawrence), 126, 127
"Forget" (D.H. Lawrence), 133
Forster, E.M., 124, 277; on the "greenwood," 242; on language, 211; and D.H. Lawrence, 223
—*Howards End*, 124
Four Quartets (T.S. Eliot), 258; *Burnt Norton*, 265; *East Coker*, 266
"Fox, The" (D.H. Lawrence), 228
Francis, Saint, 29, 51
Freedom and Culture (John Dewey), 98–104
Freedom and the Tragic Life (Vyacheslav Ivanov), 188
French Revolution, 77, 84, 164
Freud, Sigmund: and Herbert Marcuse, 155; and Karl Marx, 150, 151, 155; sexual materialism of, 155; on Woodrow Wilson, 245
—*Thomas Woodrow Wilson*, 245
Friedberg, Maurice, 202
Friendship, ix; and Bloomsbury, 241–44; of D.H. Lawrence and S.S. Koteliansky, 220; of Karl Marx and Friedrich Engels, 150, 193–202; in war, 220–31, 236; and Austin Warren, ix; and Simone Weil, 43, 44

Gallup, Donald: *T.S. Eliot: A Bibliography*, 86
Galsworthy, John, 247
Garaudy, Roger, 153
Gardner, W.H.: *Poems of Gerard Manley Hopkins* (ed.), 142
Garnett, David, 258
—*Carrington* (ed.), 238–44
Gasset, José Ortega y. *See* Ortega y Gasset, José
Geissbuhler, Elisabeth Chase, 185
Genius: of D.H. Lawrence, 139, 174;

Genius (*cont.*)
223; of F.R. Leavis, 267; of Karl Marx, 193; of Bertrand Russell, 223; of William Shakespeare, 174; Leo Tolstoy on, 116; Simone Weil on, 37, 39–40
Ghiselin, Brewster, 126
Gide, André: and F.M. Dostoevsky, 179; homosexuality of, 247, 248
Giese, Rachel, 78
Gill, Eric, 41
"Gladness of Death" (D.H. Lawrence), 134
God, 10, 33, 112, 116, 152, 154, 164, 178, 193, 236, 238; and F.M. Dostoevsky, 180, 182, 187, 188; and D.H. Lawrence, 125, 126, 127, 133, 134, 135, 222, 225, 231; and Nikolai Lenin, 201; and Leo Tolstoy, 115, 119, 120, 124; and Simone Weil, 20, 21, 22, 29, 36, 42–43, 44, 45, 46, 47, 48, 49–50, 51, 52, 186, 244
—"Concerning the Our Father" (Simone Weil), 52–53
"God" (D.H. Lawrence), 134
Goethe, Johann Wolfgang von, 174; and Irving Babbitt, 55, 68, 72, 79; and Karl Marx, 200
—*Faust*, 200
Gogol, Nikolai: and F.M. Dostoevsky, 116, 118
—"Three Masters" (Georges Florovsky), 122, 183
Good: and evil, 131, 175–76; Leo Tolstoy on, 121; Simone Weil on, 26, 34, 39–40, 44–45, 52, 53, 151
Goodbye to All That (Robert Graves), 221, 236
Gorky, Maxim: on Leo Tolstoy, 116, 119, 124
—*Reminiscences of Tolstoy, Chekhov, and Andreev*, 119
Gospels, The, 118
Gosse, Edmund: and his father, 245–48
Grand Inquisitor (*The Brothers Karamazov*): and Christianity, 177–88
Graves, Robert: soldier–memoirist, 221, 233, 236
—*Goodbye to All That*, 221, 236
Gravity: and grace, Simone Weil on, 22, 42, 45, 102
Gravity and Grace (Simone Weil), 102
"Great Beast, The": and Plato, 186, 192; and Simone Weil, 24, 45, 186, 192

Great Tradition, The (F.R. Leavis), 253

Great War. *See* World War I

Greek spirit: and D.H. Lawrence, 125–29; and Simone Weil, 32. *See also* Hellenism, Homer, Plato, Platonism

"Greeks Are Coming, The" (D.H. Lawrence), 126

Greene, Graham: *Collected Essays*, 180

Gregory, Horace: on D.H. Lawrence's *Last Poems*, 125

—*D.H. Lawrence: Pilgrim of the Apocalypse*, 125

Grenfell, Julian: and World War I, 221

Gross, John: *The Rise and Fall of the Man of Letters*, 253, 254, 255

Guardini, Romano, 152

Haig, Douglas, 223

Hard Times (Charles Dickens), 260

Hardy, Thomas, 264; T.S. Eliot on, 91, 92, 93

—"After a Journey," 264

Hassall, Christopher: "D.H. Lawrence and the Etruscans," 140

Hasse, Friedrich Rudolf: and Karl Marx, 195

Hawthorne (Henry James), 217

Hayward, John, 91

Hazlitt, William, 69

Hedgehog and the Fox, The (Sir Isaiah Berlin), 116

Hegel, Georg Wilhelm Friedrich, 150, 197

Heilbroner, Robert L.: *An Inquiry into the Human Prospect*, 189–92; on Marxism, 202; on the modernist impasse, 189–92, 202

—*Marxism*, 202

Heine, Heinrich: and Karl Marx, 150, 153

Hellenism: Christian Hellenism of Simone Weil, 20, 35, 43, 44, 50; and Norman Foerster, 104–105; D.H. Lawrence on the ancient Greeks, 125–29; and Lewis Mumford, 271–72; of George A. Panichas, ix, xiii

—*Early Greek Philosophy* (John Burnet), 126

—*Epicurus* (George A. Panichas), 196

—*Five Stages of Greek Religion* (Gilbert Murray), 125

—*Intimations of Christianity among the Ancient Greeks* (Simone Weil), 185

Heller, Erich: on quality and quantity,

Heller, Erich *(cont.)* 113

Heller, Joseph, 278

Hemingway, Ernest, 275; on World War I, 171

Henry James: Letters (ed. Leon Edel): Volume I, 211; Volume II, 215

Herbert, George: "Love," 29

Herodotus, 116

History: and F.M. Dostoevsky, 180; Jerrold Seigel's psychohistorical criticism of Karl Marx, 148–55; antihistoricism of Leo Tolstoy, 120; Simone Weil on, 32

—*War and Peace* (Leo Tolstoy), 120, 124

History of Russian Philosophy, A (V.V. Zenkovsky), 122

Hitler, Adolf: Simone Weil on, 32, 33; and World War II, 95, 184, 237

Hobbes, Thomas, 187

Hobhouse, L.T., 92

Homer, 277; and Irving Babbitt, 67; and Christ, 188; and F.M. Dostoevsky, 187, 188; and D.H. Lawrence, 226; and Leo Tolstoy, 187; and Simone Weil, 40

—*Iliad, The*, 34–35, 187–88

—"*Iliad*, Poem of Might, The" (Simone Weil), 34–35, 185–86

Homosexuality: of J.R. Ackerley, 245–49; of André Gide, 247, 248; of Lytton Strachey, 241–44; of Oscar Wilde, 248

—*My Father and Myself* (J.R. Ackerley), 245–49

Hopkins, Gerard Manley: on death, 142

—*Poems of Gerard Manley Hopkins*, 142

House of the Dead, The (F.M. Dostoevsky), 185

"Houseless Dead, The" (D.H. Lawrence), 131

Howards End (E.M. Forster), 124

Howe, Irving: *Politics and the Novel*, 177

Howells, William Dean: and Henry James, 214, 217

Hulme, T.E., 85

"Human Personality" (Simone Weil), 41

Humanism, 6–7; atheist humanism, 177–88; of Irving Babbitt, 54–84, 93; G.K. Chesterton on, 106; critical humanism, 3–15; and T.S. Eliot,

Humanism (cont.)
85–108; Norman Foerster on,
104–105; and Jacques Maritain, 105;
and Paul Elmer More, 83; of George
A. Panichas, ix–xiii; values of, 5; and
Edmund Wilson, 59
—"Religion Without Humanism" (T.S.
Eliot), 105
—"Revival of Humanism, A" (Paul
Elmer More), 83
—"Second Thoughts about Humanism"
(T.S. Eliot), 105
Humanism and America (Norman
Foerster), 105·
"Humanism and Religion" (Norman
Foerster), 104
"Humanism of Irving Babbitt, The"
(T.S. Eliot), 105
Hume, David, 180; and Dora
Carrington, 244
—Essay on Suicide, 244
Huxley, Aldous, 131; on Dora
Carrington, 242; on Edmund Gosse's
father, 246
—Crome Yellow, 242
Hyams, Edward: Pierre—Joseph
Proudhon, 197

Idea of a Christian Society, The (T.S.
Eliot), 95–101
Ideas Have Consequences (Richard M.
Weaver), 207–208
Idiot, The (F.M. Dostoevsky), 181, 183
Iliad, The (Homer), 34–35, 187–88
"Iliad, Poem of Might, The" (Simone
Weil), 34–35, 185–86
In the Country of the Young (John W.
Aldridge), 206
Inge, W.R.: The Philosophy of Plotinus,
125
Inquiry into the Human Prospect, An
(Robert L. Heilbroner), 189–92
Interpretations and Forecasts (Lewis
Mumford), 269–72
Intimations of Christianity among the
Ancient Greeks (Simone Weil), 185
"Is There a Marxist Doctrine?" (Simone
Weil), 24
Isaiah. See Old Testament, The
Ivanov, Vyacheslav: and F.M.
Dostoevsky, 188; on The Iliad, 188
—Freedom and the Tragic Life, 188

Jackson, Robert Louis: Dostoevsky's
Quest for Form, 185
James, Henry, 56, 274; his character,
215–16; on discrimination, xi, 256;

James, Henry (cont.)
and George Eliot, 212, 213; and T.S.
Eliot, 219; father of, 217, 218; and
William Dean Howells, 214, 217; on
Italy, 214; letters of, 211–19;
manliness of, 215–16; on marriage,
218–19; mother of, 216, 217, 218;
and Charles Eliot Norton, 213, 216;
and Grace Norton, 218, 219; parents'
deaths, 217–18; and Ezra Pound, 219;
on John Ruskin, 212, 213; on sorrow,
213–14, 219; and Edmund Wilson,
218; on World War I, 236
—American, The, 215
—Confidence, 215
—Daisy Miller, 215
—Europeans, The, 215, 217
—Hawthorne, 217
—Henry James: Letters (ed. Leon Edel):
Volume I, 211; Volume II, 215
—Notebooks of Henry James, The (ed.
F.O. Matthiessen and Kenneth B.
Murdock), 218
—Portrait of a Lady, The, 215
—Washington Square, 215
James, William: on The Europeans,
217; love of Germany, 214; and
Henry James, 214, 216, 217
Jarrett–Kerr, Father Martin: D.H.
Lawrence and Human Existence, 137
Job. See Old Testament, The
John, Saint, 113
John Bull, 227
John of the Cross, Saint, 51
Jones, James, 277
Joubert, Joseph: Irving Babbitt on,
70–71
Journey's End (R.C. Sherriff), 236
Joyce, James, 116
—Ulysses, 277
Judaism: T.S. Eliot on, 92:
anti–Semitism of T.S. Eliot, 92; and
Karl Marx, 195–96, 201:
anti–Semitism of Karl Marx, 195–96;
and Simone Weil, 25, 29–30
—Karl Marx: Racist (Nathaniel Weyl),
195
—"On the Jewish Question" (Karl
Marx), 152, 201
—Simone Weil Reader, The (ed. George
A. Panichas), 19–53
—"What Is a Jew?" (Simone Weil), 30

Kafka, Franz, 165
Kangaroo (D.H. Lawrence), 173, 227
Karl Marx (David McLellan), 201
Karl Marx: Racist (Nathaniel Weyl),

Karl Marx: Racist (cont.)
195
Keats, John: letters of, 116, 212
Kepler, Johannes: hero of Karl Marx,
201
Keynes, John Maynard: on H.H.
Asquith, 234; and Bloomsbury, 242;
on David Lloyd George, 234; and
Bertrand Russell, 242
—*Essays in Biography*, 234
King Lear (William Shakespeare), 124
"Know–All" (D.H. Lawrence), 133
Koteliansky, S.S.: and D.H. Lawrence,
220
Kreutzer Sonata, The (Leo Tolstoy), 121

Lady Chatterley's Lover (D.H.
Lawrence), 125, 228, 260
"Ladybird, The" (D.H. Lawrence), 228
Lafargue, François: and Karl Marx, 199
Lafargue, Paul: and Karl Marx, 199;
fiancé of Laura Marx, 199
Lalley, J.M.: on Jean–Jacques Rousseau,
120
—"Solipsistic Saint, The," 120
Language: American language, 211;
barbarization of, 211–12; English
language, 211; E.M. Forster on, 211;
Simone Weil on, 37–39
—"Power of Words, The" (Simone
Weil), 37
Language as Gesture (R.P. Blackmur),
135–38
Lao–tzu, 118
Lassalle, Ferdinand: and Karl Marx, 200
Last Poems (D.H. Lawrence), 125–47
Lattimore, Richmond, 188
Lawrence, D.H.: A. Alvarez on, 138;
R.P. Blackmur on, 135–38; and
William Blake, 28, 171, 228, 260,
261; and Bloomsbury, 93; with Earl
Brewster in Italy, 139–40; and Christ,
139; Christianity of, x;
"conservatism" of, ix, x; and Harry
Crosby, 143–44; on culture, 126; and
Dante, 171; death–poetry of, 125–47;
and F.M. Dostoevsky, 266; and T.S.
Eliot, 92–93, 137–38; on the Etruscan
concept of death, 126, 128, 140–44;
on evil, 131, 175–76; and E.M.
Forster, 223; genius of, 139, 174;
Georgian influences on, 138–39; and
God, 125, 126, 127, 133, 134, 135,
222, 225, 231; and the ancient
Greeks, 125–29; and Homer, 226; and
S.S. Koteliansky, 220; and F.R.

Lawrence, D.H. (*cont.*)
Leavis, 225, 256, 258, 260, 261, 263;
letters of, 116, 125–26, 131, 138–39,
212: war letters of, 220–32; on David
Lloyd George, 223; anti–militarism
of, 225–26; and J. Middleton Murry,
221; mysticism of, 133, 136–37; and
Robert Nichols, 225; and Plato, 126;
Protestant sensibility of, 136; as a
religious artist, 112, 209; his religious
quest, 112, 125–47; and Bertrand
Russell, 94, 170, 223; and William
Shakespeare, 174; and M.L. Skinner,
131; on soldiers, 225–26, 228–30; on
suicide, 143–44; and Thucydides,
125–26; on time, 142; on Leo
Tolstoy, 117; visionary insight of, 28,
51, 139, 146, 261; and Simone Weil,
51; and World War I, 168, 220–31
—*Aaron's Rod*, 230
—"All Soul's Day," 130
—*Apocalypse*, 139, 142
—"Argonauts, The," 127
—*Assorted Articles*, 132
—"Bavarian Gentians, " 128, 129
—"Beware the Unhappy Dead!,"
131–32
—*Birds, Beasts and Flowers*, 131
—"Blind Man, The," 228
—"Breath of Life, The," 138
—"Captain's Doll, The," 228
—"Cerveteri," 141
—*Collected Letters of D.H. Lawrence,
The* (ed. Harry T. Moore), 220
—*Collected Poems of D.H. Lawrence,
The*, 128, 131, 140, 141, 224
—"Cypresses," 131
—*D.H. Lawrence: A Composite
Biography* (ed. Edward Nehls), 126
—*D.H. Lawrence and Human
Existence* (Martin Jarrett-Kerr), 137
—"D.H. Lawrence and the Etruscans"
(Christoper Hassall), 140
—*D.H. Lawrence: Pilgrim of the
Apocalypse* (Horace Gregory), 125
—*D.H. Lawrence: Portrait of a Genius,
but . . .* (Richard Aldington), 126
—*D.H. Lawrence: Reminiscences and
Correspondence* (Earl and Achsah
Brewster), 125, 140
—*D.H. Lawrence: Selected Poems* (ed.
Kenneth Rexroth), 146
—*D.H. Lawrence's Nightmare* (Paul
Delany), 221
—"Death," 130
—"Difficult Death," 130
—"End, the Beginning, The," 133

—"England my England," 256
—*Etruscan Places*, 139, 140
—*Fantasia of the Unconscious*, 133, 223
—"For the Heroes are Dipped in Scarlet," 126, 127
—"Forget," 133
—"Fox, The," 228
—"Gladness of Death," 134
—"God," 134
—"Greeks Are Coming, The," 126
—"Houseless Dead, The," 131
—*Kangaroo*, 173, 227
—"Know–All," 133
—*Lady Chatterley's Lover*, 125, 228, 260
—"Ladybird, The," 228
—*Language as Gesture* (R.P. Blackmur), 135–38
—*Last Poems*, 125–47
—*Letters of D.H. Lawrence, The* (ed. Aldous Huxley), 131, 139
—*Life and Works of D.H. Lawrence* (Harry T. Moore), 140
—*Man Who Died, The*, 139
—"Middle of the World," 127
—*Mornings in Mexico*, 128
—*Movements in European History*, 126
—"Mozo, The," 128
—"New Heaven and Earth," 224
—*New Poems*, 138
—"Nottingham and the Mining Countryside," 229
—"On Human Destiny," 132
—*Pansies*, 125
—*Phoenix*, 128, 230
—"Piano," 263
—"Prussian Officer, The," 228, 229
—*Rainbow, The*, 143, 225, 226, 227
—"St. Mawr," 132
—"Self–Sacrifice," 144
—"Shadows," 134
—"Ship of Death, The," 135–36, 139–47
—"Sleep," 133
—"Sleep and Waking," 133
—"So Let Me Live," 129
—"Song of Death," 133
—*Sons and Lovers*, 225, 229
—*Studies in Classic American Literature*, 226
—"Tabernacle," 133
—*Tales of D.H. Lawrence, The*, 132
—"Thorn in the Flesh, The," 228
—"Two Ways of Living and Dying," 131

—"Virgin Mother, The," 141
—"War Again, The," 230
—*Women in Love*, 133, 167–76, 190, 225, 260
Lawrence, Frieda: *Not I, but the Wind . . .*, 140, 227, 228; and Manfred von Richthofen, 227
Leavis, F.R., ix, x; and John W. Aldridge, 278; and Matthew Arnold, 256, 257, 261; on W.H. Auden, 255; and William Blake, 255, 260; on Bloomsbury, 242; critical style of, 254–55, 278; on discrimination, 263: Christian discrimination, 111; on education, 106, 256; on T.S. Eliot, 257–58: *Four Quartets*, 264–66; genius of, 267; on judgment, 255; and D.H. Lawrence, 225, 256, 260, 261, 263; letters of, 235, 254–56; and Vivian de Sola Pinto, 267; and religion, 254, 267; and C.P. Snow, 90, 260, 261; and Virginia Woolf, 258; on World War I, 235
—*Common Pursuit, The*, 253
—*Education and the University*, 253
—*English Literature in Our Time and the University*, 260
—*F.R. Leavis: Letters in Criticism* (ed. John Tasker), 254–56
—*For Continuity*, 253
—*Great Tradition, The*, 253
—*Living Principle, The*, 253, 262–67
—"Logic of Christian Discrimination, The," 111
—*Nor Shall My Sword*, 253, 258–59
"Legend of the Grand Inquisitor, The" (F.M. Dostoevsky), 266
Lenin, Nikolai: and God, 201; on David Lloyd George, 235; and Leon Trotsky, 201–202
—*Young Lenin, The* (Leon Trotsky), 201, 202
Lessing, Gotthold Ephraim, 150
Letter to a Priest (Simone Weil), 24
Letters: epistolary art, ix; of Henry James, 211–19; of John Keats, 116, 212; of D.H. Lawrence, 116, 125–26, 131, 138–39, 212: war letters of, 220–32; of F.R. Leavis, 235, 254–56; of Norman Mailer, 212; of Karl Marx, 193–202; of George A. Panichas, ix, 235; of Rainer Maria Rilke, 115; of Leo Tolstoy, 115–24; of Vincent van Gogh, 116; of Austin Warren, ix; of Simone Weil, 22, 27, 28; of Edmund Wilson, 59

—*D.H. Lawrence: Reminiscences and Correspondence* (Earl and Achsah Brewster), 140
—*F.R. Leavis: Letters in Criticism* (ed. John Tasker), 254–56
—*Henry James: Letters* (ed. Leon Edel): Volume I, 211; Volume II, 215
Letters of D.H. Lawrence, The (ed. Aldous Huxley), 131, 139
Letters of Fyodor Michailovitch Dostoevsky to His Family and Friends (trans. Ethel Colburn Mayne), 187
Letters of Karl Marx, The (trans. Saul K. Padover), 193–202
Letters of Rainer Maria Rilke (trans. Jane Bannard Greene and M.D. Herter Norton), 115
Letters of Tolstoy and his Cousin Countess Alexandra Tolstoy, The, 115
Letters on Literature and Politics, 1912–1972 (Edmund Wilson), 59
Lévy, Bernard–Henry: on politics, 177
Lewis, Sinclair, 240
Lewis, Wyndham, 242; on Irving Babbitt, 79
Liberal Middle Class, The (Richard L. Cutler), 203–208
Liberalism: conservative critique of, 203–208; and John Dewey, 86, 88–90, 92, 107, 108; and T.S. Eliot, 85–108; John Henry Newman on, 85; and Lionel Trilling, 107, 268
—*After Strange Gods* (T.S. Eliot), 88–96, 137
—*Gravity and Grace* (Simone Weil), 102
—*Liberal Middle Class, The* (Richard L. Cutler), 203–208
Liberalism and Social Action (John Dewey), 88–90, 91
Life and Works of D.H. Lawrence (Harry T. Moore), 140
Life of One's Own, A (Gerald Brenan), 248
Lippmann, Walter, 103
Literature: T.S. Eliot on, 113; and politics, 159–76; and psychology, 148–50; and religion, 111–14; and science, 111
—*Letters on Literature and Politics, 1912–1972* (Edmund Wilson), 59
—"Religion and Literature" (T.S. Eliot), 95

Literature and the American College (Irving Babbitt), xii, 65
"Literature of Politics, The" (T.S. Eliot), 86
Living Principle, The (F.R. Leavis), 253, 262–67
Lloyd George, David, 173; and John Maynard Keynes, 234; and D.H. Lawrence, 223; and Nikolai Lenin, 235
Locke, John, 90, 255; and William Blake, 260
"Logic of Christian Discrimination, The" (F.R. Leavis), 111
"Love" (George Herbert), 29
Love, Freedom, and Society (J. Middleton Murry), 221
Lovejoy, Arthur O., 63
Lowell, Robert, 262
Loyalty: of Friedrich Engels to Karl Marx, 150, 193–202; and Austin Warren, ix. *See also* Devotion
Lubbock, Percy: *The Craft of Fiction*, 187
Lucretius, 116
Luther, Martin, 188

McCarthy, Mary, 277, 278
McDonald, Edward D., 128
Machiavelli, Niccolò: T.S. Eliot on, 86
McLellan, David: *Karl Marx*, 201
Madness: in Dostoevsky's novels, 182; of Joseph Stalin, 237; and Leo Tolstoy, 118
Mailer, Norman: John W. Aldridge on, 277–78; letters of, 212
"Man of Letters and the Future of Europe, The" (T.S. Eliot), 87
"Man of Letters in the Modern World, The" (Allen Tate), 269
Man Who Died, The (D.H. Lawrence), 139
Manchester, Frederick, 78
Manifesto of the Communist Party, The (Karl Marx), 196
Mann, Thomas: on F.M. Dostoevsky, 179
Mansfield, Katherine, 222
Mansions of the Spirit (ed. George A. Panichas), 122, 183
Marcuse, Herbert, 182; and Sigmund Freud, 155; and Karl Marx, 155
—*Eros and Civilization*, 155
Maritain, Jacques: and humanism, 105

—*Paysan de la Garonne, Le*, 152

Marriage: of Dora Carrington and Ralph Partridge, 241, 243–44; Henry James on, 218–19; of Frances Marshall and Ralph Partridge, 241, 243; of Karl and Jenny Marx, 198–201; of Leo Tolstoy, 115–18

Marsh, Edward: and Georgian poetry, 138–39

Marshall, Frances: and Dora Carrington, 241, 243; and Ralph Partridge, 241, 243; and Lytton Strachey, 241, 243

Martin, Hugh: *Revelation* (ed.), 94

Marx, Edgar: death of, 198

Marx, Eleanor: suicide of, 201

Marx, Jenny (Marx's daughter): death of, 201

Marx, Karl, 182; and Aeschylus, 200; aestheticism of, 200–201; appearance of, 194; atheism of, 153; Amiri Baraka on, 193, 196, 199, 200; bastard son of, 198; on Canterbury Cathedral, 200; and children, 198, 201; and Christ, 124, 151–55, 172, 193; and Christianity, 148–55; and Communism, 148–55, 193–202; and Democritus, 194; and Friedrich Engels, 150, 193–202; and Epicurus, 194, 196; and Ludwig Feuerbach, 150; and Sigmund Freud, 150, 151, 155; funeral of, 195, 196; and Johann Wolfgang von Goethe, 200; and Friedrich Rudolf Hasse, 195; health of, 198, 201; and Heinrich Heine, 150, 153; and Judaism, 195–96, 201; and Johannes Kepler, 201; and François Lafargue, 199; and Paul Lafargue, 199; and Ferdinand Lassalle, 200; letters of, 193–202; and Herbert Marcuse, 155; marriage of, 198–201; materialism of, 150, 155; poetry of, 195, 196; and Pierre–Joseph Proudhon, 197–98; and Jerrold Seigel, 148–55; anti–Semitism of, 195–96; and William Shakespeare, 200; and Ignazio Silone, 153; and Socrates, 193; and Simone Weil, 20, 32, 33, 151, 200

—*Contribution to the Critique of Political Economy, A*, 149, 198

—*Das Kapital*, 199, 201–202

—"Domesticated Marx, The" (Amiri Baraka), 193

—"Is There a Marxist Doctrine?" (Simone Weil), 24

—*Karl Marx* (David McLellan), 201

—*Karl Marx: Racist* (Nathaniel Weyl), 195

—*Letters of Karl Marx, The* (trans. Saul K. Padover), 193–202

—*Manifesto of the Communist Party, The*, 196

—*Marx's Fate* (Jerrold Seigel), 148–55

—*Misère de la philosophie, La*, 197

—"On the Jewish Question," 152, 201

—"Paris Manuscripts," 200

Marx, Laura: and Paul Lafargue, 199; suicide of, 201

Marx, Mrs. Karl: death of, 201; on Karl Marx's bastard son, 198

Marx (Robert Payne), 195

Marxism, 172; and Christianity, 148–55; and Paul Tillich, 154. *See also* Marx, Karl

—*On Synthesizing Marxism and Christianity* (Dale Vree), 148–55

—*Secular City, The* (Harvey Cox), 152

Marxism (Robert L. Heilbroner), 202

Marx's Fate (Jerrold Seigel), 148–55

Master Builders (Stefan Zweig), 122

Masters of Modern French Criticism (Irving Babbitt), 70

Materialism: Freud's sexual, 155; of Karl Marx, 150, 155; of Leo Tolstoy, 123; Simone Weil on, 32

Matthiessen, F.O., 218; on criticism, 251

—*Notebooks of Henry James, The*, 218

Maugham, Somerset: and Harold Acton, 240

Mayne, Ethel Colburn: *Letters of Fyodor Michailovitch Dostoevsky to His Family and Friends*, 187

Memoirs: of J.R. Ackerley, 245–49; of Sir Harold Acton, 238–41: Harold Acton on, 240; of Dora Carrington, 238, 241–44; of Anthony Eden, 232–37; of Edmund Gosse, 245–48; of Leo Tolstoy, 116–17

—*Autobiography* (Bertrand Russell), 242

—*Autobiography of Carl Schurz* (abridged by Wayne Andrews), 194

—*Cab at the Door, A* (V.S. Pritchett), 248

—*City That Shone, The* (Vivian de Sola Pinto), 248

—*Confession, A* (Leo Tolstoy), 117

—*Confessions* (Jean–Jacques Rousseau), 120

—*Downhill All the Way* (Leonard Woolf), 236

—*Goodbye to All That* (Robert Graves),

Goodbye to All That (cont.)
221, 236
—*Life of One's Own, A* (Gerald
Brenan), 248
—"Spiritual Autobiography" (Simone
Weil), 29, 30
—*Spots of Time* (Basil Willey), 248
Memoirs of a Dutiful Daughter
(Simone de Beauvoir), 20
Memoirs of an Aesthete (Sir Harold
Acton), 238–41
Memoirs of an Infantry Officer
(Siegfried Sassoon), 221
Memories, 1898–1936 (Sir Maurice
Bowra), 248
Mencius, 118
Mencken, H.L.: and Irving Babbitt, 268
Merejkowski, Dmitri: and Leo Tolstoy,
122, 123
—*Tolstoi as Man and Artist*, 122
"Metaphysical Poets" (T.S. Eliot), 258
"Middle of the World" (D.H.
Lawrence), 127
Might. *See* Power
Mill, John Stuart, 107, 108
Millay, Edna St. Vincent, 142
Milton, John: and Leo Tolstoy, 121
Miracles: Leo Tolstoy on, 119; Simone
Weil on, 31
Misère de la philosophie, La (Karl
Marx), 197
"Modern Education and the Classics"
(T.S. Eliot), 101–104
Modernism: Matthew Arnold on, 179;
chaos of values of, 12, 120; death of
modern civilization, 173–76, 220–37;
of F.M. Dostoevsky, 179–80; E.M.
Forster on the "greenwood," 242;
Robert L. Heilbroner on the
modernist impasse, 189–92, 202; and
Marxism, 148–55, 172; and Lewis
Mumford, 269–72; and Aleksandr
Solzhenitsyn, 154, 234, 268;
technologico–Benthamism of, 87,
107, 191, 255, 260, 261, 268; and
Paul Valéry, 232
—*Cocktail Party, The* (T.S. Eliot), 258,
266
—"Factory Work" (Simone Weil), 27,
28
—*Inquiry into the Human Prospect, An*
(Robert L. Heilbroner), 189–92
—*Interpretations and Forecasts* (Lewis
Mumford), 269–72
—"Man of Letters in the Modern
World, The" (Allen Tate), 269
—"Modern Education and the Classics"

"Modern Education and the Classics"
(cont.)
(T.S. Eliot), 101–104
—"Sketch of Contemporary Life"
(Simone Weil), 26, 27
—*Waste Land, The* (T.S. Eliot), 258
—*Women in Love* (D.H. Lawrence),
133, 167–76, 190, 225, 260
Moffatt, James, 125
Moltmann, Juergen, 152
Montaigne, Michel Eyquem de, 116
Moore, Harry T., 140, 220
—*Life and Works of D.H. Lawrence*,
140
More, Henry: Platonism of, ix
More, Paul Elmer: and Irving Babbitt,
65, 74, 82, 85, 206; on Christianity,
83; and T.S. Eliot, 258; on
humanism, 83; on Platonism, 83; on
religion, 83
—*Aristocracy and Justice*, 204
—*Catholic Faith, The*, 83
—*Christ the Word*, 83
—"Revival of Humanism, A," 83
Mornings in Mexico (D.H. Lawrence),
128
Morrell, Lady Ottoline: and D.H.
Lawrence, 223
Morris, William, 212
Morris, Wright, 277, 278
Moses, 196
Movements in European History (D.H.
Lawrence), 126
"Mozo, The" (D.H. Lawrence), 128
Mumford, Lewis, xi; and Hellenism,
271–72; and modernism, 269–72; and
wisdom, 271–72
—*Interpretations and Forecasts*, 269–72
Munich, 95
Murdock, Kenneth B.: *The Notebooks
of Henry James*, 218
Murray, Gilbert: *Five Stages of Greek
Religion*, 125
Murry, J. Middleton: and criticism,
273; and D.H. Lawrence, 221
—*Love, Freedom, and Society*, 221
Muse in Arms, The (E.B. Osborn), 221
Mussolini, Benito, 95
My Father and Myself (J.R. Ackerley),
245–49
Myers, Henry Alonzo: *Systematic
Pluralism*, 101
Mysticism: and asceticism, 21; of D.H.
Lawrence, 133, 136–37; and reason,
136–37; and Simone Weil, 27, 29, 36,
42, 45: her ascetic mysticism, 21

Need for Roots, The (Simone Weil), x, 24, 31, 35

Nehls, Edward: *D.H. Lawrence: A Composite Biography* (ed.), 126

Nevins, Allan, 194

New England: and Irving Babbitt, 56, 58

"New Heaven and Earth" (D.H. Lawrence), 224

New Humanism: of Irving Babbitt, x, 93, 104–105

New Orpheus, The (ed. Nathan A. Scott, Jr.), 249

New Poems (D.H. Lawrence), 138

Newman, John Henry: on the Antichrist, 85; on liberalism, 85

Newton, Sir Isaac: and William Blake, 260

Nichols, Robert: and D.H. Lawrence, 225

Nietzsche, Friedrich, x

1914 (Rupert Brooke), 222

Nor Shall My Sword (F.R. Leavis), 253, 258–59

Norton, Charles Eliot: and Henry James, 213, 216

Norton, Grace: and Henry James, 218, 219

Not I, but the Wind . . . (Frieda Lawrence), 140, 227

Notebooks of Henry James, The (ed. F.O. Matthiessen and Kenneth B. Murdock), 218

Notes towards the Definition of Culture (T.S. Eliot), 99–103

"Nottingham and the Mining Countryside" (D.H. Lawrence), 229

Nouvelle Héloïse, La (Jean–Jacques Rousseau), 120

O'Brien, Conor Cruise, 24

Observer, The, 254

O'Connor, Flannery, 40

Odysseus, 127

Old Testament, The, 30, 51, 92, 245

—Isaiah, 51, 118

—Job, 46, 51

—Psalms, 51, 220

"On Human Destiny" (D.H. Lawrence), 132

On Synthesizing Marxism and Christianity (Dale Vree), 148–55

"On the Jewish Question" (Karl Marx), 152, 201

Ong, Walter J.: on T.S. Eliot, 99

Oppression: Simone Weil on, 32–33

Oppression and Liberty (Simone Weil), 24, 31, 200

Origen: and Simone Weil, 53

Orioli, Giusèppe, 126

Ortega y Gasset, José, xi, 17, 85

Orwell, George, 240; and John W. Aldridge, 278; and Leo Tolstoy, 116

—*Animal Farm*, 258

Osborn, E.B.: *Muse in Arms, The*, 221

Padover, Saul K.: *The Letters of Karl Marx* (ed.), 193–202

Panichas, George A.: conservative criticism of, ix–xiii; and F.R. Leavis, 235; letters of, ix, 235; and Austin Warren, ix–xiii

—*Epicurus*, 196

—*Mansions of the Spirit* (ed.), 122, 183

—*Promise of Greatness* (ed.), 233, 235

—*Reverent Discipline, The*, x

—*Simone Weil Reader, The* (ed.), 19–53

Pansies (D.H. Lawrence), 125

"Paris Manuscripts" (Karl Marx), 200

Partisan Review, 106, 278

Partridge, Ralph: bisexuality of, 241–44; and Bloomsbury, 241–44; marriage to Dora Carrington, 241, 243–44; marriage to Frances Marshall, 241, 243; and Lytton Strachey, 241, 243–44

Pascal, Blaise, 116; and Irving Babbitt, 80; and Simone Weil, 25, 30

Pasternak, Boris: on art, 113

Pater, Walter: "Arnold and Pater" (T.S. Eliot), 107

Paul, Cedar, 122

Paul, Eden, 122

Paul, Saint, 272

Payne, Robert: *Marx*, 195, 198

Paysan de la Garonne, Le (Jacques Maritain), 152

Peirce, Charles Sanders: empiricism of, 90

Pericles, 105

Perrin, Father J.-M.: and Simone Weil, 29, 30

Persephone, 128, 129

Pétrement, Simone: and Simone Weil, 24

—*Simone Weil*, 21

Petrie, John, 200

Philosophy of Plotinus, The (W.R. Inge), 125

Philosophy of Poverty, The (Pierre–Joseph Proudhon), 197

Phoenix (D.H. Lawrence), 128, 230

"Piano" (D.H. Lawrence), 263

Picasso, Pablo, 240

Pierre–Joseph Proudhon (Edward Hyams), 197

Pinker, J.B., 224

Pinto, Vivian de Sola, 233; and F.R. Leavis, 267

—*City That Shone, The*, 248

Plato, 116; and Aristotle, 161; and Irving Babbitt, 66, 81; and the "Great Beast," 186, 192; and D.H. Lawrence, 126; earliest novelist, 161; and Simone Weil, 40, 186, 192

Platonism: and Christianity, 81, 83; Christian Platonism of Simone Weil, 43–44, 182; of Paul Elmer More, 83; of Henry More, ix

Pluto, 128, 129

Poems of Gerard Manley Hopkins (ed. W.H. Gardner), 142

Poetry: Georgian influence of Edward Marsh, 138–39; D.H. Lawrence's death–poems, 125–47; of Karl Marx, 195, 196; and Simone Weil, 24, 32

—"Metaphysical Poets" (T.S. Eliot), 258

Points of View (T.S. Eliot), 91, 93

Polanyi, Michael, 109, 189

Political Apocalypse (Ellis Sandoz), 177–88

Political Thought of Pierre–Joseph Proudhon, The (Alan Ritter), 197

Politics: of F.M. Dostoevsky, 165, 177–88; Bernard–Henry Lévy on, 177; and literature, 159–76; William Shakespeare on, 33; and Simone Weil, 20, 27, 31, 32, 33, 35; her anti–politics, 24

—*Democracy and Leadership* (Irving Babbitt), xii, 70, 75–77

—"Is There a Marxist Doctrine?" (Simone Weil), 24

—*Letters on Literature and Politics, 1912–1972* (Edmund Wilson), 59

—"Literature of Politics, The" (T.S. Eliot), 86

—*Oppression and Liberty* (Simone Weil), 24, 31, 200

—*Political Apocalypse* (Ellis Sandoz), 177–88

—*Political Thought of Pierre–Joseph Proudhon, The* (Alan Ritter), 197

Politics and the Novel (Irving Howe), 177

Pope John XXIII, 152

Porter, Katherine Anne: John W. Aldridge on, 275–76

—"Flowering Judas," 276

Portrait of a Lady, The (Henry James), 215

Pound, Ezra, 92; and Henry James, 219

Power: and F.M. Dostoevsky, 181–88; of good and evil, 184; Simone Weil on might, 19, 34–35, 182, 185–86

"Power of Words, The" (Simone Weil), 37

Prisoners of War (J.R. Ackerley), 248

Pritchett, V.S.: *A Cab at the Door*, 248

Promise of Greatness (ed. George A. Panichas), 233, 235

Prophecy: and Irving Babbitt, 79; and crisis, 167–68; Paul Tillich on the prophetic spirit, 261

Protagoras, 61

Proudhon, Pierre–Joseph: and Karl Marx, 197–98

—*Philosophy of Poverty, The*, 197

—*Pierre–Joseph Proudhon* (Edward Hyams), 197

—*Political Thought of Pierre–Joseph Proudhon, The* (Alan Ritter), 197

"Prussian Officer, The" (D.H. Lawrence), 228, 229

Psalms. *See* Old Testament, The

Psychology: epic, 187; and literature, 148–50; of Karl Marx, 148–55

Quiller–Couch, Sir Arthur: and T.S. Eliot, 107–108

Racine, Jean: and Simone Weil, 30, 40

Radcliffe, Lord, 192

Radford, Dollie: and D.H. Lawrence, 226

Rahv, Philip: and T.S. Eliot, 106–107

Rainbow, The (D.H. Lawrence), 143, 225, 226, 227

Rascoe, Burton, 59

"Rational Study of the Classics, The" (Irving Babbitt), 64, 65

Rationalism: of Leo Tolstoy, 118–19, 124

Read, Sir Herbert: and T.S. Eliot, 108; and World War I, 233, 235

Reason: and mysticism, 136–37; and religion, 119

"Reflections on the Right Use of School Studies with a View to the Love of God" (Simone Weil), 27

Relativism: and standards, 253

Religion: and Vissarion Belinsky, 187–88; and Martin Buber, 114; criticism of, 149; and criticism,

Religion *(cont.)*
111–14; of the Etruscans, 126, 128, 140–44; Norman Foerster on, 104–105; of the ancient Greeks, 125–29; and D.H. Lawrence, 112, 125–47, 209; and F.R. Leavis, 111, 254, 267; and literature, 111–14; and Karl Marx, 153, 195–96, 200–201; and Paul Elmer More, 83; and reason, 118–19; of the Romans, 126; and science, 111; of Leo Tolstoy, 116–24: his excommunication, 116. *See also* Christ Jesus, the, God, Roman Catholicism

—*After Strange Gods* (T.S. Eliot), 88–96, 137

—"Concerning the Our Father" (Simone Weil), 52–53

—*Courage To Be* (Paul Tillich), 179–80

—*Five Stages of Greek Religion* (Gilbert Murray), 125

—"Humanism and Religion" (Norman Foerster), 104

—*Mansions of the Spirit* (ed. George A. Panichas), 122, 183

—*New Orpheus, The* (ed. Nathan A. Scott, Jr.), 249

—"Spiritual Autobiography" (Simone Weil), 29, 30

"Religion and Literature" (T.S. Eliot), 95

"Religion and the Mission of the Artist" (Denis de Rougemont), 249

"Religion Without Humanism" (T.S. Eliot), 105

Reminiscences of Tolstoy, Chekhov, and Andreev (Maxim Gorky), 119

"Responsibility of Writers, The" (Simone Weil), 38

Revelation (ed. John Baillie and Hugh Martin), 94

Reverent Discipline, The (George A. Panichas), x

"Revival of Humanism, A" (Paul Elmer More), 83

Rexroth, Kenneth: on D.H. Lawrence, 146

Richthofen, Frau Baronin von: and D.H. Lawrence, 140

Richthofen, Manfred von: and Frieda Lawrence, 227

Rilke, Rainer Maria: letters of, 115; on World War I, 112

—*Letters of Rainer Maria Rilke* (trans. Jane Bannard Greene and M.D. Herter Norton), 115

Rimbaud, Arthur: and Simone Weil, 40

Rise and Fall of the Man of Letters, The (John Gross), 253

Ritter, Alan: *The Political Thought of Pierre–Joseph Proudhon*, 197

Roman Catholicism, 152; of Simone Weil, 24, 25, 26, 30

—*Catholic Faith, The* (Paul Elmer More), 83

Roman Empire: D.H. Lawrence on its religion, 126; and Simone Weil, 24, 30, 32, 45

Romanticism: Irving Babbitt on, 61–63, 68; of Friedrich Schlegel, 81; of Paul Verlaine, 68; of Oscar Wilde, 68. *See also* Rousseau, Jean–Jacques

—*Rousseau and Romanticism* (Irving Babbitt), 64, 77, 192

Rosenberg, Isaac: and World War I, 221

Rosenthal, Raymond, 21

Rossetti, Dante Gabriel, 212

Rousseau, Jean–Jacques, 90, 124, 150, 182; and Irving Babbitt, 60, 61, 62, 63, 64, 68, 71, 72, 77, 84; J.M. Lalley on, 120; and Leo Tolstoy, 119–22, 124

—*Confessions*, 120

—*Émile*, 120

—*Nouvelle Héloïse, La*, 120

—*Rousseau and Romanticism* (Irving Babbitt), 64, 77, 192

Rousseau and Romanticism (Irving Babbitt), 64, 77, 192

Ruskin, John: and Henry James, 212, 213

Russell, Bertrand: and Bloomsbury, 242; and T.S. Eliot, 105; genius of, 223; and John Maynard Keynes, 242; and D.H. Lawrence, 94, 170, 223; and liberalism, 86

—*Autobiography*, 242

—*Conquest of Happiness, The*, 105

Russian Revolution, 234

Saint. *See* saint's forename

"St. Mawr" (D.H. Lawrence), 132

Sainte–Beuve, Charles Augustin, 70

Saintliness: of Simone Weil, 21, 26, 29, 31, 53

Sakharov, Andrei D., 202

Sandoz, Ellis: on F.M. Dostoevsky's Grand Inquisitor, 177–88

—*Political Apocalypse*, 177–88

Sassoon, Siegfried: on J.R. Ackerley's *The Prisoners of War*, 248; and World War I, 221, 233, 248

—*Memoirs of an Infantry Officer*, 221

Schlegel, Friedrich: romantic Buddhism

Schlegel, Friedrich *(cont.)*
of, 81
Schopenhauer, Arthur: pessimistic
Buddhism of, 81
Schumann, Maurice: and Simone Weil,
22, 25, 28
Schurz, Carl: on the physical
appearance of Karl Marx, 194, 197
—*Autobiography of Carl Schurz*
(abridged by Wayne Andrews), 194
Science: German scientific spirit, 64;
and religion, 111; and technology,
111
Scott, Nathan A., Jr., 249; on the crisis
of criticism, 112
—*New Orpheus, The* (ed.), 249
"Second Thoughts about Humanism"
(T.S. Eliot), 105
Secular City, The (Harvey Cox), 152
Seigel, Jerrold: psychohistorical
approach to Karl Marx, 148–55
—*Marx's Fate*, 148–55
Selected Philosophical Works
(Vissarion G. Belinsky), 188
"Self–Sacrifice" (D.H. Lawrence), 144
Seneca, 118
Sexuality: of Alfred Roger Ackerley,
247–48; Freud's sexual materialism,
155; Leo Tolstoy on, 120–21; Simone
Weil on carnal love, 52; Simone Weil
on passion, 21; sexual scenes in
Women in Love, 174. *See also*
Bisexuality, Homosexuality
—*Kreutzer Sonata, The* (Leo Tolstoy),
121
"Shadows" (D.H. Lawrence), 134
Shakespeare, William, 256; genius of,
174; and D.H. Lawrence, 174; and
Karl Marx, 200; on politicians, 33;
and Leo Tolstoy, 121, 124
—*King Lear*, 124
—*Timon of Athens*, 200
—*What is Art?* (Leo Tolstoy), 124
Shelley, Percy Bysshe: and Irving
Babbitt, 62; and World War I, 236
Sherriff, R.C.: *Journey's End*, 236
"Ship of Death, The" (D.H. Lawrence),
139–47; analyzed by R.P. Blackmur,
135–36
Silone, Ignazio: and Karl Marx, 153
Simone Weil (Simone Pétrement), 21
Simone Weil Reader, The (ed. George
A. Panichas), 19–53
Sin: Leo Tolstoy on, 121
Sitwell, Edith: and Gertrude Stein, 239
Sitwell, Osbert: and Gertrude Stein,
239

Sitwell, Sacheverell: and Gertrude
Stein, 239
"Sketch of Contemporary Life"
(Simone Weil), 26, 27
Skinner, M.L.: and D.H. Lawrence, 131
"Sleep" (D.H. Lawrence), 133
"Sleep and Waking" (D.H. Lawrence),
133
Smith, T.V.: and Irving Babbitt, 76
Snow, C.P.: and F.R. Leavis, 90, 260,
261
"So Let Me Live" (D.H. Lawrence), 129
Socrates, 126; and Irving Babbitt, 59,
72, 76; and Karl Marx, 193
Soldiers: D.H. Lawrence on, 225–26,
228–30
"Solipsistic Saint, The" (J.M. Lalley),
120
Solzhenitsyn, Aleksandr: and
modernism, 154, 234, 268
—*August 1914*, 234
"Song of Death" (D.H. Lawrence), 133
Sons and Lovers (D.H. Lawrence), 225,
229
Sophocles, 40
Sorrow: Henry James on, 213–14, 219
Spanish Character and Other Essays
(Irving Babbitt), 78
Spectator, The, 254
Spencer, Theodore: and Irving Babbitt,
74
Spenser, Edmund, 71
Spingarn, J.E.: and Irving Babbitt, 72
Spinoza, Baruch, 196
"Spiritual Autobiography" (Simone
Weil), 29, 30
"Spleen" (Charles Baudelaire), 141–42
Spots of Time (Basil Willey), 248
Staël, Madame de: Irving Babbitt on, 77
Stalin, Joseph, 152, 184; madness of,
237
Standards: of John W. Aldridge, 278;
Irving Babbitt on, 74–77;
compromised, xi; of criticism, ix–xiii,
3–15, 113, 204, 214, 253–69, 278;
T.S. Eliot on, 204; and F.R. Leavis,
253–67; and relativism, 253; Allen
Tate on, 269; of Austin Warren,
ix–xiii
Stein, Gertrude: and Sir Harold Acton,
239; and Edith Sitwell, 239; and
Osbert Sitwell, 239; and Sacheverell
Sitwell, 239; and Alice B. Toklas, 239
—"Composition as Explanation," 239
Steiner, George, 38
—*Tolstoy or Dostoevsky*, 187
Stephen, Leslie, 212

Strachey, Lytton: and Bloomsbury, 241–44; and Dora Carrington, 241–44; death of, 244; and F.M. Dostoevsky, 244; homosexuality of, 241–44; and Frances Marshall, 241, 243; and Ralph Partridge, 241, 243–44
—*Carrington* (ed. David Garnett), 238–44
Strakhov, N.N., 121
Studies in Classic American Literature (D.H. Lawrence), 226
Styron, William: and John W. Aldridge, 277–78
Suicide: of Dora Carrington, 244; of Harry Crosby, 143–44; D.H. Lawrence on, 143–44; of Eleanor Marx, 201; of Laura Marx, 201
—*Carrington* (ed. David Garnett), 238–44
—*Essay on Suicide* (David Hume), 244
Systematic Pluralism (Henry Alonzo Myers), 101

T.S. Eliot: A Bibliography (Donald Gallup), 86
"Tabernacle" (D.H. Lawrence), 133
Taine, Hippolyte, 70
Tales of D.H. Lawrence, The, 132
Tate, Allen, 269
—*Essays of Four Decades*, 269
—"Man of Letters in the Modern World, The," 269
Technologico–Benthamism, 87, 107, 191, 255, 260, 261, 268
Tennyson, Lord Alfred, 127
Teresa, Saint: and Simone Weil, 53
Thibon, Gustave: and Simone Weil, 23
Thomas, Saint, 153
Thomas Woodrow Wilson (Sigmund Freud and William C. Bullitt), 245
"Thorn in the Flesh, The" (D.H. Lawrence), 228
"Three Masters" (Georges Florovsky), 122, 183
Thucydides: and D.H. Lawrence, 125–26
Thurneysen, Eduard, 180
Tillich, Paul, 180, 206; on the crisis of faith, 154; on Marxism and Christianity, 154; on the prophetic spirit, 261
—*The Courage to Be*, 179–80
Time: D.H. Lawrence on, 142; pagan conception of, 142; Simone Weil on, 47
Timon of Athens (William

Timon of Athens (cont.) Shakespeare), 200
Tiverton, Father William. *See* Jarrett–Kerr, Father Martin
Toklas, Alice B.: and Gertrude Stein, 239
Tolstoi as Man and Artist (Dmitri Merejkowski), 122
Tolstoy, Count Leo: antihistoricism of, 120; Irving Babbitt on, 116; on Christ, 118–22, 124; Christian socialism of, 117; on Dante, 121; death of, 117–18, 124; on death, 122–24; and F.M. Dostoevsky, 122–24; on evil, 121; excommunication of, 116; and his family, 115, 117–18; Georges Florovsky on, 116, 122; on genius, 116; and God, 115, 119, 120, 124; and Homer, 187; and D.H. Lawrence, 117; letters of, 115–24; madness of, 118; materialism of, 123; memoirs of, 116–17; and Dmitri Merejkowski, 122, 123; on Milton, 121; on miracles, 119; and George Orwell, 116; rationalism of, 118–19, 124; religion of, 116–24; and Jean–Jacques Rousseau, 119–22, 124; and Shakespeare, 121, 124; on sin, 121; on Nikolay Tolstoy, 122–23; on truth, 123; and Simone Weil, 34; and Edmund Wilson, 115–16; and Stefan Zweig, 122–23
—*Confession, A*, 117
—*Father Sergius*, 123
—*Hedgehog and the Fox, The* (Sir Isaiah Berlin), 116
—*History of Russian Philosophy, A* (V.V. Zenkovsky), 122
—*Kreutzer Sonata, The*, 121
—*Letters of Tolstoy and his Cousin Countess Alexandra Tolstoy, The*, 115
—*Master Builders* (Stefan Zweig), 122
—*Reminiscences of Tolstoy, Chekhov, and Andreev* (Maxim Gorky), 119
—"Three Masters" (Georges Florovsky), 122, 183
—*Tolstoi as Man and Artist* (Dmitri Merejkowski), 122
—*Tolstoy or Dostoevsky* (George Steiner), 187
—*War and Peace*, 120, 124
—*What is Art?*, 124
—*Window on Russia, A* (Edmund Wilson), 115
—*Youth*, 121

Tolstoy, Nikolay: death of, 122–23; and
Leo Tolstoy, 122–23
Tolstoy or Dostoevsky (George Steiner),
187
Tragedy: Greek, 187
—*Freedom and the Tragic Life*
(Vyacheslav Ivanov), 188
Tragic vision: of Dante, 121; of Milton,
121; of Shakespeare, 121
Trahison des clercs, La (Julien Benda),
192
Trilling, Lionel: on liberalism, 107, 268
Trotsky, Leon: and Nikolai Lenin,
201–202
—*Young Lenin, The*, 201, 202
Truth: Leo Tolstoy on, 123
"Two Ways of Living and Dying" (D.H.
Lawrence), 131

Ulysses (James Joyce), 277
Undertones of War (Edmund Blunden),
221
Updike, John: *The Centaur*, 277
"Upon Westminster Bridge" (William
Wordsworth), 264

Valéry, Paul: on modernism, 232
Values: and Irving Babbitt, xii; chaos
of, 12, 120; of critical thought,
ix–xiii, 3–15; higher values, xi, 3–15;
of humanism, 5
Van Gogh, Vincent: letters of, 116
Vergil: and T.S. Eliot, 85
Verlaine, Paul: and romanticism, 68
Viereck, Peter: and T.S. Eliot, 87
Villon, François, 40
Vinci, Leonardo da, 239
"Virgin Mother, The" (D.H. Lawrence),
141
Visions of Order (Richard M. Weaver),
99
Voegelin, Eric, 182
Voltaire, 150, 182; and Irving Babbitt,
54; and Vissarion G. Belinsky, 188;
and Bloomsbury, 244
Vree, Dale: *On Synthesizing Marxism
and Christianity*, 148–55

Waley, Arthur, 240
"War Again, The" (D.H. Lawrence), 230
War and Peace (Leo Tolstoy), 120, 124
Warren, Austin: on beauty, xi; on
conservatism, ix–xiii; on courage of
judgment, xi–xiii; on criticism,
ix–xiii; on culture, xi; on friendship,
ix; letters of, ix; on loyalty, ix; and
George A. Panichas, ix–xiii; on

Warren, Austin *(cont.)*
wisdom, xii
Washington Square (Henry James), 215
Waste Land, The (T.S. Eliot), 258
Waugh, Evelyn, 240
Weaver, Richard M.: conservative
criticism of, 99, 157, 207–208; on
culture, 99; and Richard L. Cutler,
207–208; and World War II, 207
—*Ideas Have Consequences*, 207–208
—*Visions of Order*, 99
Weil, Simone: on affliction, 26, 28, 42,
48, 50; on art, 39, 40–41; on
attention, 27, 31, 46–47; and beauty,
44; "beauty of the world," 50–52;
and capitalism, 32; on carnal love,
52; on Catharism, 30; on Christ,
46–49, 53; Christian Platonism of,
43–44, 182; and Christianity, 23, 24,
25, 29–30, 43–44, 46, 47, 51, 53, 182;
and contemplation, 23; conservatism
of, ix; as a critic, 36–37; death of, 25;
on death, 35, 41; on decreation, 22,
46, 48; on diabolism, 34; and F.M.
Dostoevsky, 28, 40; and T.S. Eliot, x,
21, 35, 40, 102; and evil, 26, 34,
39–40, 44–45, 52, 53; on factory
work, 27–28; on friendship, 43, 44;
on genius, 37, 39–40; and God, 20,
21, 22, 29, 36, 42–43, 44, 45, 46, 47,
48, 49–50, 51, 52, 186, 244; and good
and evil, 39–40, 44–45, 52, 53; on
gravity and grace, 22, 42, 45, 102; and
"the Great Beast," 24, 45, 186, 192;
on the Greeks, 32; headaches of, 29;
and Hellenism, 35, 37, 43; her
Christian Hellenism, 20, 35, 43, 44,
50; on history, 32; on Adolf Hitler,
32, 33; and Homer, 40; on
humiliation, 28, 29; on *The Iliad*,
34–35, 185–86; and Judaism, 25,
29–30; on language, 37–39; letters of,
22, 27, 28; and D.H. Lawrence, 51;
on machines, 26; and Karl Marx, 20,
32, 33, 151, 200; on Marxism, 151; on
materialism, 32; on might, 19, 34–35,
182, 185–86; on miracles, 31; and
mysticism, 27, 29, 36, 42, 45; her
ascetic mysticism, 21; on oppression,
32–33; and Origen, 53; pacifism of,
28; parents of, 29; and passion, 21;
on patience, 46; and Father J.M.
Perrin, 29, 30; and Simone
Pétrement, 24; physical appearance
of, 23, 25; and Plato, 40, 186, 192; on
poetry and religion, 24, 32;
anti–politics of, 24; and politics, 20,

Weil, Simone (*cont.*)
27, 31, 32, 33, 35; and Jean Racine,
30, 40; on reflection, 19; and the
Roman Empire, 24, 30, 32, 45;
Roman Catholicism of, 24, 25, 26,
30; saintliness of, 21, 26, 29, 31, 53;
and Maurice Schumann, 22, 25, 28;
on silence, 53; on the soul, 36, 41,
42, 51; on suffering, 22; on
surrealism, 39; as a teacher, 27; and
Saint Teresa, 53; and Gustave
Thibon, 23; on time, 47; and Leo
Tolstoy, 34; on waiting, 47; on war,
28–29, 34–35; on wisdom, 31, 41–43,
44, 45, 51; on work, 22, 27–28
—"Concerning the Our Father," 52–53
—"Factory Work," 27, 28
—*Gravity and Grace*, 102
—"Human Personality," 41 ·
—"*Iliad*, Poem of Might, The," 34–35,
185–86
—*Intimations of Christianity among
the Ancient Greeks*, 185
—"Is There a Marxist Doctrine?," 24
—*Letter to a Priest*, 24
—*Memoirs of a Dutiful Daughter*
(Simone de Beauvoir), 20
—*Need for Roots, The*, x, 24, 31, 35
—*Oppression and Liberty*, 24, 31, 200
—"Power of Words, The," 37
—"Reflections on the Right Use of
School Studies with a View to the
Love of God," 27
—"Responsibility of Writers, The," 38
—*Simone Weil* (Simone Pétrement), 21
—"Sketch of Contemporary Life," 26,
27
—"Spiritual Autobiography," 29, 30
—"What Is a Jew?," 30
Well–Remembered Voice, A (James
Barrie), 235
Wellek, René: on literary criticism, 111
Welty, Eudora, 277
Weyl, Nathaniel: *Karl Marx: Racist*,
195
"What Is a Jew?" (Simone Weil), 30
What is Art? (Leo Tolstoy), 124
Whibley, Charles, 258
Whitehead, Alfred North, 74
Whitman, Walt, 226
Wilde, Oscar: homosexuality of, 248;
and romanticism, 68
Wilder, Amos, 112
Willey, Basil: *Spots of Time*, 248
Wills, Arthur, 35, 200

Wilson, Edmund: on criticism, 274;
humanism of, 59; and Henry James,
218; letters of, 59; pragmatism of,
115; on Leo Tolstoy, 115–16
—*Letters on Literature and Politics,
1912—1972*, 59
—*Window on Russia, A*, 115
Wilson, Elena, 59
Wilson (Thomas) Woodrow, 66;
Sigmund Freud on, 245
—*Thomas Woodrow Wilson* (Sigmund
Freud and William C. Bullitt), 245
Window on Russia, A (Edmund
Wilson), 115
Winter Notes on Summer Impressions
(F.M. Dostoevsky), 187
Winters, Yvor, 265
Wisdom: and Irving Babbitt, 59; and
Robert L. Heilbroner, 192; and Lewis
Mumford, 271–72; and Austin
Warren, xii; Simone Weil on, 31,
41–43, 44, 45, 51
Wolfe, Thomas, 276
Women in Love (D.H. Lawrence), 133,
167–76, 190, 225, 260
Woolf, Leonard: and Bloomsbury, 242;
on World War I, 236
—*Downhill All the Way* (Leonard
Woolf), 236
Woolf, Virginia, 233; on Dora
Carrington's death, 244; and F.R.
Leavis, 258
Wordsworth, William: "Upon
Westminster Bridge," 264
World War I: and J.R. Ackerley, 247;
Irving Babbitt on, 78; and Joë
Bousquet, 27; and Rupert Brooke,
221, 222, 231; and Anthony Eden,
232–37; frontline conditions, 235–36;
and Julian Grenfell, 221; and Ernest
Hemingway, 171; Henry James on,
236; and D.H. Lawrence, 168,
220–31; F.R. Leavis on, 235; and Sir
Herbert Read, 233, 235; Rainer Maria
Rilke on, 112; and Isaac Rosenberg,
221; and Siegfried Sassoon, 221, 233,
248; and R.C. Sherriff, 236; and
Leonard Woolf, 236
—*Another World, 1897–1917* (Anthony
Eden), 232
—*D.H. Lawrence's Nightmare* (Paul
Delany), 221
—*Goodbye to All That* (Robert Graves),
221, 236
—*Journey's End* (R.C. Sherriff), 236

—*Memoirs of an Infantry Officer* (Siegfried Sassoon), 221

—*1914* (Rupert Brooke), 222

—*Prisoners of War* (J.R. Ackerley), 248

—*Promise of Greatness* (ed. George A. Panichas), 233, 235

—*Undertones of War* (Edmund Blunden), 221

—"War Again, The" (D.H. Lawrence), 230

—*Well–Remembered Voice, A* (James Barrie), 235

World War II, 87; and T.S. Eliot, 95, 99–100; and Adolf Hitler, 95, 184, 237; and Richard M. Weaver, 207

Yeats, William Butler, 92

Young Lenin, The (Leon Trotsky), 201, 202

Youth (Leo Tolstoy), 121

Zenkovsky, V.V.: *A History of Russian Philosophy*, 122

Zweig, Stefan: and Leo Tolstoy, 122–23

—*Master Builders*, 122

The Courage of Judgment was composed on the Mergenthaler Lino-tron 202N Phototypesetter in ten-point Trump Medieval type with two-point line spacing. The calligraphic display was hand lettered. The book was designed by Jim Billingsley, composed by Williams, Chattanooga, Tennessee, printed by offset lithography at Thomson-Shore, Inc., Dexter, Michigan, and bound by John H. Dekker & Sons, Grand Rapids, Michigan. The paper on which the book is printed bears the watermark of S.D. Warren and is designed for an effective life of at least three hundred years.

THE UNIVERSITY OF TENNESSEE PRESS : KNOXVILLE